A PHILOSOPHY OF MUSIC EDUCATION

Advancing the Vision

Third Edition

Bennett Reimer
Northwestern University

Prentice
Hall

Upper Saddle River, New Jersey 07468

Library of Congress Cataloging-in-Publication Data

REIMER, BENNETT.
  A philosophy of music education : advancing the vision / Bennett Reimer.—3rd ed.
    p. cm.
  Includes index.
  ISBN 0-13-099338-7
  1. Music—Instruction and study. 2. Music—Philosophy and aesthetics. I. Title.

  MT1 .R435 2003
  780'.71—dc21

                                              2002066341

Senior acquisitions editor: *Christopher T. Johnson*
Editorial assistant: *Evette Dickerson*
Project manager: *Carole R. Crouse*
Prepress and manufacturing buyer: *Benjamin Smith*
Copy editor: *Cheryl Smith*
Marketing manager: *Chris Ruel*
Cover designer: *Bruce Kenselaar*

This book was set in 10/12 Berkeley Medium by Stratford Publishing Services, Inc.,
and was printed and bound by Courier Companies, Inc.
The cover was printed by Coral Graphics.

 © 2003, 1989, 1970 by Pearson Education, Inc.
Upper Saddle River, New Jersey 07458

Printed in the United States of America

10 9 8 7 6 5 4 3 2 1

ISBN: 0-13-099338-7

PEARSON EDUCATION LTD., *London*
PEARSON EDUCATION AUSTRALIA PTY, LIMITED, *Sydney*
PEARSON EDUCATION SINGAPORE, PTE. LTD.
PEARSON EDUCATION NORTH ASIA LTD., *Hong Kong*
PEARSON EDUCATION CANADA, LTD., *Toronto*
PEARSON EDUCACÍON DE MEXICO, S.A., DE C.V.
PEARSON EDUCATION--JAPAN, *Tokyo*
PEARSON EDUCATION MALAYSIA, PTE. LTD.
PEARSON EDUCATION, *Upper Saddle River, New Jersey*

You must say something new and yet nothing but
what is old. You must indeed say only what is old—
but all the same something new!
　　　　　　—Ludwig Wittgenstein, *Culture and Value*

Contents

4

THE CREATING DIMENSION OF MUSICAL EXPERIENCE   103

5

THE MEANING DIMENSION OF MUSICAL EXPERIENCE   133

6

THE CONTEXTUAL DIMENSION OF MUSICAL EXPERIENCE   168

Preface

In both the first (1970) and the second (1989) editions of this book, I began by stating the fundamental premise on which my philosophy was based: that the nature and value of music education are determined primarily by the nature and value of music. To the degree that music educators are able to construct a convincing explanation of what music is like—its diverse yet distinctive features and the many contributions it makes to human welfare—the profession will understand the domain to which it is devoted and be able to implement programs that effectively share its special values.

That premise continues to undergird the philosophy I offer in this edition. I continue to believe that music has characteristics that make it recognizably and distinctively a subject, or a field, or a practice, or an "art"; that these characteristics can be identified to a reasonable and useful degree (but no doubt never definitively); that music is of value to humans and their communities in a variety of ways related to these characteristics; and that the primary mission of music education is to make musical values widely and deeply available.

Why, then, another edition?

In the time span of almost two decades between the first and second editions, a good deal of work was accomplished in the cognitive sciences, work that I felt added muscle to the philosophy I had articulated and that needed to be incorporated so that the implications of the philosophy could be drawn more clearly. I was also aware of stirrings in the field of aesthetics, or, if one prefers, philosophy of the arts (see the discussion of these terms in Chapter 1), along with important related work in education, social theory, psychology, and various other fields, that had begun to expand and shift previous interests and positions. But at the time I was writing the second edition I was not yet ready to incorporate such emerging ideas because they had not become sufficiently articulated and reasoned (at least to me) as to cause me to adapt to or adopt them.

In the intervening dozen or so years many of those ideas have become clearer, more defensible, and more urgently in need of recognition and application to music education philosophy and practice. These changes in aesthetic thinking include alterations of existing ideas, expansions into previously little explored territory, rebalances in emphases among various dimensions of the aesthetic enterprise, disputes among positions previously not seen to be in tension, and on and on with all the natural, inevitable, and healthy developments within the ongoing domain of aesthetic theorizing and within all the many domains that influence it.

In this book I have related the modifications in thinking to their implications for the practice of music education. That is because, as a devoted music educator who happens to specialize in matters theoretical, I *always* relate theoretical ideas to practices of music education. That is, after all, what makes me a music educator, albeit of a somewhat peculiar stripe. It is as natural to me as breathing to view and understand emerging ideas in terms of their use in improving the field of music education (and, in my more ambitious if clearly less practical moments, the larger field of the arts in education as well). So I have more than a speculative interest in ideas relating to music and education. I have a pressing sense of vocation to use my expanding theoretical understanding to help clarify what music education is all about so that it can be more valid and effective in its actions. As my understanding grows, so grows my sense of what an effective music education might consist of.

The present revision is significantly more thoroughgoing and extensive than the previous one, reflecting the remarkable activity in aesthetics and related fields during the past decade or so. Readers acquainted with the previous versions will find that I have added a good deal of newly emergent material, have rebalanced several positions, have explained several key ideas in somewhat different or substantially different ways, and have accommodated myself to interests and ideas previously either nonexistent, not noticed, or not considered convincing to me. In a real sense my philosophy has changed, but in just as real a sense it has retained fundamental convictions I continue to find persuasive. Above all, I have maintained and recommitted myself to the belief that the experience of music itself—how musical sounds influence human lives—is the cornerstone of a viable philosophy of music education and of an effective and valid program of music learning. My philosophy is founded now, as it always has been, on my belief in the power of musical experience, in its many manifestations, to deepen, broaden, and enhance human life.

THE INCLUDE–EXCLUDE PROBLEM

I must confess the same sense of frustration in offering this revision as with the first. On almost every page of this book ideas are raised that practically beg for several more books to be written exploring their implications. The philosopher knows, better than most others, the layers that exist below anything he or she asserts. If one tried to deal with all those layers as one went along, one's writing would become so heavy that readers could only go into a trance trying to read it, and, also, one's book would soon become a multivolume epic. So one is forced to plunge ahead, ruthlessly leaving out all sorts of relevant material, trying desperately to keep things reasonably uncluttered yet sufficiently inclusive. Sometimes I feel this book has achieved some success at paring things down to manageable dimensions. Some readers, I am sure, will not agree. At other times I wish I had gone more deeply into some matters. Some readers, I am just as sure, would have wished that also. To those who will feel that there is too much here I offer apologies. To those who will feel just as strongly that there is not enough I apologize as well. In a real sense both are correct. So beware, those of you who attempt to write philosophy for anyone else to read!

I am indebted to a great many people who have influenced my thinking over the years—my teachers, my university colleagues, my students, music educators in many specializations around the United States and all over the world, and scholars and practitioners in a variety of disciplines, all of whom have supplied precious grist for my mill. I am particularly grateful to the following professionals, who offered useful insights in their reviews of selected sections, early chapters, or the completed first draft of the book. Their critiques allowed me to fashion a more cogent and convincing philosophy—a task, I am afraid, never to be fully completed: James Daugherty, University of Kansas; Harriet Hair, University of Georgia; Forest Hansen, Lake Forest College (emeritus); Jerome J. Hausman, School of the Art Institute of Chicago; Nancy K. Klein, Old Dominion University; John Kratus, Michigan State University; Steven J. Morrison, University of Washington; Carlos Xavier Rodriguez, University of Iowa; James Standifer, University of Michigan; and Iris Yob, Indiana University.

Bennett Reimer

1

From Philosophical Concurrence to Diversity: Problems and Opportunities

MAIN THEMES

- A philosophy of music education provides grounding for our professional lives, both in explaining our value as a field and in giving direction to our actions.
- In the second half of the twentieth century, the profession tended to be unified by the philosophy of "aesthetic education."
- The National Content Standards for Music Education were an important outgrowth of the aesthetic education movement.
- Recent arguments of postmodernism as an alternative to modernism have eroded previous philosophical, educational, and musical certainties. There are important implications for music education, needing to be understood by professionals.
- In the current period of conflicting philosophical positions, a synergistic (cooperative) approach to ideas can serve to maintain philosophical balance and professional cohesion.

WHY DO WE NEED A PHILOSOPHY?

Why should we music educators bother to deal with philosophy—to read it, discuss it, write it, try to develop our own professional version of it? After all, philosophy requires "language-think." Music requires "sound-think." Philosophy creates word-meanings. Music creates sound-meanings. Both philosophical thinking and musical thinking are hard work. Both call for great care to be taken with their materials (words or sounds). Both require effort and skill to be brought to bear in shaping the words or sounds to make them as convincing, as powerful, as "right" as they can be made to be. Both also require care and close attention to gain their meanings. Isn't it sufficient for music educators to be concerned with music, to be proficient in think-ing musically?

The answer is unequivocally no. Music educators must, of course, be proficient in all the aspects of music they are responsible for teaching, a daunting task in itself. They must also be well versed in many aspects of education: curriculum, evaluation, methods of teaching, human development, and so forth. They must possess a variety of interpersonal skills and attitudes conducive to being effective, trusted, admired teachers and leaders. And they also require a set of guiding beliefs about the nature and value of their subject—that is, a philosophy.

The purpose of the philosophy I will propose in this book is to provide a sys-tem of principles for guidance in creating and implementing useful and meaningful music education programs. Our profession needs such guidance at both the collec-tive and the individual levels. The profession as a whole needs a set of beliefs that can serve to guide the efforts of the group. The impact the profession can make on society depends in large degree on the quality of the profession's understanding of what it has to offer that might be of value to society. There is a continuing need for a better understanding of the value of music and of the teaching and learning of it. An uncomfortable amount of defensiveness, of self-doubt, of grasping at straws that seem to offer bits and pieces of self-justification, has always seemed to exist in music education. It would be difficult to find another field so active, so apparently healthy, so venerable in age and widespread in practice, and at the same time so worried about its inherent value.

The tremendous expression of concern about how to justify itself—both to itself and to others—that has been traditional in this field reflects a lack of philosoph-ical "inner peace." What a shame this is. For, as will be made clear in this book, justi-fication for teaching and learning music exists at the very deepest levels of human value. Until we in music education understand what we genuinely have to offer, until we are convinced that we are a necessary rather than a peripheral part of human cul-ture, until we "feel in our bones" that our value is a fundamental one, we will not have attained the peace of mind that is the mark of maturity. Until then we cannot reach the level of operational effectiveness that is an outgrowth of self-acceptance, of security, of purposes understood and efforts channeled.

A philosophy is necessary for overall effectiveness and serves as a sort of "col-lective conscience" for music education as a whole. But the strength of the field ulti-mately depends on the convictions of its members. The individuals who constitute the group must have an understanding of the nature and the value of their individual endeavors.

Individuals who have a clear notion of their aims as professionals and of the importance of those aims are a strong link in the chain of people who collectively make a profession. Music education has been fortunate in having leaders who have held strong convictions, who have helped enormously in forging a sense of group identity. But too many of our convictions have been based on platitudes, on attractive but empty arguments, on vague intimations that music education is important with little in the way of solid reasoning to give backbone to beliefs. Many individuals have enormous dedication to this field but little more to base it on than fond hopes. That is why the profession gives the appearance—a very accurate appearance—of tremendous vitality and purposefulness and goodness of intentions while at the same time harboring the nagging doubt as to whether it all makes much difference. Individuals who *do* have convincing justifications for music education, who exhibit in their own lives the inner sense of worth that comes from doing important work in the world, become some of the profession's most prized possessions. To the degree that individual music educators are helped to formulate a compelling philosophy, the profession will become more solid and secure.

Another reason for the importance of strengthening individual beliefs about music education is that the understanding we have about the value of our profession inevitably affects our perception of the value of our personal lives. To a large extent, we are what we do in life. If our occupation seems to us an important one, one that we respect and through which we can enrich both ourselves and society, we cannot help but feel that a large part of our lives is important and respectable and enriching. If, on the other hand, we have the feeling that our work is of doubtful value, that it lacks the respect of others in related fields, that the contribution we make through our work is inconsequential, we can only feel that much of our life is of equally dubious value.

Undergraduates preparing to enter the profession of music education need to develop an understanding of the importance of their chosen field. Perhaps at no other time in life is the desire for self-justification as pressing as when you are preparing to take your place as a contributing member of society. There is an urgent need for a philosophy that provides a mission and a meaning for this new professional life, even more so when, as in music education, the value of the field is not fully understood by its members and is perhaps even less understood by professionals in related music and education fields. Given the lack of convincing arguments about the importance of music education and attendant philosophical insecurity manifesting itself in superficial bases of self-justification, it is all too clear why so many music education undergraduates are insecure about their choice of profession.

Students deserve to be introduced to a philosophy that is more than wishful thinking. College students are far too sophisticated to be satisfied with superficial reasoning and far too involved with life to be able to accept a philosophy that does not grasp their imaginations and tap their zeal. The need to feel that life is significant, that actions do matter, that good causes can be served and good influences felt, can be met more effectively and immediately by a sound philosophy than by any other aspect of their education. Developing a sense of self-identity and self-respect requires that college students be given the opportunity to think seriously about their reasons for professional being. The return on the investment made in developing a professional philosophy is extremely high, not only in providing a basis for self-respect, but also in channeling the natural dedication and commitment of students into a dedication and commitment to music education.

All that has been said about the purposes a philosophy serves for the music educator in training applies as well to the music educator in service. No matter how long one has been a professional, the need for self-understanding and self-esteem exists. In some ways these needs become more complex with time, as professional duties, responsibilities, and problems become more complex. For the veteran music educator (and some would argue that surviving the first year of teaching qualifies the music educator as "veteran"), a goal is needed that focuses efforts toward something more satisfying than another concert, more meaningful than another contest, more important than another class, broader than another lesson or meeting or budget or report. All these obligations and pleasures need to head somewhere. They need to be viewed as the necessary carrying out in practice of an end that transcends each of them, adding to each of our duties a purpose deep enough and large enough to make all of them worthwhile. It becomes progressively more difficult, very often, for music educators to see beyond the increasing number of trees to the forest that includes all of them. Without the larger view, without a sense of the inherent value of our work, it is very easy to begin to operate at the level of daily problems with little regard for their larger context. Inevitably, an erosion of confidence takes place, in which immediate concerns never seem to mean very much. Having lost a sense of purpose, perhaps not very strong to begin with, music teachers can begin to doubt their value as professionals and as individuals.

One of the major benefits of being a music educator is the inspiring, rejuvenating, joyful nature of music itself, a strong barrier to loss of concern among us who deal with it professionally. Yet, if we music educators are to function as more than technicians, a set of beliefs clearly explaining the reasons for the power of music remains necessary. Too often beliefs about music and arguments for its importance have been at the level of the obvious, with the secret hope that if one justified music education by appeals to easily understood, facile arguments, its "deeper" values would somehow prevail. Just what these deeper values are usually remains a mystery, but they are sensed. So one plugs along, using whatever arguments turn up to bolster oneself in one's own and others' eyes, trusting that all will turn out well in the end. But as time goes along, for us as individuals and for the profession as a whole, it becomes less and less possible to be sustained by hazy hopes. A time for candor presents itself, when the question can no longer be avoided: "Just what is it about my work that really matters?"

The function of a professional philosophy is to answer that question. A good answer should be developed while a person is preparing to enter the profession. If not, any time is better than no time. If the answer is a convincing one, it will serve to pull together our thoughts about the nature and value of our professional efforts in a way that allows for those thoughts to grow and change with time and experience. A superficial philosophy cannot serve such a purpose—a philosophy is needed that illuminates the deepest level of values in our field. At that level we can find not only professional fulfillment but also the personal fulfillment that is an outgrowth of being a secure professional.

Everything we music educators do in our jobs carries out in practice our beliefs about our subject. Every time a choice is made a belief is applied. Every music teacher, as every other professional, makes hundreds of small and large choices every day, each one based on a decision that one thing rather than another should be done. The quality of those decisions depends in large measure on the quality of our understanding of the nature of our subject. The deeper this understanding, the more consistent, the more focused, the more effective our choices become. Those who lack a clear understanding of their subject can make choices only by hunch and by hope, these being a reflection of the state of their beliefs. Those who have forged a philosophy based on a probing analysis of the nature of music can act with confidence, knowing that whatever they choose to do will be in consonance with the values of the domain they represent.

These values must be sought in a concept about the primary value of music and the teaching of music. As it happens, such a concept has been formulated over a period of several decades and has been given added impetus in recent years by a variety of contributions from psychology and philosophy and educational theory. Put simply, it is that music and the other arts are basic ways that humans know themselves and their world; they are basic modes of cognition. The older idea, prevalent since the Renaissance, that knowing consists only of conceptual reasoning is giving way to the conviction that there are many ways humans conceive reality, each of them a genuine realm of cognition with its own validity and unique characteristics. We know the world through the mode of conceptual rationality, indeed, but we also know it through the musical mode.

Further, the older notion that human intelligence is unitary, being exclusively a manifestation of the level of ability to reason conceptually as measured by IQ tests, is also undergoing a profound revolution. The idea now gaining currency is that intelligence exists in many manifestations. The argument is being advanced that an education system focused exclusively or predominantly on one mode of cognition—the conceptual—which recognizes only conceptual forms of intelligence as being valid, is a system so narrow in focus, so limited in scope, so unrealistic about what humans can know and the ways humans function intelligently, as to be injurious to students and even dehumanizing in its effects on them and on the larger society it is supposed to serve.

These burgeoning ideas allow music educators to affirm, with great courage, with great hope, and with great relief, that music must be conceived as all the great disciplines of the human mind are conceived—as a basic subject with its unique characteristics of ways to know and ways to be intelligent, that must be offered to all children if they are not to be deprived of its values. This affirmation has the power to strengthen the teaching and learning of music in the schools. At one stroke it establishes music as among the essential subjects in education, prescribes the direction music education must take if it is to fulfill its unique educational mission, gives the profession a solid philosophical grounding, and provides the prospect that music education will play a far more important role for society in the future than it has in the past.

The philosophy offered in this book will explain the foundational dimensions of music on which these claims can be built. It will also attempt to bridge the gap between philosophy and practice by suggesting, at the level of general principles, how music education can be effective in bringing the unique values of music to all students. Throughout the book the methods of philosophical work will be employed—critical analysis, synthesis, and speculative projection of ideas—and the purpose of philosophical work will be pursued, to create meanings by which we can live better lives.

A WORD ABOUT SOME WORDS

What is "philosophy"? The word itself comes from the Greek (*philo* = loving, *sophy* = science of, and wisdom). Philosophy is a way of loving wisdom by thinking carefully and exactingly about it. It is not science as we have come to understand that word in the modern world but science in the sense of systematic, precise reflection about ideas, beliefs, values, and meanings. Over the centuries a number of branches of philosophy have evolved, each focusing on a particular subset of human interests, such as epistemology, dealing with issues of knowledge; ontology, focusing on ideas of being; axiology, studying ideas of value; and logic, which investigates systems and principles of reasoning.

The branches of philosophy of most direct relevance for music education are aesthetics, or philosophy of art, and education. This book will draw many (but not all) of its positions and arguments from the systematic study of ideas about the arts, music in particular, and from such study of education. A bit of clarification about "aesthetics" and its relation to "philosophy of art" will help explain how I understand and use those terms.

Aesthetics as a separate field within philosophy emerged during the eighteenth century in Europe, at a time when the arts of music, poetry, painting, sculpture, and dance were being conceived as related—as the "fine arts." Distinctions between the particular interests that arose in aesthetics—aesthetic attitude and experience, the aesthetic object, aesthetic value—and the broader and much older interests of philosophy of art—the nature of beauty, how to define art, how art is to be understood and appreciated, how it is created, and so forth—are blurred, and to a large degree are no longer useful. In *The Cambridge Dictionary of Philosophy,*[1] the comments are made that questions of aesthetics overlap with those in philosophy of art, and that "aesthetics also encompasses the philosophy of art." Wayne D. Bowman, in his *Philosophical Perspectives on Music,*[2] contrarily says that "philosophy of music is broader than aesthetics, and subsumes it." Other writers, such as Susan Feagin and Patrick Maynard, editors of *Aesthetics,*[3] equate the two, using them as synonyms. Monroe C. Beardsley,

---

[1] Robert Audi, ed., *The Cambridge Dictionary of Philosophy* (New York: Cambridge University Press, 1995), 10. Reprinted with the permission of Cambridge University Press.
[2] Wayne D. Bowman, *Philosophical Perspectives on Music* (New York: Oxford University Press, 1998), 6.
[3] Susan Feagin and Patrick Maynard, eds., *Aesthetics* (New York: Oxford University Press, 1997), 6–8.

in his book *Aesthetics from Classical Greece to the Present,*[4] says, "I have no quarrel with those who wish to preserve a distinction between 'aesthetics' and 'philosophy of art.' But I find the shorter term very convenient, and so I use it to include matters some would place under the second. I claim sufficient warrant in prevailing competent usage—e.g., the *Journal of Aesthetics and Art Criticism* and the *British Journal of Aesthetics.*"

I want to make clear that when I use the term "aesthetics" I do so in the broadest possible sense, encompassing all past and present philosophical discourse on the entire range of issues related to aesthetics and philosophy of art, whether conceived as separate or concurrent domains. I particularly want to clarify that my use of the term aesthetics in no way commits me to positions taken by thinkers associated with aesthetics in the narrow sense of a historical movement during which particular conceptions of music and the arts were developed. I find some positions from aesthetics in that narrow sense useful, some not useful, some persuasive, some untenable. The term aesthetics will be used in this book as shorthand for philosophical (as distinct from, say, experimental, or historical, or anthropological) treatments of issues connected to music (primarily) and to other arts and related aspects of human experience. Though materials from outside aesthetics will be incorporated, they will serve primarily to add complementary insights to those dealing with the nature and value of music, and to clarify their educational implications.

Clarification of the terms "artistic" and "aesthetic" is also needed at the start. As John Dewey explained,

> We have no word in the English language that unambiguously includes what is signified by the two words "artistic" and "esthetic." [The "ae" spelling tends to be more accepted in recent writings.] Since "artistic" refers primarily to the act of production and "esthetic" to that of perception and enjoyment, the absence of a term designating the two processes taken together is unfortunate. Sometimes, the effect is to separate the two from each other, to regard art as something superimposed upon esthetic material, or, upon the other side, to an assumption that, since art is a process of creation, perception and enjoyment of it have nothing in common with the creative act. In any case, there is a certain verbal awkwardness in that we are compelled sometimes to use the term "esthetic" to cover the entire field and sometimes to limit it to the receiving perceptual aspect of the whole operation.[5]

Discussions of music often use the word "aesthetic" to include both the artistic/creative aspects (composing, performing, improvising, conducting, and so forth) and the responding aspects (primarily listening.) But these two aspects are also often separated out into the artistic as distinguished from the aesthetic. To further complicate the matter, the term "aesthetic education" was usually used to encompass

---

[4]Monroe C. Beardsley, *Aesthetics from Classical Greece to the Present* (New York: Macmillan, 1966), 14.

[5]John Dewey, *Art as Experience* (New York: Capricorn Books, 1934), 46.

all aspects of teaching the arts, including their artistic, responsive, historical, critical (and so forth) dimensions. That is the way I have always used the term. However, the word aesthetic in aesthetic education seemed to be taken by some to refer to only the responsive/appreciative aspects.

I will try to avoid confusion about the artistic/aesthetic terminology, usually referring to the music-making roles as being artistic, and to the listening/responding/critiquing roles as being aesthetic. But having to repeatedly use both terms when the term aesthetic is clearly referring to all aspects would be labored and so will be avoided. I hope the reader will be patient with this inevitable clumsiness our language imposes on us.

The word "performing" also suffers from ambiguity, often being used for what I consider two distinctive ways in which this musical role is carried out: the performance of composed music, and improvisation. (There is more on this in Chapter 4.) Usually I will use the word performance, or performing, to refer to the composed music setting, reserving improvisation for those musics in which the composer function is not present or primary. Again, given the overlaps of the two situations in some music, and the common use of the single term "performing" to cover both roles, some ambiguity will no doubt creep in. I hope the confusion will be kept to a minimum.

A TIME OF CONCURRENCE
IN MUSIC EDUCATION PHILOSOPHY

In both previous editions, I mentioned that, given that beliefs change over time, and that at any single time there will be differences in belief, it still remains possible to characterize the general state of beliefs at particular times. There existed in the decades from the 1960s through the 1980s a strikingly high level of agreement about the nature and value of music and music education among those who had given serious thought to such matters. What music education seemed to need, I felt, was not persuasion about this or that alternative philosophy, but continuing refinement and careful application of ideas commonly held at that time throughout the profession.

Those common ideas had been accumulating since the late 1950s, especially after the publication of two very influential books—*Basic Concepts in Music Education,* in 1958, and Leonhard and House's *Foundations and Principles of Music Education,* in 1959, both of which contained chapters with serious philosophical content.[6] These books had revelatory effects on me as a (very) young music educator with growing interests in matters philosophical, magnified by my graduate study with Charles Leonhard at the University of Illinois. His powerful influence helped propel me into a career of reflective scholarship.

---

[6]Nelson B. Henry, ed., *Basic Concepts in Music Education,* Fifty-seventh Yearbook of the National Society for the Study of Education, part 1 (Chicago: University of Chicago Press, 1958). Charles Leonhard and Robert W. House, *Foundations and Principles of Music Education* (New York: McGraw-Hill, 1959).

Those books were followed by a number of important and complementary national initiatives, such as the Contemporary Music Project begun in 1963, the Comprehensive Musicianship Program dating from 1965, the Yale Seminar of 1963, the Tanglewood Symposium of 1967, and the Goals and Objectives project begun in 1969.[7] All these and many other events during those years, including the publication of the first edition of this book, helped forge a widely shared sense of why music was important, why music education was therefore important, and what music programs in schools should look like if they were to be in consonance with those beliefs. This movement, both theoretical and practical, and central to thought and action in all the arts in education fields, became known as "aesthetic education."[8]

Needless to say, not every music educator embraced the emerging and developing ideas of aesthetic education in those years, or even was aware of them. Some, even many, music educators went about their jobs with no knowledge of the philosophical work being done and little interest in professional events reflecting that work, or unconvinced by or even negative about the premises of aesthetic education. Music education, after all, is a broad and heterogeneous field, both in its beliefs and in its practices. It is unlikely that all music teachers will involve themselves in issues and initiatives in the broader profession beyond their own daily obligations. It is equally unlikely that those who do will be unanimously approving of any particular philosophical position, especially in a democratic culture where diversity of belief is encouraged rather than deterred or even forbidden as in some societies. Nevertheless the aesthetic education movement did become an important, perhaps a dominant, factor in the profession's self-image during those decades.[9]

Pinpointing the defining characteristics of aesthetic education is difficult, given various interpretations of it, its aversion to being dogmatized as consisting of a particular set of doctrines to be rigidly followed, and its avoidance of anything smacking of a "method." As I explained in a paper on aesthetic education given at a conference on "The Philosopher Teacher in Music," at Indiana University in 1990, a year after my revised edition was published,

> Aesthetic education is sometimes viewed as a set of dogmas incapable of being breached and doctrines incapable of being changed. I want to argue that there are no such dogmas

---

[7]For descriptions of these initiatives, see Michael L. Mark, *Contemporary Music Education*, 3rd ed. (New York: Schirmer, 1996), 28–48.

[8]Ibid. Chapter 33, "Intellectual Currents in the Contemporary Era," 54–61, gives a brief but cogent overview of the aesthetic education movement in music education. An ongoing record of thinking related to the broader field of aesthetic education is most directly to be found in *The Journal of Aesthetic Education*, which began publication in 1966.

[9]For a discussion of ideas and influences leading to the rise of the aesthetic education movement, and a bibliography of its early important writings, see the two chapters by Ralph A. Smith, "The Philosophical Literature of Aesthetic Education" and "Bibliography," in Bennett Reimer, Organizing Chairman, *Toward an Aesthetic Education* (Washington, DC: Music Educators National Conference, 1971), 137–90. Two essays on aesthetic education, dealing with its history (by Ronald Moore), and its contemporary manifestations (by Ralph A. Smith), are contained in *Encyclopedia of Aesthetics*, ed. Michael Kelly (New York: Oxford University Press, 1998), 89–96.

or doctrines, although I will suggest my own candidates for what, in my opinion, are typical characteristics of aesthetic education. I will propose that aesthetic education is not a body of immutable laws but instead provides some guidelines for a process that, by its very nature, must be both ongoing and open-ended. . . . [We] require a philosophy amenable to and dependent on change as an essential characteristic, because it is a given that the philosophical problems considered to be fundamental to music education will change over time, the availability of viable solutions to them will also continually change, and the social-cultural nature of music education will also continue to change. It must be an essential characteristic of aesthetic education as a professional philosophy, then, that it not consist of one particular set of problems or issues, resolved in one particular fashion, relevant to one particular institutional Zeitgeist as it exists at any one particular period in history.[10]

Aesthetic education as I conceive it, therefore, is changeable and flexible, attempting to capture the best thinking about music and to apply it to practices of music education. Nevertheless, several characteristic beliefs of aesthetic education in music may be identified:

1. Aesthetic education strives to be both convincing philosophically and useful across the entire spectrum of applications to the teaching and learning of music. It attempts to wed theory with practice.
2. Aesthetic education is applicable to all children in schools—not just to the small percentage who demonstrate unusually high competencies in music.
3. A useful and valid music curriculum, K–12, is comprehensive, including all possible ways people interact with music—listening, performing, composing, improvising, and so forth—and also embraces all the ways people think about and know about music, including its history, its cultural contexts, relevant criticism of it, its many functions in people's lives, and the many issues related to its nature.
4. Any single aspect of the music program—a performing group, a general music class, a composition lab, a listening-focused course, and so on—can be, in and of itself, a valid instance of aesthetic education. Aesthetic education attempts to nurture characteristic interactions with music, and those interactions can be achieved in any and all aspects of a total music curriculum.
5. Interactions with music of any sort, at any age or competence level, should be dominated by, or at least inclusive of, an aspect of experiencing called "musical," in which the particular characteristics that set music apart as a recognizable domain are an important dimension of the learning and of the interaction.
6. Central to music as a domain is its capacity to create structures of sounds that are capable of incorporating all manner of materials (conventional symbols,

---

[10]Bennett Reimer, "Essential and Nonessential Characteristics of Aesthetic Education," *The Journal of Aesthetic Education*, 25, no. 3 (Fall 1991), 193–214.

cultural beliefs, political statements, moral views, stories, emotions of every-day life) and to add something to them that is "musical"—that is, charged with meanings uniquely available from music.

7. The "beyond-the-commonplace" experience, or the "transformation" of experience that music makes available in its unique way, and that should be an important dimension of teaching and learning, has been achieved in all cultures throughout history. Whatever the culture, music shapes individual and communal experience into unique meanings able to be created and shared by those who participate in that culture.

8. The music used in school, therefore, should be far more comprehensive than the narrow spectrum of "school music" traditionally assumed to be appropriate, and should openly reflect the realities of our multimusical culture. All the world's musics provide valuable sources for musical learning and experiencing.

A definition of aesthetic education as applied to music would reflect the preceding beliefs along with others this book will elucidate. Definitions, however, tend to delimit by stipulating a definitive, exclusionary set of conditions. In the case of aesthetic education, the word "description" is likely to be more useful than "definition" in that it calls attention to salient features without requiring that they be fixed or exhaustive. (In Chapter 5 I will apply these comments to a description of music and of art.) I offer the following description of aesthetic education, or summary of propositions about it, as a tool for thought, mapping out the terrain for an ongoing agenda amenable to change as new insights continue to arise and be found persuasive:

> *Aesthetic education in music attempts to enhance learnings related to the distinctive capacity of musical sounds (as various cultures construe what these consist of) to create and share meanings only sounds structured to do so can yield. Creating such meanings, and partaking of them, requires an amalgam of mind, body, and feeling. Musical meanings incorporate within them a variety of individual/cultural meanings transformed by musical sounds. Gaining its special meanings requires direct experience with music in any of the ways cultures provide, supported by skills, knowledge, understandings, and sensitivities education can cultivate.*

Clearly such a description requires "untangling." This book will consist largely of my attempts to do so.

Ideas such as this, beginning to be developed in the late 1950s, were generally and widely (although certainly not unanimously) accepted in American music education as being both theoretically persuasive and practically useful. That concordance of belief led, in due course, to an important practical consequence of an educational philosophy—generation of a clear picture of what the knowledge base consists of for the domain with which it deals. If, in the case of music education, a philosophical position is able to yield a grounded specification of those knowings and doings related to a comprehensive and satisfying incorporation of music into people's lives, it will have served an important purpose for its profession, providing powerful guidance as to the teachings and learnings on which the profession needs to focus. The relationship of a philosophy of music to a philosophy of music education becomes clear in this conception. The former provides a cohesive picture of the complex nature and diverse values of music. The latter, based on that set of understandings, provides a cohesive picture of those learnings most relevant to the nature of music and to the values it offers.

Fortunately, an opportunity to translate philosophy into educational action embracing the arts education profession at its broadest, most inclusive, level was presented as part of a congressional bill titled "Goals 2000: Educate America Act," passed in 1994. Stipulated in that bill as required learning for all students, along with English, mathematics, science, foreign languages, civics and government, economics, history, and geography, was "arts." Representing a triumph of the advocacy expertise of the Music Educators National Conference (MENC) (the arts were not included among the core subjects in the original version of the bill but were added largely as a result of MENC efforts), the arts were now, finally, recognized at the federal level as being basic subjects in American schooling.

An enormous opportunity, as well as an equally enormous challenge, presented itself. Each subject matter field in education quickly began to define the central learnings relevant to its nature and value, using as a model the materials developed by the National Council of Teachers of Mathematics.[11] The arts education fields—dance, music, theater, and visual arts—galvanized into action by MENC, organized themselves for the task of creating documents stipulating what students needed to know and be able to do if they were to be empowered to incorporate each art into their lives in effective ways. There was a palpable sense of urgency for the arts to get the job done as quickly as possible, to demonstrate that, having for the first time in history been given "official" recognition as basic subjects, they were as capable as any other subject of defining the learnings and doings appropriate to them, and that they could do so without endless debate and argument such as has characterized aesthetics since the ancient Greeks. We did not have twenty or so centuries to spend on resolving all our philosophical dilemmas (which are unlikely to be resolved even if we did). We had to do what everyone else in education was busily doing for their subject—to describe with reasonable specificity what needed to be learned if students were to engage themselves meaningfully with each art, as that is understood in the world and times in which we are now living. We had to put up or, if not shut up, at least be muted in one of the great educational events of recent history.

---

[11]*Curriculum and Evaluation Standards for School Mathematics,* 1989, and *Professional Standards for Teaching Mathematics,* 1991 (Reston, VA: National Council of Teachers of Mathematics).

A task force was appointed in 1992 to write the music document—Paul Lehman (chair), June Hinckley, Charles Hoffer, Carolynn Lindeman, Scott Shuler, Dorothy Straub, and myself. All these people had well-established backgrounds as thinkers/activists in music education, and all were known to have firm beliefs and commitments as to what music education was all about. Yet within a period of a year, this group of strong-minded individualists was able to forge a document charting nine content areas as constituting the fundamental knowledge base of music—the learnings and doings essential for valuable musical engagements as we are best able to understand what that means in our times.[12] (Interestingly, the arts content documents, called "standards"—the common terminology at that time—were the second to appear, after mathematics, later followed by a dozen or so others.) With no time for philosophical debate, let alone solving age-old quandaries, these people were able to translate deeply shared values, beliefs, and commitments about music into a set of contents that are teachable, learnable, and foundational for musical experiencing. A shared philosophy of music (implicit in this case) had served to forge a shared philosophy of music education (also implicit) capable of focusing the profession's efforts on fundamental learnings in music education. Truly, philosophy had served its purpose well in this case.

Notably, reservations about and criticisms of the standards movement in education (generally and in the arts) have focused on related political and social issues, such as providing equal opportunity to learn, standardization as a possible undesirable consequence, allocation of time to teach all that is required, preparing teachers for raised expectations, and on and on with all the difficult, complex issues surrounding such a large, unwieldy educational movement. I fully share in these reservations and concerns. (In Chapter 8 I will return to these matters in my treatment of the standards as a basis for curriculum content.) In music education, however, despite the subsequent rise of diverse philosophical views (to be discussed below and more fully in Chapter 2), few if any criticisms of or alternatives to the nine content areas delineated in the standards have been offered. There seems to be widespread agreement, approaching unanimity, that a comprehensive concept of a music curriculum would have to include knowings and doings related to (1) singing, (2) playing, (3) improvising, (4) composing and arranging, (5) notation skills and understandings, (6) listening, (7) evaluating, (8) understanding relationships of music to other arts and other disciplines, and (9) understanding music in its historical and cultural dimensions. These nine have been acknowledged by music educators in a great variety of cultures as being an ideal for comprehensive music learnings. I will attempt in chapters 8 and 9 to explain how the national content standards represent a radical,

---

[12]Dance, theater, and visual arts followed the same pattern as music in establishing their standards, and were similarly able to do so quickly because of the high level of shared values they had achieved. The collected standards were published as *National Standards for Arts Education: What Every Young American Should Know and Be Able to Do in the Arts* (Reston, VA: Music Educators National Conference, 1994).

far-reaching transformation of the profession's traditional conception of what music education is and does, a transformation now able to be understood as an inevitable consequence of the rise and influence of the aesthetic education movement. The standards (in a reconstructed form I will offer) give specific, programmatic guidance for achieving the aspirations of aesthetic education, including, in the skills, knowledge, and understandings they foster, the bases for mind, body, and feeling to be fully and interactively engaged in satisfying musical experiences.

Does the aesthetic education movement, in and of itself, remain viable after so many years of influence? I wondered about that in my concluding remarks in the paper to which I referred previously. Is it important or helpful to retain the term "aesthetic education"? Or has it done its work, so that now it would be well to move on to other conceptualizations?

> I confess to a good deal of ambivalence in this matter. On the one hand, one grows accustomed to a much-used phrase as to a comfortable pair of old shoes, its tears and scuffs and loose threads and worn spots being perceived not so much as imperfections but as signs of its adaptability to the rough-and-tumble to which it has been subjected and the durability of a wise initial investment. On the other hand, one is tempted by some of the snappy new styles. Conceived this way, one vacillates.
>
> Conceived differently, however, and in a more rigorous intellectual manner, aesthetic education can be taken to symbolize a process rather than an entity. In that sense I suspect it might serve a useful or even essential function, reminding us as scholars and practitioners to keep our eye on what matters and helping us define what it is that matters. For me, the most essential value of aesthetic education is not its name but its agenda. It is as a reminder and symbol of that agenda that the term "aesthetic education" may continue to prove useful.[13]

The aesthetic education agenda was given tangible and specific formulation in the national content standards, and I suspect that the influence of the standards will continue for quite a long time, especially since their potential for broadening and deepening the content of instruction in music education has barely begun to be realized. But in the fullness of time, alternative philosophical views have begun to be articulated in music education and need to be examined as to what their promises and problems might be. In the final section of this chapter I will explain the perspective I will take in that examination (in Chapter 2), proposing a philosophical stance that can serve our profession well in a time of diversity of philosophical views such as has begun to occur. But before I present that discussion and those proposals, it is important to recognize an important historical shift in philosophical beliefs far larger and more encompassing than the events in the small corner of the philosophical enterprise that music education philosophy occupies.

---

[13]Reimer, "Essential and Nonessential," note 10, 213.

THE CHALLENGES OF POSTMODERNISM

A sea change in philosophical perspective has occurred across Western cultures, and influential in the world beyond their boundaries. Confusing, messy, unclear, but not to be denied or ignored, that change is generally referred to as a movement from modernism to postmodernism. Music educators have not generally paid a great deal of attention to this shift in philosophy, but it is important to do so for several very significant reasons.

First, our tendency to let the larger world of philosophy outside music education go its own way, largely unnoticed, keeps us at the sidelines of the culture of which we are a part. That is unhealthy both for us and for our culture. For us, we tend to suffer from being parochial in our interests, in a narrowness of thought and action we display in our single-minded concentration on the techniques and methods of music making. We lose sight of broader issues, and people engaged in those issues lose sight of us as possible contributors. It is not good for us, individually or as a profession, to be as isolated from the intellectual life of our times as we sometimes tend to be.

It is also not good for our culture, which misses out on the valuable perspectives we can offer from the vantage point of our expertise in music and education. Our views need to be heard in the marketplace of ideas, because we have a great deal to offer. For this to occur we must be knowledgeable about the currents of thought swirling around us.

Second, music itself—our subject—is being influenced in a variety of ways by postmodernism, ways we are obligated to be aware of so we can reflect our awareness in what and how we teach. If we are to be up to date about our subject we must be up to date on how it is changing as a result of recent philosophical tendencies. We are being inundated with musics from popular and multicultural sources, often strange and even threatening to music educators steeped in the Western classical tradition. Arguments are being made that these musics deserve and require as much respect and as much representation in music education as the standard literature to which we are accustomed. Traditional notions of musical value, musical purpose, musical "truths" are being challenged by postmodern thinkers. It is being claimed that many of our comfortable beliefs are no longer supportable and should even be abandoned because of their exclusionary and self-serving nature, hidden from view until postmodernism swept the cobwebs from our eyes. Music is politics, it is argued by some, and teaching music is a political act as much as or more than an artistic one.

On and on go the challenges to long-held assumptions. We as a profession cannot afford to ignore these challenges or dismiss them without giving them an educated hearing so that we can make informed decisions about them. We cannot adopt ideas we might find valuable, or argue against ideas we might find harmful, if we are unacquainted with the serious debates going on about the strengths and weaknesses of postmodern ideas. Knowledge, as the saying goes, is power—to judge, accept, deny, as our informed insights lead us to do. Being uninformed leaves us powerless to cope with the many effects on music, the arts, education, and society that postmodernism is having. The following discussion will, I hope, provide the beginnings of understanding for those not acquainted with this significant contemporary way of thinking, and serve as a useful review for those who are.

The Postmodern Mind-Set

I use the term "mind-set" because postmodernism is a diverse collection of reactions to ideas and positions that developed in the period generally referred to as "modern." I specifically do not call it "a philosophy" because it does not fulfill the usual expectations of what that term might mean. For example, one generally accepted notion of what is required to be considered a philosophy is a reasoned, structured set of propositions about an important aspect of the human condition and human practices. In the postmodern view, reason is seriously and severely questioned as to its primacy or even validity. Structure, conceived as coherent thinking, is also regarded as at least questionable if not misguided. However, as we shall see, propositions, made with conviction, definitely remain the basis for postmodern thinking, even though they are offered without a belief in the validity of reason or of coherence. Whether this makes postmodern propositions unreasonable and incoherent is an issue at the core of the debate about its intellectual status.

The "modern" against which postmodernism stands is, itself, quite uncertain as to just when it existed and just what it entails. As to the "when," various answers can be found. In one sense the modern period began with the ancient Greeks and their (particularly Plato's) employment of reasoned argument as the preferred way of understanding the world and acting responsibly within it. In another sense the modern period may be understood to have begun with the Renaissance, the period beginning in fourteenth-century Europe when a great revival of interest in and production of learning, literature, the arts, and philosophy marked the decline of the medieval ages. In still another sense modernism may be conceived as beginning with the Enlightenment, that time in the eighteenth century when human reason began to replace the religious faith of previous centuries as the authoritative guide to the ways humans should make sense of their world and of themselves. But other conceptions of modernism put its advent at the time of the Industrial Revolution, beginning in England in the late eighteenth century, or with the rise of avant-garde experimental art in the early years of the twentieth century, or when that period came to an end in the middle of the twentieth century. Given all this confusion, it is difficult or impossible to stipulate with assurance just what period of history postmodernism can be said to be "post" to.

The "what" that is supposed to characterize modernism and therefore be opposed by, of no interest to, or seen as no longer relevant for postmodernists is similarly murky. A great many ideas attributed to modernism have been called into question by postmodernists, but there is little agreement among these thinkers as to what, exactly, the central or defining ideas of modernism were that needed to be abandoned or replaced. However, it is possible to provide an overview of many of the positions postmodernists have taken, yielding a general picture of the postmodern mind-set. This picture makes it clear that there are, indeed, substantial issues at stake in the claims made by postmodern thinkers, issues of real and pressing concern not only for philosophers, whose business it is to take philosophical debates seriously, but also for practitioners in a variety of fields, education clearly among them and music education just as clearly as one of its subdivisions.

I will attempt a rather brief overview and explanation of ideas fueling the postmodern position, followed by a critique and then an appreciation of those ideas. This will lead me to my argument that a useful mechanism that might help diminish conflicts among competing philosophical ideas would be of great value in a time of seemingly increasing discordance in philosophy generally and music education philosophy in particular. I will offer a proposal for such a mechanism and will use it throughout the remainder of this book to demonstrate its utility and its power.

Postmodern Propositions

One recurring belief among postmodernists is that there can be no "essentialisms." Essentialisms are universal, foundational, defining characteristics of objects (including ideas), in which an object is taken to have an individual essence, or inner nature, or true substance that defines it and that pertains to no other object. In its application to the human condition postmodernism asserts that there is no essential "human nature," in the sense of a defining, stable, core set of human characteristics.[14]

Closely tied to an anti-essential stance is the equally strong belief that there can be no transcendental arguments or points of view—that is, arguments and positions that go beyond and stand above the localized, unpredictable contexts in which ideas must necessarily be grounded. All ideas are conditional, bounded, and provisional: there are no ultimate, "real" truths applicable to all people at all times and in all situations. So there can be no conclusive verities or criteria, taken to be axiomatic, self-evident, or universally binding. "Metanarratives," or "grand theories"— explanations, doctrines, and arguments above and beyond the limitations of time, place, and conditionality—are therefore rejected. There are no universal principles, or distinctions, or categories, or consistencies underlying and regulating human thought and behavior, and "the traditional dream of a complete, unique, and closed explanatory system" is only that—an unrealizable dream.[15]

Reason, for postmodernists, can never be neutral but only historical, cultural, and in much recent thinking, gendered. Therefore reason is not to be taken as supreme in human affairs. People are not independently acting and thinking creatures,

---

[14]For an explanation and history of the very complex and continually changing idea of essentialism, see the *Cambridge Dictionary,* note 1, 241–43. It should be noted that, contrary to the postmodern assertion that there is no "human nature" as such, some recent thinkers have argued the reverse, and that until we are clearer about what it essentially is, we will continue to be less effective in our actions and institutions than we need to be. See, for example, Edward O. Wilson's books *On Human Nature* (Cambridge: Harvard University Press, 1978) and *Consilience: The Unity of Knowledge* (New York: Knopf, 1998).

[15]*Cambridge Dictionary,* 634. Reprinted with the permission of Cambridge University Press.

separate from and above their particularities of place, time, moral assumptions, personal preferences, and limited understanding of what the world is like. It is not that some higher, more universal level of truth is available if we were only willing and able to grasp it—the point is that such an idea is itself misguided.

Also misguided is the modernist belief in progress toward a more just, more secure, more liberated world, guided by growth in knowledge, aided by technology, and celebrated in the arts. A more rational, more peaceful, more equitable, more humane world, achieved through the application of reason and of principles of justice, has not only not occurred, it is a false hope to think that it ever can. Further, such ideals were not free from self-interest and questionable motives. Instead, political gain and protection of entrenched power structures were behind all such seemingly noble aspirations. Those aspirations were cynically proposed and imperialistic—a way to impose Western notions of goodness on "backward" cultures—and therefore an expression of cultural arrogance, the assumption that Western modernist thinking is primal and superior. In that sense, modernist ideals can be viewed as oppressive and controlling.

Without secure beliefs to anchor ideas or actions, without faith in reason as a way to achieve desired goals, without hope that unity, or coherence, or regularity in human thinking and doing can be achieved, postmodern views present a picture of extreme diversity, disunity, multiplicity, even chaos as the inevitable condition under which human life must be lived. Uncertainty—about *everything*—pervades our lives, because its alternative—order—always implies power and therefore loss of freedom. So postmodernism proposes no solutions to issues: solutions, by nature, foreclose possibilities. Stabilization is not the goal. Destabilization reveals all the defects in the crumbling structure modernism has built, a structure ready to be broken apart. And if postmodernism offers no alternatives, it is because alternatives are, in and of themselves, simply substitute structures awaiting their own decay. Disruption is desirable, and dismantling beliefs serves a positive role in revealing the injustices, faulty premises, and oppressive motivations of existing structures humans have built. All comes down to political struggle, multiplicity of beliefs that are irreconcilable, life in the here and now of social strife, ideas as suspect and judgments as only preferences. After all, what is "better"? And what is "worse"? Why should particular values be privileged over others, or some conventions over others, or some views of reality over others, or predictability over unpredictability, or certainty over uncertainty?

If all this leaves us with nothing on which to rely, well, we can respond in an appropriate way—with irony. An ironic attitude allows us to live with, even enjoy, contradiction as inevitable, because it lets us detach ourselves from and put ourselves above the strife, viewing it with humor, with a shrug of the shoulder, a sense of the absurdity of it all. It also gives us permission to think and act pretty much as we choose (given that it would be a mistake to run afoul of the law). We can borrow or "appropriate" ideas from others, combine them in unintended ways, substitute unsystematic ways of thinking for attempts to systematize, informality in scholarship for formality. In opposing or simply ignoring the structures built by modernism, postmodernists find the freedom—even though empty of dependable values—to think and act as liberated beings.

Postmodernism, the Arts, and Music

The influence of the postmodern mind-set on the arts has been widespread and deep; indeed, the arts may be the fields most directly affected by this viewpoint. I have already discussed the ambiguities of dating modernism: the same ambiguities exist in dating modern art. And characterizing or defining the features of modern art that make it "modern" is equally difficult, given the broad spectrum of styles, approaches, agendas, beliefs, and practices within each separate art and across the arts before postmodernism became a recognizable movement. The fact is, any and all postmodern convictions about the arts can be found to exist as well in modernism, no matter when one claims it existed. (And, of course, modernism is alive, well, and, many would say, thriving, in the present.) Nevertheless, several characteristic features of postmodern thinking about the arts can be identified.

First, political issues tend to be front and center, the arts being regarded primarily or at least significantly as agents of political change and reform. Art should be judged, then, primarily or at least in large part for the reformist political stances it takes and how effectively it argues for them. Given this agenda for the arts, it is not surprising that the verbal arts, most notably literature, have been the most actively involved in postmodern ideas, followed by the visual arts.[16] These are the ones most directly involved with, or most amenable to, the construction and communication of political-social messages and attitudes. Music also can be political, of course (and always has been), although perhaps not quite as obviously.

What should the role of music education be in regard to political issues? Should we teach music for its political attitudes and positions? What would that do to the ways we normally teach music now, and the generally nonpolitical interests of most music educators? Which political issues should be dealt with through music education? And what positions about them should be taken? How, exactly, would our teaching be made to be "political"? What, exactly, about musical experience can be considered political? Should all of our interests be focused on political matters, or only some? Would each teacher determine what political issues should be dealt with, and how, and what should be taught about them?

One important political agenda for the arts is to erase false and harmful distinctions between "high" and "popular" expressions. Such elitist thinking, postmodernists are likely to argue, represents a way to privilege some people, some cultures,

---

[16]Visual art education theorists have been very active in the modern/postmodern debate, far more than their counterparts in music education. For an extended, penetrating discussion, explanation, and critique of postmodernism in visual art, see Ralph A. Smith, *Excellence II: The Continuing Quest in Art Education* (Reston, VA: National Art Education Association, 1995), 139–59. Also see, for helpful descriptions of the postmodern influence on art and art education, Michael J. Parsons and H. Gene Blocker, *Aesthetics and Education* (Urbana: University of Illinois Press, 1993).

some ideologies, and some social institutions over others, the arts serving as a power-ful reinforcer of the dominance of those social classes and cultures in power. So the arts need to be "leveled," reflecting an egalitarian view of social justice. The "canon," those artworks regarded to be the highest examples of excellence, is an elitist device intended to raise one particular tradition, that of the ruling class and its culture, above all others, and to instill its values as being "superior." Instead, postmodernists argue, there are many traditions in the arts, and none is inherently superior to others.

All artistic expressions, then, deserve equal respect: pluralism, not a singular standard of goodness, is the aim. All political, social, and cultural interests need to be represented by arts that plead their case. Feminism, civil rights, religious ideolo-gies, and class struggles can and should use the arts, or regard the arts, as existing to serve their causes. Because no single class, tradition, social group, culture, or gen-der is privileged, and there are no objective criteria for judging artistic value, all people are free to employ the arts to serve their political needs, and all such arts are equally valid.

Should music education abandon its emphasis on the classical music of the Western tradition? Are all musics equally good just because each music has its own characteris-tics? If all music is equally valuable, how do we choose what is most worth teaching? Must we choose music to equally represent all possible political agendas? Would that be acceptable to our students and communities? Is that what they expect of us? Is that what we really want to do as music educators? What kind of teacher education would prepare music educators for such teaching? Who would be capable of providing it?

Another concept of influence in postmodern thinking is that those who respond to art create art as much as artists do. What an artist does—a novelist, painter, choreographer, composer, and so forth—is just one aspect of art. Of equal or greater importance is what the responder does, because art does not "exist" until a respondent creates something in herself. There can be no agreement among people, including so-called experts, as to what the value, meaning, purpose, or "interpreta-tion" (often called the "text") of any artist's production might be. That is the right of the individual percipient, who can then be regarded as creatively equal to, or perhaps superior to, the artist. Far from being a kind of heroic figure bringing new meaning into existence, the artist is only a mediator of culturally supplied meanings that then need to be brought to reality by those who respond to her suggestive impulses.

If each person (each student) is as creative as the composers and performers and improvisers of the music we teach, what do we teach about that music? Do we just "present" it by listening to it, playing it, singing it, and let everyone make of it what they "creatively" care to? What would it mean, then, to make a performance "better"? Would we be imposing our own personal opinions and eliminating our students' creativity if we rehearsed a piece to make it sound the way we think it ought to, according to what we know of the composer, the style, the accepted practices of performing in which we are steeped? And what do we say about a piece we listen to? Would any attempt to point out this or that musical occurrence delimit our students' equal right to make of the music whatever they care to "create" out of it? What, exactly, did Beethoven, or Louis

Armstrong, or Sondheim create, if anything? Can we acknowledge their creativity without depriving our students of the right to create their own experiences of the music?

An extensive and insightful exploration of music from a postmodern point of view is given by Wayne Bowman in his book, *Philosophical Perspectives on Music,*[17] on which I will draw for a much more brief overview. Bowman's delineation of the postmodern view of music is summarized concisely at the beginning of his section on "The Postmodern Ethos":

> In place of the idea of "the musical" as a unitary domain of beautiful sonorous patterns, we find a multidimensional field where the personal, the political, and the moral claim genuinely musical relevance. The border between "the musical" and "the extramusical" has become severely eroded and difficult to patrol. The comforting belief that all music is evaluable by the same, strictly "aesthetic" criteria has lost its persuasiveness, as has the noble vision of music as an inherently and inevitably "humanizing" affair. The essentially musical core which "masterworks" were once thought to represent abundantly is increasingly characterized as ideological and political subterfuge. What the term "music" designates has become increasingly problematic, and its potential values have become radically multiple.[18]

For postmodernists music has no "essence" defining its assumed fundamental nature; there are only many different musics, each with its own culturally based particularities and individualities. There are no universal musical characteristics or values applicable to all the diverse musics in the world and in history, so there is no way to compare or judge the value of any one music against any others; all are incomparably valuable. The experience of music from a different culture radically confronts one's own musical value system with an equally valid alternative, thereby contradicting any belief that one's own culture is in any way musically privileged.

One particular music exemplifies the postmodern ethos—"rap." Blacks have good reason to disdain modernist assumptions that enlightenment, supported by reason, will inevitably lead to equality and justice. Bowman points out that "Potter puts it bluntly: blacks sensed the fundamental rottenness of European modernism long before the Europeans detected the first hints of indigestion."[19] Rap emphasizes not stable "works of art" but spectacular displays in graffiti-like fractures, fragments, and layers.

---

[17]From *Philosophical Perspectives on Music* by Wayne Bowman, copyright 1998 by Oxford University Press, Inc., 356–409. Used by permission of Oxford University Press, Inc.

[18]Ibid., 394. Bowman's overview of postmodern thinking (pp. 394–99) is very concise yet inclusive. His discussion of "Feminist Perspectives" and "Music from Feminist Perspectives" (pp. 360–94) as related to and influential on postmodern thinking is rich with useful insights. For an excellent overview of postmodernism from an education viewpoint, focusing on the idea of freedom, see Aaron Schutz, "Teaching Freedom? Postmodern Perspectives," *Review of Educational Research,* 70, no. 2 (Summer 2000), 215–51.

[19]Ibid., 402.

But postmodern convictions apply also to so-called classical or legitimate music (as if only one type of music could be regarded as legitimate). Bowman quotes Lawrence Kramer's assertion that classical music is in a very precarious position.

> It is no secret that [classical] music is in trouble. It barely registers in our schools, it has neither the prestige nor the popularity of literature and visual art, and it squanders its capacities for self-renewal by clinging to an exceptionally static core repertoire. Its audience is shrinking, graying, and overly palefaced. [It] holds at best an honorific on the margins of high culture.[20]

What is needed to rescue classical music, according to Kramer, is to remove it from its elitist pedestal and restore it to the real world. To do so requires that the formalist notion of musical form as the defining characteristic of music be abandoned in favor of the recognition that context, personal and social experience, emotive description, critical judgments, and "meaning" are not extramusical additions to the formal essence of "music alone," but valid dimensions of musical experience. While form "is the agent of musical closure, coherence, unity; the means of containing excess and superfluity," involvements of self with other, and form with context, allows "a more mobile and plural play of meanings." Autonomy—the work of music as a self-contained entity—"is as dead as Elvis," according to Kramer.[21]

RIFF 1

I arrive on the monorail at the Seattle Center station, home of the recently opened "Experience Music Project" (EMP), housed in a typically breathtaking structure by Frank Gehry, whose stunning Guggenheim Art Museum in Bilbao, Spain, I had visited a year ago. A postmodern architect *par excellence,* Gehry's creations defy previous definitions of "a building," in their avoidance of regularity, predictability, cohesive form, unity of impression. Especially do they thumb their nose at the simplicity and elegance of modernist buildings such as exemplified by Mies Van der Rohe, for whom "less is more" was a mantra. For Gehry, *more* is definitely more, his structures being wildly irregular in shapes, volumes, spaces, materials, overwhelming the senses rather than ordering them. One cannot see Gehry's buildings as a whole. They are indeterminate localities rather than defined structural forms.

Inside all is chaos, movement, sounds and sights and spaces intersecting dizzyingly from all directions. Reflecting the rock and roll culture to which EMP is dedicated, energy and immediacy are palpable, in the displays, the bewildering configuration of spaces in which various aspects of rock and roll are presented, the enormous video screen in the main hall on which black

---

[20]Ibid., 403.
[21]Ibid., 404.

vertical bands block out about a third of what is shown, yielding a blurred visual impression of the rock performances by famous groups rather than a clear image of them.

But look closer. In a display of rock in Seattle, a historical, step-by-step story is told: the early days of jazz and rhythm and blues, the rise of heavy metal, the advent of hip-hop and punk and grunge, and the diverse present scene. Visuals and audios trace this history in the format of an illustrated lecture as in a traditional museum. Same for the Guitar Gallery, in which the development of the electric guitar is traced, in a linear fashion over time, as any good historian would surely approve. In the Sound Lab I don earphones and tinker with a programmed electronic keyboard. "Find the note C on your keyboard," the announcer says. "It is lit up. Notice how the white keys go up in steps named by the letters of the alphabet—C, D, E, F, G, A, B, and then C again. Play those keys. What you played is called a major scale." And so forth. The so-called fundamentals, alive and well!

Within the shell of postmodernism, modernism supplies the blood and guts of music history, theory, performance, cultural backgrounds, influential people; all the ways of encountering music and understanding its workings and settings we have long ago devised. Enormous amounts of effort and talent (not to mention money) have gone into enlivening the experience, as appropriate for the topic. Equal resources have been spent on making it coherent—on making sense of what seems, on the surface, bewildering. A fruitful blend, it seems to me, of virtues of modernism and of postmodernism into an exhilarating whole. But I do seek, when I leave, a solitary bench where I can sit in quiet and try to restore a sense of calm.

A CRITIQUE OF POSTMODERNISM, AND AN APPRECIATION

I hope my overview of postmodernism, however brief, gives the flavor of its concerns. I hope also that the seriousness of its critiques of many assumptions in recent and contemporary culture will unsettle those who have not considered such matters. It is not pleasant to have one's beliefs challenged, and postmodernism exists precisely in order to challenge. Those who take ideas seriously cannot avoid the challenges it presents. These challenges directly confront music education, such as in the italicized questions in the preceding section.

But postmodernism can be, should be, and has been itself challenged, from a variety of standpoints. One could easily retrace my explanation of postmodern beliefs, sentence by sentence, and find abundant occasions for disagreement, for questioning the validity of what is claimed, for pointing out unsupportable exaggerations and distortions, and for outright rejection as being untrue. Here I want to give an overview of frequently made challenges to postmodernism, and some extensions of them, partly to highlight important weaknesses in its arguments but more importantly to serve as a basis for the philosophical position I will recommend in the following section of this chapter. We need a way to cope with philosophical antinomy—the clash of seemingly opposing views, both of which have claims to be taken as persuasive. I believe such clashes are characteristic of the time in which we live and are likely to persevere for some time into the future (although there is no reason to assume that this condition is inevitable). Having a useful way to navigate the choppy philosophical waters surrounding us will be both personally and professionally valuable, I believe, in allowing us, as people and as music educators, to accept, honor, and value diversity of belief while also building and maintaining a sense of unity of purpose with other professionals pursuing shared aspirations. The modern–postmodern dilemma serves as a powerful basis from which to develop principles for maintaining stability despite uncertainty, an agenda as valid as any other amid a multitude of conflicting views.

Underlying the many critiques of postmodernism is the continuing confusion about what, exactly, the term means. Because practically every one of its positions can be found, often easily, to have existed in the modernist period (however defined) that postmodernists claim is no longer relevant, the remark is often made that the only thing new about postmodernism is its name. Indeed, it is difficult to identify any particular claim made in its name as being peculiar to it, leading Richard Rorty, the important contemporary (neo)pragmatist philosopher and social commentator, to have said, "A dawning realization that I have no idea what 'postmodern' means has led me to wonder whether I ever knew what I meant by 'modernism.'"[22] But, of course, postmodernists are likely to dismiss its vagueness, or the seeming impossibility of defining it, as being either of no concern or just another ironic aspect of its nature. One might say, then, that postmodernism is not so much a distinct philosophical viewpoint as an approach to thinking with a characteristic spirit—a spirit of debunking inflated certainties, of looking for injustices masquerading as truths, and of being willing to abandon convictions that now seem doubtful even if no substitutes are available.

It also is a spirit of welcoming—even reveling in—contradictions and absurdities as being inevitable elements in human thought and action while assuming that its own positions are not at all contradictory or absurd; in abandoning reason as foundational in human affairs while simultaneously depending on it to make and explain its claims; and taking the stance that finally, with postmodernism, the "truth" about the human condition has been reached while at the same time denying, if not ridiculing, the concepts of both truth and progress. For many critics this is not a pretty picture.

Bowman offers a useful summary of the bewildering tangles postmodern views present to us.

---

[22]Quoted by Morris Grossman in his review of Hugh Mercer Cutter, *Rediscovering Values: Coming to Terms with Postmodernism* (Armonk, NY: M. E. Sharpe, 1997), in *The Journal of Aesthetics and Art Criticism,* 56, no. 4 (Fall 1998). Rorty's comment was made in *The New Republic,* December 2, 1996.

Compared to the centered, stable, secure vantage point of modernity, feminist and post-modern critiques are disturbingly relativistic and chaotic. And they precipitate a host of thorny issues. If all musical choices are equally good, none inherently better than others, how does one choose? If there are no absolutes that can claim our common loyalty in any but an arbitrary manner, how do postmodernists justify their deeply held conviction that pluralism and diversity are more descriptive of the way things "really are" than unity and uniformity? If claims to philosophical reason only serve to dignify rhetorical persuasion; if all claims to "absolutes" serve to sustain illusions of inevitability for particular sociopolitical interests; if "truth" is only "belief" given a fancy and influential name; if "objectivity" is just a politically motivated cover for "subjective" interests; then on what grounds do these voices presume their pluralistic vantage point is more adequate than those that once presumed to speak for everyone everywhere?[23]

Bowman's final point in that quotation raises the issue of extremes—of bipolar opposites that apparently are irreconcilable. Postmodernists, Bowman points out, take a pluralistic vantage point seemingly opposed to and incompatible with the view that there are universals that "speak for everyone, everywhere." But are these really the only possible choices, leaving us with only the prospect of conflict between total pluralism and total uniformity? In his defense of postmodernism following the quotation, Bowman raises the aspect of bipolar extremes as seeming to be the only alternatives. On the one hand, he points out, postmodern foundations are fluid and temporary, rejecting bipolar oppositions. But in face of that assertion he states several such bipolar opposites as if they were inevitable. Postmodern thinking, he says, "regards situatedness and fallibility not as contaminants but as crucial characteristics of human experience."[24] This implies that modernists regard situatedness (being dependent on time, place, and culture) and fallibility (being open to error) as contaminating the human condition, which is simply and obviously not the case. The postmodern acceptance of situatedness and fallibility "clearly render[s] impossible continued subscription to modernist myths and the sociocultural orders they sustained,"[25] Bowman asserts, as if those "myths" and "orders" were devoid of a sense of their situatedness and fallibility, instead being blindly accepted as being completely free of any sense of time, place, and possible error. Is this not exaggerated, as if no subtlety or complexity exists and always has existed in matters of values and their basis? Postmodernism "does not pretend its vantage point is value free or value neutral,"[26] Bowman points out. But, apparently, its valuing of situatedness and fallibility are found nowhere else before postmodernism came into existence, allowing it to utterly reject previous sociocultural orders not enlightened by its apparently invented, original values.

This one-sided, historically inaccurate standpoint is found in much post-modern theorizing. For a clear picture of its invalidity one need only read Felipe

---

[23]Bowman, *Philosophical Perspectives*, note 2, 405.
[24]Ibid., 406.
[25]Ibid.
[26]Ibid.

Fernandez-Armesto's account of "The Death of Conviction" in his book *Truth: A History and a Guide for the Perplexed*,[27] in which he examines the rise, before the advent of postmodernism, of skepticism about unsituated, infallible, objective truth, tracing its development from Descartes, to Kant, Helmholtz, Schiller, Schopenhauer, Nietzsche, Kierkegaard, William James, Ayer, Wittgenstein, and Einstein and his theory of relativity and its influences on contemporary science as in Poincaré, Russell, Bohr, Heisenberg, Kuhn, and Gödel. This history gives a sense of the long-standing struggle to forge alternatives to the four bases on which the belief in objective truth has historically depended, as Fernandez-Armesto explains them in his book: the truth of feeling (including feeling in the arts), of authority (including oracles, shamans, commandments, scriptures, and so forth), of reason, or logic, and of the senses, as in empiricism and modern science.

Fabricating an extreme division between the modern and the postmodern, a division unsustainable logically or historically, reduces complexity to simplicity, to black and white with no shades of gray, and to conflict rather than concordance. This may satisfy the postmodern enjoyment of controversy, but it does little to help clarify what is at stake in our dealings with the difficult issues of, say, situatedness and fallibility, so that we might reach conclusions about them, and take action on them, more solidly grounded than bipolar extremes will allow. Of course, this implies that it is possible to be more solidly grounded about anything, a belief rejected in extreme forms of postmodern thought. We must remember, however, the irony that postmodern assertions are presented under the assumption that they are worthy of belief—that they are solidly grounded. Which way does one face in this hall of mirrors?

In an impassioned plea that postmodern theory should be heeded (he includes feminism as part of it although some feminists might object), Bowman presents its beliefs as if they were foundational truths, or universal essences, or transcendental arguments to be taken as axiomatic, based on reason and aimed toward progress—all the basic characteristics that postmodernism, at least in theory, thoroughly rejects.

> Both feminist and postmodern theory urge us to recognize and accept the fact of music's radical plurality and dynamic fluidity, as well as music's importance in constructing and reconstructing social and personal identities that are themselves always plural and fluid. They urge us to recognize music as an instrument of power, to divest ourselves of belief in the idea of musical autonomy that would exempt music from social criticism, and to deconstruct the elaborate system of oppositional hierarchies that idea has spawned. They urge us to deny in ourselves the totalizing tendency to represent as unitary what is fundamentally diverse. They urge greater tolerance for things like instability, change, multiplicity, and difference, while at the same time alerting us to ideological biases that can no longer be tolerated. They disrupt dreams of unity and uniformity, and expose the interests served by appeals to musical essences, absolutes, and authenticity. Perhaps most importantly, they urge that fallibility and partiality be recognized not just as

---

[27]Felipe Fernández-Armesto, *Truth: A History and a Guide for the Perplexed* (New York: St. Martin's Press, 1997), 161–202.

ineradicable parts but as preconditions of human knowledge and understanding. In so doing, feminist and postmodernist discourses defy the institutional and ideological arrangements that isolate music from life and [that] oppose popular/vernacular musical practices to those deemed worthy of serious study.[28]

I do not question the validity of some or many of the claims Bowman makes here. I, and I suspect many others in music education, share with him his devotion to aspects of what he is arguing for, although I would (and will throughout this book) explain them differently and balance them differently. What I am concerned about in his presentation of these ideas is his assumption, along with many postmodernists, that they are the property of a newly minted philosophical position rather than aspects of belief long present in human history. Understanding them as embedded in history lowers the level of intellectual arrogance of much postmodern theory; softens the bipolar, destructive opposition of the "virtuous new" against the "wicked old"; allows a search for resolutions as intricate as the complexities actually are, rather than seeing them as simplistic binaries;[29] and promotes a spirit that is positive for helpful action, by enlisting the sympathies and efforts of like-minded professionals aware that the problems posed by postmodern thinking are and have for a very long time been their problems as well, that some progress has in fact been made with them (despite the postmodern claim that progress is a myth), and that shared, cooperative efforts continue to be needed to move toward better resolutions than have so far been devised.

If all this sounds suspiciously "modern" rather than "postmodern," one must ask why the latter is preferable to the former. I am suggesting that extreme views in each position need not and should not be understood as defining each position; there is a vast area in between extremes in which modernism and postmodernism make not-so-strange bedfellows. We can appreciate the postmodern skepticism toward glib, self-serving systems of belief that have caused untold human suffering while also recognizing that some belief systems have provided hope, meaning, and a vision of a better life. We can agree that universal, ultimate truths are human inventions while also recognizing the need for and possibility of reaching better clarity in matters that concern human well-being. Of course, reason is a slippery beast, capable of being misused with disastrous consequences, but it can also be a powerful ally in combating the evils with which humans are regularly confronted. Coherent thinking has allowed us to achieve valued results in countless human endeavors: incoherence may be inevitable but it need not be desired. Human life may be limited to what particular places and times allow, but that is one important truth among others, such as that in many fundamental respects humans share characteristics, such as being musical, that are innate, transcultural, and transhistorical. And on and on with all the

---

[28]Bowman, *Philosophical Perspectives*, note 2, 406.
[29]For an egregious example of the complex reduced to the simplistic, see the table of "Attributes of Modernism and Postmodernism" in Arthur D. Efland, Kerry Freedman, and Patricia Stuhr, *Postmodern Art Education* (Reston, VA: National Arts Education Association, 1996), 42. This book is rife with examples of extremist thinking.

postmodern claims that can be appreciated, valued, recognized to be convincing, curative of inflated modernist attitudes in need of being punctured, of entrenched beliefs equally in need of being shaken up, of truisms no longer convincing, useful, or benign and needing to be abandoned. Between the modernist beliefs needing re-examination, and postmodern reactions to them also requiring careful assessment, lies a territory in which more secure, more useful beliefs can be reached than are available in immoderate, exclusive stances for modernism or postmodernism.

Can postmodernism sustain its critique of aesthetic/artistic values, so cherished by so many for so long? There are signs that even among devoted and highly visible postmodern theorists, a return to recognition of the validity of long-standing aesthetic beliefs is occurring. In an essay in the *New York Times Book Review* section titled "The Play's the Thing, Again," Shakespeare scholar Ron Rosenbaum describes a meeting of the Shakespeare Association of America. This group has for some time embraced the standard postmodern position that Shakespeare's works are not the product of his genius, but instead that he is greatly overrated (a kind of "Bardolatry") and that any artistic value of his writings is irrelevant, as is the entire idea of artistic value. According to those for whom "theorizing Shakespeare replaced reading, seeing, or enacting Shakespeare," Rosenbaum explains, Shakespeare was "a slave to the power relations of his moment in history," and his works simply represented those oppressive forces.[30]

A strong sense of disillusionment with postmodern theory was felt at the meeting, with even the most influential proponents of it admitting that they were weary of its pedantry in dismissing as beyond contempt the ideas of essentialism, humanism, and personal autonomy. As one influential theorist, Linda Charnes, put it, in her presentation on Harold Bloom's best-selling anti-postmodern book *Shakespeare: The Invention of the Human,*

> We all avow we speak for oppressed voices of class, race, gender, nationality . . . but is this all we have to offer as critics? It's time to get beyond the institutionalized debunking of the bourgeois autonomous or essentialist humanist self. The time to make a career of beating that horse has passed. . . . If Bloom's right about anything it's this: the world doesn't give a fig for our critiques of its epistemology. Post-humanism may exist in the academy but it won't be found in the hearts and minds of the book-buying public. For at least in Bloom's zesty world there's some humor, some poignancy, and some openly avowed love of art."[31]

"Love of art! Astonishing for a theorist to even utter such a retrograde formulation," says Rosenbaum. The demonizing of beauty, of genius, of "the aesthetic," he points out, seems to have peaked, allowing a return to questions of value, of aesthetic

---

[30]Ron Rosenbaum, "The Play's the Thing, Again," *New York Times Book Review,* August 6, 2000, 12–13.
[31]Ibid.

judgments, of a liberating perspective that recognizes the power of beauty in art, and art as personally humanizing. This "return of the aesthetic," says Rosenbaum, suggests a third way beyond the excesses of stereotypical modernism and postmodernism; "not a quaint return of the past, but something new: the post-postmodern, perhaps."

The return to recognition of beauty as a determining factor in art and life is also acknowledged by philosopher Alexander Nehamas. In his essay "The Return of the Beautiful," he reviews three recent books on beauty and comments on the issues they raise. In postmodern thinking, Nehamas explains,

> In all its forms, beauty came to seem morally and politically suspect as well as intellectually embarrassing. And now, as the millennium ends, beauty is suddenly back. It is impossible to keep up with the books that address it. . . . Beauty is emerging in different domains, from divergent directions, along diverse paths, in disparate manners and styles. . . . Why, once again, are we willing to acknowledge that beauty is worthy of love?[32]

It is comforting to begin to find, now, that even among those who have argued strongly for abandonment of long-cherished aesthetic values and beliefs, those values and beliefs continue to exert such a powerful pull as to force acknowledgment of their validity, thereby tempering excessive overreactions to them. Excess may have its place, but often, in ideas as well as in life, it is destructive, choking off any possibility of reaching accommodations sorely needed if inclusive rather than dogmatic understandings are to be gained. Truth, conceived as somewhat less than perfect or pure in this complicated, imperfect world, can often be better approached through an attitude of conciliation than one of opposition. As Mary Lefkowitz puts it in her appreciative review of Fernandez-Armesto's book, "One place to begin to look for the truth is in between the extremes of authoritarianism and skepticism, the middle ground that Aristotelian logic is reluctant to explore: something is not entirely false just because it cannot be shown to be entirely true, or entirely true because it cannot be shown to be entirely false."[33] In that middle ground, I believe, we are more likely to achieve a strong union of like-minded professionals able to act cooperatively toward mutually desired goals than can ever be accomplished by a state of intellectual and operational warfare between extreme, unbending positions. What would it take to achieve such a community of shared beliefs? And what are the complexities and hazards entailed in trying to do so?

---

[32]Alexander Nehamas, "The Return of the Beautiful: Morality, Pleasure, and the Value of Uncertainty," *The Journal of Aesthetics and Art Criticism*, 58, no. 4 (Fall 2000), 393.

[33]Mary Lefkowitz, "Believe It or Not," a review of *Truth* (note 27), *New York Times Book Review* section, January 23, 2000, 18. For an incisive analysis of extremist thinking in education research, and a plea for balance, see Kenneth R. Howe, "The Interpretive Turn and the New Debate in Education," *Educational Researcher*, 27, no. 8 (November 1998), 13–20.

TOWARD A SYNERGISTIC PHILOSOPHICAL STANCE

The term "synergy," or "synergism," from the Greek "working (or acting) together" (*syn* = together; *ergon* = work; *energia* = activity), indicates the possibility of cooperative rather than oppositional thinking and acting, in which "the interaction of elements, when combined, produce a total effect that is greater than the sum of the individual elements, contributions, etc."[34] As applied to philosophy, a synergistic position assumes that many or most beliefs or "isms" (doctrines, theories, systems, or practices), rather than being conceived as fixed, dogmatic, self-sufficient, axiomatic, and unable to be adjusted to take account of alternatives, are likely to be more valid and useful if understood as being open to variations, modifications, and adaptations to a variety of positions ranging from those similar to those seemingly oppositional. What is to be avoided whenever possible is an "either–or" mentality that forecloses helpful accommodations, as if beliefs, to be valued, must be absolute and unassailable or else not worth having. There may indeed be issues seemingly incapable of any resolution between the "either" and the "or" (one thinks of the abortion issue as an example), but these are likely to be exceptions.

A synergistic attitude begins with the premise that complete opposition is likely to occur only when extreme positions are taken—positions excluding any possibility of adaptation to other views that can strengthen, widen, and add dimensionality to those rigidly held. It also takes the position that usually—perhaps always—an open, accommodating attitude is to be preferred to one that opts for conflict as the desired or inevitable way to deal with ideas. Yes, conflict may be necessary. Opposition may be inevitable. But both may be reduced if possibilities for concordance are explored. It is likely that reconciliation of different views will yield more convincing solutions than those reached through the exclusion of alternatives. So a synergistic mind-set is one open to cooperation as an alternative to contention, to searching for points of agreement or confluence as an alternative to fixating on discord, to recognizing nuances in which seemingly opposed views are capable of some level of reconciliation. It accepts the fact that ideas and beliefs can and perhaps sometimes must be irreconcilably opposed to each other. But it also recognizes that many or most need not be entirely so, or even largely so, when attention to details reveals overlapping, compatible elements that can be built on toward creating a more rather than less accordant position.

As already mentioned, the modernist/postmodernist controversy provides an excellent test case for the usefulness of a synergistic posture. Each view can position itself at an extreme from which no concordance is possible; one is then forced to choose between the either and the or, the black and the white with no shades of gray in between. As Judith Grant puts it in her book *Fundamental Feminism: Contesting the Core Concepts of Feminist Theory,* "Postmodernist theory often sounds suspiciously as though it is reflecting some more authentic reading of texts: as though difference is

---

[34]*Random House Dictionary,* 2nd ed., s.v. "synergism."

more authentic than oneness."[35] Rather than seeking only difference, one can understand the two positions as overlapping both historically and intellectually, with a great many points of compatibility. Resistance to the either–or stance is increasingly being felt among thinkers about this important philosophical debate, as in this heartfelt plea for balance by Susan Haack, in the Introduction to her book *Manifesto of a Passionate Moderate*:

> In these essays I have tried to expose the flaws of recent fads, fashions, and false dichotomies: *either* scientistic philosophy, *or* philosophy as "just a kind of writing;" either metaphor as an abuse of language, *or* metaphor as ubiquitous, and philosophy, even the sciences, as genres of literature: *either* the Old Deferentialism, *or* the New Cynicism; *either* scientific knowledge as a mere social construction, *or* a denial of the significance of the internal organization and external context of scientific work; *either* the scholastic rigidities of analytic epistemology, *or* wild and woolly "feminist epistemology;" *either* preferential hiring of women, etc., *or* the Old Boy Network; and so forth and so on.[36] (Emphases in original)

From the field of visual art education a synergistic position toward the modern/postmodern debate is also being taken by some thinkers. In their book *Aesthetics and Education*, Michael J. Parsons and H. Gene Blocker suggest that

> it appears that many of the differences between modernism and postmodernism are in fact not unbridgeable. When we look at the work of actual modernists we see many anticipations of postmodernism and it seems that the more sophisticated modernists have been evolving for years in that direction. And when we look at the actual analysis of artworks by postmodernists we see that they retain some very traditional elements of modernist analysis. . . . The problem for most of us, therefore, is not whether to accept modernism or postmodernism, but how to strike the right balance between those approaches and take from them what is most valuable to us.[37]

And in music education proper, Paul Woodford's rigorous critique of postmodern excesses pinpoints its dangers.

> Postmodernists recognize, and even valorize, the concept of democratic community, although with their emphasis on diversity and plurality they generally prefer to conceive of society as consisting of many different communities. Each of these communities has its own particular political agenda and interests. What postmodernists have yet to satisfactorily address, though, is what happens when those groups disagree. Any society, due to its complexity, must necessarily entertain a plethora of competing and often conflicting claims. Without some minimal notion of public reason, which implies a spirit of mutuality, tolerance, and civility, but also rules of evidence, claims to oppression

---

[35]Judith Grant, *Fundamental Feminism: Contesting the Core Concepts of Feminist Theory* (New York: Routledge, 1993), 149.

[36]Susan Haack, *Manifesto of a Passionate Moderate* (Chicago: University of Chicago Press, 1998), 5.

[37]Parsons and Blocker, *Aesthetics and Education*, note 16, 62, 63.

become nonfalsifiable and society runs the risk . . . of becoming increasingly fragmented and incapable of collective action.[38]

In music education, Woodford points out, recent controversies have exacerbated differences in philosophies unnecessarily, causing rifts and quarrels. A change of attitude from one of contention to one of accommodation can restore a much needed sense of community and shared values, while at the same time respecting inevitable disagreements. He eloquently pleads for what I am calling a synergistic approach to music education philosophy.

> What gets many contemporary critics and theorists into trouble, I think, are their monolithic and dogmatic assertions that all authority is arbitrary and, therefore, suspect, and that absolutely everything is socially constructed (Barbara Riebling refers to these as totalitarian theories of truth). A more reasonable proposition is that we are both processes and products of some complex, even chaotic, mix of biological nature and lived experience. But aside from this, and their contention that it is necessary for philosophers and teachers to overtly engage in politics and social engineering, I see no irreparable gulf, no irreconcilable chasm separating our respective musical and educational agendas.[39]

In the next chapter I will address some striking examples of extreme views relevant to music education philosophies, attempting to show how they may be mediated and thereby strengthen music education. But it remains to discuss possible disadvantages of a synergistic posture. After all, there seems to be no sure cure for all the ills besetting humans, including those besetting a needlessly combative culture in recent music education philosophy. Inevitably, attempts to seek concordance can be undesirable, or can go astray.

The most important disadvantage of philosophical synergism is that it is much more difficult than either–or approaches. Philosophy attempts to probe beneath the surface of superficial observations and ideas to deeper, more explanatory, more complex concepts that are as insightful as intelligence and effort can devise. In trying to deal with the endless intricacies of the ideas every philosopher faces it is easy and appealing to cope with the challenges by portraying a position being examined as simpler than it is. The way to do this is to push the position toward a more "pure," or unadulterated, or uncomplicated state by exaggerating a single, obvious aspect and ignoring its subtle, or shaded, aspects—by portraying a set of ideas at its extreme, stripped of nuance. Extremes oversimplify. Black is black, white is white, good is this, bad that, either has nothing to do with or, certainty is unrelated to yes, but. Modern or postmodern—take your pick. How comforting—an endlessly puzzling, terribly convoluted set of interacting notions becomes, well, chocolate or vanilla.

---

[38]Paul G. Woodford, "Living in a Postmusical Age: Revisiting the Concept of Abstract Reason," *Philosophy of Music Education Review,* 7, no. 1 (Spring 1999), 8.
[39]Ibid., 12–13.

Synergism resists this simplifying tendency. In doing so it confronts the real work of philosophy—the hard, slogging attempt to discriminate carefully among differences and similarities of ideas, to avoid portraying alternative views in simplistic, unshaded ways in order to score points in an assumed argument, to attempt to be as subtle as required for the complexities in question but also as precise as possible so that the proposals can be grasped with clarity and directness. This kind of work, I am suggesting, is weakened by oversimplification, or exaggeration, or misrepresentation of the ideas being examined. These are difficult things to avoid because it is so much easier to oversimplify. The challenge I am presenting, to myself and to others, is to rise above that tendency.

That also has its hazards, however. An overly cautious approach can add complexity to what is actually relatively simple, making too much of what can and should be taken at face value. In search of confluence, one can overlook what is, really and simply, disagreement. If there is no middle ground between position "a" and position "b," one must accept that fact and act accordingly, not manufacture agreement for the sake of some larger principle: that, too, is misrepresentation.

Is synergy the same as eclecticism? I do not think so. Eclectics choose what they want from a variety of sources, picking here and there according to what seems most valuable. The point of eclecticism is not to create a philosophical system with its own identity but to gather items together from a variety of systems. I have elsewhere characterized those who depend on this approach as "philosophical raga-muffins," which is no doubt unkind in that appropriating others' ideas is both valid and convenient. All philosophers do this to some extent. But eclecticism as the sole or major mechanism of philosophizing avoids the creative work of forging one's own structure of propositions and using others' ideas as supportive elements. That is what synergism attempts to do, but with a sympathetic rather than an antagonistic attitude toward philosophical differences.

Synergism is compatible with pluralism but goes beyond it. A pluralistic stance recognizes what is obvious—that on any significant issue there are likely to be diverse positions. But it does little more, simply accepting, and attempting to live with, the diversity. The "more" that is needed is to examine alternative positions as to their similarities and differences, seeking to locate overlaps and agreements and also to clarify which disagreements seem not to be amenable to resolution. This *makes something* of diversity, attempting to do what philosophical work should do, probing beneath the surface of differing positions for what makes them tick and how they might, in ways not always obvious, be less antagonistic toward each other than a surface view of them would reveal. Synergism is a thoughtful, probing, analytical form of pluralism.

Synergism is similar to but perhaps not identical with a "dialectical" (or "dialogical") approach to issues. In her book *In Search of Music Education,* Estelle Jorgensen implies that divergent views can be either reconciled or tolerated, as follows:

> In proposing such a broad concept of music education, I am also committed to the idea that music educators need to embrace the many discontinuities, dissonances, and

dialectics of their world. The multiplicities and pluralities of individuals bring us face to face with the challenges of reconciling differences in language, culture, religion, life-style, age, and color, among a host of other boundaries that separate people. . . . The best way to meet these challenges is to take a dialectical and dialogical view of music education, recognize tensions in need of resolution, and hope that through dialogue these tensions can be worked through and either reconciled or tolerated.[40]

Later in the book, however, she argues that instead of attempts to achieve reconciliation we must learn to live with disunity.

[The] dialectical approach offers a synthesis of a particular sort. Rather than attempting to bring conflicting ideas or tendencies into reconciliation, unity, or harmony, educators may sometimes need to be content with disturbance, disunity, and dissonance. Things in dialectic do not always mesh tidily, simply, or easily. Nor necessarily ought they. The resultant complexity, murkiness, and fuzziness of the dialectical relationships, however, greatly complicate the task of music educators.[41]

In another discussion Jorgensen rejects the "either–or" position as too limiting, and the "both–and" synthesis as neglecting the difficulties of synthesizing things in tension. "The this-with-that solution, drawing as it does on a dramatic metaphor in which alternatives teachers face are actors on a stage seems closest to the process I am trying to articulate."[42] "This" and "that" retain their identity and their opposition, but each sometimes occupies the foreground of the stage and sometimes the background. Reconciliation seems to have disappeared as an option. In response to a criticism by Iris Yob, she says, "Yob regards my this-with-that solution of holding things in tension as problematical because the flaws of each alternative still remain and the weaknesses as well as the strengths of each are multiplied. I concur, but plead that, practically speaking, I cannot see how this can be avoided."[43] Later in this discussion, she reiterates that there are cases "in which alternatives are irreconcilable and mutually contradictory, in which this cannot be combined with that."[44] But then she switches back to the possibility of reconciliation: "I am inclined to the view that many apparently dichotomous cases turn out to be fuzzier than on first glance . . . the dialectical approach constitutes a process whereby teachers and their students explore their alternatives and the possibility of the ground between them before fore-closing either option."[45]

It is difficult to assess whether Jorgensen's dialectical approach is different from what I am calling synergism, or the same, or similar in some respects. What is important here is not so much the comparison between or harmonization of the two as the

---

[40]Estelle Jorgensen, *In Search of Music Education* (Urbana: University of Illinois Press, 1997), xii–xiii.
[41]Ibid., 68–69.
[42]Estelle Jorgensen, *Renewing Education Through Music*, unpublished manuscript, 20.
[43]Ibid., 23–24.
[44]Ibid., 26.
[45]Ibid., 27.

recognition that serious, thoughtful attempts, such as Jorgensen's, are being made within the philosophical community to deal in some reasonable way with the emergence of what has seemed by many to be an "argument by way of opposition" approach to philosophy. In that approach the goal appears to be to "win" rather than to illuminate similarities and differences among views and proposals. Philosophy by warfare is no doubt an option, but it is an unattractive and ultimately self-defeating one, both substantively and professionally.

A synergistic point of view should not be equated with a belief that "moderation in all things" is the most desirable position. Yes, moderation has its benefits, although it suggests that even moderation should be approached with moderation! We do not always want to feel moderately, or love moderately, or believe moderately, or enjoy moderately. In some things and in many ways we want and need passion, commitment, and devotion. As professionals we do not want moderate allegiance to the cause of music education. We want to value what we do with all our hearts, as appropriate to the subject that has so smitten us with its significance and grandeur. A philosophy of music education should intensify rather than moderate our devotion to a cause we can treasure.

RIFF 2

"Excuse me, Dr. Reimer. Would you be so kind as to autograph my copy of your book?" A young man holds out *A Philosophy of Music Education,* second edition, a hopeful look on his face. We are in the lobby of the headquarters hotel at an MENC convention, people milling around, talking, greeting each other happily. I smile and take the book. As always when I am asked to do this I'm a bit embarrassed, flattered, amused. Since when does a philosopher get treated like some sort of celebrity?

"I'm a sophomore in music education," the young fellow says, "and I've never read a book before." I hope he does not notice my startled look. "So it's not been easy for me to read your book—it really has stretched me. I try really hard to understand it, and sometimes I have to read a chapter a few times before I get the hang of it. But I wanted to tell you how much it's meant to me to start getting a philosophy. It's made me love music in a way I never did before. And to be excited about teaching it, which I really wasn't before. It's changed my life, and I'd be honored if you'd sign it."

I'm touched by his request, and by his honesty. (How did he get to be a college sophomore and never have read a book? Am I living in a different world from the one I thought I knew?) Also by his excitement about ideas, and the passion he displays about becoming a music educator, a world of possibility opening to him. "It's still happening," I think. "Young people continue to be enthralled with learning, with their first glimpse of how important music is, how noble it is to teach music. What a joy to be reminded of this." I reach for my pen. "It's my honor," I tell him.

Finally, a synergistic approach does not require, or assume, or desire that all who adopt it will wind up at some middle point, or "average philosophy," or grand consensus foreclosing the need for continued debate. Those who are willing and able to work with others in an accommodating spirit are likely to have fewer hard edges in their work—edges that bruise or draw blood. That, I am suggesting, is to be desired, psychologically and morally as well as philosophically. But there is no chance that synergistic thinkers will become so homogeneous that distinctions among them will fade away just because they treat one another's ideas with respect rather than condemnation. Synergism does not require or value agreement for its own sake, nor does it in any way assume that substantive disagreement is negative. It does deplore the manufacture of disagreement for its own sake or for the sake of falsely shoring up an argument being made. Philosophy will no doubt continue to be, and should continue to be, a discourse about alternatives, even if it succeeds in being more cooperative (synergistic) than it often has been in its history.

Music education philosophy has moved from a period of relative concurrence (roughly the 1960s through the 1980s) to one of relative diversity. In that earlier period philosophers of music education were rare birds indeed, so philosophical diversity was minimal. That had its advantages, as I discussed early in this chapter, but also its disadvantages in a lack of fruitfully contending ideas. In recent years the number of music educators devoted to philosophy, and the level of expertise they have achieved, have risen dramatically. This is a healthy state of affairs—a coming to maturity our profession has greatly needed and from which it stands to benefit substantially. But there are dangers when a profession's basis for being—its philosophical underpinning—becomes not only diversified but also conflicted. Discord in its foundations can throw the entire profession into disarray, threatening its equanimity and its effectiveness. I have argued for an approach to establishing reasonable and reliable philosophical bases for music education, despite major movements in our culture recently toward less secure beliefs. My hope is that diversity of convictions, which is inevitable, can be dealt with in a manner that makes us more rather than less secure. In Chapter 2 I will turn to an explanation of several contentious issues and how a synergistic approach toward them can help us achieve strength and identity in a period of philosophical variety.

ETUDES

1. Think of some (nonprofessional) beliefs you had earlier in your life that have had to be altered or abandoned along the way. Was it difficult to do? A relief to do?

   Now think of any of your assumptions about music education that have changed over time. Were those changes also difficult to make? Relieving? How did the changes affect your actions as a professional (or pre-professional)?

2. What are some beliefs about music education that have changed over the course

of the profession's history?[46] Do you think the changes caused a struggle in the profession as they were being made?

    Can you identify changes going on now at the professional level causing difficulties (or relief) in adapting to them? What changes in actions will be needed to reflect changing beliefs?

3. Suppose the music education profession, all over the world, was able to agree substantially on a particular philosophy. What benefits to the international profession might ensue? What dangers, or drawbacks, might be entailed? Do you think such a philosophy is ever likely to be developed? Overall, would it be better, or worse, for music education if it were?

4. What level of comfort do you have with the postmodern argument that life is inevitably confusing, incoherent, disunified, and unstable? Do you seek these qualities, or value these qualities, in your life? What positive effects might they have on people's lives? Can you conceive of a reasonable, or workable, balance of such qualities with their opposites (clear, coherent, unified, stable) as bases for a satisfying life?

5. Play out a projection of a completely, extremely postmodern music education program as it would actually work in schools.

    Try the same with its opposite—not modernism as such, given the many overlaps between the two views, but an extreme of unity and rationality in a music education program.

    Does each picture leave something to be desired? What aspects of each might yield a satisfying and practical combination?

6. Can you identify beliefs or ideas in your life that tend to be based on an "either–or" position rather than on a "both–and" stance? Are some such beliefs or ideas acceptable and satisfying to you despite their one-sidedness? Are you uncomfortable with some of them, especially when recognizing their exclusiveness?

7. What are some specific beliefs or ideas in present-day music education that seem to be at odds with each other? How might a synergistic approach to them help reduce unnecessary opposition between them? Would taking such an approach always be desirable, or might seemingly irreconcilable differences between them be sometimes better preserved rather than softened?

---

[46]A good source is Michael L. Mark and Charles L. Gary, *A History of American Music Education*, 2nd ed. (Reston, VA: Music Educators National Conference, 1999).

2

Several Alternative Views and a Synergistic Proposal: An Experience-Based Philosophy of Music Education

MAIN THEMES

- A synergistic stance is demonstrated in an examination of several key aspects of musical value:
  - Music as formed sounds.
  - Music as practice.
  - Music as a means for social change.
  - The boundaries of music and of music education.
  - Music as serving a variety of utilitarian values.
- Musical experience is an amalgam of "inherent" (the actual music people create and share) and "delineated" (what we as individuals-in-context make of that music).
- Musical experience is multidimensional. At its core, distinguishing it from other experiences, is its use of sounds to "make special" in the way only sounds can do.
- To achieve this specialness, people must create and share it; that is, engage in musical experience.
- One way to state the purpose of music education is that it exists to make musical experiences, in all their various manifestations, as widely available to all people, and as deeply cultivated by each individual, as possible.

APPLYING SYNERGISM

In his introduction to the book *What Is Music?*, editor Philip Alperson suggests that "the philosophy of music consists in the sustained, systematic, and critical examination of our beliefs about the nature and function of music."[1] Throughout history, people have wondered about music—what it is all about, and why humans seem to care about it so much. What is this thing called music (its nature)? What good is it (its functions or value)? And, for music educators, how can we teach it to best reflect what it is and best share the values it offers people?

These questions, seemingly so simple, are actually so profoundly complex as to have bedeviled a host of philosophers and others in the past, and they will no doubt continue to do so in the future. Added to the complexity has been the postmodern challenge to long-held beliefs, as explained in Chapter 1, causing an undermining of security about how, or whether, we can achieve solidity in our understandings of music's nature and value. Nonetheless, we can hope that enough sense can be made of music's roles in human life to provide a belief system sufficiently grounded, sufficiently inclusive, sufficiently useful, and sufficiently clear as to allow music educators in our time to act with shared understandings toward shared aspirations; that is, to form a community of beliefs, discourse, values, practices, and goals. Such a community will have enough homogeneity of thought and action to make it viable and enough heterogeneity of thought and action to keep it vital.

In this chapter I will provide a broad overview of several issues of pressing concern in aesthetics (or philosophy of music) that have direct relevance for a philosophy of music education. Each of the issues I will identify can be and has been dealt with in extreme ways in the past or at present—ways that insist on solutions I regard as exclusive and exaggerated. In such positions one is faced with mutually contradictory, one-sided decisions, as if there are no ways to find accommodations among alternatives. In a synergistic spirit, I will attempt to explain how it is often or usually possible, if one is able to get beyond unitary stances, to recognize sufficient overlaps among seemingly contending views to allow a more inclusive position to be attained.

After these discussions I will propose a philosophy of music education—a reasoned, coherent set of propositions about how music and its values can be shared and cultivated through education—in which the notion of musical experience will play a major role. Musical experience, I will explain, includes aspects of form, practice, and social agency, is bounded in a particular way, and inevitably serves some functional purposes. An experience-based philosophy of music education, I propose, allows for, honors, and cultivates a broad array of characteristics particular to music and the ways people engage themselves with it, while also recognizing how such engagements can musically incorporate and transform many dimensions of life and culture. An experience-based philosophy, I believe, can be inclusive yet distinctively musical.

---

[1]Philip Alperson, ed., *What Is Music?* (New York: Haven, 1987), 3.

MUSIC AS FORM

"To me, the greatest objective is when the composer disappears, the performer disappears, and there remains only the work."[2]

This comment, by the famous and influential composition teacher Nadia Boulanger, embodies several assumptions and attitudes shared by a great many people, musicians and others. The nature and value of music, it suggests, can be found in the autonomous, self-sufficient musical work. Music is the product of the labor of composers and performers (and others), to be sure, which means it must also reflect the lives, times, beliefs, aspirations, intentions, genders, races, religions, and so forth, of those humans. But all those matters should disappear, leaving only the work in its pristine isolation, as sound with value strictly as sound, separated from the worlds and experiences of the people who created it.

The idea that music, or all the arts, can or should attain a "selfness," or "isness"—a "beingness" of its own—has intrigued thinkers for many centuries. Music, after all, does seem to create its own distinctive world, different in important respects from all others. And we often enjoy music—find it meaningful and satisfying—with no knowledge of the people who were engaged in its creation and little if any knowledge of its cultural or historical context. We frequently just enjoy it "for what it is." But what *is* that?

A century or so ago, a very strong and distinctive answer to that question arose among several people who pondered it. Their answer was that the nature of music—its essential being—lay in its form. By "form" they meant not only the overall structure of a particular work (sonata allegro, rondo, theme and variations, and so forth), although that is one aspect of form, but also the many interrelations of all the sounds of every piece: how the music "goes" and how the sounds create meaningful sonic gestures that "hang together." Sounds "make sense" musically because of the ways they relate to one another in whatever musical relationship system is being used, such as the Western twelve-note scale, the Indian *raga,* and the Javanese *slendro.*

Because of their emphasis on the relations of sounds to one another as the basis of music, and the comparable internal relationships of colors, shapes, lines, and so on as the basis for the visual arts, these "formalists" asserted that the meaning of the arts—the experience of "sensibleness" they give us—is unique to the arts and therefore like no other meaning in all of human experience. Artistic events, such as sounds in music, mean *only themselves:* the meaning of music is completely and essentially different from anything in the world that is nonmusical.

[T]o appreciate a work of art we need bring with us nothing from life, no knowledge of its ideas and affairs, no familiarity with its emotions. Art transports us from the world of

---

[2]Nadia Boulanger, quoted in Alan Kendall, *The Tender Tyrant: A Life Devoted to Music* (London: MacDonald and James, 1976), 115.

man's activity to a world of aesthetic exaltation. For a moment we are shut off from human interests; our anticipations and memories are arrested; we are lifted above the stream of life.[3]

The experience of art, for the formalist, is primarily an intellectual one; it is the recognition and appreciation of form for its own sake. This recognition and appreciation, while intellectual in character, is called by formalists an "emotion"—usually, the "aesthetic emotion." But this so-called emotion is a unique one—it has no counterpart in other emotional experiences.

> [H]e who contemplates a work of art, inhabit(s) a world with an intense and peculiar significance of its own; that significance is unrelated to the significance of life. In this world the emotions of life find no place. It is a world with emotions of its own.[4]

Formalists do not deny that many art works contain references to the world outside the work. But they insist that all such references are totally irrelevant to the art work's meaning.

> [N]o one who has a real understanding of the art of painting attaches any importance to what we call the subject of a picture—what is represented . . . all depends on *how* it is presented, *nothing* on what. Rembrandt expressed his profoundest feelings just as well when he painted a carcass hanging up in a butcher's shop as when he painted the Crucifixion or his mistress.[5] (Emphases in original)

In music, because it is capable of being entirely untainted with nonartistic subject matter, the formalist finds the clearest example of artistic meaning: "Definite feelings and emotions are unsusceptible of being embodied in music."[6] Instead, "The ideas which a composer expresses are mainly and primarily of a purely musical nature."[7] There is no correspondence whatsoever between the beauty we find in the nonartistic world and the beauty we find in art, for the beauty in art is a separate kind. This is especially the case in music, in which the nature of the beautiful "is specifically musical. By this we mean that the beautiful is not contingent upon nor in need of any subject introduced from without, but that it consists wholly of sounds artistically combined."[8]

Formalism concentrates so exclusively on the internal qualities of music and their inherent, unique meanings as to deny that other factors, such as political opinions, references to particular people or events, the use of various signs and symbols, suggestions of ideas, ordinary emotions, and so forth, contribute anything of

---

[3]Clive Bell, *Art* (New York: Putnam's, 1914), 25.
[4]Ibid., 26, 27.
[5]Roger Fry, *The Artist and Psycho-Analysis,* Hogarth Essays (London: Hogarth Press, 1924), 308.
[6]Eduard Hanslick, *The Beautiful in Music,* trans. Gustav Cohen (Indianapolis: The Liberal Arts Press, 1957), 21.
[7]Ibid., 23.
[8]Ibid., 47.

significance to music and the experience of it. Perhaps the musical/cultural influences surrounding the work can be recognized, but these too are considered insignificant or at least secondary. What really matters is the internal interplay of sound-relations and the incomparable experience they can give.

In the estimation of extreme formalists, few people are able to enjoy the peculiar, special, esoteric kind of experience the contemplation of formal relationships offers. So most people, being inherently incapable of pure musical enjoyment, satisfy themselves with nonmusical reactions to music; that is, with reactions to the referents in music—the stories, images, ideas, and so forth they imagine to be in the music or to which the music suggests it might refer, such as "program music" does. For formalists this completely misses the point of music, of course, but they assumed that this is to be expected. Given the special nature of music and the general insensitivity of most people, these formalists believed, we should not be too concerned if the value of music is available only on a limited basis, and we should not have any illusions that most people will ever understand that the real value of music is quite different from what they think it is.

The extreme formalistic position taken by writers such as Hanslick, Bell, and Fry during the nineteenth and early twentieth centuries represented a particular historical and culturally embedded view, as all positions about music and the arts are likely to do. These thinkers conceived of music in terms of their own culture's music—that of Western Europe, which, despite being multiethnic (British, French, Italian, Spanish, German, and so forth), shared a common aesthetic stance. In that music, large, complex forms, expressed in an elaborate notation, conceived by composers able to master the enormous intricacies entailed in creating it, performed by specialists, often in large groups requiring the coordination of a conductor, and offered for the edification and delight of an audience capable of appreciating all this complexity, were the norm of what music was considered to "be." So conceiving of music as essentially "significant form" can be understood to be a natural conclusion under these particular cultural conditions.

Also influencing this conception was the position of the great philosopher Immanuel Kant (1724–1804), who

> insisted that the only thing relevant to determining the beauty of an object is its appearance, but within the appearance, the *form*, the *design*: in visual art, not the colors but the design the colors compose; in music, not the timbre of the individual sounds but the formal relationships among them. It comes as no surprise that theories of music have tended to be much more formalist than theories of literature and drama, with theories of the visual arts located in between.[9] (Emphases in original)

Formalist attention to the "interiority" of music—its selfness and significance as dependent on what the sounds are actually doing in relation to one another—has

---

[9]Robert Audi, ed., *The Cambridge Dictionary of Philosophy* (New York: Cambridge University Press, 1995), 9. Reprinted with the permission of Cambridge University Press.

proven to be a powerful and long-lasting construct. It has also proven to have useful application far broader than the particular cultural setting in which it took on its most extreme manifestation. Applied in a general way to all music, the argument that, to be "music" (whether or not that particular word is used for the phenomenon), the sounds must have been created to be, in and of themselves, significant as interrelated sounds no matter what other functions they might also fulfill, makes a good deal of sense. The sounds themselves must, to some degree and in some way, be part of the meaning, or significance, of the phenomenon.

The formalists elevated form to the highest degree of importance. But even those thinkers who did so had to recognize that the product containing the formed sounds—the "work"—was the result of the processes that made it, that no product can exist except as the result of processes. Even the ultraformalist Clive Bell quite naturally and unquestioningly included recognition of the artist's role as the source of the created forms. "Is it possible that the answer to my question, 'Why are we so profoundly moved by certain combinations of lines and colours?' should be, 'Because artists can express in combinations of lines and colours an emotion felt for reality which reveals itself through line and color'?"[10]

So it is not that for the formalist the product focus *eliminates* process; it is that the role of the former extremely overshadows the role of the latter.

Further, it is important to understand that the historical attention to form as a dimension of music exists on a continuum. The extreme views expressed by a few thinkers at a particular time and in a particular place, despite being influential beyond that time and in other places, were not accepted to that extreme by all subsequent (or previous) thinkers, most of whom acknowledged the role of form as an aspect of music but not to the same extent. Various views of music place more or less emphasis on the role of formed sounds as the determining factor in what is thought of as being music. At one extreme, form is predominant. At the other, form is insignificant. In between is a large space where form can be understood to play an important role among others, and therefore to be attended to in various degrees depending on the particulars of different musics, different cultures, different interests, and different motivations.

Form, I would suggest, is denied at great peril. It is overemphasized at equally great peril. Music is too complex, too inclusive, too multifaceted, to be entirely dependent on just one of its dimensions, necessary as each of its dimensions might be. Form, along with other musical dimensions I will be discussing here and in subsequent chapters, is, I would argue, a necessary component of music but not a sufficient one.

Many contemporary writers on music would agree with the claim that form plays an obligatory role in music. For example, Lucy Green, in her books *Music, Gender, and Education,* and *Music on Deaf Ears,*[11] makes a fundamental distinction

---

[10]Bell, *Art,* note 3, 46.
[11]Lucy Green, *Music, Gender, Education* (Cambridge: Cambridge University Press, 1997); *Music on Deaf Ears* (Manchester: Manchester University Press, 1988).

between what she calls "inherent" and "delineated" musical meanings. Inherent meanings—the organization of the musical materials—"are 'inherent' in the sense that they are contained within the musical materials, and they are 'meanings,' in the sense that they are perceived to have relationships."

> Listeners' responses to [inherent meanings] and understanding of them are dependent on the listeners' competence and subject-position in relation to the style of the music. A piece of music whose materials are highly meaningful or very rewarding to one individual might be relatively meaningless or lacking in interest to another. There are thus multiple possible inherent meanings arising from any one piece of music. In sum, the *materials* of music physically inhere; the *inherent meanings* of music arise from the conventional interrelationships of musical materials, in so far as these interrelationships are perceived as such in the mind of a listener.[12] [I would add performer, composer, improviser, conductor, and so forth.] (Emphases in original)

But although inherent meanings are necessary in musical experience, according to Green, they are partial, and dependent on a variety of delineated meanings. These meanings include the social, cultural, and historical contexts in which every instance of music resides.

> These contexts are not merely extra-musical appendages, but they also, to varying degrees, form a part of the music's meaning during the listening [and so forth] experience. Without some understanding of the fact that music is a social construction, we would ultimately be unable to recognize any particular collection of sounds as music at all. When we listen to music, we cannot separate our experience of its inherent meanings entirely from a greater or lesser awareness of the social context that accompanies its production, distribution or reception. I will therefore suggest a second category of musical meaning, qualitatively distinct from the first, which I will call "delineated meaning." By this expression I wish to convey the idea that music metaphorically sketches, or delineates, a plethora of contextualising, symbolic factors.[13]

In her books Green pleads for a balanced, nonextremist position in regard to the roles of these two dimensions of musical meaning, especially in regard to feminist agendas. I will discuss this matter further in the section of this chapter on music as social agency. Here, I am interested only in pointing out the ongoing recognition, even among highly socially conscious thinkers such as Green, of the "formal," or "inherent" dimension of musical meaning as being necessary (but not sufficient) in an inclusive theory of musical experience.[14]

---

[12]Green, *Music, Gender, Education,* 6.

[13]Ibid., 7.

[14]Other discussions of this matter, in which the role of significant form is recognized as important in music, include Stephen Miles, "The Limits of Metaphorical Interpretation," *College Music Symposium,*

Another important aspect of the formal dimension of musical experience is its identification in the minds of many with the idea of "music for music's sake," or, more broadly, "art for art's sake." Extreme formalists, as pointed out, tended to regard the ability to find significance in form as the property only of those who were gifted in this way, or, at least, highly educated so as to be able to find this significance. The elitist flavor of this idea seems obvious—formal meaning is not for everyone, and, because all art depends largely on form, art is also not for everyone. To value music for "its own sake" as formed sounds, then, is to be an elitist—a musical aesthete for whom the real world is of no interest but is instead an intrusion on the purity and preciousness of a "higher" world of formal delight.

I suggest that this understanding of music for music's sake is both extremist and inaccurate. Many if not most people actually enjoy and treasure music not for what it says about social issues, or for ethical purposes, or to gain any practical results from it, but for the sheer delight musical sounds afford. Starting in infancy (probably in the womb) and lasting throughout life, people naturally, spontaneously, and joyfully "groove" with—relish and are enchanted with—sounds they form or others have formed to give musical pleasure, or significance. Music for the sheer pleasure of its formed sounds is a benefit deeply and innately valued by people—a human benefit serving human needs for joyful experience. No, it is not the only benefit of music. But it is surely one of its most precious and one of its most sought after because it is one of its most *immediately accessible* qualities—the quality of organized sound as deeply satisfying in being, in and of itself, organized sound. It seems to me perverse to regard this inherent human capacity to enjoy musical sounds for the sheer sake of their musicality as in some way "elitist." However, the view that the only music worthy of being experienced this way is that of the Western classical tradition certainly *is* elitist. Recognizing that *all* music is "musical" in this way (along with other ways) liberates us from the limitations of the extreme formalist position.

---

39 (1999), 9–26; Bohdan Dziemidok, "Artistic Formalism: Its Achievements and Weaknesses," *The Journal of Aesthetics and Art Criticism*, 51, no. 2 (Spring 1993), 185–93; Marjorie Grene, *The Knower and the Known* (London: Faber and Faber, 1966); Wayne Bowman, "The Values of Musical Formalism," *The Journal of Aesthetic Education*, 25, no. 3 (Fall 1991), 41–60, as well as Chapter 4 of his book *Philosophical Perspectives on Music* (New York: Oxford University Press, 1998), 133–97; Leonard B. Meyer, *Emotion and Meaning in Music* (Chicago: University of Chicago Press, 1956), and "Exploiting Limits: Creation, Archetypes, and Style Change," *Daedalus*, 109, no. 2 (Spring 1980), 177–205 (as well as practically everything else he has written); Edward Cone, "Music and Form" in *What Is Music?*, note 1; Casey Haskins, "Paradoxes of Autonomy; or, Why Won't the Problem of Artistic Justification Go Away?" *The Journal of Aesthetics and Art Criticism*, 58, no. 1 (Winter 2000), 1–22; Constantijn Koopman and Stephen Davies, "Musical Meaning in a Broader Perspective," *The Journal of Aesthetics and Art Criticism*, 59, no. 3 (Summer 2001), 261–73; and, of course, Susanne K. Langer's monumental *Feeling and Form* (New York: Scribner's, 1957). Unfortunately, space considerations forbid me from treating these and other such sources with the respect and attention they deserve. Readers interested in this issue will be greatly rewarded by a perusal of them.

RIFF 3

On the way from the airport to my hotel in Cleveland, I get into a conversation with the cabby, a middle-aged man. "So what are you doing here in Cleveland?" he asks. "Well, I'm attending a meeting of people involved in teaching music in colleges and universities (The College Music Society)," I reply. "Oh yeah? You gonna go to the rock and roll museum? I get a lot of business taking people there." "Yes, I plan to go there some time during the conference. Do you like rock and roll?"

"Oh, hey, that's the music I grew up with," he says. "There's nothing I don't know about it. I got practically every important recording ever made. All those hippies and druggies, they were terrific musicians, invented a whole new kind of music, then they threw it all away with drugs. They got so famous and made so much money they didn't know how to handle it, they kind of went nuts. But that's music you can really relate to, you know? What kind of music do you like?" "Well," I say, "I like lots of different kinds of music. I was trained to be a classical musician, so that's kind of my stuff. But I like jazz also, some popular music, different music from around the world."

"Oh, jazz," he says. "Don't tell me about jazz. They start off and you get an idea of what they're doing. Then they start messing around and pretty soon you don't know what's going on. They just play stuff and you can't tell what it is. Do they know what they're doing? Who knows? I don't know what they're doing. They're off in la la land. So how do I know how to listen to it? Crazy, if you ask me."

"What about classical music?" I ask.

"Huh. That can be even worse. Most of the time I can't tell where they are, you know? Sometimes you get a nice melody you can hold on to. Some of it is easy to listen to because there's lots of melodies, so I can tell what's going on. Then I really enjoy it. But then they start going off in all directions and I can't follow it. If I can't follow it how can I enjoy it? And some of it there's no melodies at all I can hang on to, you know what I mean? So what am I supposed to do with it?" He shrugs his shoulders. "I guess I never learned to listen to that stuff. Rock I can understand. I know where I am, I know what they're doing. So it makes sense to me."

I contemplate his thinking. A natural-born formalist, this guy. He needs form, sense, the recognition of where the music is, where it is going, how it is ordered. That is enjoyment for him. Without that sense, too challenged by musics in which form is not easily evident, he is lost, and he loses his pleasure. The music has no "meaning" for him then. Is he unusual? He's salt of the earth, probably the rule rather than the exception. He wants form, and he gets it where he can. What would those old formalists, Bell and Fry and Hanslick, have made of him?, I wonder.

I propose an additional meaning to those usually ascribed to the word "form," a meaning going beyond the limitations of the exaggerated view of form explained previously. Sounds formed musically, as that is defined by and within the cultural settings in which music always exists, achieve a materiality—a substantiality—that, although made of sounds and therefore not able to be "touched," are nevertheless experienced as having a physical presence. That presence to the body, or "embodiment," is the basis for the power of music to engage our bodies, which also entails engaging our minds and our feelings. I will return to this idea of music's reliance on and challenge to the human condition of thinking and feeling as corporeal—as situated within and dependent on the body—in several appropriate discussions throughout this book. Here I want to emphasize that forming sounds is the fundamental way music achieves this embodiment, this appeal to the bodied mind and its accompanying feelings. At the core of music, I believe, is the power of sounds to "in-corp-orate" [from the Latin *corpus* = body] meanings—to give meanings corporeal actuality for humans to experience. As Mikel Dufrenne explains in his classic book *The Phenomenology of Aesthetic Experience,*

> The aesthetic object is above all the apotheosis of the sensuous, and all its meaning is given in the sensuous. Hence the latter must be amenable to the body. Thus the aesthetic object first manifests itself to the body, immediately inviting the body to join forces with it. . . . The schemata organizing the sensuous seek to confer on it not only brilliance and prestige but also an ability to convince the body. . . . It is through the body that the aesthetic object is first taken up and assumed in order to pass from potentiality to act.[15]

Here, in meaning made a presence in the body, musical sounds, in and of themselves, serve one of their precious purposes. This purpose, I believe, is what was in anthropologist Robert Plant Armstrong's mind when he defined aesthetics as "the theory or study of form incarnating feeling."[16] Musical form—sounds organized to be musically meaningful within a cultural context—is the basis for the characteristic experience music provides, "giving body to" (incarnating) feeling through sounds intended to do precisely that. (The breadth and depth of the concept "feeling" will be addressed in some detail in Chapter 3.)

But necessary as the "formed sounds" dimension of music is to the experience of music it is not, by itself, sufficient for a full understanding of the complexities of music and the meanings it makes available. Music education, I would argue, must attend to the materiality of music as one major factor in its goal of enhancing every person's ability to experience the power of music as fully as possible. (I will discuss,

---

[15]Mikel Dufrenne, *The Phenomenology of Aesthetic Experience* (Evanston, IL: Northwestern University Press, 1973), 339.

[16]Robert Plant Armstrong, *Wellspring: On the Myth and Source of Culture* (Berkeley and Los Angeles: University of California Press, 1975), 11.

in Chapter 5, a movement in the arts that downplays materiality in favor of ideas.) But other dimensions of music are also necessary and must also be made available in effective teaching and learning of music. One of these is the "practice" of music—the "making" music requires for it to come into being and be available for sharing.

MUSIC AS PRACTICE

> *What music is, at root, is a human activity. . . . Fundamentally, music is something people do.*[17] (Emphasis in original)

Compare this quote, by David J. Elliott, with that of Nadia Boulanger at the beginning of the previous section. Boulanger isolates the product as the essence of music. Elliott, conversely, isolates the process as music's essential characteristic. To focus on process is to emphasize what people do and how they do it. In music, it is to emphasize, as central to the enterprise, those people who "make" music—who bring musical sounds into being—and how they go about doing what they do. The product of the making, the "piece" or "work" they produce by their doings, is not really the point. The point, or value, or essence of music is *in the doing* of it. So when we approach music we should attend to the doings—the actions of musicians—as of primary interest. And when we teach music we should do the same; that is, attend to helping people do what musicians do, because those doings, those "practices," are what is valuable about music.

Which musicians do things we can observe? Composers generally work in isolation, as writers of fiction or poetry (or philosophy) do. We don't normally observe such people at their work because there is nothing we can learn by directly observing them (except, perhaps, if we are psychological researchers or clinicians). The proof of their pudding is what they produce, not the acts of thinking they go through as they fashion their products.

Performers, on the other hand, whether performing composed music or improvising, must by the very nature of what they do display their doings publicly (after readying themselves privately, of course). So a focus on performance—the public doings of people engaged in the process of making (sounding) music—would best fulfill a philosophical position emphasizing "practice" as what music is all or primarily about.

Boulanger, though focusing on the product—the "work"—as primary, had to recognize that the product could not exist except through the processes that brought

---

[17]David J. Elliott, *Music Matters: A New Philosophy of Music Education* (New York: Oxford University Press, 1995), 39. Elliott's "praxial" philosophy, emphasizing process rather than product, is indebted to an essay by Francis Sparshott, in which Sparshott suggests that process should be viewed as fundamental to music: "Aesthetics of Music: Limits and Grounds," note 1, 33–98. For a discussion and critique of this essay (and of the book in which it appears), see my review in *The Journal of Aesthetic Education*, 27, no. 1 (Spring 1993), 105–8.

it into being. The composer and the performer, having done their necessary work, should then, she feels, disappear, leaving us with what their processes created—the work. Elliott, who emphasizes process more than anyone ever has in music education philosophy, has to recognize that the process always produces a product, but he attempts to reverse Boulanger's priority.

> In the case of Beethoven's "Eroica" Symphony, or the *Bete* drumming of the Asanti people, or a Zuni lullaby, or Duke Ellington's *Cotton Tail*, and in every example of a musical product that comes to mind, what we are presented with is more than a piece of music, a composition, an improvisation, a performance, or a "work" in the aesthetic sense. What we are presented with is the outcome of a particular kind of intentional human activity. Music is not simply a collection of products or objects.[18]

Elliott is here trying to stake out a position contrary to Boulanger's. As we have seen, that concept was given an extreme formulation at a particular time and place, a formulation (an appropriate word in this context) called "Formalism." Further, according to Elliott, "music education as aesthetic education" is an attempt to apply an extreme formalist philosophy to education. He makes this claim even though the aesthetic education movement, especially as articulated in the previous editions of this book, specifically and directly repudiated formalism as a basis for music education because of its extremist posture. But although I rejected formalism in its puristic manifestation, the contribution it made in identifying form as one important component of music and musical experience was indeed acknowledged. That acknowledgment, apparently, was sufficient for Elliott to reject aesthetic education entirely and to search for a "new" philosophy untainted by respect for the formed outcomes of musical processes as being a precious, necessary dimension of music.

One of the major drawbacks of an approach to philosophy that depends on portraying various views in their most extreme manifestations, rather than on more accurate, inclusive portrayals, is that to counteract an extreme there is a tendency to adopt an opposite one, setting up an either–or confrontation. Once the aesthetic concept of music is portrayed in the most extreme formalistic way possible (as it is by Elliott), a very strong antidote is apparently needed to correct its drastic imbalance— an antidote just as imbalanced in the opposite direction. A position focusing on process as the be-all and end-all of music, opposite to a (presumed) focus on product, will serve the purpose. In place of thinking of music as consisting of "autonomous objects," we can conceive of it as consisting of activities in which people engage. We must choose, then, between *either* music as form *or* music as practice.

A practice-based, or "praxial," philosophy (in Greek, *praxis* = deed, act, action) is, then, the needed remedy for the disease of formalism, and a praxial music education is the necessary corrective to a formalistic music education. In a praxial philosophy of music education, or at least in Elliott's construal of what that is, we would focus not on finished, formal objects as "revered pieces" or "esteemed works" but on

---

[18]Ibid.

music as "a matter of singing and playing instruments,"[19] as if a choice between two incompatible dimensions of music had to be made. If the choice is practice *instead of* its results (rather than as interdependent dimensions), the focus of music education becomes the doing rather than what is done. We have now accomplished a leap from one exclusionary position to another, from one extreme to another.

Suppose that, instead of pitting one extreme against another, we adopt a synergistic attitude and ask, Are there more moderate views about product and process than extreme formalism or extreme praxialism entertain? Must we abandon our enjoyment of—even treasuring of—particular musical products that we enjoy for "what they are"? Or is it possible to continue to treasure these ends of musical processes while also confirming, treasuring, and honoring the processes that make all the products possible in the first place? It would not seem a betrayal of the importance in musical experience of either form (product) or practice (process) to recognize not only that both are necessary for any inclusive understanding of music but also that *each depends on the other*. Just as Clive Bell had to recognize the role of the composer, whose processes form the products, Elliott also has to—and does, therefore—recognize that processes produce products or else they are meaningless, that processes are processes of doing *something*: "Music, then, is a four-dimensional concept at least . . . involving (1) a doer, (2) some kind of doing, (3) something done, and (4) the complete context in which doers do what they do."[20] The "something done," of course, is the musical work, to which Elliott devotes a chapter. And although, characteristically, his explanation of the musical work focuses resolutely on its performative nature, its "design" being just one dimension, he cannot explain music, as Bell and everyone else cannot, without acknowledging the interdependence of work on maker and maker on work, a codependency music shares with every other productive human activity.

Extreme views are usually extreme in emphasis. They put so much emphasis on one or another aspect of a larger, more complex whole as to tend to exclude or severely diminish other aspects, yielding a skewed vision. That is why I believe it is often possible to find a synergistic accommodation, giving due recognition to aspects called to attention by those who put extreme emphasis on them, but conceiving other balances that are more flexible and more appreciative of the contributions of factors not necessarily in opposition. In this case, viewing form and action as compatible—even as codependent—rather than contradictory, allows one to give appropriate attention to both, sometimes focusing on one, sometimes on the other, and often focusing on their necessary interrelationship. This, I would argue, portrays music more faithfully and realistically than the severely imbalanced positions of extremist thinkers, and benefits our students in helping them to understand and to enjoy the multidimensionality of music. Musical performance, understood as "per-*form*-ance"

---

[19]Ibid., 39.
[20]Ibid., 40.

(giving form to), along with all the other creative actions music requires to be brought into being and experienced, is an essential dimension of music and therefore of music education. But performance is not sufficient for doing all that music education is required to do, contrary to what Elliott insists.

Not all thinkers attracted to the praxial view take Elliott's excessive stance on it, of course, just as those who find formalism compelling do not all align themselves with the thinkers who gave it its most overstated expression. Most people of a praxial bent are likely to value the "doing" aspects of music highly, of course, which is the traditional, long-standing position of American music education. So in a real sense, praxialism as the view that performance should be central is the oldest (not the newest) position in American music education; in fact, it has been the dominant view throughout its history. Another claim of present-day thinkers attracted to praxialism is that music is always culturally grounded (Elliott explains this dimension thoughtfully and extensively) and that it serves many social functions. These beliefs are central to my own philosophy. On the other hand, some praxialist thinkers give the impression that listening to music as an involvement in and of itself is passive, inferior to and less creative (if creative at all) than "making" music (although some praxialists include listening as one of the ways to actively "do" music). Elliott goes so far as to say, in his discussion of listening, "In sum, educating competent, proficient, and expert listeners for the future depends on the progressive education of competent, proficient, and artistic music makers in the present."[21] This view of listening as entirely a subsidiary of performing and the other music-producing roles, as if the practicing musician's way of listening is the only valid or "musical" way to experience music, has plagued music education in the United States since its earliest days, accounting in large part for the irrelevance of our offerings for the great majority of students in American schools. I will attempt to dispute this and other extremist praxial views in several discussions throughout this book, becase I find them unreasonable and destructive of the relevance of music education for all people.

The claims of praxialism, including those I heartily endorse and those I cannot, have marked American music education from its very beginnings. In that sense one is tempted to say what is often said about postmodernism (as mentioned in Chapter 1)—that the only thing new about praxialism is its name. However, the concerns this orientation raises and the positions it tends to promote are important to any full, balanced view of music and music education, and must be taken seriously into account along with the concerns of the other views presented here. Active involvement in music making—the practices of music as each culture has devised them—must certainly (obviously) be a major component of music education, balanced with and in concordance with the component of the products of music making. Process (praxis) and product (form), each dependent on the other, are necessary components of the experience-based philosophy I will propose.

---

[21]Ibid., 99.

MUSIC AS SOCIAL AGENCY

In her poem "The Images," Adrienne Rich speaks of her inability to romanticize music or other arts (painted ceilings, Pietàs, frescoes), "romanticize" meaning to regard them for their beauty alone. That is because they all translate victimization and violence into artistic/aesthetic patterns that, being so powerful and pure through their beauty, cause us not to ask what should be asked about works of art—whether they are true for us, whether the violent gender messages they give, victimizing women, should be accepted by us. Those messages are not necessarily explicit. They can be, instead, hidden within the seemingly innocent sounds.

> This passage from Adrienne Rich's 1978 poem "The Images" evokes a problem that I think bedevils all of us engaged in what Elaine Showalter has called "feminist critique"—the deciphering and demystification of gender messages in our repertoire's canonic works.[22]

The passage of poetry and Suzanne G. Cusick's comment on it transport us to a point of view seemingly quite different from those of formalism and praxialism, seeming to cast a very different light on the issue of the nature and value of music (and all art). Here, we are not concerned with the experience of formed sounds as satisfying for what they allow us to undergo, or with the practices of creating and sharing such sounds, but with figuring out—deciphering and demystifying—particular *messages* in music, in this case in the standard repertoire of Western classical music. The particular focus of "feminist critique," Cusick suggests, is the attempt to decipher messages relating to gender in general and to female gender in particular. Other critiques, or critical examinations, can be made from a variety of alternative standpoints, of course, such as race, age, social class, ethnicity, culture, sexuality, religion, economic status, ecological concerns, locality, personality type, disabilities, relationship status, and on and on. For each, attention would be paid to what messages—information, attitudes, values, positions, and so forth—are being given or taken or suggested in the works in question: what the works *refer to*. Such references, in the social agency view, are an important means for redressing societal injustices. Music, as well as the other arts and all human endeavors, should be seen as serving social-political purposes, to be critiqued when those purposes are harmful and to be celebrated when helpful. At bottom, music exists as a political phenomenon, and should be treated and understood—and taught—as such.

For the poet Adrienne Rich the message, or reference, of music, or of any form created (painted ceilings, Pietàs, frescoes), is one of victimization and violence (we presume in regard to women). This message is found by deciphering—decoding—the images or, in the case of music, the formed sounds. But not only the "work," or

---

[22]Suzanne G. Cusick, "Gender and the Cultural Work of a Classical Music Performance," *repercussions*, 3, no. 1 (Spring 1994), 77–78. The poem passage referred to is from Adrienne Rich, "The Images," in *A Wild Patience Has Taken Me This Far: Poems 1978–81* (New York: W. W. Norton, 1981), 3–5.

"product," is amenable to such decoding; processes of music can also yield messages if decoded appropriately. For Cusick, "the cultural work of all classical music performances, regardless of the explicit or implicit content of any particular piece, might be understood to be the public enactment of obedience to a culturally prescribed script."[23]

This script forces the performer to abide by—be faithful to—the composer's instructions in the score, with all the hidden messages relating to gender such compliance entails. "Unless it is possible to imagine resisting performers as well as resisting listeners, musical works will always have an enormous (and insidious) power to force either submission to their image of gender or complete refusal to participate in it."[24] So both products and processes can be implicated in conveying messages, in this case having to do with gender but in other cases, with other agendas, having to do with whatever interests one takes in music (or any of the arts).

As pointed out in Chapter 1, those interests, under the influence of postmodernism, have become strongly political for many thinkers, rebalancing the age-old aesthetic topics of form, practice, and cultural context in the direction of that aspect of context having to do with social justice. Though the arts, including music, have always been recognized as being socially engaged in a variety of ways, overtly political engagement has become far more dominant than previously, sometimes or often overshadowing attention to the nature of products and processes. We live in a time of the politicization of much of our lives, the arts included. The question often asked about a particular work or performance is "Whose interests are being served by this?" By "interests" is meant political interests—interests having to do with power, influence, advantage, subjugation, oppression, exclusion, and so forth. Of course, one may reply to that question with another question: "Whose interests are being served by asking that question?" The answer is likely to be "The political interests of the particular person(s) asking it."

A variety of people have asked the "interests" question from a variety of political standpoints, or agendas, but the feminist standpoint has generated a strikingly extensive and searching literature, now constituting an important domain within philosophy and other fields. Therefore I will use feminism as one example of approaching music from a social agency perspective, recognizing that parallel examinations can be carried out for diverse other social standpoints. I urge music educators devoted to other social issues to use my discussion of this particular one as a basis for their examination of those to which they personally relate, thereby broadening my discussion beyond the limitations of space this book imposes.

While the justice and equity issues in regard to gender are complex, deep-rooted, and pervasive, they exist at the political level—that is, as matters calling for all the actions, persuasions, confrontations, and strategies required in the messy, contentious arena of social change. That arena is certainly not a simple one, nor one

---

[23]Ibid., 80–81.
[24]Ibid., 80.

lacking in demands for courage and for perseverance. The rise of political action in regard to feminist issues in music education following the rise of a variety of other social justice issues, especially racism, is testament to the need for our field, no less than others, to face the realities of the imperfect social organism it is and to work vigorously toward improving itself.

In addition to the need for political action (a need shared with many other constituencies with histories of unequal treatment), the feminist movement has raised particular dilemmas having to do with the way humans identify themselves and how such identifications might affect the way they experience the world, how they act within it, and how they are expected to "be" in the world. Humans are typically and overtly identified as being either female or male (sex), and their sex has been a major determinant of societal role expectations in all cultures (gender). So questions arise as to what and how much of the perceived differences are due to nature (sex, or biology), and what and how much are due to nurture (gender, or culturally assigned values and expectations). In the case of music, are musical experiences, as various cultures make them available, different for females and males? If so, why? Is it sex or gender that causes the differences? If they are not different, why are perceptions of difference and the many musical practices based on those perceptions so widespread in all human societies? Perhaps any differences are caused not by nature alone, or nurture alone, but by some combination of the two, as seems to be the case in just about every other aspect of human affairs. If that is the case, how do we identify what is "natural" and what is "cultural"? Are any differences between males' and females' musical experiences a matter of degree rather than of kind? Should differences in musical ways of being (assuming that they exist) be celebrated and enjoyed? Or should they be condemned and stamped out, especially if the differences lead to unequal treatment?

These questions and others of the same sort, obviously applicable to all aspects of life, not just to music, have generated an important field of inquiry, far too extensive and complicated to be dealt with here in any way respectful of its seriousness. Only a few points will be made, relating to extremist views and why it is important for the future of music education to have a philosophical mechanism to mediate them.

To take a feminist view toward music, approaching it to critique its messages about gender, is to pay a particular kind of attention to music and to look for a particular kind of thing from it. (The same would be true, of course, if one adopted any other social agency perspective.) One extreme view would be to insist that the feminist view is privileged above all others: that feminism should be the exclusive or at least the dominant way people should approach music. That would force all people, of both sexes and all racial, ethnic, and other identifications, to regard music from a stipulated point of view rather than from whatever identification was germane to them. And music education would follow suit, teaching music to all students from the perspective that music is a way, or opportunity, or mechanism, of raising issues concerning female-male political relations and of dealing with those issues as the point and purpose of learning music.

But many people, females included, do not desire to view music as a source of messages about gender politics, especially when the music they are engaged with does not have overt, obvious gender content such as words that deal with gender, or a title clearly calling attention to a gender issue, or a program so literal as to plainly depict a gender situation. When music has none of this, as often is the case, finding a gender issue in it requires an act of "interpretation," which means, in this context, an imaginative projection onto the music of one's preexisting interest, or an equally imaginative deduction from the music that it contains and is giving such and such a message in which one has a preexisting interest. Adopting such an interpretive stance, as directed by a political agenda, has serious consequences for the ways music can be experienced. Following the quotation from Cusick with which I began this section, in which she defines feminist critique as deciphering gender messages in music, she continues as follows:

> Once we've begun the deciphering, many of us feel with gathering regret that we can never listen to music again. Our urge to eschew classical music amounts to the temptation of separatism. Like separatism, it promises our psyches temporary safety from and moral superiority over misogynist and homophobic messages. But like separatism it threatens to rob feminist musicology of its political power, its power to challenge classical music's complicity in sustaining ideas of gender and sexuality we find anachronistic and oppressive. Worse, a separation from classical music threatens to rend from us a music we have loved passionately for most of our lives; a music we have found to be a source of pleasure and power; a music that once seemed to grant our psyches a safe field for the play of deep feelings with deep thought. Our instinct to flee the implied misogyny of so much classical music is thus an instinct that threatens us with wrenching and self-inflicted psychic pain; yet how can we justify to ourselves a continued sanctioning (through listening, teaching, performance) of objectionable repertoire? Can we listen to this music again, now that we can no longer romanticize it?[25]

This calls attention to another extreme in addition to that of assuming that all musical experience should be undergone from a feminist perspective (or, of course, from any other perspective in which music serves a social agency function). To disallow music from its role as "a source of pleasure . . . a safe field for the play of deep feeling with deep thought," as Cusick puts it so eloquently, is to face the loss of that pleasure and not be able to retrieve it. That loss, I believe, would be an extreme one, not to be lightly accepted. The consequence is very great. Is there a position that would provide space for both musical experience and social justice, recognizing that both are compelling (at least for some people) and, perhaps, are not entirely incompatible?

If it *is* impossible to take, say, a feminist view of the sort Cusick (and others) seem to take without also abandoning the musical pleasures of classical music (or any other music deemed repressive, a good deal of rock and popular music clearly

---

[25]Cusick, "Gender," note 22, 78–79.

included), a serious issue immediately arises. Should a person who believes that a feminist view does indeed exclude the musical pleasures Cusick describes take the initiative to persuade others to share her or his view? Remember, that view precludes the coexistence of political (delineated) and musical (inherent) responses: one or the other must be chosen. Is one, then, being ethically responsible if one *teaches* that such a choice must be made? Would such a teacher be putting his or her students at risk of a serious musical loss in order to adopt the teacher's particular political perspective?

Cusick struggles with this dilemma in the article from which I have quoted. The questions raised in the quotation "gnawed at my students" in a seminar she taught on "Women, Music, and Feminism," and she desired to "ease my students' pain." To do so, she asked them to listen to several different performances of Schumann's song cycle *Frauenliebe und Leben,* "to engage my students in the idea that singers might make choices of dynamics, phrasing, timbre, and so on that would re-read even so offensive a work as [this] in a way that would allow us to keep it in the repertoire. If one could re-read it into acceptability, I reckoned, we could re-read anything."[26] (In *Frauenliebe und Leben*—"Woman's Life and Love"—composed by Schumann in 1840, the woman falls so deeply in love with the man who reciprocates that love as to devote her entire life and being to him and the gift of love they share, the only hurt from that love being his death, leaving her forsaken. This heart-rending poem by Chamisso is typical of the romantic period and its life-view. Its ravishingly beautiful musical setting (in my and many others' opinions) reflects Schumann's singular compositional genius as well as his historically and culturally based image of romantic love.)

Notice that the agenda here is to make something else of the music than it seems to be, through performing it in such a way as to make it politically "acceptable," meaning no longer containing offensive (to her) messages about gender, or, at least, counteracting such messages by the way a performer resisted them. If the "meanings" of the music (that is, according to Cusick, messages about gender) are fixed within works and irresistible, and if performers "must be faithful to [music's] inherent meanings," there is little one can do except abandon works one finds offensive. But if we remove the premise that performers should be faithful to the work, "musical works automatically become open texts. For then implied meanings [political] can be resisted and contested by an endless variety of performative acts that create the meanings available to receiving listeners."[27]

So musical works, performances of them, and responses to those performances all need to be governed by a higher good than musical pleasure and power—the good served by correcting offensive gender messages. And teaching, to be good, should focus the attention and skills of students on how to go about serving that purpose. But how can we reconcile such a position about music with the compelling view that

---

[26]Ibid., 79.
[27]Ibid., 80.

music does not simply state social messages, even when words are present as in songs, but creates something in which "deep feeling and deep thought," as Cusick aptly puts it, become deep *musical* feeling and deep *musical* thought; that is, the work of composers, and the supportive work of performers, aimed toward producing experiences that transform any real (or assumed) messages into a feeling-thinking amalgam only music can accomplish? Must "interpretation" displace the musical pleasures we have "loved so passionately for most of our lives," as Cusick states it so poignantly?

Susan Sontag does not think so. In her famous essay "Against Interpretation," she characterizes our culture as one that elevates intellect—ideas, messages, theories—over immediate, sensuous experience such as the forms of art allow us to have.

> Interpretation is the revenge of the intellect upon art. . . . To interpret is to impoverish, to deplete the world—in order to set up a shadow world of "meanings." The world, our world, is depleted, impoverished enough. Away with all duplicates of it, until we experience more immediately what we have. . . . Interpretation, based on the highly dubious theory that a work of art is composed of items of content, violates art. It makes art into an article for use, for arrangement into a mental scheme of categories.[28]

Instead of seeking messages in art, Sontag argues, we should focus on how art "dissolves considerations of content [messages] into those of form." Rather than mucking about in the "meanings" of art—the interpreted messages it supposedly gives us—we need to "experience the luminousness of the thing in itself, of things being what they are."

> What is important now is to recover our senses. We must learn to *see* more, to *hear* more, to *feel* more. Our task is not to find the maximum amount of content in a work of art, much less to squeeze more content out of the work than is already there. Our task is to cut back content so that we can see [hear] the thing at all. The aim of all commentary on art now should be to make works of art—and, by analogy, our own experience—more, rather than less, real to us. The function of criticism [we can add "teaching"] should be to show *how it is what it is,* even *that it is what it is,* rather than to show *what it means.*[29] (Emphases in original)

Between the poles of message-seeking as the be-all and end-all of music, and messages, interpretations, "content" seen as impoverishing music, it may be possible to find a link that preserves the validity of both views. Yes, we are tempted sometimes to want to ignore the realities of political issues as connected to music. As Stephen Miles puts it, "Weary of politics and touched by nostalgia, we long for a time when we can return to the tasks of making music—purely, simply, and undisturbed. . . . Few would deny that music possesses deep cultural significance, that it even can bear

---

[28]Susan Sontag, *Against Interpretation* (New York: Farrar, Straus & Giroux, 1961), 7, 10.
[29]Ibid., 12–14.

philosophical meaning, yet many recoil at the idea that a Beethoven symphony is irreducibly political."[30] Yet life is not so simple, and music is not exempt from the dilemmas and inequities and bruises our world supplies in abundance. We cannot dismiss the need to embroil music in the important social debates of our times, despite that many of us, social activists as well, might wish to use music as a retreat from them.

An attempt at a synergistic resolution of this seemingly oppositional issue is offered by Miles in his penetrating examination of absolute music and contextualism. In the "music means itself" position of formalism, he explains, the social function of music is taken to be that it *has no* operational social function: its aesthetic autonomy is the "grandest achievement" of absolute music. But "in an effort to fully explicate music's technical functioning, formalists disregard all 'irrelevant' factors, such as music's emotional, social, and political significance."[31] Unfortunately, doing so not only reveals but conceals—conceals the contexts that also make the music what it is.

Contextualists, in their focus on social and political significance, make an invaluable contribution, balancing the overly internal concentration of formalism.

> The real problem is when the issue of causality is not faced squarely. Contextualists all too frequently leave doubts as to their claims, implying a causal relationship where one is undemonstrable. If contextualists simplify, it is usually on not one but two levels: the musical *and* the social. Just as formalists call attention to certain features of music at the expense of others, so do contextualists through the use of metaphor. The great challenge of the metaphorical interpretation of absolute music is to enhance our understanding of this repertoire's social embeddedness without diminishing our understanding of its formal integrity. A concerto may indeed be structurally analogous to a social dialogue, but it is much more as well. To reduce a complex phenomenon to such an equation is to substitute one meaning for another, a move that denies music its legitimate aesthetic autonomy.[32]

So although formalist and contextualist understandings of music each contribute a necessary dimension, each is incomplete without the other and each benefits from including the other.

> Theorists and musicologists [and, I would add, music educators] are not presented with a choice between formalism and contextualism; only when these methods of analysis are followed simplistically are they truly antithetical. If contextualists first attend rigorously to the details of musical meaning before interrogating music's social implications, they are not projecting politics onto music; rather, they are elaborating the significance of music in a variety of social and political contexts. Likewise, if formalists acknowledge that music exists only in social contexts and that formalist analysis is

---

[30]Miles, "The Limits of Metaphorical Interpretation," note 14, 9.
[31]Ibid., 15
[32]Ibid., 23.

necessarily incomplete, their project need not be understood as an implicit denial of music's social meaning.[33]

I am grateful to Miles for his thoughtful, incisive explanation that seemingly contradictory aesthetic positions can be understood to be mutually supporting if single-minded positions can be moderated so as to recognize other perspectives, even those at first glance appearing irreconcilable. It is not always easy to achieve this synergy, as I have mentioned, but when it is achieved we gain a much firmer grounding for our beliefs than unitary positions can yield. In this case we can respect the distinctive contributions of the formal and the contextual, or, as Green puts it, the inherent and the delineated aspects of music, but in addition we are led to recognize and honor their interdependence. Doing so provides a more inclusive philosophical understanding of the complexities and values of music, and, as well, the complexities and values of teaching it inclusively.

As I will suggest further on in this book, musical meaning, at bottom, is meaning individuals choose to give to and take from music, based on their life experiences and their musical orientations. There is, to be explicit, no "one right way" everyone must experience music, freedom of choice being here, as in many other aspects of our lives, a fundamental prerogative. When feminists choose to emphasize that dimension of music, even in the face of possible loss of the values of inherence, they are exercising their right of freedom to do so (as are others who emphasize different delineated values).

My philosophy will emphasize the synergistic capacity of music to encompass delineated meanings and also to take them into the realm of inherence as only music can do. This capacity, I believe, accounts for the uniqueness of music in human life and therefore its powerful, indispensable value. Implications for music education will be drawn from this position. But this does not negate or repudiate the fact that other values, such as from a variety of delineated aspects of music, can be and often should be honored and attended to as important dimensions of musical meaning and experiencing.

THE BOUNDARIES OF MUSIC

Is music a unique, incomparable phenomenon unlike any other in all of human experience? Some have argued that it is, taking the position that any comparison between music, the other arts, and fields outside the arts is bound to misrepresent the singular nature of music and therefore to weaken the impact it exists to make.

---

[33]Ibid., 25. For a discussion of formalist and contextualist positions in visual art education, and the need to regard them as mutually reinforcing rather than mutually exclusive, see Tom Anderson and Sally McCrorie, "A Role for Aesthetics in Centering the K–12 Art Curriculum," *Art Education*, 50, no. 3 (May 1997), 6–14.

Nothing else in human experience, this argument goes, uses sounds to create a world of its own, with its own ways to be meaningful, its own ways to think, act, and feel, its own ways to transform individual and cultural beliefs and values into experiences both reflecting them and enriching them. There is a "music-world," in this view, a world in which all young people need to be involved so they can experience the ways of being that music makes possible, ways treasured by humans for the special qualities they add to our lives. All of us who have devoted our lives to music, whether as performers, composers, improvisers, teachers, scholars, and so on, are aware that we dwell in the world of music, a realm with its own identity. And although all who live in the world of music must also deal with surrounding worlds, we know that when we want to, or need to, we can depend on music for its power, its joy, its comfort, its nourishment; all those gifts that music offers in a way nothing else can.

On the other hand (that inevitable "other hand") is the position that at the core of music is its close relation to and incorporation of many other aspects of life. It is how music is *connected* to life that makes it so important for people. First, it is connected by blood ties to the other arts, all of which share the same reasons for existence—to create meanings and to engage with individual and cultural values as all the arts do, deepening them, critiquing them, exploring their nuances, making them vivid for all to share. Music, in this view, is one member of a family of human activities, all contributing to the same artistic/aesthetic/cultural goals of heightened awarenesses, understandings and experiences. What unites the arts, then, is far more important, more fundamental, than the superficial differences in their materials and modes of production.

Second, this argument goes, music is intimately related to worlds outside the arts, the worlds of politics, religion, commerce, nationhood, psychology, history, sociology, science, philosophy, and so forth. All these worlds interact, intermesh, and are mutually dependent on one another: human experience cannot be pigeonholed except artificially. To understand music is to understand its intimate connections to all of human experience. To experience music is to experience how we as individuals are connected to all other humans in our communities and all other communities in the world and in history. Music is all-encompassing.

The first view draws a tight, hard boundary around music, separating it as a circumscribed domain different from all others. The second wants no boundaries at all for music, viewing it as subsumed within the totality of human life and history. And each view has strong implications for how music would be dealt with in education. In the first, music would be taught as a separate subject by specialists trained to do so, with its own curriculum, its own goals and objectives, its own evaluations, its own methodologies, all centered on and determined by the nature of music conceived as a unique domain. In the second, musical learnings would be attached to and approached through learnings in other arts and other subjects, with the curriculum, evaluations, methods, goals and objectives all shared with those in the other domains. Music would be "integrated" in the larger sphere of education. So take your choice. Hard boundaries? No discernible boundaries at all? Or, perhaps, soft boundaries that mediate synergistically between those two extremes?

In her book *Soft Boundaries: Revisioning the Arts and Aesthetics in American Education,*[34] Claire Detels argues against the rigidity that has characterized music education throughout its American history. She decries the specialization mentality that assumes all students need to or want to study music as if they were aiming to become musicians, as David Elliott does (see the previous discussion of praxialism), thereby causing their musical experiences in schools to be narrowly conceived and technically oriented. She also regrets the existence of hard boundaries between music-making and conceptual understandings about music. In her discussion of how performing and conceptual understandings need to interrelate, Detels points out that David Elliott's approach to performing, in his *Music Matters,* has been characterized as neglecting historical, philosophical, or cultural contexts, and my approach has been characterized as "purely intellectual inquiry into the relationship of aesthetic concepts of form and style in music and the other arts."[35] This portrayal of Elliott's and my positions is extreme and inaccurate—in fact, a caricature (as Detels correctly points out). Elliott writes extensively about the many understandings relevant to performance, especially in regard to cultural contexts, and insists that all such understandings must become part of the performer's cognition-in-action, a position I wholeheartedly endorse. And I write extensively on musical creation (Chapter 4 in the previous editions and this one) and specifically on performance (Chapter 9 in the previous editions, in several chapters in this one) as essential components of music education, with conceptual understandings being a necessary dimension *supportive* of artistry—not as a substitute for it. In this matter, Elliott and I are very much in agreement. Where we disagree is on the issue of whether (according to Elliott) performance must be the essential mode of musical learning or whether (according to me) it is one of a variety of ways musical learnings can and must occur.

Detels also discusses the hard boundaries existing between teaching the musically talented and the general population; between historical and philosophical inquiry; between the historical canon of what "good music" is and other musics that do not make the grade; between various specializations within music, fragmenting the field into unrelated splinters; and the same fragmentation in music education. All these and other ills of music and music education are traced to overly rigid separations into "either–or" of what needs to be conceived as interrelated—having soft rather than hard boundaries. What Detels urges, as a cure for the ills of separatism, is an "Integrative, Interdisciplinary Education in the Arts and Aesthetics" (her Chapter 8). However, she says,

> The trouble is, under the single-disciplinary structure of American education today, there is almost no opportunity to consider interdisciplinary approaches or challenges in the arts, no matter how important they may be for improving that education. . . . [T]he arts exist in our educational institutions as separate disciplines of art (visual arts),

---

[34]Claire Detels, *Soft Boundaries: Revisioning the Arts and Aesthetics in American Education* (Westport, CT: Bergin and Garvey, 1999).
[35]Ibid., 19.

music, dance, and drama, in which concepts and competencies are defined and evaluated by single-disciplinary specialists. Single-disciplinary specialization in the arts has led to extraordinary levels of complexity and virtuosity in the areas of research and practice, but it has also had the effect of isolating the specialists who teach about the arts from each other and from contacts and influences from other academic disciplines. The result of this isolation has been an ever-widening gap between arts specialists and the public that has in turn been devastating to public understanding and support for education in the arts.[36]

I will return to some of the issues raised by Detels later on in this book, especially in regard to my theory of intelligence in Chapter 7. For purposes of the present discussion, the point to be made is that an extreme of hard-boundary thinking has indeed characterized music (and other arts) education throughout American history. However, an opposite extreme that erases distinctions among the arts, or between the arts and other subjects, would be unsupportable philosophically and practically. In a synergistic resolution, music, and each art, would be recognized as unique in one sense and related in another, as would the domain of the arts in relation to the nonart world. In this matter, I suggest that a reasonable softening of boundaries to include substantial exploration of the connections of music and the arts to the larger world in which they reside, while insisting on protecting the integrity of each art and the arts as a family, would represent a major shift toward maturity for music education and arts education, and a major repositioning toward their security and importance in the education enterprise. A change from hard to realistically soft boundaries would be revolutionary—a revolution quietly and unsuspectingly lurking within the potentials of the national standards. I will attempt to shine some light on that latent radical dimension of the standards in my discussion of them in chapters 8 and 9.

MUSIC AND UTILITARIAN VALUES

What is music "good for"? The philosophy to be offered in this book provides a particular answer to this question, an answer focusing on the kind of multifaceted experience music makes available and why such experience has many valuable

---

[36]Ibid.,119–20. A detailed description of a "soft-boundary" program of arts study, along with related issues such as teacher education for it, a philosophical rationale for it, evaluating learnings in it, and so forth, is given in my article "A Comprehensive Arts Curriculum Model," *Design for Arts in Education*, 90, no. 6 (July/August 1989), 2–17. An excellent book covering all aspects of music in interdisciplinary settings, worth careful attention by all music educators, is Janet R. Barrett, Claire W. McCoy, and Kari W. Veblen, *Sound Ways of Knowing* (New York: Schirmer Books, 1997). Detels's own "interdisciplinary arts" course, which she devised and teaches at her university, spends two weeks discussing aesthetic terms and issues, and then breaks into two weeks devoted to each separate art—Drama, Visual Arts, Musical Arts, Environmental Arts—then a week on Photography and Film, and a week on Other New Art Forms. A final two weeks is devoted to the Present and Future, including student reports on twentieth-century arts movements (ibid., 131–33). Though softer in boundaries than completely separate arts courses, this rather traditional approach retains aspects of strong-boundaried art study. (I do not intend for that comment to be perceived as a criticism.)

consequences for humans. Here, I intend for the question to refer to purposes music might serve for anything and everything other than the multiple valuable effects musical experience itself has on people. (I will explain what the term "musical experience itself" means in this and subsequent chapters.) That is, what good is music for securing values for which it is entirely a *means* rather than in any relevant sense an *end*?

The values I have in mind by the term "music as utilitarian" are, for example, that music is useful for raising test scores in the "basic" subjects, for improving spatial-temporal reasoning (the so-called Mozart effect),[37] for making people "smarter," for supporting the teaching of a variety of other subjects, for instilling discipline, improving social skills, and on and on with the many uses music has been claimed to serve throughout the history of music education.[38] A workable way to identify what I mean by "utilitarian" in this context is to ask to what extent the content areas of the national standards are the pertinent learnings for achieving the goal being claimed. Those learnings (or ways to experience music), I suggest, are not at all the point of most utilitarian uses of music as I am defining that term.

Utilitarian claims for music's value are a major—perhaps *the* major—tool for advocacy efforts by the music education profession. Advocacy consists of "the act of pleading for, supporting, or recommending; active espousal."[39] Advocacy arguments, intended to persuade the larger community to support music programs as part of schooling rather than as an out-of-school activity for those who choose it, have tended to focus on whatever values happen to be important to people at various times, attempting to convince people that music can serve those values and therefore should be allowed a place at the education table. This has caused the music education profession, actively supported by our national organization, MENC: The National Association for Music Education, to keep a sharp eye on current values, and to develop a great deal of expertise about how to exploit music's contributions to them (whether or not such contributions can be validated).

RIFF 4

In Los Angeles, at a conference sponsored by the J. Paul Getty Trust, I gather with an invited group of some thirty-five attendees to review and discuss Ellen Winner and Lois Hetland's just-finished research study titled "The Arts and

---

[37]For my discussion of this claim, see "Facing the Risks of the 'Mozart Effect,'" Grandmaster Series, *Music Educators Journal,* 86, no. 1 (July 1999). Reprinted in *Arts Education Policy Review,* 101, no. 2 (November/December 1999). Reprinted in *Phi Delta Kappan,* 81, no. 4 (December 1999).

[38]In 1837, a committee appointed to determine the value of vocal music instruction for the Boston public schools concluded that music served three values: intellectual ("It may be made, to some extent, an intellectual discipline"), moral ("the natural scale of musical sound can only produce good, virtuous, and kindly feelings"), and health ("exercise in vocal Music, when not carried to an unreasonable excess, must expand the chest, and thereby strengthen the lungs and vital organs.") Michael L. Mark and Charles L. Gary, *A History of American Music Education,* 2nd ed. (Reston, VA: Music Educators National Conference, 1999), 142–43.

[39]*Random House Dictionary,* 2nd ed., s.v. "advocacy."

Academic Achievement: What the Evidence Shows."[40] This is an exhaustive, meticulously detailed review, with meta-analyses of all the relevant research on how the arts (music, visual arts, dance, theater) affect academic learning (SAT scores, creative thinking, spatial-temporal reasoning, mathematics learnings, reading skills, verbal skills, nonverbal reasoning, and visual-spatial skills). It is likely to be the model and authority for this hot-button issue for some time to come: it is unlikely that such a massive, expensive, and painstaking review will be carried out again any time soon. A prestigious group, including Howard Gardner, Elliot Eisner, Sam Hope, David Perkins, Richard Colwell, and Joyce Gromko, has been summoned to discuss the findings. Ten were asked to present formal responses to assigned chapters: my responsibility is to respond to the two dealing with music and spatial-temporal reasoning, no doubt because my article on it (note 37) had received a good deal of attention.

The Winner-Hetland study reveals that of ten areas in which the research was reviewed, seven showed no reliable causal links: arts-rich education and verbal and mathematical scores/grades; arts-rich education and creative thinking; playing music and mathematics; playing music and reading; visual arts and reading; dance and reading; and dance and nonverbal reasoning. Three areas showed causal links: listening to music and spatial-temporal reasoning (insofar as what was measured had anything whatsoever to do with reasoning); playing music and spatial-temporal reasoning (ditto); and drama and verbal skills. However, the listening–spatial-temporal reasoning result has little if any relevance for education, because it is very short-lived, it cannot be produced by other researchers who have tried to do so, and there is no evidence that what was measured would influence learning in the fields where S-T reasoning is applicable (such as math, physics, engineering). The results of the playing–spatial reasoning review are also equivocal and uncertain as to what caused the result and why.

Throughout the report, the authors stress that arts education cannot and should not be justified on the basis of its contributions (few and meager) to academic learnings. But the need to be vindicated—to be given a "hard" (scientific) rather than "soft" (philosophical) justification for existence— is so great among arts educators, thirsting for respect, that any excuse for acceptance is likely to be embraced, even if demeaning to their art.

The authors say, in their Introduction, "Studying the arts should not have to be justified in terms of anything else. The arts are as important as the sciences: they are time-honored ways of learning, knowing, and expressing."

---

[40]"Special Issue: The Arts and Academic Achievement: What the Evidence Shows," *The Journal of Aesthetic Education,* 34, nos. 3–4 (Fall/Winter 2000). A report of the Getty conference, with all the papers and responses, is *Beyond the Soundbite: Arts Education and Academic Outcomes* (Los Angeles: The Getty Trust, 2001). A follow-up set of discussions about the arts and academic learning is in *Arts Education Policy Review,* 102, no. 5 (May/June 2001).

"Amen," I think when I read this (although I'm grateful, as well, for any other positive effects studying the arts might have). I contemplate how long I have been arguing the same point, and I dig out one of my first published articles, "What Music Cannot Do," in the *Music Educators Journal,* September/October 1959, which caused a firestorm of controversy because it urged the profession to concentrate its justifications on the experiences only music can give rather than all sorts of other contributions made as well or better by other fields. It has been over forty years, and we're still plowing the same ground, hoping to uncover something that will "save" us. Here I am, involved again in this latest spasm of interest in how the arts can be conceived to be important as an instrumentality, now focusing on academic learning (meaning "basic" learning, the arts, obviously, not being "basic"). We seem to go round and round over the years, ending up in the same old place. "Courage," I say to myself. "Keep your eye where your heart is, on the unique power of music to make life special, meaningful. Underneath, that's what music educators bank on, just as I do. The surface politics can be disheartening. The depths remain nourishing."

Do efforts to advocate for music on utilitarian grounds also provide a philosophy of music education? As previously discussed, a philosophy of music education as I conceive it attempts to build a structure of grounded convictions about the nature of music as a domain with characteristics particular to it, and how that nature can best be shared through education. To accomplish this one must look to the thinking, in the past and in the present, that has attempted to explain why and how music is what it is as a singular human endeavor, treasured as such by people at all times and in all places, and what the implications of that explanation might be for effective education. Is there any substantive relation, then, between philosophy and advocacy?

Philosophy and advocacy, I suggest, can complement each other. Music education needs both. We need to recognize that utilitarian values of music can indeed be achieved as outgrowths of an education devoted to the particular values music offers. We also must recognize that without a clear sense of the special values of music, and the pursuit of them as our primary professional obligation, we are left with no foundation for our presence in education. The ongoing debate within music education as to whether we should make the case for our value on aesthetic/artistic bases or utilitarian bases is fruitless and self-defeating. It is never a case of one or the other. Philosophy as such, unadapted to political considerations, is seldom sufficient at the level of politics, while political arguments ungrounded in a philosophy or that do violence to a philosophy are dangerous. The question for effective advocacy is always how to balance philosophical honesty with practical efficacy, and this is never an easy question to answer. It requires people who understand the basic values of music education deeply yet are sensitive to the many other concerns held by various nonmusic constituencies. Recognizing this, we can end the tiresome, inappropriate pitting against each other of two dimensions that must be used to support each other. And we can get on with the work of building a philosophy that establishes the primary values of music education so that the secondary values have a leg to stand on. I now turn to beginning that task.

A PHILOSOPHY BASED ON MUSICAL EXPERIENCE: SETTING THE STAGE

> . . . *music heard so deeply*
> *That it is not heard at all, but you are the music*
> *While the music lasts.*
> > T. S. Eliot[41]

> *When you listen, you hear what you are.*
> > Carl Seashore[42]

These two thoughts, the first by a great poet, the second by an important early psychologist of music, call attention to seemingly contradictory assertions about musical experience. In the first, music is said to cause the experience we have of it, and to be able to do so at a level so powerful and so intimate as to make us *be* the music, rather than ourselves, at least as long as we are deeply engaged with it. In the second, we cause the music to be what we bring to it, the music being a projection of ourselves. We create the musical experience, not the music.

Each view, by itself, is true but only partially so, I would suggest. T. S. Eliot is correct: music does indeed cause us to experience, deeply, widely, and subtly, by doing something special to us when we listen, or perform, or improvise, or compose. That, I think, is why music exists—to give us experiences we otherwise could not have. But Seashore also has his finger on the truth, in that everything we experience in our lives, music or anything else, comes to us through the screen of our selfness— the personal ways of being through which we construct our lived world. We experience *music*. We experience music. Together, Eliot and Seashore provide a more complete description of musical experience than either can do separately.

In involving something that is both presented to us and created within us, music is like all other experience in human life. We live in a world outside us that impinges on us constantly. We also live in an interior world, a world of individual, private undergoings. The outside world and the interior world intersect continuously: life as we experience it is an interplay between the two. As John Dewey puts it, "Experience occurs continuously, because the interaction of live creature and environing conditions is involved in the very process of living."[43] In a real sense, music,

---

[41]T. S. Eliot, *The Waste Land* (New York: Faber and Faber, 1944), 33.
[42]Carl Seashore, *In Search of Beauty in Music* (New York: Ronald Press, 1947), 201.
[43]John Dewey, *Art as Experience* (New York: Capricorn Books, 1934), 35.

like everything else in our lives, is an "environing condition" with which we interact, whether we are creating it or sharing what others have created. But although music is one of many things in our world that causes us to have experience, there is something about it that is distinctive, that allows us to recognize that it is not identical to everything else in our experienced lives and that not everything else is music. What are the qualities of music that identify it?

Several of those qualities have already been discussed. First, music entails sounds, and those sounds are formed, or composed, or put together, in ways that are both culturally and individually determined. When we experience sounds organized to be meaningful because of the ways they are interrelated to one another, we are likely to call the sounds we are undergoing "music" and the experience we are having of them "musical."

The process of organizing musical sounds, on the basis of how a culture has devised means for doing so, requires us to think and act in particular ways—to put into practice the ways of making music our culture (or another) has provided. Practicing music making—creating sounds that are considered music in a particular context—is experienced in a way nothing else in the world precisely matches. When we are engaged in such practices we are experiencing music through our creation of it.

The organized sounds of music, and the ways, or practices, by which they are created, are situated in particular contexts: communities of people who share traditions and beliefs about what music properly is and how to properly create it. Those traditions and beliefs affect the sounds of music in a great many ways—how they get organized, what skills are needed to do so, how they are to be responded to, what meanings they are considered to make available, what values are to be ascribed to music, what functions it is intended to serve, how important or unimportant it is, how desirable or undesirable it is, how it relates to or does not relate to other cultural activities, and so forth. All these contextual influences affect the experience we have of music. Music does not exist in a vacuum; it is saturated with stated (conscious) and unstated (preconscious) assumptions. As members of a culture we bring with us to musical experience all our culture has made us, as well as all the individual ways we have internalized our culture into our own personality. The sounds of music, and the practices of music, are experienced through the filter of who we are as both communal and individual beings.

Music as achieved sounds, as practices of achieving those sounds, as meaningful, useful, valuable, important, in ways and to degrees people collectively and individually determine, is clearly a multidimensional phenomenon offering multidimensional experiences. Yet in a real and very important sense all those experiences share a common core, a core that identifies music as music despite all its countless ways to exist and all its countless ways to be experienced. It is difficult, perhaps reckless, to try to identify that core of music, given the diversity of ways it has been understood in the past and present. But I shall attempt to do so nevertheless because I believe there is something common to human beings and something common to their musics, a human quality and a musical quality that remains constant despite the endless diversity in how it is manifested and how it is explained.

That quality, I suggest, is what Ellen Dissanayake (in one example among others I will mention as this book proceeds) calls "making special." In her book *What Is Art For?* she argues that among the many attempts to answer the questions of what is art, and what art does for people, one answer in particular stands out as most deeply explanatory. Her notion of art

> rests on the recognition of a fundamental behavioral tendency that I claim lies behind the arts in all their diverse and dissimilar manifestations from their remotest beginnings to the present day. It can result in artifacts and activities in people without expressed "aesthetic" motivations as well as the most highly self-conscious creations of contemporary art. I call this tendency *making special* and claim that it is as distinguishing and universal in humankind as speech or the skillful manufacture and use of tools.
>
> In whatever we are accustomed to call art, a *specialness* is tacitly or overtly acknowledged. Reality, or what is considered to be reality, is elaborated, reformed, given not only particularity (emphasis on uniqueness, or "specialness") but import (value, or "specialness")—what may be called such things as magic or beauty or spiritual power or significance.[44] (Emphases in original)

What, then, is particular to art and not to other ways of making special? Dissanayake argues that art, unlike other human activities,

> seeks to shape and embellish reality (or experience) so that it appears otherwise additionally or alternatively real. . . . Reality is converted from its usual unremarkable state—in which we take its components for granted—to a significant or specially experienced reality in which the components, by their emphasis or combination or juxtaposition, acquire a meta-reality.[45]

The "components" of art—the materials and qualities each art utilizes as its basic materials—are, by "emphasis or combination or juxtaposition," "made something of"; they are organized in ways to intentionally lift (or, if one prefers, deepen) the experience of them to the level of the special, significant, powerful, beautiful, meaningful, *as a function of the intentional ways the components have been treated.* Art, Dissanayake is suggesting, is different from other things humans do in its dependence on formed materials, created according to particular practices within culturally provided expectations, for the purpose of embodying within their created conditions the potential for out-of-the-ordinary experience. (I will return to this description of art in Chapter 5, in my discussion of art and meaning.) The key aspect in anything that can be called art is that the person creating it, no matter what that person thinks about, feels, or believes, absorbs all of that into the materials being used, into their look, their sound, their intricate, meaningful embodiment of interactive forces that make the resulting experience special, or significant, *as a function of that embodiment.*

---

[44]Ellen Dissanayake, *What Is Art For?* (Seattle: University of Washington Press, 1988), 92.
[45]Ibid., 95.

Such experience makes the ordinary extra-ordinary, the usual unusual, the commonplace vivid, whether a simple creation by a child, a complex achievement by a master, a casual encounter by a spectator, or an engrossed involvement of a connoisseur. Every experience of art, whether creating it or sharing it, "makes special" in the way only art can accomplish.

Music does this with sounds, thereby establishing its individuality among the arts. Thereby, as well, it establishes both its limitations and its power. Sounds, even when they incorporate visuals, words, drama, or movement, cannot do everything: if they could we would not need and therefore would not have other arts. But sounds, in their endless capacity for invention, their dynamic qualities, their infinite subtlety, their intimate relation to the body and its undergoings in feelings, and their capacity to absorb and transform ideas, beliefs, and values, provide humans with a powerful mode of meaningful experience treasured as such throughout history.

An experience-based philosophy of music education is one that focuses on and cherishes all the many ways music can be experienced and all the many musics offering the special experience music provides. Any philosophy less inclusive than this, such as a performance-based philosophy, or a singing skills philosophy, or one based on one particular style or type of music such as that of the Western classical tradition or that of pentatonic music, or one devoted to a particular social issue or to social utility as the end, or to ethical conduct as the end, or to the use of music to enhance learnings not particular to music; any such single-focus philosophy cannot do justice to the diversity of ways music can be experienced and to the diverse musics that offer such experiences. An experience-based philosophy of music education is inclusive of all musics and of all ways of being engaged with it because every particular kind and type of music, and every particular way music is made and received, represents a particular opportunity for musical experience. All such opportunities are precious. The central task of music education, I propose, is to make musical experience in all its manifestations as widely available to all people, and as richly cultivated for each individual, as possible.

A philosophy of music education should clarify the major dimensions of musical experience so music educators can effectively offer them to, and nurture them within, their students. In the following chapters I will focus on what I understand to be fundamental aspects of musical experience, each of them one dimension of a larger whole encompassing them all. In Chapter 3 I will discuss music and its relation to feeling. Chapter 4 will focus on creating music. The meaning of music—the special ways music allows us to experience—will be the topic of Chapter 5. In Chapter 6 I will discuss music as a culturally grounded endeavor. Chapter 7 will explain how music is a domain of multiple intelligences and why the cultivation of these intelligences may be conceived to be a central aim, or goal, of music education. The final chapters will apply the philosophy to the issues of creating an optimal music curriculum devoted to enhancing the musical experiences of every individual. That devotion, I propose, is worthy both of music and of people, providing music educators with a solid, secure basis for their values and actions as professionals.

ETUDES

1. Why do you think that a formalist position about art, stressing the internal construction of the work's materials, has tended to be more influential in music than in visual arts, dance, theater, and literature? Is that a strength of music, or a weakness?

2. The idea of "art for art's sake," or "music for music's sake," has had an elitist connotation, seeming to suggest that art or music is relevant for only a few people. I argued that this is unfortunate and mistaken. Assuming for the sake of clarification that I am correct, how would you argue to a group of parents, or a school board, or nonmusic faculty members in a school, that *all* people can and do treasure music "for its own sake"? How would you try to clarify this argument for them?

   Then take the opposite view: that only a few people can or want to enjoy music that way. What explanation would you offer to nonmusic constituencies as to why this view is persuasive?

   Which argument appeals to you more?

3. In a few paragraphs, or in an oral explanation, make an argument that performers of composed music create, in their practice of performing, the dynamic form of the piece being brought to actualization. Can this argument be understood to demonstrate the unity of form and practice? If so, what would a good teacher do to help all students learn that performance requires the achievement of an optimum balance of form with practice?

4. Do you think it is possible for people to listen actively, sensitively, and musically if they are not performers or composers or improvisers? If you think that is possible, what are some very practical implications for music education, especially in teaching for enhanced listening abilities? If you think it is not possible, what teaching implications then suggest themselves?

5. I used feminism as a way to illustrate issues connected with music as social agency. Try doing this using racism instead, playing out how music can be and has been used to call attention to racial problems in America and elsewhere. What are some parallels between feminist issues and race-related issues? What are some differences? What issues arise from a race-focused approach to music, as they do in a feminist approach? What other issues in our society can be used to illustrate the role of music in social criticism and change?

6. Many people believe that there are hard boundaries around music, that it constitutes a world of its own with its own ways to be, act, and know. Do you find this view attractive? What are some ways in which music does indeed seem to be a separate activity in life, deserving to be valued for its own qualities? Are there hazards in this understanding of music?

   Take a "no-boundaries" position about music, contrasted to the hard-boundaries view. Are there hazards also in this position? Can a moderately "soft-boundary" position help overcome the problems of extreme views in this matter?

7. In a debate, you are assigned the proposition that stressing the utilitarian values of music is the sole way to guarantee a secure place for music in the schools. How would you argue this position? Now do the same for the proposition that musical values have nothing to do with utilitarian values, and that only musical values can justify having music in the schools.

   Are there arguments from each position that can be aligned to strengthen, rather than weaken, the other? Is it acceptable, in your opinion, to sometimes stress utilitarian values and sometimes more philosophically grounded values without being hypocritical about either?

8. Music, I claim, "makes experience special." Try stating this idea in a variety of ways, as if you were addressing a variety of groups interested in learning more about what makes music so attractive to people. Explain to these imaginary groups what the particular, singular power of music is, to be able to do this as nothing else can. Be specific in your examples, citing (or using recorded examples of) various musics and various musical roles (performer, composer, listener, etc.) to illustrate how some people regard each kind of music, and each musical role, to be a source of important, deeply significant, life-enhancing, very "special" experiences.

3

The Feeling Dimension
of Musical Experience

MAIN THEMES

- The emotional dimension of music—its power to make us feel, and to "know" through feeling—is probably its most important defining characteristic.

- Attempts to explain exactly why and how music is experienced as emotional have never yielded a definitive solution, so complex are the issues.

- Emotion and intellect have historically been conceived to be different and even incompatible, accounting in large degree for the lesser status of music (and the arts) in education.

- Recent work in a variety of fields has revealed that the old idea that body and mind are separate can no longer be sustained. Body, mind, and feelings are integrally related, in fact interdependent. In one important explanation, feelings are the bases of consciousness itself.

- Music (and the arts) may be conceived as ways to refine and extend conscious experience, accounting for the widespread acknowledgment of their potential to enhance the quality of human life.

- Emotion and feeling are not identical. Feeling takes emotion further, to the stage at which music functions. Music allows us to create and share subjective experiences available in no other way.

- Musical feelings come from within the sounds of music and how they are configured, and from the outside world in which music resides. Inside and outside interplay in a great variety of ways.

- Music education, in its attempts to make musical feeling more accessible and more deeply internalized, may be regarded as an education of feeling. Helping all people to "know within" music more effectively is a primary goal of the enterprise.

MUSIC AND FEELING: AN INTRICATE RELATIONSHIP

If someone from a civilization without music were to ask us why our civilization supported so much musical activity, our answer would surely point to this capacity of music to heighten emotional life. Of course there are other reasons for individuals or societies to make use of music. Because much musical activity is also social activity it can come to have many social meanings, offering a variety of social rewards to those who participate in it. . . . However, we may label these social motivations as secondary, if only because they are so closely tied to particular cultures. The emotional factor is, however, transcultural. It seems unlikely that music could have penetrated to the core of so many different cultures unless there were some fundamental human attraction to organized sound which transcended cultural boundaries.[1]

[T]he structural properties of music are found culturally significant and everywhere cultivated because of the complexity, subtlety, and strength of the emotional life that only music sustains, and that life is sustainable only by the refinement and extension of musical means.[2]

These two assertions—the first by John A. Sloboda, a cognitive psychologist with particular expertise in music, the second by Francis Sparshott, a philosopher of the arts who often writes on music—converge in several ways. Both call attention to the emotional dimension of music as being a defining characteristic of it. Both point out that this characteristic of music makes it so central, so significant to humans, that music penetrates to the core of all cultures. And both pinpoint the same aspect of music as being the basis for its power to heighten, sustain, refine, and extend human emotional life—its organization of sounds, or structural properties, or musical means. Recall from Chapter 2 that Ellen Dissanayake also identified the way art "makes special" by the ways its components are emphasized, or combined, or juxtaposed—that is, their structural organization. The sounds of music, these thinkers suggest, given structure in the ways each culture devises, have a special power to enhance the "complexity, subtlety, and strength" of human emotional experience.

But what, exactly, is meant by associating music so closely with emotions, feelings, affections, and so forth? And where, exactly, does emotion, or feeling, come from in musical experience? Sloboda, Sparshott, and Dissanayake, along with a host of other thinkers throughout history, attribute the "emotional life" of music—its seeming to be "alive" with emotion—to what the sounds of music actually do. Musical sounds move through time and interrelate with each other as they do so, in ways organized to accomplish the purpose of heightening, refining, extending (and so forth) emotion, or feeling. But how do sounds, which are, after all, just sounds, have the power to so deeply move those involved with them?

---

[1]John A. Sloboda, *The Musical Mind: The Cognitive Psychology of Music* (Oxford: Clarendon Press, 1985), 1.
[2]Francis Sparshott, "Music and Feeling," *The Journal of Aesthetics and Art Criticism*, 52, no. 1 (Winter 1994), 26.

The ways musical sounds interplay and are structured within particular cultur-ally supplied expectation systems may be, as so many thinkers have argued, a neces-sary condition for music to be experienced as emotional, but is it a sufficient or exclusive condition? Those who view music as primarily a practice might seek its emotionality in the acts of making it, focusing on the exhilaration that producing musical sounds affords, the feelings of satisfaction, challenge, cooperation, achieve-ment, success and failure, that being involved in the "doing" of music entails. Are these not also legitimate sources of musical feeling?

Those who approach music from a social agency perspective are likely to be involved emotionally with it in still a different way. When music propounds points of view about ethical issues, equality, subjugation, violence, and so forth, emotions rele-vant to the music's message, positive or negative, will be undergone. In that case, what is emotional about music is its references to or associations with political-social matters about which strong feelings exist.

We have not yet exhausted the possibilities. Music is used in a great many ways in cultures—at weddings, funerals, celebrations of all sorts, social gatherings, reli-gious occasions, sports events, all the many societal functions in which music plays a role. Our responses to music in such settings are likely to be appropriate to the set-ting, the emotions we undergo being inseparable from the emotional context in which the music is serving a supporting role. Music is also used to enhance the emo-tional experience in film, dance, and theater, the feelings one gets from the music being largely dependent on what is going on in the medium to which it is contribut-ing. Music as a background for exercise, piped into a restaurant, or doctor's office, or shopping mall, is experienced in ways relevant to the purposes of exciting or sooth-ing people (or getting them to spend more money).

Additionally, each individual is likely to feel music in ways particular to that individual's personality, mood, physical condition, and so forth. Nothing is so per-sonal as what we feel, and how we personally feel music at the time we are involved with it. Whatever the music or its purpose or setting, all individuals are likely to experience it emotionally in ways particular to them.[3] But at the same time, we are aware that others are also feeling the music and that at least part of what we are feel-ing is felt as well by all those experiencing it now and in the past. In fact, the strong belief that the feelings we as individuals have in musical experience are also being had by others is the basis for successful group performance and for the powerful sense of community generated by performing and also by audience involvements. Emotion coexists as individual and as communal in musical experience, each dimen-sion strengthening the other.

Given this bewildering array of ways to account for how music and emotion are related, what are music educators' responsibilities in this matter? After all, if any single value of music underlies the commitment and passion of music educators it is

---

[3]For an insightful discussion of individuality in music listening, see Kathleen Marie Higgins, "Musical Idiosyncrasy and Perspectival Listening," in *Music and Meaning,* ed. Jenefer Robinson (Ithaca and London: Cornell University Press, 1997), 83–102.

likely the capacity of music to enhance human feelings, and the desire to make this gift of music as richly available to people as possible. Music educators have been transformed by the power of music: music has touched our lives deeply. We are devoted to the cause of sharing with others the emotional depths music so uniquely makes available. How can we go about doing this effectively when there is so much confusion about what musical emotion is, how it works, and where it comes from?

I cannot promise to dispel all the confusions about music and its involvement with emotion, for the simple reason that no one ever has. Many attempts have been made and many useful insights have been offered, but no ultimate or definitive solution has appeared. What can be done is to explain what seem to be helpful ideas that offer a reasonable degree of clarity, enough for music educators to be reasonably secure about the topic and reasonably comfortable with the ways we teach music to accomplish what we are likely to particularly wish—to help students be engaged more thoroughly in the emotional dimension of music.

THE EMOTION/INTELLECT DICHOTOMY

To better understand the interrelations of music and emotion, it is first important to acknowledge that, at least in Western history, there has been a strong tendency to regard emotion as different from, and of lesser value than, intellect. Until the advent of postmodernism at the end of the twentieth century, as explained in Chapter 1, the belief was (and continues to be) widespread that reason, or rationality, is the epitome of human functioning, and that the emotions or feelings have little or nothing to do with reason. In fact, emotions are often believed to get in the way of reason's proper workings. This belief has largely accounted for the arts being regarded as less important in education than those subjects clearly based on reasoning. These are considered "the basics" because they entail thinking and intelligence. The arts, on the other hand, have mostly to do with the feelings, and require a kind of talent rather than intelligence to be successful with them. Including the arts as enrichment—as one of the "specials"—is a good thing, in this view, but they certainly do not deserve to be taken seriously as being essential for all students, especially those not particularly gifted in the ways the arts peculiarly require.

In recent years a turnaround has begun to occur in our understandings of the workings of intellect, intelligence, and emotion. From a variety of sources, including the cognitive sciences, philosophy, psychology, physiology, and neuroscience, the old idea that emotion is separate and different from human mindful processes has begun to be eroded. It is rapidly becoming evident that human cognition, or intelligence, exists and is demonstrated in diverse forms, is directly tied to the functions of the body, and is pervaded throughout with feeling. The human mind, we are now beginning to understand, is a complex amalgam of dimensions previously thought to be separate—dimensions of thinking, feeling, acting, and context, each contributing essentially to what we can know and experience. The implications of these emerging insights for how we understand music and the values of musical experience are profound. Musical thinking, doing, and feeling, in their necessary interdependence and their exercise of genuine, high-order intelligence, may well be a paradigm of human mindful functioning at its optimal level.

FEELING, COGNITION, AND CONSCIOUSNESS

Among the many studies in recent years of how and why emotion is implicated in mindfulness,[4] one in particular is strikingly pertinent for clarifying the primal role feeling plays in human mentality and why musical feeling seems to be so significant in all cultures. This is the explanation by research neurologist Antonio R. Damasio of how feeling is likely to be the key factor in human consciousness itself and an essential ingredient in human cognition. A brief introduction to his thinking will lead me to a hypothesis that suggests, in a gripping way, why musical feeling has served humans so well in the ways so many thinkers throughout history have recognized.

In his first book, *Descartes' Error: Emotion, Reason, and the Human Brain*,[5] Damasio explained the unfortunate legacy of Descartes' attempt to separate the mind from the body and its attendant feelings. What was Descartes' error? Or, to be more exact, which of his many errors is Damasio's focus? Descartes' position was summarized in his claim "I think, therefore I am." (*"Cogito, ergo sum."*)

> The statement [is] perhaps the most famous in the history of philosophy. . . . Taken literally, the statement illustrates precisely the opposite of what I believe to be true about the origins of mind and about the relation between mind and body. It suggests that thinking, and awareness of thinking, are the real substrates of being. . . . This is Descartes' error: the abyssal separation between body and mind . . . the suggestion that reasoning, and moral judgment, and the suffering that comes from physical pain or emotional upheaval might exist separately from the body. Specifically: the separation of the most refined operations of mind from the structure and operation of a biological organism.[6]

Damasio's insistence that the body is the basis for thought, contrary to Descartes' claim, leads directly to the centrality of feeling in his theory of mind and consciousness.

---

[4]For an exhaustive overview of the literature on the cognitive dimension of emotion up to 1990, see W. Ann Stokes, "Intelligence and Feeling: A Philosophical Examination of These Concepts as Interdependent Factors in Musical Experience and Music Education" (Doctoral diss., Northwestern University, 1990). The Index listings under "Emotion" and "Feeling" in Wayne D. Bowman, *Philosophical Perspectives on Music* (New York: Oxford University Press, 1998), provide further sources and discussions. An excellent essay on the relation of cognition and emotion, which she calls "a conspiracy of the mind and heart," with commentary on Israel Scheffler's notion of "cognitive emotions," is Iris Yob's "The Cognitive Emotions and Emotional Cognitions," in *Reason and Education: Essays in Honor of Israel Scheffler* (Dordrecht, Boston: Kluwer Academic Press, 1997), 43–57.

[5]Antonio R. Damasio, *Descartes' Error: Emotion, Reason, and the Human Brain* (New York: Putnam's, 1994).

[6]Ibid., 248–50.

For feeling serves as the body's sensor system—the body's regulatory mechanism connecting it to thinking and consciousness.

> Feelings, along with the emotions they come from, are not a luxury. They serve as internal guides, and they help us communicate to others signals that can also guide them. And feelings are neither intangible nor elusive. Contrary to traditional scientific opinion, feelings are just as cognitive as other percepts. They are the result of a most curious physiological arrangement that has turned the brain into the body's captive audience.
>
> Feelings let us catch a glimpse of the organism in full biological swing, a reflection of the mechanisms of life itself as they go about their business. Were it not for the possibility of sensing body states that are inherently ordained to be painful or pleasurable, there would be no suffering or bliss, no longing or mercy, no tragedy or glory in the human condition.[7]

In his examination of the role of the body in reasoning and knowing, Damasio begins, in his first book, to make important distinctions between emotion and feeling, distinctions useful for understanding the nature of music. He explains that as our bodily states change from moment to moment we "get to know about" their existence and can monitor their continuously evolving condition.

> That process of continuous monitoring, that experience of what your body is doing *while* thoughts about specific contents roll by, is the essence of what I call a feeling. If an emotion is a collection of changes in body state connected to particular mental images that have activated a specific brain system, *the essence of feeling an emotion is the experience of such changes in juxtaposition to mental images that initiated the cycle.* In other words, a feeling depends on the juxtaposition of an image of the body proper, to an image of something else, such as the visual image of a face or the auditory image of a melody.[8] (Emphases in original)

Note that there are both quantitative and qualitative differences between emotion and feeling, emotion being at a large level of activation and a broad level of awareness, whereas feeling is the actual, specific awareness of what is transpiring and its connection with the details of whatever is triggering it—a face, or a melody. An emotion, we might say, is general: feeling is the "specifics" of an emotion. "A feeling about a particular object [say, a melody] is based on the subjectivity of the perception of the object, the perception of the body state it engenders, and the perception of modified style and efficiency of the thought process as all of the above happens."[9] "Feeling a melody," this suggests, is an amalgam of one's subjective interaction with the qualities of the melody itself, undergoing what that interaction does to one's body, and

---

[7]Ibid., xv.
[8]Ibid., 145.
[9]Ibid., 147–48.

sensing the changes in thought processing (in this case musical) the experience of the melody entails—that is, thinking/feeling musically along with the melody. Feeling, body, and mind are combined in such an act.[10]

Feelings, then, are awarenesses of the body and of the body undergoing its life. They "let us mind the body 'live.'" This capacity pervades and directs all we undergo as living, aware creatures.

> I see feelings as having a truly privileged status. They are represented at many neural levels, including the neocortical, where they are the neuroanatomical and neurophysiological equals of whatever is appreciated by other sensory channels. But because of their inextricable ties to the body, they come first in development and retain a primacy that subtly pervades our mental life. Because the brain is the body's captive audience, feelings are winners among equals. And since what comes first constitutes a frame of reference for what comes after, feelings have a say on how the rest of the brain and cognition go about their business. Their influence is immense.[11]

The influence of feelings on what humans know and how they know it led Damasio, through further study of people with various brain conditions impeding their ability to feel, to a second book more detailed and precise than the first. In *The Feeling of What Happens: Body and Emotion in the Making of Consciousness*,[12] a new concept is introduced—that feeling is the key to the occurrence of, and workings of, consciousness. Our awareness of ourselves as we relate to our inner and outer worlds is based on feeling. Without it we would undergo without perceiving, or realizing, that we are doing so. This perception, or realization, or awareness of what is happening to us, caused by feeling, is consciousness.

> I write about the sense of self and about the transition from innocence and ignorance to knowingness and selfness. My specific goal is to consider the biological circumstances that permit this critical transition. . . . It is easy to envision how consciousness is likely to have opened the way in human evolution to a new order of creations not possible without it: conscience, religion, social and political organizations, the arts, the sciences, and technology. Perhaps even more compellingly, consciousness is the critical biological function that allows us to know sorrow or know joy, to know suffering or know pleasure, to sense embarrassment or pride, to grieve for lost love or lost life. Consciousness is, in effect, the key to a life examined, for better and for worse, our beginner's permit into knowing all about the hunger, the thirst, the sex, the tears, the laughter, the kicks,

---

[10]Damasio also discusses the existence of "background feeling" as a dimension of brain function and awareness. This is the "feeling of life itself, the sense of being." More restricted in range than the feelings connected with broad emotional experience, background feeling provides the sense of oneself living a life—of "individual identity"—that acts as the stage, or backdrop, for the playings-out of emotions and their particularities of feeling.

[11]Damasio, *Descartes' Error,* note 5, 159–60.

[12]Antonio Damasio, *The Feeling of What Happens: Body and Emotion in the Making of Consciousness* (New York: Harcourt Brace, 1999).

the punches, the flow of images we call thought, the feelings, the words, the stories, the beliefs, the music and the poetry, the happiness and the ecstasy.[13]

What most makes human life "human," then, is our consciousness. And our consciousness, Damasio hypothesizes, is built on "three distinct although closely related phenomena: *an emotion, the feeling of that emotion, and knowing that we have a feeling of that emotion*"[14] (emphasis in original). In a tightly reasoned yet colorfully humane manner he traces these phenomena throughout his book, referring along the way to the extensive brain research that led him to his conclusions. I can here only mention a few points from his sizable book, to clarify his hypothesis and its implications for music and music educators.

Consciousness, Damasio explains, has several dimensions. The simplest is "core consciousness," concerned with the here and now, the existent present. It is a simple biological phenomenon, present throughout life, allowing the self (the "core self") to interact in an immediate way with the environment. As it does so, the self *feels* itself interacting, and *knows* that it is the one interacting. This "feeling of knowing" oneself is the "first triad" of consciousness. It is probably what T. S. Eliot had in mind in his line "you are the music while the music lasts," Damasio suggests. In core consciousness there is "the fleeting moment in which a deep knowledge can emerge—a union, or *incarnation*, as [T. S. Eliot] called it"[15] (emphasis added). Knowledge, here, is incarnated. Knowing occurs in and through the body, in and through the feelings caused by the body's undergoings, and the awareness that the self is undergoing what the body and feelings are experiencing.

We may be the music while it lasts, but a residue of memory remains after the music stops, Damasio reminds us, a memory related to others in an aggregate of all those the self stores up throughout life. This aggregate constitutes the "autobiographical self," which changes continuously as a result of one's lived, *felt* history. This history consists of "telling stories," registered in the form of brain maps. Telling stories precedes language and is in fact a precondition for language. The buildup of mapped stories—the feelings of what happens to a self immersed in an environment—creates an individual.

On the basis of this (necessarily very brief and sketchy) description of Damasio's theory of consciousness and the central role of feelings in it, I want to propose that humans have devised a way to explicitly build on and extend their capacity for felt experience, their reveling in and finding primally meaningful the gaining and storing (or "storying") of lived, felt undergoings, that are the basis of that most precious aspect of the human condition—consciousness. That way to extend feeling for the sake of the enhancement of consciousness it provides—the depths and breadth of felt meaning it makes available—is called "music" (and, of course, in a broader sense, "the arts"). An essential ingredient in the creation of a storied individual, I would

---

[13]Ibid., 4–5.
[14]Ibid., 8.
[15]Ibid., 172.

suggest, is the story of musical experiences that individual has undergone, an impoverished story if such experiences are very limited, a rich one if they are abundant. Because musical experience is quintessentially *felt* experience, such experience is as directly tied to the quality of conscious life as anything can be.

Music makes feeling conscious, not by being "about" feeling, as psychological knowledge is (such as Damasio provides); it adds to felt consciousness through the *immediate experiences of feeling it affords*. As Damasio says, "*Explaining* how to make something mental or something ours in scientific terms is an entirely different matter from *making* that something mental and ours *directly*"[16] (emphases in original). Direct experiences of feeling are embodied in music and made available to the bodied experience of those engaged with it. Such experience is as extensively and powerfully gained from musical involvements as from anything else humans can possibly do. Music, I suggest, is perhaps our most effective mode for cultivating, extending, and refining the felt undergoings that are the basis for human consciousness and cognition.

In that light, the assertion by Francis Sparshott at the beginning of this chapter takes on its full significance: that music is "culturally significant and everywhere cultivated because of the complexity, subtlety, and strength of the emotional life that only music sustains, and that life is sustainable only by the refinement and extension of musical means." Damasio's research begins to provide a warranted basis for this claim, and for Sloboda's, Dissanayake's, and all the many, many others who have also made it.

RIFF 5

Intuition. Knowing something before evidence of it is available. Sensing it, glimpsing its veracity without being able to fully explain why in scientific terms. The great philosophers astound me by the depth and convincingness of their intuitions, their ability to grasp truths long before science comes along and "mops up"—provides the evidential basis for what had long been known intuitively.

As I read Damasio's books I am stunned by the familiarity to me of what his research has led him to propose. "I know this stuff," I find myself thinking. "Not in neurological terms but certainly ideationally. I've been steeped in these ideas without the brain-function evidence to back them up." It hits me. "This is Susanne Langer! This is precisely what she was suggesting all along. No wonder it all seems so recognizable—so evident to me." In my early years as an aspiring scholar the work of Langer was the hottest stuff going, and, for me, revelatory. *Philosophy in a New Key* widened my eyes. *Feeling and Form* knocked me out. *Problems of Art* deepened my respect. *Mind: An Essay on Human Feeling* (three volumes) was flat-out awesome.

---

[16]Ibid., 308.

I dig out my article "Langer on the Arts as Cognitive," in the inaugural issue of the *Philosophy of Music Education Review,* entirely devoted to reflections on her work. I read through it, shaking my head at how she anticipated Damasio and neuroscience as we now know it by over three decades. Of course, her explanation of how feeling is the essential underpinning of consciousness and of mind was, necessarily, incomplete and imperfect (as is still the case). Yet over and over, in detailed language, she explains how feeling arises from bodily awareness and, at a certain point in evolution, enters a new phase: consciousness arises. "That is why I make feeling the starting-point of a philosophy of mind," she says. "The study of feeling—its sources, its forms, its complexities—leads one down into biological structure and process until its estimation becomes (for the time) impossible, and upward to the purely human sphere known as 'culture.' It is still what we feel, and everything that can be felt, that is important."[17]

Just so, as Damasio is now able to confirm in ways Langer could only anticipate. I read on in my article, being reminded again and again of her astounding intuitions now being verified. Later, on page 287 of Damasio's second book, I come across this comment, in his discussion of background feelings: "That notion was first hinted at by the remarkable but unsung American philosopher Susanne Langer, a disciple of Alfred North Whitehead."

"Thank you, Mr. Damasio," I say to myself. "Thank you for recognizing this extraordinary thinker, a precursor in philosophy to the ideas you are now propounding based on brain research. She beat you to it, out there, on a wing and a prayer, guided only by the depth of her intuitions, intuitions I long ago intuited as being seminal, and that guided my earlier understandings of feeling as cognitive. Now your work, and others', is supporting her creative intuitions. What goes around comes around."

EMOTION AND FEELING

Damasio's distinction between emotion and feeling helps explain the abundant power of music to "refine and extend" our felt experiences. Emotion and feeling are linked, feeling being the "playing out" in actual experience of what the body is emotionally undergoing. That playing out—the intricacies of felt experience as we interact with environing conditions—is what consciousness "notices," or "is aware of." What music does, then, is to make available for awareness, in how its organized sounds move and interrelate, the infinitely extendable, infinitely subtle, infinitely

---

[17]Quoted in Bennett Reimer, "Langer on the Arts as Cognitive," *Philosophy of Music Education Review,* 1, no. 1 (Spring 1993), 48.

"complexifiable" possibilities of the feelings we are capable of having and so crave to have to fulfill our capacities for consciousness and cognition. Emotions in and of themselves are not extensible this way: emotions require felt, aware feelings to carry out their potentials. Emotions can be thought of as broad categories of possible feelings—as guideposts marking off feeling-potentials.

These guideposts are broad enough and stable enough to have acquired names—joy, sadness, fear, and so on. When they are played out in felt experience, however, they become attached to the specificities of what we are interacting with, specificities so complex, fluid, linked to one another in a variety of ways, as to leave behind the capacity of language to keep up with their subtleties. As Damasio says, "The idea of consciousness as a feeling of knowing" stems from brain and body structures. "All of those structures operate with the *nonverbal vocabulary of feelings.* . . . The mysterious first-person perspective of consciousness consists of *newly minted knowledge, information if you will, expressed as feeling*"[18] (emphases added).

Emotions are nameable in words. Feelings are the nonverbal, "newly minted" crossings into consciousness of felt information, or knowing, consisting of "feeling-beyond-language." It is such knowing—knowing through experiencing what ordinary language cannot express—that music is so potently able to bring to the level of awareness. Such knowing is, in the fullest sense of the word, *cognitive* in the post-Descartes sense, the sense in which the body and feelings are recognized to be essential components in what humans are capable of knowing.

Such knowing in and through feeling could not occur and need not occur (and therefore there would be no need for music) if what we were capable of knowing in this way were limited to the level of emotion. So the distinction between feeling and emotion is an important one, especially for those who teach music.

An analogy can help make the distinction between emotions and feelings clearer.

All of human experience is permeated with the feelings on which consciousness is based. Far from being little computers on legs, humans are creatures whose every act and every thought, from birth to death, is suffused with feeling. Much of what we know about our world—of what our world seems to us to be like—we know about by feeling about it. Our feelings are not just added on to our human existence as a separate element overlaying our physical or intellectual being; feeling saturates everything we are and do and is inseparable from everything we are and do. The nature of the human condition is very largely a nature of organisms that have the capacity to feel and are aware that they are feeling.

Let us call the feelingful aspect of human life "subjectivity"—the element in human reality of affective responsiveness. Human subjectivity is endlessly varied and infinitely complex. Its possibilities are inexhaustible, both in breadth and in depth. And subjectivity is part of all human experience: there is nothing that is real for human experience without the involvement of subjectivity

---

[18]Damasio, *The Feeling of What Happens,* note 12, 313.

In the vast realm of human subjectivity some guideposts exist, marking off large areas of feeling that are somewhat related to one another or that share a particular quality. These guideposts, which are little more than occasional buoys in an ocean of subjective responses, have been given names. One of them, for example, is called "love." Love is a category word, and what it categorizes is an infinite number of possible ways to feel. The breadth and depth of feeling that falls under the category love is so large and complex, so subtle and varied, that the word used as a category for it can only indicate its most general character. Even if one qualifies the word by adding others—parental love, romantic love, puppy love, platonic love—one is only adding a few more buoys to the ocean, each one surrounded by a huge expanse of water. Parental love is another category word for another limitless domain of possible feelings. In fact, trying to narrow down feeling by using more descriptive category words has the opposite effect: each new verbal category calls attention to a whole new realm of possibilities of feeling.

Another factor makes the realm of human subjectivity infinite in complexity and scope. This is the compound nature of human feeling. Think of the possibilities of feeling categorized by the word hate. Surely, as the history of humankind shows, these must be infinite. Now think of the possibilities of fear. Again, an infinite realm of feeling. But are these two categories really separate? Is there not a great deal of fear in hate? Could we not add a few more category-words to flavor the pot? How about envy and suspicion? Each word categorizes a huge realm of possibilities of feeling, and each overlaps and fuses with the others. Our affective experiences are seldom if ever discrete; instead, our feelings mingle and blend in countless, inseparable mixtures that the words of language cannot begin to describe because they are inherently not designed to do so.

Still another characteristic of subjectivity makes it unable to be captured by words—its fluidity. We do not feel in a static, unchanging way. At every moment our feelings are in motion, developing, changing, waxing and waning, gathering energy to a peak, then fading to quietude. As our feelings move continually, just as life itself moves on in continuous energy from moment to moment, they are constantly shifting in their mixtures, so that it is impossible to say at any single point, "Well, now I am feeling 62 percent happiness, 12 percent joy, and 26 percent anticipation." Our feelings are better envisioned as the surging waters underneath the buoys that have been given names, the waters mingling, moving, deep in some places (so deep we are not sure how far down our feelings might take us), shallow in others. Feelings are dynamic and organic, as are the forces of life itself.

For purposes of clarity let us agree to call all the possible category words (every buoy floating on the turbulent ocean) "emotions." And let us call what takes place in our actual, subjective, conscious experience (the dynamic waters themselves) "feelings." Feelings themselves—experienced subjectivities—are incapable of being named, for every time we produce a name we are only producing a category, a buoy reminding us that underneath it lies a vast realm of possible ways to feel.

So the difference between emotion and feeling is a real one—it is the difference between words on the one hand and experiences on the other, the one being a symbol (or sign) of certain possibilities in the other.

> Save nominally, there is no such thing as *the* emotion of fear, hate, love. The unique, unduplicated character of experienced events and situations impregnates the emotion that is evoked. Were it the function of speech to reproduce that to which it refers, we could never speak of fear, but only of fear-of-this-particular-oncoming-automobile, with all its specifications of time and place, or fear-under-specified-circumstances-of-drawing-a-wrong-conclusion from just-such-and-such-data. A lifetime would be too short to reproduce in words a single emotion [what Damasio and I are calling feeling].[19] (Emphasis in original)

Human experience is always accompanied by feeling, but our ability to stipulate what is being felt is bound by the extreme limitations of category words, which are incapable of pinpointing the immense complexity and fluidity of subjective responsiveness.

> We are given to thinking of emotions as things as simple and compact as are the words by which we name them. Joy, sorrow, hope, fear, anger, curiosity, are treated as if each in itself were a sort of entity that enters full-made upon the scene, an entity that may last a long time or a short time, but whose duration, whose growth and career, is irrelevant to its nature. In fact emotions are qualities, when they are significant, of a complex experience that moves and changes. . . . Experience is emotional [feelingful] but there are no separate things called emotions in it.[20]

Music can present a sense of human feeling because music is, in Dewey's words, *"a complex experience that moves and changes."* When attention is paid to the unchanging or constant aspect of music, a particular emotional shading can sometimes be identified that characterizes a piece. This particular identifiable emotional quality is usually called "mood," as Leonard B. Meyer explains.

> Because music flows through time, listeners and critics have generally been unable to pinpoint the particular musical process which evoked the affective response which they describe. They have been prone, therefore, to characterize a whole passage, section, or composition. In such cases the response must have been made to those elements of the musical organization which tend to be constant, e.g., tempo, general range, dynamic level, instrumentation, and texture. What these elements characterize are those aspects of mental life which are also relatively stable and persistent, namely, moods and associations, rather than the changing and developing affective responses [feelings] with which this study is concerned.[21]

---

[19]John Dewey, *Art as Experience* (New York: Capricorn Books, 1958), 67.
[20]Ibid., 41–42.
[21]Leonard B. Meyer, *Emotion and Meaning in Music* (Chicago: University of Chicago Press, 1956), 7.

Meyer's study has been, throughout his long career, about the ways musical sounds go beyond moods (emotions) and associations (references) to affective (feelingful) responses. Such responses are caused by the ways sounds, within culturally determined style possibilities, cause us to expect what might happen to them and then deviate from those expectations so as to cause us to get involved with them—to pay attention and open ourselves to the tensions and resolutions of feeling they present. This happens with musics of all cultures, Meyer makes clear, not just with music in Western styles. In close analyses and discussions of music from China, Japan, Java, India, and Africa, of Jewish and Byzantine chant, and of Chippewa singing, he emphasizes that the expressive devices that cause expectations and deviations "are by no means confined to the tradition of Western music," and he cautions against "the danger of reading Western meanings and expectations into passages where they are not relevant."[22] Every cultural music, *on it own terms*, "captures" and engrosses us by not giving us, immediately, all of its possibilities on a silver platter: that would be too easy, too predictable and therefore uninvolving. The "specialness" music arouses requires creative *work* to bring it into being, and to share that specialness requires, also, creative *work* by those listening to it. In creating music, both as artists and as listeners, people explore and discover feeling through experiences that require, if they are to be successful, an adventure of imagination into new possibilities of undergoing.

MUSIC AND FEELING

If the only means available to humans to help them explore their subjective nature were ordinary language, a major part of human reality would be forever closed off to our conscious development. The subjective part of reality—the way life feels as it is lived—cannot be fully clarified or refined in our experience solely through the use of ordinary language. This is not because no one has taken the time to think up enough words to name all possible ways of feeling; it is because the nature of feeling is ineffable in essence. This is what Leonard Bernstein meant when he explained, during the first of his "Young People's Concerts," that music does what language cannot do.

> The most wonderful thing of all is that there's no limit to the different kinds of feelings music can make you have. Sometimes we can name the things we feel, like joy or sadness or love or hate or peacefulness. But there are other feelings so deep and special that we have no words for them, and that is where music is especially marvelous. It names the feelings for us, only in notes instead of words.[23]

"Only in notes." Bernstein is saying, here, what so many have said and continue to say: that musical feeling can be found "in the notes"—what the sounds of

---

[22]Ibid., 197–232.
[23]Leonard Bernstein, "What Does Music Mean?" Young People's Concert, January 18, 1958.

music actually do. Once again we are presented with the same claim made by thinkers about music throughout history: that the feelings of music are properties of the ways it organizes sounds, structures sounds through musical means, emphasizing, combining, juxtaposing sounds, and so forth. In light of Damasio's explanation, and of countless complementary explanations long before Damasio and neuroscience appeared on the scene, it seems clear that music affords us a very powerful way to embody and share the infinite subtleties and complexities of feeling. Music is able to do this by creating an environment in which "what happens"—what the music does—is experienced as felt knowledge at the aware, conscious level. In music, *the feeling of what happens* (the title of Damasio's book) is the feeling of what happens *musically*—what happens to the sounds as they do what they do.

How do those sounds become transformed into felt experience? While the struggle to answer this question theoretically has gone on for centuries,[24] the practice of doing it has gone its merry way quite unconcerned about an explanation. In every culture, in all the countless styles and types of music people have invented and shared, success at doing so always depends on whether the music "works," on whether it engages people in meaningful feeling. Such engagements, whether through composing, performing, listening, or whatever, range in power from the casually pleasant, or enjoyable, to the deeply spiritual, or profound.[25] In all of them, the sounds of music are arranged to *"make sense"* as each culture, style, and type regulates. These sounds capture and exhibit the intricacies of feeling as only musical sounds can do.

How do sounds "make sense" musically? Sparshott adds still another explanation to the many that have attempted to link musical sounds with feeling. "We experience musical works," he says, "as objects—in creating them, in performing them, in listening to them, we are aware of them as full realities."[26] The distinctive nature of musical objects and of the way we experience them (completely different from the notion of an object as something separate and distanced from the experience within a person confronting it) stem from three characteristics of music, according to Sparshott.

> First, music is music, a system all its own: keys, scales, intervals defined as "fifths" and so on, tones defined as "dominant" and so forth, are elements not found in nature. Since musical qualities are derived from formal properties that are generated by artificially constituted entities in constructed relationships, it is to be expected that the affective character we experience in a piece of music should be *sui generis,* not to be described in terms derived from other areas of experience and hence not to be effectively described at all . . . music remains music and its affectiveness is distinctive of it.

---

[24]Much of Wayne Bowman's book *Philosophical Perspectives on Music,* note 4, can be read as a history of the attempt to explain how created sounds also create felt meanings.

[25]My attempt to clarify musical experience at its deepest levels is "The Experience of Profundity in Music," *The Journal of Aesthetic Education,* 29, no. 4 (Winter 1995).

[26]Sparshott, "Music and Feeling," note 2, 25.

Second, "musical works are experienced as belonging to a world of their own." In this musical world the feelings one has not only are distinctive to it but also are experienced, for many people,

> more directly and intensely than any other sort of object. Probably it is the very fact that music as such has no reference, no descriptive content, and no subjectivity [emotions], that makes it directly affectual [feelingful] . . . the affectivity of music is its own and has its own precisions, which are not dependent on the range of named responses to the practical world. Mendelssohn's famous observation that the emotional meaning of music is too precise to be put into words is best understood in this light.[27]

Musical experience, Sparshott explains, though it comes to us from an external source, is heard "inside us," as "not located or identified as itself other or elsewhere than [in] the listener." Music is experienced as "a sounding structure or a structured sound, indwelling in the listening mind."[28] It is important to understand, here, that "the listening mind" is the composer's, the performer's, the improviser's, as well as the listener's. All engagements with music activate the "listening mind," each in its own way and each calling for its own creativity and intelligence, as will be explained in chapters 4 and 7.

MUSICAL FEELING FROM WORLD TO SOUND

While the listening mind in all its manifestations is involved with music as a special system of thinking, doing, and feeling that creates its own virtual world, the experience of music also takes place, simultaneously, in the larger world in which each of us dwells. Musical boundaries are usually not hard enough to completely shut out the rest of the world, or lacking enough to eliminate our awareness that the special sort of thing called musical experience is going on. In the usual soft-boundary musical experience the musical world and the rest of the world interpenetrate in all sorts of ways and to a variety of degrees. The feelings we have in musical experience, then, though based on "what happens" musically, are affected as well by whatever else we ourselves add to that experience. As Carl Seashore reminded us (Chapter 2), "When you listen, you hear what you are." And "what we are" when having musical experience is the sum total of all we have experienced in our lives.

Most directly, the musical role we are playing (composer, performer, listener, teacher, critic, historian, theorist) affects our experience profoundly. Also, the lifetime of feeling that has made us who we are does not simply disappear when we are

---

[27]Ibid. Mendelssohn's observation was "What any music I like expresses for me is not *thoughts too indefinite* to clothe in words, but *too definite*." Quoted in Edmund Burney, *The Power of Sound* (New York: Basic Books, 1966), 357 (emphases in original). Compare this comment by the novelist Saul Bellow about his protagonist Ravelstein: "He loses himself in sublime music, a music in which ideas are dissolved, reflecting these ideas in the form of feeling." Saul Bellow, *Ravelstein* (New York: Penguin, 2001), 232.

[28]Sparshott, 25.

musically involved, any more than it does when we are involved with anything else. And if our life has caused us to adopt a particular perspective that permeates our being, one focused on race, or gender, or religion, or whatever, we are likely to apply that perspective to music as we might to much else in our life. Musical experience is not exempt from being influenced by who we are, in all our complexities, when we are having it. Certainly there are times when "we are the music while the music lasts," and those are very precious times indeed. But just as surely we often cause music to reflect who we happen to be, and, in the deepest sense, we *must* do so to some degree as we must with everything else.

What, then, are music educators responsible for as educators? At one extreme, we can take the position that "purely" musical feelings, untouched and uninfluenced by any others, are what we exist to cultivate, so that we should suppress or at least ignore any feelings caused by anything other than music. At the other extreme, we can use music as a kind of Rorschach test, in which it merely serves to cue feelings already part of the personality of the responder. We can go, then, 100 percent for T. S. Eliot, or 100 percent for Carl Seashore. Or we can set a proportion at a level we think is the correct one, taking a theoretical position that musical experience should be, say, 90 percent Eliot and 10 percent Seashore, or perhaps the reverse.

But we can also adapt ourselves to a variety of balances as they exist in diverse musical experiences, depending on the particularities of various musics, various occasions, various individuals, various objectives. We know from our own lives as music educators that our experiences of music depend heavily on the circumstances surrounding the ways we are engaged with it. When we are performing, a whole "performance-world" colors our felt experience. Different worlds of influence come into play when (and if) we compose, or improvise, each of those participations deeply affecting the ways we feel the music with which we are dealing. And when we are in our teaching mode we must adapt ourselves to the particulars of our work.

We are all, also, listeners. When we go to hear a musical presentation, the place, time, and type all influence how we respond, as do the size of the audience, whether we are alone or with others, and our plans for after the event. We have a very different surround when we are home, perhaps alone, and listen to recordings. Sometimes we become so deeply and intimately engaged with the sounds that we truly "lose ourselves" and "become the music." But we can just as easily feel the music in the background as we go about our household activities.

Does all this make "what the music is doing" irrelevant? If that were the case, so that the feelings people have with music were entirely predetermined by each person's particular life circumstances rather than in any way by the music itself, it would be difficult to explain why music would exist at all, and why every culture and subculture so cherishes its music as to consider it a precious possession. The music itself—sound arranged in ways that yield meaningful feeling—is at the root of our need for and value of music, despite our ascribing of our own feelings and values to it, embedding them in the sounds we make or share. The coexistence of inner and outer is the crucial factor—the interrelation between what the music actually does and what the engaged person both gets from it and makes of it.

Within that inevitable coexistence, music educators, I suggest, can and should help make what Lucy Green calls "inherent" meanings (Chapter 2)—those inhering in the interrelated sounds themselves—as available for experiencing as possible. However, doing so need not and should not deny or suppress the inevitability that "delineated" meanings—those we as individuals, and the social contexts in which we exist, add to inherent meanings—will also be implicated in how we respond to music. There is no neat "line" of either–or between the inherent and delineated aspects of musical experiencing, between *either* "musical" *or* "extra-musical," *either* "intrinsic" *or* "extrinsic" dimensions, a line that, crossed in either direction, immediately changes the nature of the experience. Instead, there is a "space" in which the two coexist in proportions impossible to delineate. In our efforts to reveal as much inherence as we can—as much of the "feeling of what is happening" in each particular musical experience we are sharing with our students—we must make room for, and give all due recognition to, what our students add to the experience from their own, individual perspective. The balance is likely to shift depending on a great many factors, sometimes emphasizing the internal events of the music, other times focusing on its political, religious, ideological, and such implications. Attention to the created sounds themselves, supplemented and enriched by all the meanings attributed to, suggested by, and incorporated within those sounds, will most genuinely represent the nature and value of music. Such attention, in our case teaching, will also best accomplish the underlying purpose of music education—to harness the power of music to enhance people's felt lives.

MUSIC EDUCATION AND THE EDUCATION OF FEELING

Throughout my discussion of music and feeling, I have used, and quoted, phrases highlighting the capacity of music to heighten emotional life; the complexity, subtlety, and strength of the emotional life that only music sustains; refinement and extension of feeling through music; cultivation, extension, and refinement of felt undergoings; newly minted knowledge, or information, expressed as feelings; and so forth. All these call attention to an important consequence of being involved in music. When we are musically involved, in any of the many ways various cultures make available, our felt awarenesses are inevitably enhanced. That enhancement of the extent and depth of what we feel, as musical experience uniquely provides and as music education attempts to cultivate, can be called an "education of feelings." As Damasio puts it, "'Feeling' feelings [knowing that we have feelings] extends the reach of emotions by facilitating the planning of novel and customized forms of adaptive response."[29] Music is a unique way of extending (refining, enhancing, deepening, etc.) our emotional lives, through the novel and customized forms of response it calls on both to create it and share it. Music education attempts to enhance the effectiveness by which people are able to extend their musical involvements.

---

[29]Damasio, *The Feeling of What Happens*, note 12, 285.

As with the difference between emotion and feeling, an analogy can help clarify the sense in which the cultivation of musical experience can be understood to be an education of feeling. To make this analogy, let us look at two activities so basic to any notion of education that it would be difficult for anyone to question their essentiality: writing and reading. If schools did nothing else, surely they would have to do this—to teach children to write and read sufficiently for functionality in the language of their culture. This is because there is a direct correlation between language and conceptual reasoning, language being the essential mode in which such reasoning takes place. In our society conceptual reasoning is so highly valued that it is usually equated with intelligence. So writing and reading, as the basic modes of language literacy, which equals conceptual reasoning ability, which equals level of intelligence, are absolutely fundamental to the entire educational enterprise as that enterprise is conceived in our culture.

How, exactly, do writing and reading improve the ability to reason, to be rational, to be logical, to be intelligent (as these words are commonly understood)? A close look at the inner workings of this process will lead to my claim that music education can be conceived as an education of feeling.

Human beings constantly think. Thoughts flood our minds in a never-ending stream or torrent, overlapping, rushing ahead or slowing down, mixing together in countless blends, whirling around then shooting off in different directions. Internal thinking is not, in and of itself, linear and logical in its organization; it is more like a whirlpool in its dynamic disorder.

If we want to "think something through," or "get our thoughts straight," or "get our ideas sorted out" (all these phrases indicate a process of bringing some ordered arrangement into the natural dynamism of inner thinking), we can sit down in a quiet place and "get our head together." So we start to formulate logical, linear, ordered ideas. Unfortunately, as we do, the torrent of thinking continues, with all sorts of related and unrelated ideas flooding in and drowning those we're trying to separate out or interfering with them because they take us away from the particular ideas into a great many other streams of thought going in different directions. And our thoughts tend to evaporate—to disappear into thin air—as soon as we have them and focus on them. The fluid nature of inner thought simply cannot be entirely controlled by the act of thinking inwardly.

What we need, to go beyond the dynamic flux of inner thinking, is some device to hold onto a thought so it cannot wash away, a means to give it permanent embodiment. We need to actualize it, that is, make it into an entity that stays as it is. So what can we do? You guessed it: we can write it down (on paper, on a computer, and so forth).

Now we have done a quite remarkable, even an astonishing, thing. As far as we know, no other living organism on earth is remotely capable of so doing. We have transformed an entirely inner process into an outer symbolic system that so closely corresponds to the form and shape and dynamic interrelations that previously existed only inwardly as to seem to us to be identical with what transpired within us.

This capacity for symbolic transformation may be the most important distinguishing characteristic of the creature we call human.[30]

Writing a thought down does not just mean that we have been enabled, by doing so, to separate it out of the ongoing stream so that it now has been made material (substantive, embodied). The incredible power and utility of written thought lies in enabling us, in addition, *to think reflectively about the thought itself.* We can examine the entity that captures the thought—we can read the sentence—and decide whether it presents the thought acceptably or poorly. And further, we can, by examining the sentence, *improve the thought itself by improving the sentence.* The act of improving the embodiment of the thought—the sentence—improves the thought we now have. The outer embodiment and the inner process become inseparable. As we work on the quality of the sentence we are also working directly and substantively on the quality of the inner process it objectifies. As our sentence improves, our thinking improves.

What constitutes "improvement"? As we ponder a sentence we have written, we may notice that a particular word seems to be weak. It does not quite express the shading of meaning we are seeking. So we try to think of a better word—one that is closer to what we want to capture but have not yet quite succeeded in capturing. We consult our memory and our dictionary or thesaurus for that better word. When we think of it or see it, it leaps out as the discovery for which we've been searching. "Ah," we say, "that's better. That's more like it. That says it right." So we change the word. What we have done is to *clarify* the sentence's meaning and thereby clarify the thought we're trying to capture. A thought that is clearer is a thought that has been improved. It is better than the thought in its unclear, muddled state.

Notice that when we write down our thought in a sentence, we then *read* the sentence to receive its meaning and to ponder whether that meaning is coming through clearly or whether it needs to be clarified. So writing also entails reading: we are constantly and continually reading and rereading each word and sentence we have written. The reading part gives us back the meaning we have written, and we can then, in receiving it, judge whether it is given well. And, of course, we can read and share the thoughts *someone else* has captured who has gone through this identical process. Reading the clarified thought another has written gives us clarified meaning to share.

As we continue to ponder our sentence we may realize that it is weak in form. It dawns on us that if we were to reorganize it by starting it in a different place and finishing it differently, the meaning would be strengthened. Or perhaps it is a group of sentences that needs to be shifted around. So we make the shifts—we *organize* the sentence or sentences differently and it works (if things are going well for us that day). The thought or thoughts have now been strengthened. We have given better organization to the sentences bearing the thoughts, and the thoughts themselves are

---

[30]An early and extremely influential explanation of the process of symbolic transformation was given by Susanne K. Langer, *Philosophy in a New Key* (New York: Mentor Books, 1942).

now better organized. Better-organized thoughts are improved over those less well organized. And, of course, when we read a complex set of thoughts organized by someone else we are able to share them as organized thinking.

The act of writing, and improving the writing, and reading the writing of someone else who has done so, *broadens* our thinking. One thought suggests another we could not have thought of until the first was captured. We are often amazed at where our thoughts lead us because we sense that we are discovering new thoughts enabled by previous ones. Thinking that is broader is improved over thinking that is narrow and limited. We are taken by such thinking beyond where we were in our thinking before, whether we or someone else has written those thoughts.

Writing and reading *deepen* our thinking. We are able to probe beneath the surface of our thoughts by the act of thinking about them more penetratingly, as writing allows us to do. We can work on a thought, turning it over, examining its implications, getting further into its implied meanings, and finally restating it in a way that captures its depth rather than its surface. And we are taken deeply into thoughts when we read those another writer has succeeded in capturing more deeply.

The same processes allow thoughts to be more *concentrated*—to be rid of extraneous ideas that weaken rather than strengthen the unfolding concepts. Writing and reading *refine* reasoning and *sensitize* reasoning in the same ways.

They also *discipline* thinking. They require the thinker, whether she or he is writing and reading her or his own thoughts or reading those of another, to conform to the veracity of those unfolding thoughts, doing what the words and sentences require to have done as they both create meanings and yield up their meanings. The writer (or reader) cannot just do anything, capriciously, with those thoughts as they develop. They require respect and honesty, and the person dealing with them must be persistent and self-controlled and resolute in guiding their expression or in being guided by another's disciplined expression. And this purposeful, diligent involvement with the ideas *internalizes* them. They become part of the thought structure now characterizing that person's mind.

Here is a summary of the foregoing points, illustrating that writing and reading clarify reasoning, organize reasoning, broaden reasoning, and more:

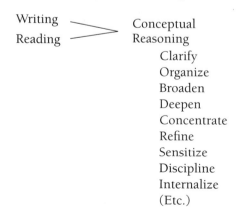

Writing ⟶ Conceptual
Reading ⟶ Reasoning
          Clarify
          Organize
          Broaden
          Deepen
          Concentrate
          Refine
          Sensitize
          Discipline
          Internalize
          (Etc.)

All these qualities of improved conceptual reasoning, and many more that could be mentioned, stem from this process of writing and reading. The higher quality of reasoning is a direct result of a process that enables thoughts to be precise, accurate, detailed, meticulous, subtle, lucid, complex, discriminating, powerful, meaningful. *In this profound sense, writing and reading educate reasoning.*

Based on that explanation of the role of writing and reading in the education of conceptual reasoning, the claim about music (and music education) as an education of feeling can now be made.

Creating music as musicians, and listening to music creatively, do precisely and exactly for feeling what writing and reading do for reasoning.

This claim is made with the full intent that every sentence in the preceding section is to apply with as much validity to feeling as it does to reasoning. That section was written precisely to encompass the claim about the relation of music to feeling. Please reread that section, substituting the word feeling (or feels, feelings, subjectivity, affect, and so on) each time a word such as thinks, thoughts, ideas, or reasoning appears. And for terms such as symbol, sentence, word, and write, substitute terms such as sounds, compose, create, notate, and record. The impact of the argument will then be understood fully. (My own realization of this exercise is given at the end of this chapter, pages 98–101.)

The summary diagram can now be completed as follows:

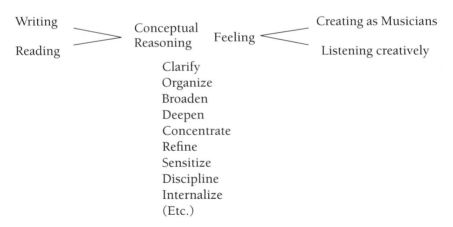

Writing   Conceptual   Creating as Musicians
Reading   Reasoning   Feeling   Listening creatively

Clarify
Organize
Broaden
Deepen
Concentrate
Refine
Sensitize
Discipline
Internalize
(Etc.)

And the last sentence of that section now reads as follows: *In this profound sense, creating music as musicians and listening to music creatively educate feeling.*

The idea that music has a special relation to feeling is pervasive in all cultures. The idea that music education is the education of feeling has been influential in music education for several decades. The argument presented here extends that idea beyond where it has been taken before in the literalness, specificity, and exactitude of its claim. It sounds perfectly reasonable to argue that reasoning can be educated in quality and depth and breadth and that we have the means to do so in education by using the forms of cognition appropriate to conceptual thinking—languages and other symbolic systems. The parallel claim being made here, that feeling can be educated in quality and depth and breadth, and that we have the means to do so in education by using the form of cognition appropriate to the affective realm—music (and the arts)—sounds remarkable or even radical. But with work such as Damasio's to add credence to the philosophical intuitions preceding it, we can now make that claim with substantial confidence. And we can organize our efforts as music educators to effectively achieve the education of feeling so powerfully available through musical experience.

TEACHING FOR "KNOWING WITHIN" MUSIC

> The affecting presence [work of art] is at least a direct presentation of the feelingful dimension of experience. It proceeds at its root not through mediation, as a symbol does—though it may do this as well—but through what we may only call *immediation*. The affecting presence is directly and presently what it is, and precisely *is* in those physical-significant terms in which it is presented for our witnessing.[31] (Emphasis in original)

These insights, by the cultural anthropologist Robert Plant Armstrong (his work will be discussed in some detail in Chapter 6), provide several key guidelines for how we can teach to enhance the power of music to be felt, and, as a consequence, to educate feelings. Experiencing music as an "affecting presence"—as a source of meanings gained through feeling—is a primary end of being involved with music. It is what provides the joy of music, the "making experience special" music accomplishes so effectively. We go to music, and do music, for a variety of reasons, of course. Underneath, I suggest, is the affective quality it adds to our experience: musical feeling becoming musical meaning. Music immerses us in the raw reality of feeling—its naked, subtle, exquisite truth, the truth of conscious being. This accounts for its charm and joyousness, and also its profundities and awesomeness—the entire spectrum of aware undergoing. That primal experience of the affecting presence of sounds is what I call "knowing within" music.

In Chapter 5 I will expand on the idea of knowing within. I will also, in Chapter 4, discuss in detail the second essential dimension of knowing that music provides—"knowing how" to create musical meanings. All these musical creativities require the involvement of knowing within. I will also, at appropriate times, explain two subsidiary, or facilitative, dimensions of knowing—"knowing about" and "knowing why"—that are necessary for enhancing the essential knowing within and knowing how.

---

[31]Robert Plant Armstrong, *Wellspring: On the Myth and Source of Culture* (Berkeley and Los Angeles: University of California Press, 1975), 19.

In my discussion of teaching for knowing within I specifically mean for all I say to apply to people of all ages from infancy to old age, in all settings in which music is learned, in all possible musical involvements, and to all musics in all cultures. Knowing within underlies all musical experience. The quote by Armstrong leads to several important implications for teaching this basic aspect of musical knowing.

First, music is a "*direct presentation* of the feelingful dimension of experience." We get the feelings *directly from the music*—not from ideas about music, information about music, the vocabulary of music, facts about music, the history of music, cultural backgrounds of music, music theory, philosophy of music, or any of the other associated learnings in the music education enterprise. All those learnings (knowing about and knowing why) *serve a purpose*—the purpose of enhancing the quality of the direct engagement with the sounds of music themselves—of knowing within music. Knowing about and knowing why are means. The end is enhanced knowing within music (and knowing how) in direct, immediate musical experiences.

So when we teach music, we must keep firmly in mind that all our efforts, which must, of course, include teaching ideas, information, and vocabulary, should be aimed toward producing something that gives all those efforts their point—the point of improving the quality of knowing within music. Whenever those necessary but subsidiary learnings begin to lose contact with musical experience itself they are becoming academic and losing their point. Whenever that happens we begin to lose our students.

Second, the direct experience of music "proceeds at its root not through mediation, as a symbol does—though it may do this as well." In Chapter 5 I will explain how symbols "mediate"—how they act as a "go-between," carrying one to meanings not contained within them, as words and numbers and notations exist to do. Here, the point Armstrong is making is that the way music accomplishes its affective presence to us is not, at root, by pointing us to something *outside* its inherent nature as "sounds-in-meaningful-configurations," but by taking us *into* these sounds directly and thereby *into* the cultural meanings they have embodied. Yes, music often contains ideas, messages, beliefs, and so on, about, for example, race, gender, religion, relationships. All these mediating functions of music, its immersion in the realities of our lives outside music and its reflection of and commentary about them, exist in musics of all cultures and all types, for music, as has been pointed out, is not separate from the larger world in which it functions and could not possibly be. But *at root* it goes beyond such functions, immersing them *as one determining factor* in the immediacy of sounds configured to be felt.

When we teach music, then, we are in the position of having to achieve a delicate balance between legitimate interests in it from its ability to mediate meanings associated with it, and the "immediation" of its inherent, embodied meanings. A synergistic attitude can help us avoid extremes.

One extreme would be to focus entirely on feelings caused by associations—by the words of songs and what they refer to, by the "program" some music incorporates or suggests by a title, by cultural associations of all sorts, by "interpretations" of what the music might mean. All these can and do influence the experience—the feelings—

we get from music. So they need to be acknowledged and incorporated as a genuine dimension of feeling possibilities music affords. The extreme, of course, is to so overemphasize them that we seem to be teaching that they are the *point* of music rather than an added dimension of music. Doing so makes music a mediator—a "go-between" to feelings not caused by music but by matters for which music serves as an indicator, or sign. In doing so, we shortchange how music makes experience special in ways nothing else but music can accomplish.

The other extreme would be to so exclude associated meanings/feelings as to make them seem illegitimate. This "formalizes" music beyond what even the archetypal formalists at the turn of the twentieth century intended. A delicate balance is called for, giving credence and attention to musical associations of various sorts while also seeking the musical experience the sounds afford, going beyond associations, or references, by the special power of those sounds to take feelings to levels nothing else can. Our emphasis, or balance, must, I think, never neglect what Armstrong (and Sloboda, Sparshott, Meyer, and so many others already mentioned) points out as the root of music, that the feelings it explores are inherent within its sounds. Music "is directly and presently what it is, and precisely *is,* in those physical-significant terms in which it is presented for our witnessing." Those "physical-significant terms," in music, are the "sounds organized" (Sloboda), the "structural properties" or "musical means" (Sparshott) that set music apart as the unique phenomenon it is, with the unique values it offers. The organized sounds of music may refer, but they also embrace and incorporate references, changing them, metamorphosing them ("changing in form, structure, or substance") into felt meanings inherent in the sounds and what they do.

RIFF 6

At the height of the civil rights movement I attend a church meeting at which a prominent black clergyman is the guest speaker. A panel of church members, both white and black, offer thoughts on the events transpiring in the United States, events we all sense are history-making. They speak thoughtfully, but with urgency and deep feeling. Personal stories of racial stereotyping and mistreatment are told, experienced by blacks, witnessed by whites, diminishing the lives of both. The open discussion following the panel is charged with a sense of the need for action to be taken, for solidarity to be achieved, for a heightened awareness of the universality of experience beyond race.

The invited speaker builds on these themes, weaving them together in the style of oratory in which he is a master, eloquent, fervent, personal yet precise, building in a long crescendo of feeling to a magnificence of impassioned expression in which he asserts his faith that, together, supporting one another, we shall indeed overcome our tragic history and achieve the splendor of democracy. "We *shall* overcome," he says. "Let us all rise and express this faith."

We need no further instruction. All stand and lock arms, and he leads us in singing the great anthem. The first, simple, declarative phrase—"We shall overcome"— begins the transformative journey of idea to music. The phrase repeats, adding to its determination. It continues, rising in pitch to "some day" with its exquisite melisma—a musical extension so specific to this art as to be unavailable to our experience in any other way, a perfect blending of idea into structured feeling. This climax slowly falls in contour to the quiet, resolved repetition of the opening assertion, now a matter of assurance rather than only hope.

In our selfness each of us has linked with other selves, transforming a shared aspiration into a shared, inner progression of feeling only music could accomplish, a making of felt meaning that the words by themselves could not possibly do. Idea, assertion, faith, need, all given shape and immediacy by making music of them—making them "sound" in a way beyond language, making them "mean" in a way beyond language. Music has worked its special magic. Again.

One more implication for teaching from the quotation by Armstrong. Its final word is "witnessing." Here is what he means by that word: "My use of this term 'witnessing' rather than 'viewing' or 'seeing' or 'hearing' or 'perceiving' is intended to suggest not only that the confrontation between man and work is an *act* but also that it is an act of consequence to which the role of witness is of critical importance"[32] (emphasis in original).

Those who "witness" what music-makers offer, Armstrong is telling us, are actors in knowing within—actors engaged in a consequential dimension of music, a dimension of critical importance. Musicians (those who compose, perform, improvise) are essential to the enterprise, obviously, because without the making of sounds no music could exist. But also essential is the sharing of those sounds, not only within the selves who make them, but also with other selves who hear them. Music is a culture-creating and individual-creating act, and those who witness are key players in its full functioning.

Witnesses—our audiences when our students are performing, our students whenever they are listening—are engaged in an *act*. They are in every sense musically active participants "of critical importance." We must remember that knowing within requires an act of inner construction of feeling. The music being listened to provides the opportunity. The taking of that opportunity requires the listener's *enactment,* both in commitment to know within and in having the wherewithal to be able to do so. Effective teachers provide both. By their choice of music, their explorations of students' choices, their attitudes of involvement, their excitement, their openness in

---

[32]Ibid., 20–21.

how they themselves listen, they honor and empower their students and audiences as creative actors in the experience of music.

A major way to encourage knowing within, or "taking within," is to help reveal to both musicians and listeners more and more of the inherent workings of music so that the possibilities of feeling they contain become more available. That is a major, foundational role for all music educators—being the expert guides to the inner workings of a great variety of musics. Those inner workings are themselves the product of cultural systems, so they must be revealed in their contexts, historical, cultural, and political, in order to be grasped appropriately; that is, "knowing about" becomes an essential ingredient of artistry and of listening. Also embodied in all music is a belief-system about what music is and does; a set of aesthetic/social/political/cultural positions underlying the music. "Knowing why:" why this particular music sounds as it does because of the beliefs it embodies, also affects the way it will be experienced. And relevant personal associations round out the meaning-complex in which musical works reside.

All these dimensions of knowing within add to the fullness of experienced feeling the active witness can attain. Few human doings are as complex. Few teaching responsibilities are as challenging. Few experiences are as satisfying, as rewarding, as self- and culture-creating, as is knowing within music, both for those who attain it and for those who help them do so more deeply—that is, music educators.

Following is my application to feeling of the material on pages 90 to 93 dealing with conceptual reasoning. I have written it from the perspective of the composer and listener. It can also be written from the performer's and improviser's perspectives, along with the listener's. Try to do so, to get a sense of how each musical role provides a way to educate feeling.

Human beings constantly feel. Feelings flood our minds and beings in a never-ending stream or torrent, overlapping, rushing ahead or slowing down, mixing together in countless blends, whirling around then shooting off in different directions. Internal feeling—subjectivity or affect—is not, in and of itself, linear and logical in its organization; it is more like a whirlpool in its dynamic structure.

If we want to "feel something through," or "get our feelings straight," or "get our feelings sorted out" (all these phrases indicate a process of bringing some ordered arrangement into the natural dynamism of inner affect), we can sit down in a quiet place and "get ourselves together." So we start to formulate logical, linear, ordered feelings. Unfortunately, as we do, the torrent of feeling continues, with all sorts of related and unrelated feelings flooding in and drowning those we're trying to separate out or interfering with them because they take us away from the particular feelings into a great many other streams of feeling going in different directions. And our feelings tend to evaporate—to disappear into thin air—as soon as we have them and focus on them. The fluid nature of inner feelings simply cannot be entirely controlled by the act of feeling inwardly.

What we need, to go beyond the dynamic flux of inner subjectivity, is some device to hold onto a feeling so it cannot wash away, a means to give it permanent embodiment. We need to "materialize" it, that is, make it into an entity so that it stays as it is. So what can we do? You guessed it: we can capture it in musical sounds—melodies, rhythms, tone colors, harmonies, textures, forms.

Now we have done a quite remarkable, even an astonishing, thing. As far as we know, no other living organism on earth is remotely capable of so doing. We have transformed an entirely inner process into an outer substance that so closely corresponds to the form and shape and dynamic interrelations that previously existed only inwardly as to seem to us to be identical with what transpired within us. This capacity for symbolic transformation may be the most important distinguishing characteristic of the creature we call human.

Giving a feeling musical embodiment—that is, capturing the dynamic flow of feeling in the dynamic flow of melody, in the energies of rhythm, in the shiftings and blendings of tone colors, in the tension and resolutions of harmonies—does not just mean that we have been enabled, by doing so, to separate it out of the ongoing stream so that it has now been made material (substantive, embodied). The incredible power and utility of creating music lies in enabling us, in addition, to *feel reflectively about the feeling itself*. We can examine the materials that capture the feeling—the melody, the tone colors, the rhythms—and decide whether they present the feeling acceptably or poorly. And further, we can, by examining the melody (etc.), *improve the feeling itself by improving the melody*. The act of improving the material embodying the feeling—the melody—actively improves the feeling we now have. The outer embodiment and the inner process become inseparable. As we work on the quality of the musical materials, we are also working directly and substantively on the quality of the inner processes they embody. As our melody improves our feeling improves.

What constitutes "improvement"? As we ponder a melody we have composed, we may notice that a particular tone or phrase seems to be weak. It does not quite express the shading of feeling we are seeking. So we try to think of a better tone or arrangement of tones—one that is closer to what we want to capture but have not yet quite succeeded in capturing. We consult our creative imagination and our storehouse of previous experiences with melodies for that better phrase. When we hear it, it leaps out as the discovery for which we've been searching. "Ah," we say, "that's better. That's more like it. That sounds right." So we change the tones. What we have done is to *clarify* the melody's dynamic form and thereby clarify the feeling we're trying to capture. A feeling that is clearer is a feeling that has been improved. It is better than the feeling in its unclear, muddled state.

Notice that when we compose our feelings into a set of tones as in a melodic phrase, we then *listen* to the phrase to receive its affect and to ponder whether that affect is coming through clearly or whether it needs to be clarified. So composing is also experiencing through listening: we are constantly and continually hearing and rehearing each tone and phrase we have composed. The listening or experiencing or responding part gives us back the feeling we have composed, and we can then, in feeling it, judge whether it is given well. And, of course, we can experience and share the feelings *someone else* has captured who has gone through this identical process. Experiencing the clarified musical feelings another has composed gives us clarified subjectivity to share.

As we continue to ponder—to reexperience reflectively—our phrase or melody, we may realize that it is weak in form. It dawns on us that if we were to reorganize it by starting it in a different place and finishing it differently, the affect would be strengthened. Or perhaps it is a group of phrases or melodies that needs to be shifted around. So we make the shifts—we *organize* the phrases or the melodies differently and it works (we hope). The dynamic interplay of feeling has now been strengthened. We have given better organization to the phrases or melodies bearing the dynamics of feeling, and the interplay of feelings is now better organized. And, of course, when we listen to a complex set of structured musical feelings organized by someone else we are able to share them as an organized, composed feelingful experience.

The act of creating with musical sounds and improving what is being created, and experiencing the creation of someone else who has done so, *broadens* our feelingful experience. One creative act—one musical decision—suggests another we could not have envisioned until the first was captured. We are often amazed at where our compositional decisions lead us because we sense that we are discovering totally new ways of feeling enabled by previous ones. Feelingful experience that is broader is improved over such experience that is narrow and limited. We are taken, by such experiences, beyond where we were in our subjective selves before, whether we or someone else has created those expanded expressive sounds.

Composing music and listening to music *deepen* our subjectivity. We are able to probe beneath the surface of our feelings by the act of experiencing them more penetratingly, as musical composition allows us to do. We can stay with a feeling, turning it over, examining its implications, getting further into its implied affects, and finally re-forming it in a way that captures its depth rather than its surface. And we are taken deeply into feelings when we experience those another composer has succeeded in capturing more deeply.

The same processes allow affective experiences to be more *concentrated*—to be rid of extraneous impulses that weaken rather than strengthen the unfolding expressive form. Listening to music and composing music *refine* feeling and *sensitize* feeling in the same ways.

They also *discipline* our subjectivities. They require the one who is experiencing music, whether he or she is creating and experiencing his or her own developing feelings or sharing the created music of another, to conform to the veracity of those unfolding dynamic structures, doing what the musical materials require to have done as they both create the conditions of feeling and yield up their embodied feelings. The composer (or listener) cannot just do anything, capriciously, with those affective events as they develop. They require respect and honesty, and the person dealing with them must be persistent and self-controlled and resolute in guiding their expression or in being guided by another's disciplined musical expression. And this purposeful, diligent involvement of the self with the feelings *internalizes* them. They become part of the inner subjective structure now characterizing that person's selfhood.

All these qualities of improved subjectivity, and many more that could be mentioned, stem from this process of composing and listening to music. The higher quality of affective experience is a direct result of a process that enables feelings to be precise, accurate, detailed, meticulous, subtle, lucid, complex, discriminating, powerful, meaningful. *In this profound sense, composing music and listening to music educate feeling.*

ETUDES

1. Are you comfortable with the idea that music is valuable in human experience largely, or at least importantly, because of its powers to refine and extend what we can feel, or "know within"? What other aspects of music also seem to you important, needing emphasis in teaching for its values?

2. If feeling comes both from inside music (the inherent dimension) and from music's relations with the rest of the world (the delineated dimension), how do those two dimensions interact in musical experience? Do you tend to emphasize one or the other in your own musical experiences? Or do you sometimes focus on one and at other times on the other? Is there an "ideal balance" of the two in which a complete merger takes place in our experiences of music, so that inner and outer can no longer be distinguished? Or is that unlikely or unnecessary?

3. There has been widespread approval in recent times of the idea that the body, the mind, and feelings are integrally related, each depending on the others. Given this, how would you explain to influential education policymakers how music (and the arts) play a central role in how young people develop in their abilities to think, feel, and act effectively and with satisfaction in their lives? Do you think arguments of this sort, for the centrality of music and the arts in educating people genuinely and completely, might win a more secure place for them in schools?

4. What other analogies explaining the differences between emotions and feelings, in addition to the one about buoys floating on the ocean, can you think of to make the same point? What analogies might best help (1) children in early grades, (2) middle school students, and (3) high school students, more clearly grasp the distinctions? Think of ways, with each of those levels, that the appropriate analogies could be applied to how they sing, play, compose, improvise, and listen, helping them become more musically sensitive in each of those roles.

5. Music listening is often considered inferior to composing, performing, and improvising, as being "merely" listening, or as being a "passive" way to experience music. How can the idea of listening as "witnessing"—as an act of critical importance in music—be used to rethink this old conception? Especially in that all our students, including all those involved in our performance programs,

no doubt listen to music more than anything else they do with it, how can we help them, both when listening to others' music and when creating their own music through composing, performing, and improvising, become more engaged witnesses—to feel more deeply and discriminatingly—as a result of our instruction?

6. Many if not all the ideas dealt with in this chapter (and the previous two) can be and should be included as basic learnings in music education programs at every level of schooling if our students are to be musically educated in the broad sense. Choose one or several ideas discussed here and try to frame it (them) in language and activities appropriate for (1) early grades, (2) middle grades, (3) high school. How can music programs, at all levels and in all activities, incorporate the dimension of thoughtful understanding of important ideas as a necessary, powerful aspect of teaching? Have we attempted to do so in the past and are we doing so effectively in the present? What changes would be needed if we are to include understandings such as these as important components of a complete music education?

4

The Creating Dimension
of Musical Experience

MAIN THEMES

- Individuals create music. This is the case even when they do so in cooperation with other individuals.

- A certain way of thinking and acting underlies musical creating. But each creative musical role a culture provides requires its own application of creativity: each role has its own integrity.

- Whichever way music is being created, the music itself makes demands on the one creating, demands that cannot be ignored if the result is to be genuine.

- Achieving this genuineness requires an attitude of honoring the music, of attending to and feeling its needs along with one's own, and doing honestly what the music requires of one. This interaction of self and not-self entails an ethical dimension.

- Musical competence is required in order to create. Each creative role calls on particular competencies, all of which are educable.

- Musical creating is a search for musical meaning, carried out distinctively in each musical role.

- A consequence of being engaged in creating music is an enhanced sense of one's self from what one has experienced in creating, an expansion of one's inner life caused by one's own creative acts. This may be understood as a spiritual maturation.

- Musical creating, in any of its manifestations, can be conceived as a distinctive way to "know"; to be engaged with musical meanings by bringing them into existence. Such engagements are instances of "knowing how" musically. Knowing within, as explained in the previous chapter, plays an essential role in knowing how.

- The characteristics of musical creativity described here apply to musics of all types and styles in all cultures around the world, including all the many musics within Western cultures. It is a Western conceit to think that genuine creativity is unique to its music, and to its classical music in particular. This is a conceit those in the West can no longer sustain.

WHAT—OR WHEN—IS "CREATIVITY"?

It is with himself that the artist debates as he thinks out his colors, harmonies, or characters. What this act of meditation, which is like the labor of childbirth, strives to fix and deliver is something which wants to *be*. The work which the artist bears within him is, on this plane, already a demand. But it is only a demand, one entirely inside the creator. It is nothing he can see or imitate. In preparing himself for the execution-performance, the artist puts himself into a state of grace, and the demand which induces it is the expression of an inner logic—the logic of a certain technical development, of a peculiarly aesthetic searching, and of a spiritual maturation. All this comes together in the artist, who is precisely that individual in whom it all merges. More deeply than other men, he creates himself by creating and he creates because he creates himself.[1] (Emphasis in original)

In this passage from his book *The Phenomenology of Aesthetic Experience,* Mikel Dufrenne identifies several important aspects of artistic creativity that are directly germane to the essential role creating music plays in music education. To begin to understand and apply Dufrenne's thinking, we must ask two questions. Who qualifies to be called "creative"? And what do such persons do when they create? I will examine the first question here and the second in the following section.

In one prevalent view the only people who fully qualify to be called creative are the world-renowned, historically eminent exemplars—the ones whose achievements have altered the course of their domain's history. Such people demonstrate creativity with a capital C, and they are the ones we should look to in defining creativity. All others are not "really" creative, although they may enjoy some of the pleasures of doing what "really" creative people do. Their creativity is definitely "small c."

This view is taken by Howard Gardner, who, in attempting to define creativity, chooses to do so, instead, by describing the creative *person*.

Let me begin, then, by offering a definition of the creative individual, which I have found useful in my work: The creative individual is a person who regularly solves problems, fashions products, or defines new questions in a way that is initially considered novel but that ultimately becomes accepted in a particular cultural setting.

Further, such persons refashion the domain in which they work "as a result of a creative breakthrough"; organize their lives "so as to heighten the likelihood that

[1]Mikel Dufrenne, *The Phenomenology of Aesthetic Experience* (Evanston, IL: Northwestern University Press, 1973), 31.

they will achieve a series of breakthroughs"; succeed in "fashioning a new kind of product, or by the discovery of an unknown or neglected set of issues or themes that call for fresh exploration," that "have been *accepted in a particular culture*. No time limit is assumed here; a product may be recognized as creative immediately—or not for a century or even for a millennium"[2] (emphasis in original). All these criteria, please notice, can be met by only the elite of the elite. Gardner recognizes this. "There is a sense—for which I do not apologize—in which this study of creativity reflects the "great man/great woman" view of creativity."[3]

In another discussion of creativity, Gardner mentions, as paradigms, people such as Freud, Shakespeare, and Tolstoy.

> In designating these individuals as creative investigators of the human mind and personality, I am making attributions that should be relatively uncontroversial. These is little dispute about those few individuals who represent the summit of creativity in a particular field—Mozart or Beethoven, Leonardo da Vinci or Rembrandt, Newton or Einstein. Yet, if I had lowered my standards of renown a few notches (Antonio Vivaldi or Jackson Pollock), or singled out an individual work (Mozart's *Magic Flute* or Freud's study of Leonardo da Vinci), I would have already skirted controversy. There may be an important lesson here. Inasmuch as creativity is difficult to define and challenging to investigate, it is prudent to begin on solid ground—with individuals and with bodies of work that are uncontroversially creative.[4]

Apparently, then, it is uncontroversial to designate as creative someone like Mozart, but saying that Vivaldi was creative somehow gets one into trouble: some might not agree. Singling out a particular work, even one so highly regarded as *The Magic Flute,* also is hazardous. Perhaps some would dispute that designation, saying, "No, that's not an instance of creativity. *Don Giovanni* is creative, not *The Magic Flute.*" So "true" creativity, in such a conceptualization, does not exist in degree. It exists only when some (uncontroversial) pinnacle has been reached, an exalted level attained by only "those few individuals who represent the summit of creativity in a particular field." When is someone creative? At the level of Mozart, surely, but not so surely at the level of Vivaldi.

Another writer about creativity who also takes the great-person perspective—the big-C perspective—is Mihaly Csikszentmihalyi, best known for his theory of "flow," which describes the sense of control, inner balance, and selflessness experienced by people engaged in a task in which the level of the challenge is matched by their level of skill to meet it.[5] In his work on creativity he identifies the historical and

---

[2]Howard Gardner, *Creating Minds: An Anatomy of Creativity Seen Through the Lives of Freud, Einstein, Picasso, Stravinsky, Eliot, Graham, and Gandhi* (New York: Basic Books, 1993), 34–36.

[3]Ibid., 37.

[4]Howard Gardner, "Creative Lives and Creative Works: A Synthetic Scientific Approach," in *The Nature of Creativity,* ed. Robert J. Sternberg (Cambridge: Cambridge University Press, 1988), 298–99.

[5]Mihaly Csikszentmihalyi, *Flow: The Psychology of Optimal Experience* (New York: Harper and Row, 1990). For a discussion of flow in the context of profound musical experience, see my "The Experience of Profundity in Music," *Journal of Aesthetic Education,* 29, no. 4 (Winter 1995), 1–21.

sociological dimensions as important factors in fostering and identifying creative individuals, as does Gardner. (This idea is not new: in 1953 an article by M. I. Stern proposed it, and others have adopted it in their conceptions of creativity.)[6]

> We cannot study creativity by isolating individuals and their works from the social and historical milieu in which their actions are carried out. This is because what we call creative is never the result of individual actions alone; it is the product of three main shaping forces: a set of social institutions, or *field,* that selects from the variations produced by individuals those that are worth preserving; a stable cultural *domain* that will preserve and transmit the selected new ideas or forms to the following generations; and finally the *individual,* who brings about some change in the domain, a change that the field will consider to be creative.[7] (Emphases in original)

The focus on field and domain, and the dimension of history, enrich our understanding of how great works of individual creativity come about and are recognized. But notice that creativity is equated with those endeavors "worth preserving," the preservation and transmission of such "new ideas or forms to the following generations," and someone whose achievement is so great as to cause "some change in the domain" worth preserving and transmitting. Looks like Vivaldi does not make the cut again, in that he did not serve as a major change agent for the music of his time. But, of course, neither did Bach, whose achievement was not change so much as elevation and expansion of existing practices. But while we may argue the fine points of whether people such as Vivaldi and Bach qualify to be labeled creative, the capital-C view puts us so high in the stratosphere of accomplishment as to eliminate at least 99.9 percent of people from consideration. According to Csikszentmihalyi, "Careful study of truly creative individuals . . . are especially needed and in short supply."[8] Note that he specifies *truly* creative—not *untruly* creative as are all those people in the world who actually do what the giants of creativity do but at levels not achieving their genius.

Uncharacteristically, Csikszentmihalyi, in a discussion of why some people seem to "produce a greater amount of variation in the domain than others," uses the term "creative children."[9] And the very use of the word "greater" shifts the concept of creativity from an absolute standard to a relative one. Can children, then, be conceived to be creative? In an interview, Csikszentmihalyi is asked for a definition of creativity. He replies,

> The definition most people usually agree on is that creativity is a new idea or product that is socially acceptable and valued, and which is brought to fruition. That is creativity

---

[6]M. I. Stern, "Creativity and Culture," *Journal of Psychology,* 36 (1953), 311–22. Cited and discussed in E. Paul Torrance, "The Nature of Creativity as Manifest in Its Testing," in *The Nature of Creativity,* ed. Sternberg, note 4, 44.

[7]Mihalyi Csikszentmihalyi, "Society, Culture, and Person: A Systems View of Creativity," in *The Nature of Creativity,* ed. Sternberg, note 4, 325.

[8]Ibid.

[9]Ibid.

with a big "C," creativity that changes the culture. Then we can talk also about creativity which is a more personal experience, which affects the way one experiences life, with originality, openness, and freshness. *That is something different,* though the two overlap.

Creativity with a small "c," the personal creativity, is what makes life enjoyable, but it does not necessarily result in renown or success. . . . It's true that we can't all be Einsteins; we can't all be Beethovens. If we think creativity includes success and recognition, then it's true, we can't all do it. But each one of us can experience the feeling of discovery that these people had . . . and at that level, *that kind of creativity* is what makes life very full and worth living.[10] (Emphases added)

We seem to be getting closer, here, to the real world, and to the real world of music education, in the recognition that all people can experience *something like* what the great ones experience. Of course, for Csikszentmihalyi "that is something different" from "true" creativity, although they overlap. The phrase "at that level" suggests that creativity is a matter of degree. But "that kind of creativity" reverts immediately to a matter of kind—a structural, essential difference between big C and small c. We have been given, here, a concession, but grudgingly, or perhaps only because of confusion.

In another interview the interviewer explains that Csikszentmihalyi insists that most people use the term "creative" too liberally. "Part-time painters, hobbyists or hot-shot music students" might be unique or "personally creative." But when it comes to what he calls "creativity with a capital C," what counts is the person's impact on society. Using that litmus test, who gets dubbed "creative"? Only a select few: "individuals like Leonardo, Edison, Picasso, or Einstein, [who] have changed our culture in some important respect. . . . They are the *creative* ones without qualifications"[11] (emphasis in original).

It should be clear that I reject the notion that creativity—true creativity—is incapable of being achieved by all people, children included. I want to argue that issues of *what* is creativity are better, more validly framed as issues of *when* is creativity. This shifts the focus from establishing absolute criteria to describing the ways people act when *being* creative. I will argue that anyone *being* creative is, at that time, creative.

Neither Gardner nor Csikszentmihalyi defines the ways of thinking and doing required to warrant the term creativity. They stipulate the *consequences* of being creative—being able to solve problems, fashion products, define new questions that achieve breakthroughs, change the domain, and so forth. But nowhere in their writings have I found a description of exactly how a person must think and act to accomplish such things. If such a description can be given, creativity will be found, I will argue, to exist on a continuum, a continuum from what children do to what the greatest exemplars do. *The difference is not in kind—only in degree.* To influence that

---

[10]Michael Toms, "The Well of Creativity: A Conversation with Mihalyi Csikszentmihalyi." Excerpt from New Dimensions audio program "Creativity Is in Your Reach," Tape #2578. Accessed via www.google.com/search?q=mihalyi+csikszentmihalyi&hl=en&lr=&safe=off&btnG=Google+search.

[11]Lou Carlozo, "Go with the Creative Flow," *Chicago Tribune,* January 3, 1997, sec. 5, p. 5.

degree for all students, no matter their age or their capacity, is, I believe, a major obligation of music education.

WHO—OR WHEN—IS AN "ARTIST"?

What is a person doing when being creative? And, given that being creative can occur in just about everything humans do, what makes creativity "artistic"?

In the Western world and far beyond it, there is an expectation that creativity requires qualities of imagination, originality, divergence, ingenuity, openness, inventiveness, nonconformity, innovation, novelty, uniqueness, fluency, flexibility, and the like.[12] But not every Western creativity theorist requires such qualities to exist at their highest reaches, such as Gardner and Csikszentmihalyi tend to do. As E. Paul Torrance points out, for L. L. Thurstone "an act is creative if the thinker reaches the solution in a sudden closure that necessarily implies some novelty to the thinker." And G. W. Stewart maintained that "creative thinking may occur even though the idea produced may have been produced by someone else at an earlier time. By this definition creative thinking may take place in the mind of the humblest [person] or in the mind of the most distinguished statesman, artist, or scientist."[13] So it is a matter of opinion as to whether the qualities of creativity can only be conceived to "truly" exist at the highest possible levels, or whether, instead, they exist anywhere and at any time such qualities are being employed. Torrance makes his position clear:

> I tried to describe creative thinking as the process of sensing difficulties, problems, gaps in information, missing elements, something askew; making guesses and forming hypotheses about these deficiencies; evaluating and testing these guesses and hypotheses; possibly revising and retesting them; and finally communicating the results.
>
> I like this definition because it describes a natural process. . . . Such a definition places creativity in the realm of everyday living and does not reserve it for ethereal and rarely achieved heights of creation.[14]

I, too, like this definition, partly because it begins to stipulate the thinking and doing actually implicated in creativity, and partly because it democratizes creativity, allowing it to be something all people have to some degree. Such a view of creativity, as existing in degree, and as constituted of particular, identifiable ways of dealing with one's world, *provides a role for education.* Whatever the level of one's capacity to be creative at something, that level can be better achieved by educational interventions designed to improve one's thinking and doing so as to make them "more

---

[12]For a searching, far-ranging study of the historical and cultural bases of the concept of creativity, tracing that concept from the Bible onward and across various cultures, see Robert Paul Weiner, *Creativity and Beyond: Cultures, Values, and Change* (Albany: State University of New York Press, 2000).

[13]Quoted in Torrance, "The Nature of Creativity," note 6, 43–44.

[14]Ibid., 47. For an extended discussion, with many illustrations, of how artists go through the processes of exploration and discovery Torrance identifies, see Vincent Tomas, "Creativity in Art," in *Creativity in the Arts,* ed. Vincent Tomas (Englewood Cliffs, NJ: Prentice Hall, 1964), 97–109.

creative." This is not to disparage the awesome achievements of the great masters of creativity. It is to place those achievements on a scale, a scale applicable to all humans because all humans are capable of being creative to some degree on that scale and are capable of improving that degree if they are helped to do so.

What, then, are the qualities, or characteristics, entailed in "being creative"? And how are they employed when "being artistic"?

The General/Specific Debate

Two assumptions are embodied in the preceding questions. First, that there are some general attributes of creativity applicable to all forms of creativity. Second, that the general attributes do not exist in a vacuum; that they exist only as theoretical until manifested in *some particular way*.

On the side of general traits, cultures all over the world recognize that when culturally specifiable characteristics of thinking and doing are in evidence, "creativity" is going on. In Western cultures and others, the traits enumerated as creative (imagination, originality, and so forth) are widely accepted both in theory and in practice. It would seem illogical, and unnecessary, to ignore that reality.

On the other side, divergent thinking manifested in a particular way, say in composing music, is recognized to be an indicator of compositional creativity because that general trait is being evidenced as composing particularly requires it to be. Or as painting requires it to be. Or cooking, or philosophy, or teaching. No wonder the trait in question does not manifest itself equally when an individual applies it in different ways! The trait itself—divergent thinking, say—requires the particularity of expression each application of it calls for. No individual is equally creative—equally able to demonstrate the same level of divergent thinking (or ingenuity, or nonconformity, and so forth)—in every possible particular application of it. In that sense, creativity is "application specific." But it also requires the application of recognized traits no matter what application is being made.

In Chapter 7, on musical intelligences, I will apply this discussion of creativity to a parallel one on intelligence, and I will offer a definition of intelligence in which a general factor and its applications are interdependent. I will also discuss how creativity and intelligence are not identical. (In this I entirely agree with Gardner, who says, "Creativity is not the same as intelligence. While these two traits are correlated, an individual may be far more creative than he or she is intelligent, or far more intelligent than creative.")[15] The questions remaining here are, to repeat, what are the qualities, or characteristics, entailed in "being creative"? And how are they employed when "being artistic"? That is, what are general factors of creativity, and how do they take on contextual reality when played out in one of the many ways creativity can be demonstrated?

The first question, as to what constitutes creativity, has already been answered in a culture-based, broad way: one is being creative when demonstrating qualities one's culture considers creative. In Western cultures, as pointed out, such qualities

---

[15]Gardner, *Creating Minds*, note 2, 20.

typically include imagination, originality, divergence, and so forth. My treatment of creativity will be thoroughly Western, not because this view of it is in some way privileged or "true," but because it is culturally acknowledged as true for those of us who are Western.

The question of how creativity becomes "artistic" requires that the generally recognized qualities of creativity be applied in a particular way. Immediately we encounter a dilemma. The term "artistic" is generally applied to work in the arts. We might assume, then, that the domain specificity of creativity, the second part of its nature, might be conceived to be, in this case, "the arts." But we must ask whether this is sufficiently specific. At one level it makes sense to think of the arts as constituting a domain. It is a sense widely understood in the Western world over at least the past three to four centuries. And it demarcates the arts from other domains with other identifying characteristics, such as, say, the sciences, or economics, or government. So it is a useful distinction, in that we expect the traits of creativity to take on particularity in ways germane to the arts when we speak of "artistic creativity." The quote from Dufrenne that began this chapter describes artistry as it applies in any art, and it pinpoints how artists, in a way particular to art, must think and act if they are to be creative as all art requires. That gives us a powerful tool to help us focus on and identify the ways artistic creativity has unique manifestations.

Helpful as it is to identify the arts as having shared domain characteristics, however, being creative as a sculptor must be is not the same as being creative as a poet, or a dancer, or a jazz improviser must be. All are artists, but it would be wildly illogical and unrealistic to expect that an accomplished sculptor would then automatically be equally accomplished as a poet and as a dancer and as a jazz improviser. Sculpting, and each of those other ways of being artistic, has its special, particular, unique way to be what it is—its unique way to carry out the general traits "being an artist" requires. We have not yet, when speaking of artistic creativity (valid as that is at one level of generality), reached the level at which artistry actually manifests itself when the concept is put into action. Clearly, we need to be more specific, especially if our primary interest in creativity is to improve it through education.

How specific should we get? Gardner and Csikszentmihalyi are satisfied with the levels of domain (or discipline) and field (the institutions within a domain or discipline that provide the appropriate judges of achievement). I have no quarrel with those concepts: they are useful in a variety of ways. But they do not accomplish what needs to be accomplished—the identification of the particular ways creativity operates when actually being manifested. Just as "artistic" serves a useful but inadequate purpose, the notions of domain and field are also useful but inadequate.

I suggest that the most useful level for understanding creativity, the most applicable to the ways music actually exists in all cultures, is the level of the musical roles each culture provides. Each of those roles is, indeed, a "role" because it requires a particular way to be musically creative (and, I will explain in Chapter 7, musically intelligent.) Together, all musical roles in a culture constitute the musical domain for that culture. And, at a larger level, all the musical roles of all cultures, past, present, and future, together constitute the domain for music as a human endeavor.

Most important for purposes of music education, *each musical role requires the education of creativity as particular to that role.* Just as general traits of creativity take their reality—their actuality—in the specifics of how they are applied, musical creativity requires specific roles in order to become "real," or "actual," and, thereby, educable. In that sense, the issue is not musical *creativity,* but musical *creativities.* Given this focus on particular creative roles, the specifics of creativity and artistry as particular to some major roles within music can now be identified. Or, to be more realistic, identified sufficiently to promote guidance for a philosophy of music education and for a program of studies in consonance with that philosophy. (A complete identification of all the traits of creative roles, even limited to the domain of music, is obviously not so much an achievable goal as a work in constant process.)

As a background for this explanation is the idea that whatever the creative musical role, it must be played by and within an individual. "It is with himself that the artist debates as he thinks out his colors, harmonies, or characters," says Dufrenne. Creativity is, at bottom, something happening within a person's experience. In music, that "something" is the coming into being of musical sounds, the outward evidence of the inner processes. And that "coming into being" requires the individual to both "think sounds" and "do sounds" with imagination, originality, divergence, ingenuity, and so forth. Each musical role requires its particular way to think and do sounds creatively.

Composing Creativity

Composers think and do creatively by imagining possibilities of sounds coming into being and by capturing them in some way (notation, computer memory, their own memory) so they can be worked on and "made something of." That making entails, as Torrance explains, sensing difficulties, problems, and gaps, making guesses, evaluating what has been imagined and where it is going or might go, revising, testing, working out. In short, a composer creates through *exploration* and *discovery* of new musical possibilities.

Of course, extramusical ideas can be and often are implicated in getting the composing process going—the words of "We Shall Overcome," the story of *Til Eulenspiegel's Merry Pranks,* descriptions of *The Seasons,* the image of a train in Duke Ellington's *Daybreak Express,* or whatever. But when composing begins, *sounds must be imagined,* and then, inevitably, *what the sounds might become.* An extramusical idea (when that happens to be involved—often none is) must, to become music, *become sounds,* inevitably taking on a life of their own, guided by the idea, in consonance with the idea, appropriate to the idea (appropriate, say, to a requiem, or a particular story, or the word-meanings of a song, and so forth), but, fundamentally, *making music* from the idea.

In addition to all the influences on a composer's decisions from ideas, words, messages of various sorts, and so on, every composer works within an expectation system consisting of composers past and present, how they have thought about composing, and what they have accomplished. Also in mind are performers, who will potentially make the actual sounds of their compositions. Performers also have a history of doing what they do, and a widely shared sense of what is proper to do in the present. Composers are keenly aware of that expectation-system as they envision their works being played and/or sung. And, of course, many compositions in recent times explicitly transfer responsibility for many substantive decisions from the composer to the performer(s), requiring of performers that they add and be accountable for a variety of events previously regarded to be entirely the prerogative of composers.

Also to be taken into account by composers is the audience—its historically and presently constituted set of expectations as to what compositions, and performances of them, are properly construed to be. Those expectations of potential audiences shape the composer's thinking, just as, when heard, the audience will shape the experience the composer offers.

Within all these interacting influences the composer brings forth meanings reflecting (or commenting upon, or opposing) the influences she lives within. But sooner or later she must go beyond those influences, incorporating them within her unfolding interaction with what the sounds are doing and what they might do next. That, after all, is what makes composing different from literature, painting, or political argumentation—its creation of meaningful musical sounds, its "making special" musically by causing original musical meanings to come into existence within compositions. That idea, that all the many influences on a composer's work are, finally, incorporated within creative decisions about sounds, is summarized powerfully by philosopher and aesthetician Nicholas Wolterstorff, who, in a detailed explanation of the many social contexts in which composers work, says, "The central suggestion I shall be making is that the artist allows social realities to *guide her* composition, doing this in such a way that those realities become *embodied* in the works"[16] (emphases in original).

The implications for music education are clear, if we take seriously our obligation to cultivate musical creativity in all the ways our culture makes available. The creativity of composing—the meaning-making that musical composition uniquely allows—can be and should be as readily accessible for development for all our students as any other way to be musically creative.

Performing Creativity

Performers of composed music are faced, by their role, with unique demands. They start with the product of the composer's creativity, and they have an ethical as well as a musical obligation (or, to put it another way, a musical obligation that is itself ethical) to give that prior act all due respect. (I will discuss the ethical dimension of musical creating further on.) How much respect? That in itself is a creative decision a performer must make, a decision ranging on a continuum from an attempt to be as

---

[16]Nicholas Wolterstorff, "The Work of Making a Work of Music," in *What Is Music?* ed. Philip Alperson (New York: Haven, 1987), 108–9.

completely true to the composer's intentions as is humanly possible (never entirely possible) to an attempt to alter the composition to make it conform to an agenda not the composer's, as was discussed in Chapter 2 in regard to *Frauenliebe und Leben*. But no matter what position a performer takes on that continuum, countless decisions must always be made about the sounds themselves and how to most effectively produce and shape them.

Performers are artists—are creative in imagining and producing musically expressive sounds—precisely because they must make creative decisions with the materials (compositions) with which they are engaged. If that were not the case—if imagination, divergence, ingenuity, and the like were not essential requirements of performing—it would correctly be regarded as a skill, or a trade, or a job, for which creativity was irrelevant. This completely misrepresents the creative demands inherent in the act of performing. It is why I reject the often-heard demarcation of music into creating, performing, and listening, as if creating is what composers do but performers (and listeners) are not creating when doing what they do. This not only entirely misconstrues the role of the performer but also demeans the artistry that is the point and purpose of performing. And it leads to many unfortunate consequences in teaching performance, too easily becoming a matter of convergent thinking/doing rather than the divergent thinking/doing that creativity—artistry—requires.

Several significant conditions affect the performer's creativity. First, as mentioned, the composition itself presents a set of possibilities awaiting realization. To achieve that realization requires that the performer possess the necessary craftsmanship to do so—the required skills of execution the composition calls for. Without that capability the performer cannot meet the first level of demands made by the music. Building, maintaining, and refining craftsmanship—the carrying forward of skill to a unity of mind, body, and feeling—is an obligation of all those who pursue performance as part of their lives, and all those who, as part of their general education in music, explore what the performer's role requires.

Second, adequate or even exceptional craftsmanship, though necessary, is not sufficient. Each composition to be performed lives in a world that must be understood in order to perform it successfully—a world encompassing the composer and his life-space. The creativity of performance requires that the composer's musical reality, necessarily including the larger cultural/societal/musical reality in which he lived or lives, be taken into account in the decisions made as to how to interpret—give musical meaning to—the notated sounds. That interpretation, by necessity, is a personal quest being made by an individual human being who also inhabits and reflects a world, a world that cannot be identical with the composer's. Two worlds of musical thinking, doing, and feeling merge in the act of performance. A new, unique musical event occurs.

When this happens—and I insist that it happens when second graders are genuinely performing a song as well as when a world-class orchestra is performing a symphony, only in different degree—a change occurs in the performers of the work. Dufrenne calls it a spiritual maturation. In this case it is a merging of the work (the song, the symphony) and its performers (the children, the professionals) in a musical experience to which both have contributed, and therefore that has created distinctive musical meaning that could not have existed before that performance. Such creation of meaning "inspirits"—infuses new meaning into all engaged in it. No wonder music educators are devoted to encouraging all people, no matter their age or capacities, to experience this inspiration.

One more point about the creativity of musical performance: it is often a shared act. The Western classical tradition, in its large-group contexts, usually entails a leader–follower dynamic, the leader (conductor) having major responsibility for creative interpretation, the followers (performers) conforming to the leader's wishes. Solo-chair performers in instrumental ensembles, and soloists in choral ensembles, have a good deal of leeway for individuality, but the majority—the section players or singers—must achieve commonality with others according to decisions made by the conductor.

We have, here, a triple layering of nonindividual demands. The first is from the composition being performed—though allowing a good deal of interpretive leeway, it cannot simply be ignored. Second, sections must sound uniform, the individuals within them conforming to the group interpretation. Third, that interpretation is largely the responsibility of the conductor rather than of individuals in sections or of sections acting autonomously. Surely "freedom" in such situations, or creativity as an expression of individual imagination, seems far in the distance for many if not most ensemble performances. Convergence, rather than divergence, seems to be a major, if not the major, condition for success.

One position about this situation is that Western ensemble music acts out the culture of oppression inherent in Western history. Music, in this history, is "an instrument of power," requiring "oppositional hierarchies," as Bowman argues in his plea that we view music through postmodern eyes. Suzanne Cusick agrees, arguing in the article referred to in Chapter 2 that although music supposedly gives the performer interpretive freedom, it then "demeans the gift" by forcing the performer to be "the one whose personality is to disappear": that the power relationship between the music and the performer of it "seems decidedly unequal," a "relationship of submission."[17]

I acknowledge the composer-work-conductor-performer hierarchy of decision making in Western (and other) musics, and its requirements of conformance to several levels of demands if performance is to be successful within this particular cultural system of musical expectations. But within this reality of ensemble performance, creativity in a genuine sense is, I claim, achievable. The key to this claim is that no matter how coordinated the playing and singing in groups must be, every performer can and should experience her or his contribution as one of individual selfness as integrated with the selfness of others. This is a paradox—the achievement, simultaneously, of selfhood and mutuality. This paradoxical yet very real experience pervades all group artistic creation. The term most apt for describing it is

---

[17]Suzanne G. Cusick, "Gender and the Cultural Work of a Classical Music Performance," *repercussions*, 3, no. 1 (Spring 1994), 90–93.

"communion" ("unity together"). In the act of ensemble performance individuals "commune" in joint creativity, a self-combined-with-other-selves experience in which individuality and community are fused in service of original musical expression.

In the best large ensembles, every performer feels as individually engaged in the act of creation, as fully responsible for creative decision making, as one would, by nature and necessity, in a small chamber group, say, a string quartet. Even in student groups at beginning levels, the sense, the flavor, the excitement of feeling the music individually and contributing that individuality to the conjoint musical expression emerging, can be experienced genuinely. So powerful is this experience in enhancing both the sense of self and the sense of self united with other selves as to change the inner lives of all who have been privileged to undergo it. Surely Dufrenne's characterization of creativity as spiritual maturation also applies to such experience, and explains the radiance felt by teachers and students who, through genuinely creative ensemble performance, undergo it.

Achieving this special dimension of creativity, I suggest, is the primary goal of ensemble performance. In the context of this chapter the affirmation that group creativity is capable of being both authentic and achievable, even with young students, is the major point to be made. Especially given the historical dominance of this form of musical involvement in American music education (and its popularity worldwide), understanding ensemble performance as potentially offering individuals a unique and powerful opportunity for musical creativity is essential for both explaining its importance and pinpointing its primary objective.

Improvising Creativity

In improvisation the performer makes substantive decisions about what the musical sounds might be and become in the very act of performing them. The combination of original generation of musical ideas, and the simultaneity of doing so within the act of playing or singing, separates improvisation from both composition and the performance of composed music.

There are, of course, some similarities. Complete freedom to do anything, whether in composing or improvising, is largely or entirely unachievable, as is the case in all other human endeavors. But although composers and improvisers make original choices within cultural/musical constraints, composers aim for a determinate (or relatively determinate) work awaiting completion or at least collaboration at another level by performers. Improvisers realize the creation of the work in the very act of performing it. Each improvised performance, even of the same piece, is expected to be, and is created to be, different from every other performance of that piece, despite the use of a well-known repertoire of sonic gestures, borrowings from and allusions to the improvisations of others, and all the other available material the improviser can employ from the rich, accumulative history and accepted ways of going about doing things each improvisatory style has developed. Within each well-established repertoire of choice making, the improviser, every time, attempts a distinctive exploration. Fertility of inventiveness—the constant search for new musical meanings *as those meanings are being made*—is the rationale, and the challenge, of improvisation.

The important understanding, I think, is that improvisation goes beyond the performance of composed music in that constitutive structural properties of the music must be created by the former but are predetermined for the latter. That is enough to cause a different way to teach in order to enable and improve each mode of musical/creative thinking and doing. The major implication for music education is that there are significant educational differences to be attended to, differences to be further delineated in my explanation in Chapter 7 of the different intelligences called for by each musical role.

Listening Creativity

Each of the previously discussed musical roles identifies a way a person can "be an artist" within the domain of music. Another way to express this is that being a musical artist is being a "musician." Musicians are people who create musical sounds in any of the ways their culture provides (and in ways that challenge or expand or even abandon cultural expectations). Musicians create by shaping sounds to embody meanings inhering within them, incorporating other meanings within their shapings. Composers, performers, and improvisers (and various combinations) clearly do this. Can listening to music be considered an act of creation? Can those who listen to music be considered "musicians"?

I suggest that listening is, indeed, an act of creation but that, unlike the other musical roles, it does not qualify to be conceived as an act of a musician, very simply because it does not do what a musician does—create music potentially shareable by others. Being a musician requires all the operations explained previously in regard to composing, performing, and improvising, and also a particular kind of "listening for a purpose" to be described in the following section. In all those cases the result of the creativity is a set of musical sounds brought into sonic existence (or potential sonic existence as in the case of a notated composition).

Listeners, on the other hand, bring a musical experience creatively to life within their own experience. Though it is possible to share aspects of that experience with others by describing it verbally, kinetically, or notationally, the listener creates no sounds shareable by others. It would be only poetic license, therefore, to call a listener a musician, a license I am not persuaded is useful or meaningful.

What, then, is "creative" about the experience listeners have of the work of musical artists (musicians)? (Of course, I mean "musicians" to apply to all, including children, who are engaged in doing what musicians do.) Don't listeners simply absorb what they are given in a kind of aural osmosis? Perhaps if they analyze music, or describe music, or notate it from listening, or perform what they have listened to, they *then* become creative, or at least active. But short of such "taking further," what is creative about listening itself?

This chapter began with a quotation from Mikel Dufrenne about the creativity of artists—people who bring meanings into existence through a particular kind of interaction with their materials. Here is a paraphrase of that quotation applied to the creativity of listening.

> It is within themselves that listeners perceive and respond as they think out musical sounds. What this act of original, creative reconstruction, which is like the labor of childbirth, strives to fix and internalize is the created music, which wants to *be* in the listener's experience. The work listeners do is, on this plane, a demand. But it is only a demand, one entirely inside each listener. In preparing themselves for the creative reconstruction listeners put themselves in a state of grace, or openness to musical meaning. The demand the music makes calls on the listener for an expression of inner logic—the logic of a certain technical development, of a peculiarly musical/aesthetic searching, and of a spiritual maturation. All this comes together in the listener, who is presently that individual in whom the work of a musician and a respondent merge. More deeply than others who do not listen to music, listeners create themselves by creatively reconstructing the work of musicians, and they listen because in so doing they create themselves.

This paraphrase gives a sense of the meaning-making listeners are responsible for achieving. The sounds composers, performers, and improvisers make are saturated with potential musical meanings—potential significant undergoings of mind, body, and feelings. Listeners are called on to make sense of the music, to "put it together" with mind, body, and feelings. Each individual listener must bring to that task his or her technical capacities to hear the complexities of the music, a "peculiarly musical aesthetic searching" for musical meaning, and a spirit of openness to inner growth as a result of doing so. In a real sense it is not possible to listen *without* being imaginative, original, inventive, and so forth—that is, creative—because no experience except one of chaotic, meaningless sounds could occur without acts of individual imagination to create meaning out of what is being heard. Jeanne Bamberger puts this idea as follows:

> I shall argue that a hearing is a performance; that is, what the hearer seems simply to find in the music is actually a process of perceptual problem solving—an active process of sense-making . . . a hearing . . . is both creative and responsive—a conversation back and forth between the music, as material, and the hearer as he or she shapes its meaning and form in some particular way.[18]

There is a catch here, of course. In some or even many cases (depending on the listener) the music presents challenges so far beyond the available perceptual problem-solving abilities to create meaning out of it as to shut down the searching

---

[18]Jeanne Bamberger, *The Mind Behind the Musical Ear: How Children Develop Musical Intelligence* (Cambridge: Harvard University Press, 1991), 8–9. The opposite position is taken by David Elliott, who argues that listening is not creative, because it produces no tangible product. (*Music Matters: A New Philosophy of Music Education* [New York: Oxford University Press, 1995], 220–21.) It is a supreme irony that in his book devoted to the supremacy of process over product, Elliott, in regard to creativity, contradicts his own fundamental premise, arguing that only product, not process, counts as being creative. This rules out, of course, any notion of creative thinking, not only in music.

and the openness required for creative response. Or, even if perceptual abilities are reasonably up to the music's demands, a listener may, for a great variety of reasons, be simply turned off to it and therefore unwilling to invest the creativity energy it takes to "make something" of it. I suspect few if any of us have not, in fact, shut down on some listening occasions, for a broad spectrum of reasons. It is harder to do so when one is performing or composing or improvising (although I suspect also that all of us have had times, when doing so, that attention and creative energy have flagged). When we listen, given the individuality and privacy of the act, inattention, passivity, indifference, unwillingness are all viable options whenever we choose.

That does not, however, alter the fact that when listening does go on creativity must be exercised at some level from little to much, just as is the case with musicianship. And we must recognize that most people, perhaps all people, often willingly and enthusiastically choose to listen—to immerse themselves in listening to their chosen musics for all the diverse pleasures musical meaning affords (and to spend considerable amounts of money to do so). Meaning-making, after all, in music as well as everything else people do, is a core need in the human condition. The meaning-making—the creative responsiveness—of musical listening is by far the most common way people involve themselves in musical creativity, and that includes those who, in addition, choose to be creative as musicians.

Viewed in this way, the obligation of music education to cultivate the most widely elected musical creativity would seem to be a core value for the profession, one that would receive a major amount of its energies, resources, and devotion. The fact that it does not, at least in typical North American programs, remains among the most pressing problems faced by the profession in that locale.

THE ROLE OF KNOWING WITHIN IN KNOWING HOW

Musical artistry, or musicianship—"knowing how"—no matter the specificities of each artistic role, requires meeting the music's demands, according to Dufrenne. Torrance spells out some of those demands: sensing, in the unfolding music, what needs to be done with it to make it work, hypothesizing about where it might go and what it might become, evaluating, revising, and retesting assumptions, and, finally, sharing the results with others. To meet a musical demand is to confront a musical possibility and decide what to do with that possibility. Each artistic musical role does that differently: all share in the requirement that it be done.

How is a musical possibility actually confronted, by a composer, a performer, an improviser, and anyone else—conductor, arranger, pop/rock performer-composer, sound engineer—engaged in musical creative artistry? Here is Dufrenne's answer:

> [T]he artist is an artist only through his act. He does not think the idea of the work but rather about what he is making and what he perceives as he creates. It is always with what is perceived that he deals, and the in-itself of the work exists for him only by being

identified with what is perceived. He knows what he has intended only when, following creation, he perceives it and judges it to be definitive—that is, *when he is at last in the position of the spectator.*[19] (Emphasis added)

Putting herself in the position of the receiver of the act of creation—in the position of knowing within—allows the musician to judge what has been done—to regard the decision she has made for its adequacy, or "rightness." "Taking the decision in"—experiencing it within—gives the immediate feedback the musician needs if progress is to be made toward bringing the unfolding musical meaning into existence. Otherwise, without the doing-experiencing-judging-redoing-reexperiencing-judging interplay between the act and the experience of the act, creation would be rudderless, meandering on without needed directionality toward the accumulation of convincing musical meaning. The experiencing—the "taking in"—illuminates the "giving out," correcting it, refining it, sharpening it, deepening it. The sure guide for this creativity—this exploration of musical possibility and discovery of musical potential—is the depth, criticalness, and exactitude of one's knowing within the musical decisions one has made. In that sense, having a "good ear" (supported by the craft to do what is needed) is the foundational requirement for all musical creativity.

A "good ear" is an ear trained to hear exquisitely subtle nuances of sound with exquisite accuracy, so the subtlety can be captured accurately (and with the necessary facility) in the music being created (composed, performed, and so on). An ear capable of hearing back to what has already transpired and hearing forward to what then is needed to carry the meaning further. An ear steeped in the historical, cultural, musical expectation system this instance of creativity resides within, so that the meanings being created are part of an artistic tradition and also an original contribution. An ear aware of the social surround in which the creative act exists, and able to incorporate—give musical body to—ideas and beliefs relevant to this particular creative act, "musicalizing" them as only music can do. An ear that hears with imagination; that hears possibilities and potentials, reveals new and fresh solutions, takes the act toward an emergence of meaning not yet achieved. An ear both in control of what is transpiring and responsive to the demands the created music is making. An ear capable of both asserting and acknowledging.

Such an ear, of course, is a mind; a mind in action in the meaning-system we call music. Musical creation—the making of musical meaning in all its forms—is deeply and powerfully an act of mind, centered in the body and in the feelings caused and shaped by each momentary, accumulating, creative act. Meaning in music is not something outside the music awaiting expression. It is what comes into being *through* the creative act of expression. Musical creation, as a unique form of meaning creation, engages individuals at the highest level of functioning of which the human organism is capable. No wonder there is a spiritual dimension to it, a "spiritual maturation" as Dufrenne puts it.

---

[19]Dufrenne, *Phenomenology,* note 1.

THE ETHICAL DIMENSION OF MUSICAL CREATING

In his deeply thoughtful book on morality, philosopher Mark Johnson identifies two positions about it that have had great influence throughout history.[20] In the more widespread view, the assumption is made that there are ultimate principles, or laws, governing our lives and how we should behave, these laws being attributed variously to God (or gods), human reason, or universal human feelings. To be moral is to have the strength of will to follow the prescribed rules meticulously.

In the opposite view, morality is considered to be entirely arbitrary, ungrounded in any ultimate laws and therefore open to whatever people care to invent. Because there are no rationally defensible moral standards, morality is itself irrational and completely subjective. So on the one hand is a kind of moral absolutism, and on the other a moral relativism.

In a synergistic posture, Johnson decries the extremism of each of these views and proposes that morality, and ethical behaviors, are, at base, products of human imagination. Issues concerning how we can be better people draw on a combination of reason and imagination (both based on bodily experience), guiding our choices in the world of others in which all of us must live.

> The absolutist/relativist split is a false dichotomy. It forces us to choose between two opposite views, both of which are false. We are forced to say that either all moral rules are absolute because they have a basis in universal human reason, or else all values and principles are utterly relative to specific cultural contexts. But empirical studies in the cognitive sciences concerning conceptual structure, meaning, and reason show that neither of these views is correct and that they do not exhaust the options we have for explaining morality. There is ample evidence to show that, although our moral understanding cannot be absolute, there are constraints on the forms it can take.[21]

In regard to the arts, Johnson suggests that we can learn some useful things about morality if we examine how it is something like aesthetic discrimination and artistic creation. He identifies four characteristics of artistic activity as being metaphorical of moral deliberation.

1. *Discernment.* The capacity to make subtle discriminations, fine-textured perceptions, "seeing a complex, concrete reality in a highly lucid and richly responsive way," are characteristics prized in the realm of the arts and are equally the basis of moral understandings. Both aesthetic/artistic engagements and moral perception "are acts of imagination and feeling for which there is no predetermined method . . . yet they are 'assisted' by general principles and constrained by the nature of our bodily, interpersonal, and cultural interactions."

---

[20]Mark Johnson, *Moral Imagination: Implications of Cognitive Science for Ethics* (Chicago: University of Chicago Press, 1993).
[21]Ibid., 5.

2. *Expression.* In expressive engagements with art, emotions, images, and desires are given definition, individuality, and clarity. Similarly, moral reasoning requires us to form and reform ourselves imaginatively through our thoughts and acts.

3. *Investigation.* Art is widely understood to be an investigation (an exploration and discovery) "of the possibilities of form, materials, language, institutions, relationships, and so forth. Thinking of moral deliberation as a form of moral investigation is enlightening, therefore, because it highlights the exploratory aspects of morality."

4. *Creativity.*

> In art we make things: physical objects, texts, tunes, events, or even conceptual entities. We mold, shape, give form to, compose, harmonize, balance, disrupt, organize, re-form, construct, delineate, portray, and use other forms of imaginative making. In a very straightforward way, this is exactly what we do in morality. We *portray* situations, *delineate* characters, *formulate* problems, and *mold* events. . . . [This] is a precise account of what morally sensitive and perceptive people must do.[22] (Emphases in original)

Notice that Johnson makes no presumption that aesthetic/artistic engagements are in and of themselves moral or ethical, or that such engagements make the people involved in them more moral, ethical people. He is simply trying to clarify the conception of morality as requiring imaginative acts, and is using those required in the arts as metaphors to assist him in that task. "I am not, thereby, collapsing morality into art. . . . I am thus not sanctioning the 'aestheticization' of life and morality." He is simply using the arts as a device to help him explain that morality requires "discriminating, balancing, composing, envisioning, projecting, exploring—matters of imaginative perception, imaginative envisionment, and imaginative action."[23]

Johnson's use of artistic creation as a metaphor, figuratively comparing it to the imaginative creation he believes morality requires, is an illuminating but unconventional approach to the creative process as it operates in both domains. More traditional views of the relation of art to morality tend to take one of two perspectives, as British philosopher Matthew Kieran explains. In one perspective, the position taken is that "art proper, however indirectly, prescribes and guides us toward a sound moral understanding of the world." In the contrary view "the spheres of morality and art are thought of as autonomous rather than complementary."[24] Both these views can be traced back to the ancient Greeks and both exert influence to this day. Kieran argues for a position in which imaginative understanding, called on whenever we are engaged with art, may indeed have moral implications, enhancing our sensibilities toward moral issues by allowing for "a distinctive and fuller exploration of possible

---

[22]Ibid., 210–12.

[23]Ibid., 215–16.

[24]Matthew Kieran, "Art, Imagination, and the Cultivation of Morals," *The Journal of Aesthetics and Art Criticism,* 54, no. 4 (Fall 1996), 337.

imaginative understandings of the world and others than can be afforded in our ordinary imaginings."[25]

Kieran's argument is that people sensitive to an art (or to several) have developed, as a result, "distinctive and fuller" ways to imagine the world and other people, and they can then apply those imaginings to moral issues. But it is not clear how aesthetic/artistic understandings, given that they are "distinctive," can be transferred to and employed in a different realm such as morality. And their "fullness" is fullness in aesthetic/artistic circumstances, distinct from moral circumstances. The assumption is often made that sensitivity in one (distinctive) domain naturally or automatically transfers to a different one. Is this feasible or persuasive? I will return to this issue after explaining how I conceive musical creativity to have an ethical dimension, a conception substantially different from those Johnson and Kieran suggest.

As I have pointed out, in all musical creativity demands are made that must be fulfilled. Whenever in human experience demands, or needs, are present, calling for an individual to respond through choices to be made, values come into play as a determinant of one's conduct. What is "right," or "better," and what is "wrong," or "worse," to do? What does my culture regard as right or wrong, better or worse? What do I as an individual regard as proper conduct, influenced by my culture's beliefs but also in my obligation to achieve selfness by accepting them, rejecting them, adapting them, altering them to fit the singular circumstances of my life while also honoring their power as bases for communal identity? Such ethical questions pervade our lives as we negotiate our actions in all the many roles each of us play.

Whenever we play a creative musical role as a musician, choices are at the center of what we are doing. Some characteristics of creative choices are matters of craft in the service of musical expression: how to achieve an effect we are after, how to heighten or diminish an emphasis, how to keep the energy going through a long phrase, how to repeat a previously improvised idea but keep it developing, how to balance a long legato line as a foil to a staccato accompaniment, and on and on with all the musically interior interpretive decisions every musical creator constantly faces.

At a broader level, subsuming all those kinds of "how to" decisions but adding another dimension to them, are matters in which ethical considerations seem to me to be clearly in play. I will identify a sample of five of them.

---

[25]Ibid., 349. Kieran's position is argued also, in a carefully presented and humanely written essay, by Ted Cohen, "Identifying with Metaphor: Metaphors of Personal Identification," *The Journal of Aesthetics and Art Criticism*, 57, no. 4 (Fall 1999), 399–409. For another thoughtful discussion of the relation of the aesthetic and the ethical, see Marcia Mueder Eaton, "Aesthetics: The Mother of Ethics?" *The Journal of Aesthetics and Art Criticism*, 55, no. 2 (Spring 1997), 355–64. A review of her article by Arnold Berleant, and her response to it, are given in *The Journal of Aesthetics and Art Criticism*, 57, no. 3 (Summer 1999), 363–66. An excellent book on morality and education is Philip W. Jackson, Robert E Boostrom, and David T. Hansen, *The Moral Life of Schools* (San Francisco: Jossey-Bass, 1993). A wide-ranging and useful discussion of various positions in ethics and an examination of ethical dilemmas in music education caused by conflicts of interest are given by John W. Richmond, "Ethics and the Philosophy of Music Education," *The Journal of Aesthetic Education*, 30, no. 3 (Fall 1966), 3–22.

1. *Trust.* Whatever our particular role as a musician we are always dependent on others who are dependent on us. A composer must depend on—must trust—the performer(s) who will bring his ideas to sonic fruition, that they will pay all due regard (depending on the particularities of the composer/performer expectation system) to the musical ideas embodied in his work. Nothing but trust binds the performer(s) to the composer: no law forces them to pay attention to his desires. He is in their hands, for better or worse, and he can only hope (and trust) that in some reasonable or acceptable or relevant or even tolerable way, his wishes will be honored.

Performers in ensembles, small or large, and whether performing composed works or improvising, must trust each other to devote the required energy and devotion to the task at hand. The spirit of mutual dedication all group performance depends on requires trust that all will fulfill their role conscientiously. When someone or some do not, chaos ensues: the enterprise falls apart. A lack of mutual trust that the group embraces the attitude of "all for one and one for all"—even a deficiency in that trust—can spell disaster. In school groups, trust between the performers and the teacher/director reflects the dependence of young performers psychologically and emotionally as well as musically and educationally. Solid confidence, built on personal and professional trust, is an absolute requirement if music is to be created successfully in school ensemble situations.

Audiences must have trust in performers (and conductors), that they are being presented with the fruits of conscientious, honest musical work. For the performers, trust is placed in their audiences, that they will attend and respond appropriately and relevantly, and give all due regard to their efforts. On and on go the many interplays of person with person, person with group, group with person(s), constituting the social structure of music as each culture and subculture devises it. Trust is the bedrock on which the musical enterprise rests, making a moral/ethical demand on all involved with it.

2. *Competence.* In every musical creative role (including that of the listener) there is an expectation that individuals will have attained, and will maintain, an acceptable if not high level of ability to do what is musically required of them. Of course, that expectation varies significantly depending on the particulars of the creative work being done, the age and experience of those doing it, the purpose of doing it, whether it is amateur or professional or educational, and so on. But whether extremely modest or extremely expert, those involved have an ethical obligation to be able to accomplish what they are called on to accomplish. No musical creation can occur without competence, and attaining it calls for work to be done. That need for accomplishment, of course, is the challenge and the joy underlying music making, which can sustain people throughout their lives if they choose to pursue it.

Music education, in an important sense, initiates and sustains students' efforts to achieve increasing competence in the know-hows of creativity, enabling parallel musical satisfactions to occur. Those efforts cannot be coerced. They must be taken on as a matter of choice, and sustained by a willingness to bend one's energies to them if the musical rewards are to be gained. As in all other aspects of learning, success in musical creativity depends on a sense of obligation to achieve whatever competence is required, an obligation of an ethical nature.

RIFF 7

It's my senior year in college. Having started to study the oboe the year before (in addition to my regular major in clarinet), I am first-chair oboe in the excellent orchestra. For the spring concert the director has scheduled Respighi's *Roman Carnival Overture,* and he informs me I am to play the English horn in it, with the famous solo that is the basis for the piece. I've never held an English horn, let alone played one. I immediately go to my teacher's studio and tell him the news. "Well," he says, " we have an English horn. We'll have to make a reed for it." There's a worried look on his face. I am to learn that he has limited experience making such reeds.

For weeks he works on one reed, then another, and another, and each one produces, when I play it, enough squawking to rival a chicken coop. My attempts at the solo are disasters, and my consternation grows at each failed effort. The conductor and the players are equally alarmed, and embarrassed for me, my reputation for solid musical competence becoming severely eroded. I can't sleep, can't eat. At the final rehearsal, the morning of the day before the concert, I repeat my dreadful sounds. Afterward, no one has enough courage to look me in the eye.

I work with my teacher frantically all afternoon and evening. By around 10:00 P.M. we have made progress. The notes are starting to come, my control is starting to solidify, the reed is responding rather than resisting. The next day, in a practice room, I play the solo through dozens of times. I go home, dress for the concert, walk shakily to the auditorium, seat myself on stage, warm up. No one looks at me.

The piece begins, with its energetic flourish and long tones in French horn and clarinet introducing the solo. I'm in a cold sweat. I begin to play. Every note speaks, projecting with liquid fluency, with color and richness of tone, with every bit of nuance I can pile on. The reed takes it all and gives back its cooperation. The conductor, who had looked away when the solo began, not being able to face me, is now emoting along with me, conducting my solo with his whole body, so relieved and happy he is almost crying. As am I. As is the entire orchestra. When the solo ends, flawlessly, all eyes are on me, expressing pride that my competence has been vindicated. Afterward hugs, handshakes, handslaps. Drinks.

Never again in my life am I able to listen to an English horn solo, especially by a student, without a tightening in the gut, a bit of a sweat, fingers crossed. The English horn literature is pretty well wiped out for me to enjoy.

It was worth it.

3. *Cooperation.* All group efforts require cooperation: working together toward mutual goals. As with trust and competence, cooperation cannot be coerced; it calls

on a choice willingly made to give one's self to a task in which others also have a stake. That choice is an ethical one, entailing a value to be adopted and self-restraint to be exercised, so that one's actions will contribute to a good larger than one's own.

Though in group musical creativity of all sorts the need for cooperation is obvious, it exists as well in solo performance when a composition is being brought to realization. The performer must "work with" the composer's ideas to give them sonic existence sharable by others. A solo improviser also "works with" ideas—her own and those of the piece she is improvising on, blending the two in a co-dependent creation. And listeners cooperate in the musical enterprise when attending genuinely so as to share what is being offered, investing themselves in mind, body, and feeling in the cooperative making and taking of musical meaning. Music is saturated with dependence on a cooperative attitude, or ethic, if it is to fulfill its meaning-making-and-receiving function.

4. *Respect.* Cooperation, trust, competence, all are grounded in the ethical need for mutual respect, the granting to others of a sense of their worth as part of a shared enterprise to which all are contributing. When respect is lacking or questionable in any aspect of musical creating, failure awaits. Retaining one's respectable-ness—one's worthiness of esteem in one's creative role—is an ethical constant, underlying every person's participation in music. Musical respect is given to a person who is cooperative, trustworthy, competent (at an appropriate level) in creating music, and is deserved by all who demonstrate those qualities. In the interactions of ethical responsibilities musical creativity depends on, mutual respect is the engine generating the power of musical expression.

5. *Courage.* Creativity originates. It takes every individual involved in it to a place that person has not yet been. In a real sense the exploration and discovery of musical possibilities that constitutes creativity calls on the individual's willingness to risk, to be open to the unexpected and the not-yet-known, and to be up to and worthy of dealing with the challenges of risking. There are no guarantees of success. A popular notion is that in the arts, including music, there are no wrong answers, no requirements, and "everything goes." Instead, creativity, as has been explained, is the skilled search, by mind, body, and feelings, for meanings, in our case musical meanings. Indeed there are wrong answers, requirements we cannot meet, musical comings into being with which we don't know how to cope. Every decision we make can be just as wrong—as inept, as insensitive, as unimaginative, as inauthentic to the musical demands—as it can be right, as all of us who have struggled to be musically creative know very well. Without the ever-present possibility of failure, of course, musical creativity would be inconsequential. The complexity and difficulty of the task makes musical creating worthy of the high regard in which it is widely held.

Musical creation calls upon our courage to be wrong as often as right, to keep working toward what is needed in face of our limitations, to be willing to grow and therefore to become what we not yet are. No doubt that is one reason we treasure it: its endless capacity to take us on a journey of becoming more fully what we can be.

Ethics and the Goal of Music Education

I leave it to the reader to add other ethical/moral dimensions to the ones I have identified: this list is intended to be suggestive. An important question must again be confronted here—whether the ethical demands made by musical creating transfer to other endeavors in life. Do composing, performing, improvising, listening, and so on, make us "more ethical"? The parallel question in regard to musical creativity itself is whether engaging in it transfers to other ways of being creative, thereby making those who do so "more creative."

In a very general sense it is reasonable to assume that whatever we do in life has some effect on us beyond its specificities, that we are not so compartmentalized that no cross-influences can occur among our many activities. So if being musically creative, and ethical in the ways that requires, may influence us to be creative and ethical in other ways, we should be pleased when and if that occurs. By the same token, being creative and ethical in every other aspect of our lives may equally lead us to be musically creative and ethical, and, if that is true, we should be equally pleased when and if that happens. I am willing to acquiesce this far: every particular good thing we do may positively influence every other particular good thing we do, making us generally "better people" as a result. And, as a necessary corollary, every bad thing we do (being uncreative, unethical, and so forth) may influence us negatively to be generally "worse people." At this level of overarching generality it is easy to go along.

Problems begin to occur when we get more specific. Does the ethical behavior entailed in musical creativity have greater force in making us "more ethical" than any or all other engagements calling for ethical conduct? Music educators sometimes tend to think so. But can we claim that there is something better or more influential about musical ethics than those required for any of the other arts, each requiring all the qualities I have discussed and many others I have not? And can we believe that the ethics entailed in fields such as government, business, religion, education, sports, research, media, and on and on, are all lesser than music in their influence? Are people devoted to musical creativity, either as professionals or active amateurs, or, say, music educators, "more ethical" as a result than other people in the world devoted to other endeavors, each of which has an ethical dimension? Is music really the center of the ethical world, radiating outward to warm everything humans do with its superior goodness? My skepticism, obviously, grows, as it does with parallel claims about music study having special power to positively influence learnings in other subjects, or with the claim that musical creativity inevitably transfers to creativity in the special ways each different subject or role entails.

Further, should it be claimed that the point and purpose of music education is to create more ethical human beings? In one sense, the argument can be made that everything humans do has as its purpose the creation of better (more ethical) people; all else is secondary and relatively unimportant. Other overarching qualities have often been identified as constituting the ultimate human values all particulars are aimed toward—loving-kindness, serving God, individuation, good citizenship, the pursuit of happiness, pleasure, and so forth. Again, at this very broad level of generality it is easy to go along (given, of course, that one can opt for the ultimate value of one's choice).

But in another sense we can conceive the good life as an accumulation of particular goods, each particular way to achieve an important value adding its particularity to the sum total of a life worth living. In that sense music offers ethical and life-enhancing values just as numberless other endeavors do, but *in the distinctive way characteristic of music*. Nothing else is quite like it. Its very particular way of "making special," of being creative, of putting ethics to work, is the ultimate value of music, in this sense. The goal, or value, or rationale for music, then, is not its contribution to what every other endeavor equally contributes to (although that is as valid and important a contribution of music as it is for every other human undertaking), but the contribution it makes *that nothing else can make*.

Focusing on the unique values of music—the unique meanings it adds to human experience, its uniqueness of creativity along with the ethical dimensions that make it possible, the unique ways it calls on the mind, the body, and the feelings—does not prevent us from recognizing that music, too, contributes to a greater good, as everything else can do. But it guides us to the core of what makes that contribution in the way nothing else can—musical experience in all its manifestations. Without music (a strictly theoretical notion, of course) all the overarching values could still be achieved. Without music, however, nothing of its values would exist to enhance human life and contribute to its goodness. That is why musical experience is the core value of the philosophy I propose and the core determinant of musical learnings on which I believe music education should focus, such as the national content standards enumerate. Musical values are uniquely available from music, and the learnings that help procure them are uniquely available from music education. Those values and learnings, in their uniqueness, contribute powerfully to the sum total of a good life, I suggest, accounting for the existence and importance of music in all cultures.

TEACHING FOR KNOWING HOW TO CREATE MUSIC

In his famous poem "Adam's Curse," W. B. Yeats describes the hard labor it takes to create a poem, ending by saying that since Adam's fall every fine thing requires great labor. Philosopher Nicholas Wolterstorff comments on Yeats's poem as follows:

> So making a poem is hard work. No doubt Yeats would say the same for a work of music, a painting, a sculpture, a novel, a drama—the making of any of these is hard work. Not always, of course; some poems of Housman and some compositions of Mozart were apparently just received by them. But our history is littered with tales of the labor, and even the agony, that have gone into the making of art. It gets washed off; but art has dripped with blood and sweat and tears.[26]

---

[26]Wolterstorff, "The Work of Making a Work of Music," note 16, 103.

Yes, creating art—composing, performing, and improvising music clearly included—is hard work, as Yeats and the commentary by Wolterstorff so powerfully express. Yet when successful, it seems to be so easy, the blood, sweat, and tears all washed off and the gleaming result clean of the labor. No one knows this better, I think, than music educators, whose labor importantly consists of enabling others to be musically creative. For, in addition to being intimately involved in the hard work of creating music, music teachers are simultaneously involved in the equally hard work of education, with all its endless, complex, demanding challenges, intellectually, psychologically, and emotionally, as well as musically.

Yet for all its difficulties, the rewards of doing all of this are so great that practically all music educators willingly and devotedly engage in teaching musical creativity, at every level and in a wide variety of contexts. It is difficult to imagine music education without the teaching of musical creativity as an essential component, especially if one includes listening as also creative, as I most emphatically do. Here are some guidelines for effective nurturing of the creativity music uniquely enables.

All teaching for musical creativity—the skilled, sensitive, imaginative, and genuine making of decisions about expressive possibilities of sounds—needs to be aimed toward helping individuals think, do, and feel music more meaningfully. Whatever the creative role, and whether it is a solitary or a group endeavor, a focus on individuals—clarifying their thinking, sharpening their craftsmanship, refining their feelings with the sounds they are imagining—will ensure that growth can take place where it must finally exist, in the experience of each person.

In music, individual instruction, so rare in systems of education for the masses, remains viable, providing an ideal context for individuality to be carefully nurtured. When that magnificent opportunity is fully taken, results can be remarkable. In group situations such as schools inevitably provide, the difficulties of individualization multiply, of course, especially given the overburdened schedules under which so many music educators labor. The success of so many in giving each participant in groups the sense that their creative selfhood is being recognized and honored is testament that even the enormous challenges of individualization in such situations can be met by those attuned to the need and skilled in providing for it. Improvement in this dimension of music education remains, I believe, one of the most critical issues the profession faces.

Growth in creative individuality requires, for all musical manifestations of it, the development of accuracy. This might seem a strange word in the context of musical creation, but it is a powerful one nonetheless. All the qualities listed as the results of educating feeling in Chapter 3—clarifying, organizing, broadening, deepening them, and so forth—come about because of more musically accurate, precise engagements of the self with meaningful sound. That thought was expressed beautifully in a comment by the poet Robert Wallace, as applied to poetry. "A poem," he said, "if it's any good, is a machine for loving with. It doesn't matter what—the ungainliest thing: a mutt, ourselves, the world. The love depends on the precision."[27]

---

[27]Robert Wallace, *Ungainly Things* (New York: Dutton, 1968), dust cover.

Applying this to music, we are reminded that musical creation, if it is successful, is a way to love; a way to feel deeply, with passion, with honesty, with directness. And not just "lovable" things—even a plain old dog (the first poem in Wallace's book is about the sculpture of a scruffy dog by Alberto Giacometti, a sculpture filled with the artist's love for this "raggy mutt"), even ourselves, even the world. But poetic love, or musical love, is not vague, or sloppy, or garbled. The composer searching, agonizingly, for that just right turn of sound, that just right rhythmic gesture, the next idea that simply must be there—that search, the rigorous work of creation, is a search for feeling captured "just right," captured precisely. The performer, or group of performers (think children learning a song), going over and over a phrase to "work it out," to capture its "love" accurately, exemplifies musical creation at its deepest and most exacting. That is the hard, demanding work of musical artistic creation, the search for a level of affective precision only these sounds, shaped precisely this way, can yield. That is what Francis Sparshott meant when he said "the affectivity of music is its own and has its own precisions," and when he quoted Mendelssohn's famous comment about the "definiteness" of music (see Chapter 3). Helping people do musical work with love—with sensitivity, devotion, and the drive for precision (definiteness), getting it to be just what it needs to be—is what music educators do when they are helping their students be creative. Artistic precision, or definiteness, never interferes with or competes with the spontaneity of artistic creation. Instead, it makes spontaneity meaningful.

Musical work occurs in every creative musical role. It is arduous work when successful, when genuine, but work filled with the gratification of loving, loving not in the sentimental sense but in the sense of devoted searching for what feeling needs to be. That sense, when it is deeply shared, sustains music educators and their students through all the hard work of creating music. It provides the spiritual dimension and also the ethical dimension of creativity, both so powerfully experienced when the work is carried on honestly; when knowing how, guided by knowing within, is being experienced authentically by each individual engaged in that work.

Every particular kind and type of music across the broad spectrum of cultural imaginings provides the potential for authentic creativity. A mistake we music educators tend to make about the music we choose to engage our students with creatively is to limit it to that kind we ourselves, because of our backgrounds, professional training, and value system, believe to be the "proper" or "appropriate" or "truly creative" kind. Given the widely shared background, training, and values of music educators in the West (and elsewhere), it is not surprising that we have tended to emphasize the successful instances of the music of the Western classical tradition and are most comfortable with teaching how to be creative within the expectation system that tradition embodies. The mistake here is not that this particular music is not worthy of the attention we tend to give it—it decidedly *is* worthy of an essential place in our efforts. Western classical music, I would argue, is an indispensable source of creative experience for all our students, both for historical/cultural reasons and for the magnitude of the achievements it represents.

The mistake is to assume it is sufficient. It is not, because each music in the world, including the many musics within the Western world, creates its own lived-in space of feeling, and each of those feeling-habitats allows us to experience the world through its body of accomplishments. Creating music within a style requires feeling out the ways of making meaning in that style, making meaning in the tradition, belief-system, constraints, and generative possibilities each style operates within, each style's world of possible encounters with feeling. One must put oneself in the shoes of a style to create within it. Doing so is a powerful way to think, feel, and act "inside" the style.

One more point about teaching for the knowing how of artistic musical creation. It is not something to be put off until "later," such as when students involved in performance or composition or improvisation achieve sufficient technique to then allow them to become creative, as if creativity cannot occur until some imagined degree of groundwork has been laid. That misconception—technique now, musicianship later—has plagued performance teaching in music education throughout its history, accounting for much of the convergent, rule-learning-and-following, technique-dominated, rote nature of the enterprise. North American music educators tend to have much less experience in teaching composing and improvising, of course, but when we do we are in danger of falling into the same trap of assuming that creative thinking/doing cannot occur until "x" degree of technique has been attained. Adding to this tendency is the heavy emphasis on teaching notation, both in performing and in composing, given its importance in our particular system of music making. This adds still another layer of technical demands—the learning of an invented, elaborate symbol-system—that can obscure the creative point of being a musician.

The irony of this situation is that technique, understood as physical and mental control over the acts and tools necessary to create music, is indeed an enabler of creativity. Deficiencies in it limit what can be created, while sufficiencies open endless possibilities. So it is not wrong, or misguided, or short-sighted to expend all the effort it takes to build technique. What is wrong is to *separate* technique from creativity and to delay the latter until the former attains some prescribed level of achievement.

The solution to this long-standing and vexing problem, I suggest, is to recognize and cultivate their interdependence *right from the start*. From the very first moments of sound-expressing in performance, and sound-imagining in composition, and imagining-expressing in improvisation, the need for technique as the servant of creativity becomes obvious: you can't do what you want to do—make music—unless you have the wherewithal to do so. The goal, the point, the purpose, is to make music—that is, to create sounds that satisfy as only music can. That is what needs to drive our instruction: the search for creative musical meaning. Technique becomes the partner in that endeavor, not an obstacle to be gotten over so one can then be creative, but the wherewithal that allows creativity to happen.

When means (technique) and ends (creativity) are mutually supportive, genuine musicianship occurs *even at its very beginnings*. When either one becomes too dominant, neglecting their necessary complementarity, both suffer, technique becoming bereft of meaning, creativity bereft of grounding. It is never a matter of either–or; always a matter of synergistic reciprocity. Of course, "practice material," understood strictly as mental/physical muscle building, can supplement and extend technique in all sorts of useful ways without pretense that it is inherently creative. It is only when that material becomes the end, absent the link to creativity, that musical meaninglessness, and hence disinterest, sets in. When a healthy balance is achieved, as so many sensitive, creative music educators successfully achieve it, musicianship flourishes, with all its attendant joys and satisfactions.

The spiritual experience inherent in creating music is available to young children being introduced to it as well as to the few who are world-class masters at it. Enhancing musical creativity with a small c—the artistic doings of all who attempt it, in all the many ways and styles music allows it to be achieved—is, I suggest, a noble responsibility. An equally noble responsibility is developing the creative listening capacities of all students, creativity that though not in itself "artistic" in the sense of being the work of "musicians" is creativity nonetheless. Some students may eventually reach the heights of big-C creativity (only a tiny fraction, by definition), but even those who will had to start at the small-c level. Whatever the age or level of ability, teaching for musical creativity requires all students to be engaged in being creative, physically, feelingfully, mindfully, in their own, personal experience. And thereby changed as human beings.

ETUDES

1. Reread the quote by Dufrenne with which this chapter begins. Can it apply to even young children in, say, first- or second-grade classrooms who are creating music by singing, playing, composing, improvising, listening? Apply each sentence in the quote, separately, to such youngsters, substituting "the young child" for "the artist." Does the quote still make sense? If so, what does this imply for effective teaching of musical creativity to youngsters of every grade level?

2. Where do you stand on the "big-C" "small-c" debate? Are there some strengths in each that the other does not have? Some weaknesses? In your own musical creativity do you feel you are genuinely able to be creative despite (let me assume) your not being among the greatest of the greats?

3. Are you comfortable with the idea that the chances of your teaching a student who will become one of the greats are quite small, but that you can, nevertheless, influence each of your students to be "more creative"? Is that enough to excite you about being a music educator? To sustain and satisfy you over the long haul?

4. Think back to when you began on the journey to becoming a musician. In those early months or years of study, were you given many, rich opportunities to make musically creative decisions on your own, with your teacher(s) as a guide? Do you feel you could have started sooner to be given that responsibility, or have been given it in more varied musical contexts, or at greater levels of challenge?

What do *you* do, or plan to do, to encourage beginners to be musicians—creative decision makers with sounds—right from the start?

5. Of all the ways your culture makes musical creativity available (the different musical roles it provides for), which were available in the schools you attended? Are you satisfied, as you look back, that your schooling gave you as many opportunities to explore your potential to be musically creative as you wish it had? What needed to be added? Have these things been added since you were there, or are the opportunities still pretty much what you experienced? If little change has occurred, why do you think that is? If change has occurred, why do you think it did?

6. What musical creativities exist in your culture beyond the four (composing, performing, improvising, listening) I discussed? Can and should schools attempt to include all those you can identify? Would that be feasible?

   Assuming for the sake of discussion that it would be feasible, who would be qualified to teach all of them? Would teacher education have to change substantially to prepare a greater diversity of music specialists than it has ever tried to do? Would you like to see that happen? Why, or why not?

7. What other ethical dimensions of musical creativity can you name, and explain, in addition to the five I identify? Where do you stand in the debate about whether ethics in musical settings necessarily transfers to nonmusical settings? Have you known excellent musicians who were also highly ethical people? Any, on the other hand, who were not exactly paragons of ethical virtue? Can you say the same about people you've known who are outstanding in fields other than music? Do you think it is (1) a good idea, or (2) a dangerous one, to argue for including musical creativity in schools on the basis of its potential to make people "more ethical"?

8. Do you agree that genuine and worthy creative experiences are available in a wide variety of musics beyond that of the Western classical literature? What are your aspirations in this regard, as to the music you hope to, or attempt to, use to engage your students? Do you feel your preparation to be a music teacher (is) (was) as enabling for your goal as it could (be) (have been)? What, if anything, would you like to change about your teacher training in this regard?

5

The Meaning Dimension
of Musical Experience

MAIN THEMES

- Language meanings and musical meanings are different in significant ways. Language is created and shared through the processes of conceptualization and communication. Music is created and shared through the process of artistic/aesthetic perceptual structuring, yielding meanings language cannot represent.

- Human knowings and meanings exist in diverse ways, including those music makes available.

- Music can be described (or defined) as sounds organized to be inherently meaningful, in which the inherence can incorporate a great variety of additional meanings.

- The preceding description (or definition) is a useful tool for understanding puzzling deviations from it.

- Teaching for musical meaning requires the use of language as a means to enhance musical experience. Language has two essential functions in music education—to disclose and to explain.

- Music means whatever a person experiences when involved with music. Music education exists to nurture people's potential to gain deeper, broader, more significant musical meanings.

[I]t is more nearly true of music than it is of anything else that it offers an alternative reality and an alternative way of being.[1]

[C]an we speak of meaning where there is no explicable signification, no represented object, and no discourse? Meaning here immediately surpasses itself toward expression. Music unveils a world invisible to the eye, undemonstrable to the intellect. Yet this

---

[1]Francis Sparshott, "Aesthetics of Music: Limits and Grounds," in *What Is Music?*, ed. Philip Alperson (New York: Haven, 1987), 89.

world can be expressed only by music, for it is a world which vanishes once the music ends. It exists in the music insofar as it is perceived, and nowhere else. Anything we may say of it in another language is pitifully inadequate to express what music expresses. . . . But this ineffable meaning still deserves to be called meaning, for it is what the musical object says. The musical object exists only by expressing this meaning. Meaning informs music, making it music rather than an incoherent succession of sounds.[2]

Sparshott again, in the first quote. Dufrenne again, in the second. This time they raise issues as difficult as any in the entire history of aesthetics or philosophy of art, difficult because they reach so far down to the nature of music that words trail off into ineffectuality, into that necessary yet frustrating gap between what language is capable of meaning and what music is capable of meaning. The gap is necessary because without it we would not need music: words or other language-symbols would serve just as well. Yet it is frustrating because it is natural to wonder about the specialness of music, its offering of an alternative way to be and to experience. That wondering finds its expression in words—questions, explanations, hypotheses, debates. For philosophers of music, whether professionals or those trying for the first time to "be philosophers," the frustration is inevitable, because language-think is their medium, and sound-think, with its meanings incapable of being expressed in language, is their subject. There is no way for philosophers of music to avoid that frustrating gap.

Music educators cannot avoid it, either. Like it or not, we are expected to clarify what music is all about, by helping our students compose, perform, improvise, listen, more adequately and satisfyingly, *and to understand what they are doing and why.* Furthermore, we work in a field—education—that consists largely of the development of people's abilities to share meanings about humans and their world. To put it another way, education increases knowledge (what is perceived and understood) so that life can be more meaningful (the significance, or import, or sense of what is known). Does music have something to contribute to this endeavor? If the answer is no, how do we justify music as an essential part of education?

For all of education, music included, language is a necessary means, an essential tool. Yet in music that gap from one kind of meaning to another always exists. As music educators, especially when we are trying to think hard about the nature of our subject, but even when dealing with routine matters of music teaching, we dwell within the gap between language-think, or language meaning, and music-think, or music meaning. That is our constant burden. But it is also our constant delight, that what we say, and help our students say, can *get them closer* to what only music can say, what only music can mean. The other side of the gap remains a mystery to language. Yet language can help us and our students get closer to the brink of the mystery.[3] It cannot take us beyond. Only musical experience can.

---

[2]Mikel Dufrenne, *The Phenomenology of Aesthetic Experience* (Evanston, IL: Northwestern University Press, 1973), 265–66.

[3]I am grateful to music theorist John Buccheri for this phrase, applied by him to analysis.

LANGUAGE MEANINGS, MUSICAL MEANINGS

In the previous two chapters the ideas of "knowing within" and "knowing how" were raised and explored. The claim was made, and discussed, that our interactions with musical sounds, both in experiencing them and in creating them, are deeply connected to human feeling, cognition, and consciousness. We "know" when we experience music, but in the special sense relevant to what music makes available to us, the sense relevant to its being an alternative reality, an alternative way than language to know ourselves and our experienced world. I claimed also that this "music-world" of meanings is inclusive of meanings from outside music itself, which enter into and influence the music-world and yet are transformed by so doing. All our musical experiences, no matter of what sort, "educate" our inner, felt life, refining, clarifying, broadening, and deepening our feelings in a way analogous to how language does the same for our conceptual reasonings.

Most people who deal professionally with knowing and meaning, whether as philosophers, psychologists, linguists, sociologists, and so forth, remain firmly within the domain of language-think—that is, language knowing and language meaning. And there are plenty of issues connected with such knowing and meaning, enough to have kept such people busy for centuries. In fact, their work has been so dominant that the term "knowing" is assumed by many people to refer exclusively to the kind of knowing language allows. Claiming as knowledge what is made available to the mind, body, and feelings through music (and the other arts, of course) is at least uncomfortable for those steeped in the common meaning of that word, and at most unacceptable to them. If knowing and the outcome of it—meaning—are not the result of language, in this very common position, how can they be called knowing or meaning at all? Surely when applied to music they must be something else—intuition, perhaps, or instinct, or, simply, emotion, which is unconnected to reasoning, allowed only by language (the fallacy discussed in Chapter 3).

Dufrenne's argument that the ineffable (incapable of being expressed in words) meaning of music still deserves to be called meaning, for it is what the music says, or expresses, takes note by his use of the word "still" of the weight of the traditional association of meaning with language meaning. "Nevertheless," he is saying, "despite that the common understanding limits meaning, knowing, and cognition, to language, still those words deserve to be used for what occurs in musical experience." I thoroughly agree with his (and others') position, but doing so requires a defense—an explanation of how and why the meanings, knowings, and cognitive functionings of music "still deserve" to be called by such terms. Such an explanation can be of enormous utility for music educators, in helping them clarify for their students and others why music is, indeed, a cognitive domain, special in nature but nevertheless grounded in human thinking and meaning. To the degree music educators are clear about how music means, they can help their students both create meaningful music effectively and gain the musical meanings in music created by others.

Creating Language Meanings, Creating Musical Meanings

A helpful way to clarify the distinctions between language meanings and musical meanings is to contrast the different processes by which meanings are created and shared in the two domains. In language, meanings are created and shared through the process of communication. In music, meanings are created and shared through the processes of artistic musical creation and aesthetic musical responsiveness, as explained in Chapter 4. Let us examine the language and music processes in turn through the lens of how meaning is made.

Several conditions must exist in order to call a process "communication." First, the person communicating must select from all possible messages a particular message that is to be transmitted. The message may be some information, an opinion, an idea, an emotion, a command, and so on.

The message is then encoded into a signal (or "sign," or "conventional symbol")—words, movements of the body, numbers, and so on—that transmit the message to someone. The receiver then changes the signal, or "decodes" the signal back into the message (the signal "please close the door" is decoded into a message about a desired action). All this may happen instantaneously as in a conversation, or it may be a prolonged process as in the writing of a book. In the latter case, the author selects a particular set of facts, opinions, or assertions and encodes them into words that are transmitted by means of ink and paper. The reader decodes the ink marks on the paper back into words that give her the author's message.

For communication to be successful, a minimum of interference should be involved between the communicator's message and the receiver's understanding of it. Interference may occur at every step along the way, unfortunately. For example, the communicator could choose a poor signal for his message. Instead of saying "please close the door," the message he wants to transmit, he might say "no one ever cares about privacy around here." The receiver may indeed get the message that the door should be closed, but a great many other possible decodings could take place instead. Because of the ambiguity involved we could say that poor communication is likely to take place.

Another opportunity for interference in the communication process arises in the decoding phase. A guest in a foreign country, being left in her hotel room by a bellhop, may say "please close the door." The bellhop cannot decode the signal because he does not understand English. He looks puzzled, trying to figure out what message is being transmitted. Again, poor communication is taking place.

If communication is to be *good* communication, the communicator must begin with a clear idea of what is to be transmitted; she must translate the message into signals that exactly represent her message; and the signals must be decoded in just the right way by the receiver. If all these things happen the message will have gotten from the communicator to the receiver intact. Good communication will have taken place.

Here is a (simplified) diagram of the process of communication:

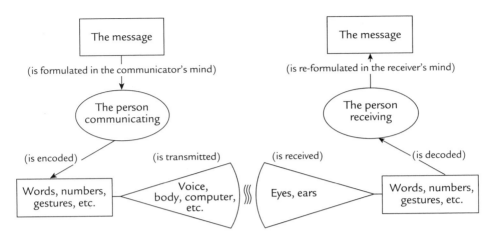

Nothing about the process just described applies to the processes of musical creation and response.

The first important difference between communication and the creation of music is that the composers or improvisers, though sometimes starting their musical creations with a message of some sort in mind, must get beyond it so as to "musicalize" it—make music out of it—if they are to be musicians. Whatever the initial impulse, it is not a formulated message—conceptual or emotional—that then is encoded into a signal. Instead, a tentative musical hunch occurs—a sense of possibility—a germinal musical idea that seems to have the power to grow. The act of musical creation lies precisely in that growth process, and this process is different from the process of choosing proper signals to transmit a message. In fact, to the extent that a musician follows the communication process rather than the creation process his work will turn out to be nonartistic: "Music that is invented while the composer's mind is fixed on what is to be expressed is apt not to be music. It is a limited idiom, like an artificial language, only even less successful."[4]

As explained in the previous chapter, the growth process that is the essential characteristic of musical creation is a process of *exploration* and *discovery*. It is a searching out and recognition of expressiveness, of musical meaning. The exploration into meaningful feeling takes place through an exploration of the expressive possibilities of the sounds the musician is using. Musical creation explores and forms the feelingful qualities of sounds. This exploring-forming process is not a process of encoding messages.

---

[4]Susanne K. Langer, *Philosophy in a New Key* (New York: Mentor Books, 1942), 125.

Creation in the fine arts is, no doubt, not a process in which an idea springs forth in the artist's mind, to be mechanically worked out in some material; it involves feeling out the possibilities inherent in the stone or the pigments [or the sounds].[5]

A diagram of the musical creation process would look like this:

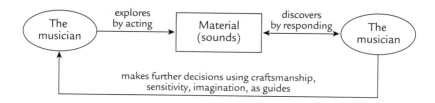

Communication tries to get a message from the sender to the receiver as directly as possible with as little interference as possible from the thing (the signal) that carries the message. The signal (words, noises, gestures, and so on) is of interest only insofar as it transmits the message. The expressive or artistic qualities of the signal are quite beside the point for communication. In fact, if the transmitting medium is too interesting in and of itself, it can only get in the way of good communication.

The diagram of musical creation indicates the reciprocal effect of the musician and his material—sounds. The musician works on the sounds and the sounds work on the musician. This ongoing interchange is precisely the condition allowing exploration to take place. In the quality, intensity, and profundity of the interchange lie the conditions for the quality, intensity, and profundity of the thing created out of it. If the musician's involvement with his medium as he explores its expressive potentials is profound, calling into play his deepest, most fully experienced feelings; of high quality—sensitive and skillful and imaginative; and intense—strong and keen and vivid—the musical product is likely to be of profound significance, high quality, and intense expressiveness. The thing created contains its profundity and quality and intensity *because of the interaction* between musician and sounds. This is far removed from the communication function of signals chosen to carry a message with a minimum of interference.

Of course, when a musician's work is being shared with others, something of what was created—the results of his explorations and discoveries of expressive meanings—is experienced by those able to discern the meaningful musical gestures captured in the created sounds. Can that interaction be called "communication"? In a general sense, because what the musician intended to be experienced is experienced (to some degree) by another, we might answer the question affirmatively.

---

[5]Monroe C. Beardsley, *Aesthetics from Classical Greece to the Present* (New York: Harcourt Brace, 1958), 33.

But in another sense the kind of sharing of experience occurring in music is poorly described as communication. The danger is to think that the purpose of music is to communicate as most people commonly understand that word—to yield "messages" consisting of singular, explicit exchanges from one person to another, as communication is supposed to do. Why is this a danger? Because it misrepresents the underlying nature of music. Music communicates in the proper sense—transferring explicit meanings—only when it uses sound-effects or other explicit signs or symbols directly referring to designated things, ideas, emotions, and so forth. In all such cases a specific reference is indeed communicated by music, and the *communicated meaning* of the music (in the sense of something referred to) is grasped when that reference is recognized. So, yes, music can and often does "communicate" in the common sense of that term.

What is missed by conceiving music as being fundamentally communication is its power to *go beyond* all such meanings to those incapable of being designated by signals operating within the communication function. The endless realm *beyond* "explicable signification," "represented objects," "discourse," as Dufrenne puts it in the quotation beginning this chapter, is where music takes us. Even when music refers, as it often does, the meaning of the music does not stop at the doorway of the referent. Here is Sparshott's explanation of how reference in music "surpasses itself" (as Dufrenne says):

> What, in general, is the significance of all these resources and devices whereby music in one way or another refers to the nonmusical? One cannot dismiss them as irrelevant or superseded: their use continues to pervade musical practice at all levels of sophistication. . . . Perhaps we should say that (as in painting) the most approved uses of the devices are those in which what is recognized and relished as referential is at the same time experienced as musical—that is, in which we feel that what we hear would be formally justified even if nothing were being referred to. . . . The characteristic musical delight in all such devices, for composers as much as for audiences, lies in the way *music is being made of them*: the exact way in which, having been what they were, they have now become completely music.[6] (Emphasis in original)

In one (limited) sense, then, music can and does communicate, and we can and should "recognize and relish" these communications when they occur. Going beyond them, however, gets us to what music does that communication does not; what music does that music is required for because nothing else can do it. What is that special quality, that special kind of meaning music produces? And how is it different from what language means? We need to get closer to the brink of this mystery.

---

[6]Sparshott, "Aesthetics of Music," note 1, 66, 67. The relation of meaning in art to reference is concisely explained by Gregory Currie, "Visible Traces: Documentary and the Contents of Photographs," *The Journal of Aesthetics and Art Criticism,* 57, no. 3 (Summer 1999), 285–97, in which he contrasts documentaries with nondocumentary photographs and paintings. His conclusion: "in a documentary meaning passes from image to narrative, while in nondocumentary meaning goes the other way." In music, we can say, "documentary"—a narrative about something—occurs when meaning passes from musical sounds to references, while in musical experience meaning goes the other way.

THE MANY MODES OF KNOWING

Is there only one way that humans can know? Or is human knowing multifaceted, in that different areas of experience and different mental-physical-psychological operations yield different ways of knowing? The most important word relating to knowing, at least for education, is cognitive, or cognition—"the act or process of knowing." Our questions can now be posed a bit differently: Is there only one form of cognition? Or is cognition multifaceted?

Since the 1960s or even earlier, the idea that cognition is diverse has been expressed and acknowledged by influential thinkers in a variety of fields, and the thought has gained power over the ensuing decades. For example, an influential book by Philip H. Phenix, *Realms of Meaning,* identified six fundamental patterns of meaning that emerge from distinctive modes of human cognition. He called them symbolics (languages and language-like systems); empirics (sciences dealing in empirical truths); aesthetics (primarily the arts, which present unique objectifications of the subjective); synnoetics ("direct awareness" or "personal or relational knowledge"); ethics (moral meaning expressing obligation); and synoptics (comprehensive, integrative meanings as in history, religion, and philosophy).[7]

An important book exploring the implications of diverse cognitive capacities for education was the 1985 Yearbook of the National Society for the Study of Education, titled *Learning and Teaching the Ways of Knowing.* It argued that there are several distinctive realms of knowing, including the aesthetic, interpersonal, intuitive, narrative-paradigmatic, formal, practical, and spiritual.[8]

No doubt the most widely known argument for diverse cognitions rather than a singular conception of cognition was Howard Gardner's *Frames of Mind: The Theory of Multiple Intelligences,* which took the position that there are seven intelligences ("frames of mind"): the linguistic, musical, logical-mathematical, spatial, bodily-kinesthetic, interpersonal, and intrapersonal. Later, Gardner added the naturalist, and, possibly, the existential or spiritual.[9] I will discuss Gardner's conception in more detail in Chapter 7.

All these proposals about the multifaceted nature of human knowing and human meaning began to influence the ways people conceive education. If the mind thinks, knows, and creates meanings in diverse ways, surely education must then represent those ways in the studies in which it engages all young people. If meaning is not limited to dealing with language and language-systems, how could all the other meaning-systems be cultivated if they are neglected in education? Should we expand our narrow conception of what is basic for schooling, a conception tending to be limited to the subjects in which knowings are mediated by language (English, foreign

---

[7]Philip H. Phenix, *Realms of Meaning* (New York: McGraw-Hill, 1964).

[8]Elliot W. Eisner, ed., *Learning and Teaching the Ways of Knowing* (Chicago: University of Chicago Press, 1985).

[9]Howard Gardner, *Frames of Mind: The Theory of Multiple Intelligences* (New York: Basic Books, 1983), and *Intelligence Reframed* (New York: Basic Books, 1999), 47–66.

languages, mathematics, science, history, geography, civics, government, economics)? Should we include subjects such as music, or the arts, now regarded as "specials" because they are not based on language-think? Is our culture ready for such a change in its understandings and priorities?

The Dominance of Conceptualization

At the present time we are still in a historical period in which the most widely recognized, most influential, most highly valued mode of cognition, based on language-think, is that called "conceptual." So powerful is the influence of conceptualization on traditional ideas of what knowledge consists of and how the human mind can know, that it is assumed by a great many people that cognition and conceptualization are one and the same. To know anything is to have a verbal or other symbol-mediated concept about it. The realm of cognition, in this still widely accepted view, is unitary: there is conceptual knowledge expressible by language, and there is mindlessness, everything we experience that is not able to be put into the form of language concepts.

The implications of this narrow view that equates knowing exclusively with verbal-symbolic conceptualizing have been profound in Western culture and education. To be intelligent, in this view, is to be able to conceptualize well. To reason is to use concepts as the sole mode of mental functioning. Conceptualizing is assumed to be the only possible way of being logical, rational, intellectual. (The intellect, in fact, is equated with conceptual functioning.) So far does this identification of knowing with conceptualizing extend that it is often accepted as a given that human mentality itself, thinking in its broadest sense, consists essentially of the process of conceptual reasoning such as language-systems allow.

The inadequacies of the traditional idea that the intellect consists of conceptualization, and that the world can be known only through conceptualization, have been recognized by major thinkers for many years. For example, Carl G. Jung (a founder of psychoanalytical theory along with Sigmund Freud) argued that

> We should not pretend to understand the world only by intellect; we apprehend it just as much by feeling. Therefore the judgment of the intellect is, at best, only a half-truth, and must, if it is honest, also admit its inadequacy.[10]

John Dewey especially was impatient with those who equated intelligence and thinking entirely with conceptualization, leaving the arts, which do not conceptualize in the way language and the other sign-systems do, in a secondary, inferior position.

> Because perception of relationship between what is done and what is undergone constitutes the work of intelligence, and because the artist is controlled in the process of his

---

[10]Carl G. Jung, *The Collected Works*, vol. 6, Bollingen Series XX (Princeton: Princeton University Press, 1971), 495.

work by his grasp of the connection between what he has already done and what he is to do next, the idea that the artist does not think as intently and penetratingly as a scientific inquirer is absurd. . . . Any idea that ignores the necessary role of intelligence in production of works of art is based upon identification of thinking with the use of one special kind of material, verbal signs and words. To think effectively in terms of relations of qualities is as severe a demand upon thought as to think in terms of symbols, verbal and mathematical. Indeed, since words are easily manipulated in mechanical ways, the production of a work of genuine art probably demands more intelligence than does most of the so-called thinking that goes on among those who pride themselves on being "intellectuals."[11]

But these were voices in the wilderness: the vast majority continued to define intelligence in the traditional way. No wonder, then, that education has been and remains dominated by the attempt to improve conceptual abilities through the subjects exemplary of this mode of cognition, the subjects called "basic," or "core." No wonder that subjects such as the arts, which do not depend on the same kind of reasoning mechanisms as language systems, have been considered secondary or even trivial in that they do not involve intelligence or intellect or logic or rationality or even *thinking* as these have been understood by this limited and outdated position as to the nature of cognition. And no wonder that those devoted to the arts can now begin to breathe more freely as it is being recognized that this older position is unsupportable. We are coming to understand that the narrow view it represented was a gross distortion of how the human mind works and how it produces knowledge. And we are better able to understand the special cognitive status of the arts and the authentic, essential ways they involve people in intelligent, mindful experiences that yield powerful meanings of their outer and inner worlds.

The Concept of Concepts

To explain these ideas, it will be necessary to take a closer look at how conceptualization is typically considered to work as a mode of cognition and then to contrast that with how the arts work as a cognitive mode. To do so I will preserve the standard or traditional definition of a concept as being an inherently verbal (or mathematical or other sign or signal) function of the mind. In this long-established and persistently influential view, concepts are considered to be those thoughts, ideas, and conceptions that language-systems mediate.

Contrary to this standard definition, it is possible to conceive a concept as including mental images or ideas *not* necessarily represented by language systems of words, numbers, notations, and codes. For example, music is perceived by people engaged with it as consisting of complex yet coherent sets of sounds formed by a number of pertinent elements—pitch, duration, dynamics, tone color, and so forth. We can attach language terms to musical sounds if we choose to do so, as I did in the

---

[11]John Dewey, *Art as Experience* (New York: Capricorn Books, 1958), 45–46.

preceding sentence. But the sounds of music are heard and understood even when we do not attach labels or notational designations to them. We can hear a trumpet in a piece, notice that it is a trumpet, but not necessarily say to ourselves, "That is a trumpet." Can the hearing of the trumpet, and the tacit recognition that it is a trumpet, be thought of as a concept despite no language term being assigned to the noticing?

When we are "knowing within" music (including "knowing how") we are not consciously and intentionally analyzing or explaining or notating or otherwise engaged in "knowing about" and "knowing why." We are, instead, "noticing without naming," or "perceptually structuring." I have made this distinction specifically to avoid using the term "conceptualizing." I want to emphasize and clarify that *language need not be and typically is not applied to the sounds we are engaged with in musical experience.* My purpose is, precisely, to avoid the common idea that all thinking requires the mediation of language—the use of concepts as that word is most commonly employed. I have no substantive objection to stretching the term concept to include the way sounds are processed in musical experience. But I am not happy to do so because it blunts the very distinction I am intent on making, a distinction confused and weakened when a word so generally understood to require language—conceptualization—is applied to a phenomenon such as music that exists to create and share meanings *unavailable through language.*

So, tactically and pedagogically, as a way to illuminate by clarification, I will retain the standard, language-connected use of the term "concept" in my explanation of how concepts function, and how musical experience, contrary to that way of functioning, occurs *nonconceptually,* in a way different from how concepts are traditionally conceived to "mean." I will then be better able to explain how, paradoxically, concepts in the usual sense of that word can be and must be employed as necessary tools for enhancing musical meaning.

A good starting point for this explanation of how musical knowing and meaning differ from conceptual knowing and meaning is a clear, unambiguous definition of what a concept is in the classical sense, so we can more clearly and unambiguously understand how musical experience differs from this sense. Here are two excellent customary definitions, saying the same thing in slightly different ways:

> A concept is a sign which points to a commonality in events and which permits the concept user to make relatively stable responses to those varied events. The signs which are vehicles for the concept are largely linguistic and conventional. The commonality in events may range from simple similarities to regularities to law-like invariance.[12]

> A concept is a triadic relation uniting a marker, counter, or vehicle, with stability in response on the part of the inquirer, and some common feature of a range of events.[13]

---

[12]D. Bob Gowin, "The Structure of Knowledge," in *Philosophy of Education,* ed. Harold B. Dunkel (Edwardsville: Southern Illinois University Press, 1970), 6.

[13]Eugene F. Kaelin, "Response to Gowin," in *Philosophy of Education,* ed. Dunkel, 19.

A diagram embodying the three essential characteristics of a concept would look like this:

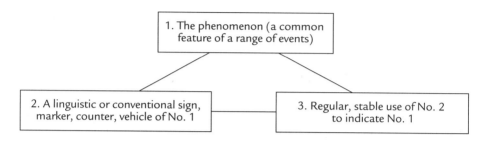

What is needed for a concept to exist is, first, something that is manifested over a "range of events." A singular instance of something cannot be a concept. A particular person—say, Bruce Springsteen—is not a concept. However, if you notice that a song or a performance is "Springsteen-like," you have identified a common feature of at least two instances and therefore are dealing with the first aspect of a concept. A particular thing—say, an apple—is not a concept. However, if you notice something about it that it has in common with other things ("fruit," "round," "edible," and so on), you are dealing with the first aspect of a concept. A particular event—say, a walk through the woods—is not a concept. However, if you notice something about it that is like other events ("path," "hill," "blackbird," "shadows"), you are dealing with the first aspect of a concept. The sound of a trumpet as one hears it is not, in and of itself, a concept. However, when the sound is perceived as common to a particular kind of instrument—trumpets—the "common feature" aspect of a concept is indeed present.

The second thing needed for a concept in the traditional sense to exist is some sort of sign, or symbol, or name, or indicator of the common feature being noticed. When you are experiencing a piece or a performance by Springsteen, *no such linguistic or conventional device need be part of the experience whatsoever.* No words or any other symbols characterizing the music need be present for you to be immersed in the ongoing experience. However, if you choose to call attention to some common feature of the sounds by giving it a name (protest song, husky voice, driving beat), you are now dealing with a concept in two aspects: a common feature within the sounds and a name for it.

Similarly for the examples of the apple, the walk, and the trumpet. No words or any other symbols need be present as you eat the apple or take the walk or hear the trumpet, and so long as no such vehicles are present, the experience is nonconceptual according to the common understanding of the term. This is not to say, however, that the experiences are not meaningful or mindful or insightful or intelligent. As a matter of fact, it is now being recognized that our minds are actively structuring our experiences in all sorts of complex ways that often never become named by symbols. These ways are not lesser than conceptualization; they are of a different order.

Some of these mental structurings lend themselves to conceptualization because they deal with common features over a range of events. But many others are not of this sort at all in that they are responses to particular, immediate instances that are themselves deeply meaningful. Spiritual experiences, for example, are resonant with complex, profound meanings captured in the depth and height of a singular moment—a "now" that seems timeless because of the powerful sense of significance contained within it. Such an experience is "vertical" in its affect: it is rich with knowing as a singular presence rather than as a horizontal commonality with similar things. The knowing or awareness or import or comprehension in such an experience is nonconceptual in all three dimensions of a concept. Experiences of love share this nonconceptual status, as do many other interpersonal and intrapersonal meaningful, cognitive experiences. In all these the richness and complexity of *what is immediately felt* is the essential characteristic and content of their meaning.

Experiences of music also yield this verticality of the "now" felt as significance. But in music this comes from an interaction with structured sounds. These structures of interrelated phenomena are very much like the first condition for a concept in that there are many features of music that are common across a wide range of events both within a particular work and from one work to another. We hear a melody in a song as a unified feature of sounds and recognize the connections when the melody is restated, varied, extended, contrasted. We perform a musical gesture in an improvisation, relating it to a previous one and then extending it to lead to a different gesture for contrast. We explore a rhythmic idea in a piece we are composing, looking for ways to link it to a previous rhythm by incorporating some of its accents. But there are two essentially different characteristics of such mental operations from the operations in typical conceptualization. First, no linguistic or conventional sign is applied. We experience the embodied sound-structures directly and immediately; there are no intermediating signs, symbols, or vehicles, as would be required in conceptualization as commonly understood. Second, the perceived structures are inseparable not only from their embodiment in sounds but also from *what is felt* in the act of perceiving them. Structured sounds are experienced simultaneously as both structured material and structured feeling, one inseparable from the other.

The ability of our minds to process the complex structures of music—to notice their embodied interrelationships and to feel what we are noticing, all without the use of any intervening symbols or signs—has been given the name "intuition."[14] This word, however, has a passive ring to it, as if it were something that just happens, a kind of gift from on high or from biology. Music educators know that this ability can be developed through all the activities that good music instruction provides. So it would seem more useful to understand this mental process as being one of *perceptual structuring* to contrast it with conceptualizing. A particular phenomenon occasioning the perceptual structuring process, say, the motive in the first movement of Beethoven's Fifth Symphony, or the rhythmic/melodic initial phrase in Glenn Miller's

---

[14]Rudolf Arnheim, "The Double-Edged Mind: Intuition and the Intellect," in *Learning and Teaching,* ed. Eisner, note 8. The active nature of artistic intuition is explained and richly discussed in Susanne K. Langer, *Problems of Art* (New York: Scribner's, 1957), Chapter 5, "Artistic Perception and 'Natural Light.'"

"In the Mood" (choose your own favorite example), may be called a *perceptual construct*. These terms, calling attention to our mindful engagement with meaningful sounds, emphasize the active, educable nature of this form of cognition, and they are also more true to what this complex function of the mind consists of than is the term "concepts."

The third aspect of a concept has to do with how well a person associates a particular symbol or name with the phenomenon to which it refers. If a person regularly names a thing with a correct symbol even though the thing exists variously across a range of common qualities, the person "has the concept." For example, if a child is shown a red apple and she says "apple," one is led to infer that the child has the concept of what an apple is. If, however, you show her a green apple and she says "grape," you would have some reason for doubt. If you continued to show her different shapes and colors of apples and continued to get different names, you would be convinced that she did not, in fact, have a concept of "appleness." If, however, she were able to notice that all the variations were of a common set of qualities, and demonstrated that noticing by correctly identifying all the different kinds of apples as apples, you would be convinced that the concept "apple" had been attained.

In music, a person able to notice the common features of the sounds of Thelonious Monk's music, give the proper name to that noticing ("that's Monk"), and do so regularly whenever a performance of Monk's is heard can be assumed to have the concept of "Monkness." And so on for all concepts, no matter how simple or how complex.

A concept, as typically understood, then, is a mechanism by which one can refer to a noticed phenomenon. A concept is *about* the phenomenon. It does not constitute the phenomenon itself or the internal experience of the phenomenon. A child may be taught that all things with certain qualities are called apples, and she may get the concept perfectly. But the experience of an apple when she eats it is of a different order. The concept is *about* the apple. The eating is *of* the apple, or "within" the experience of "appleness."

Concepts yield *knowledge about* (and why). Music yields *knowledge within*. The experience music exists to provide is of the immediate, singular, unnamed, dynamic interplay of structured forces embodied in sounds. In the experience of them we are engaged in a process of *affective/perceptual structuring*. Such an experience is not "about" anything. It is "within" a particular configuration of sounds yielded by a particular interaction with them at a particular moment in time.[15]

A diagram of the knowing within character of music, as contrasted with the knowing about and why character of concepts, diagrammed earlier, is as follows:

---

[15]The issue of the role of conceptualization in perception is among the most complex in the realm of the cognitive sciences. Those interested in acquainting themselves with those complexities, or in probing them more thoroughly, will be rewarded by reading William P. Alston, "Perception and Cognition," in *Pragmatism, Reason, and Norms*, ed. Kenneth R. Westphal (New York: Fordham University Press, 1998), 59–87, and Mark DeBellis, *Music and Conceptualization* (Cambridge University Press, 1995), as well as the many sources each cites. These represent only a brief glimpse at the complexities of the topic but are particularly germane to my discussion.

```
┌─────────────────────────────────────┐
│          1. The phenomenon:          │
│       a perceptual/affective event   │
│       (a perceptual construct) embodied │
│       in a structure of expressive sounds. │
└─────────────────────────────────────┘
                    │
┌─────────────────────────────────────┐
│          2. The experience:          │
│     perceptual/affective response to │
│    (perceptual structuring of) the event as │
│    part of its larger musical embodiment. │
└─────────────────────────────────────┘
```

The Distinctiveness of Each Cognitive Mode

The claim is often made, particularly by advocates of the arts attempting to convince people that the arts have utilitarian value, that artistic/aesthetic thinking leads to better thinking in the "basics," such as mathematical thinking or reasoning, or spatial-temporal reasoning, or verbal reasoning. Study the arts, the claim pleads, and the mind will be better able to think in nonart subjects. For example, visual art educator David Olson argued as follows:

> The arts involve the conscious and systematic comparison and organization of forms. The arts, then, are responsible for the elaboration of these forms whether verbal or visual. Once elaborated, this "language of forms" . . . is then available for the more declarative representation of objects and events. . . . The arts develop, elaborate, and refine language, and then the language is used for representation. In this way, art precedes and leads both ordinary and scientific cognition.[16]

This claim, that artistic thinking leads to better nonartistic thinking, is made by many people in many ways. It is very probably not true. What we are learning about mental functioning is that it is more diverse than we had thought and that its many realms of meaning are more disparate than we had thought. Thinking in one mode develops the capacity to think in that particular mode but has little influence on other modes of thought because each is distinctive. As Howard Gardner asserts, "It appears probable that the ways we deal with . . . syntax in language share few fundamental properties with our transformations of spatial images or our interpretation of musical expressiveness." There is likely to be in psychology "separate studies of language, music, visual processing, and the like, without any pretense that they fit into one supradiscipline."[17]

---

[16]David Olson, "The Role of the Arts in Cognition," *Art Education*, 36, no. 2 (March 1983).

[17]Howard Gardner, *The Mind's New Science: A History of the Cognitive Revolution* (New York: Basic Books, 1985), 132–33. An excellent and detailed discussion of the relation of language to music, and of the ineffable nature of musical meaning, is given by Leo Treitler, "Language and the Interpretation of Music," in *Music and Meaning*, ed. Jenefer Robinson (Ithaca and London: Cornell University Press, 1997), 23–56. Other chapters in this book also deserve careful study.

The argument that the study of music will pay off in better conceptual functioning as called for in the traditional school subjects is intended to build a stronger advocacy position for music in the schools. But if the argument is based on a false premise it cannot do anyone any good. Even if there was some measure of overlap between music and the concept-based subjects the argument would still be suspect. First, it would work both ways; that is, conceptual learnings in other subjects would be as helpful for musical learnings as the reverse, music then requiring *less* time rather than more. Second, the argument does not recognize that music exists not to cause nonmusical learnings but to provide profound human meanings unavailable in any other way. Developing this mode of mentality through education is essential if education is to help children become what their human condition enables them to become. If other purposes are served by this primary value, that is fine, but as in all other claims for the value of music in education we cannot rest, philosophically and professionally, until we have uncovered what is most characteristic of music. At bottom that is its function as a mode of cognition operating in importantly different ways than do language-based systems of thought.

A DESCRIPTION OF MUSIC AND ART

In previous chapters, from a variety of vantage points, I have identified characteristics of music that make it the distinctive (or "special") phenomenon it is. In the following discussion I want to expand on my explanation of musical meaning and go further toward specificity about music and its nature, leading to a summary description of music and, using that as a basis, to a summary description of art. Such summary descriptions are usually regarded to be definitions.

Definitions of art (and of music) are notoriously risky, because art is a domain notorious for ongoing attempts to surpass, even destroy, any inclination to pin it down to a conceptual characterization.[18] Especially in the twentieth century, and on into the twenty-first, many artists have tried to break the boundaries of established notions of what art "properly" consists of, as a definition (by definition) attempts to establish. There is something distasteful, even repulsive, to many artists about being specified, as definitions attempt to do, and it is taken sometimes as an artist's mission to violate, often gleefully, accepted notions of what art is and does.

On the other hand, those who think hard about the arts are equally driven to make some sense of the chaos confronting them, and nothing is so helpful to sense making as a handy definition. Definitions are not the be-all and end-all of theorizing. They serve as tools—as useful devices in our attempts to achieve clarity in confusing, complex situations such as the arts exemplify.

---

[18]For a searching discussion of attempts to define music, see Bruno Nettl, "Music," in *The New Grove Dictionary of Music and Musicians,* 2nd ed., ed. Stanley Sadie and John Tyrell (New York: Grove's Dictionaries, Inc., 2001).

In that spirit, and with modest expectations (given how often art has rendered definitions of it irrelevant), I am emboldened to use the previous discussions of conceptualization and artistic/aesthetic perceptual structuring as a basis for what I offer, not so much as a definition, but as a description of salient features of music, and more generally, art. Avoiding the term definition in favor of description can help keep me out of trouble (although, realistically, not entirely.) More important, a "description" avoids, somewhat, the sense that art can be defined conclusively, definitively, and finally.

In his famous discussion of the difficulties of defining art, aesthetician Morris Weitz suggested that definitions of it, or descriptions of it, should be regarded as "seriously made recommendations to attend in certain ways to certain features of art."[19] I intend my description to be such a recommendation. Given that the arts can be regarded from a great variety of vantage points—sociologically, psychologically, politically, economically, historically, anthropologically, physiologically, neurologically, and on and on—each based on a different interest in them and therefore a different way to attend to them, the description I offer can be only one among many. Nevertheless I believe it gets to, or at least tries to get to, features of music and the arts that separate them substantively from the other ways humans create meanings. That, I argue, is what makes the arts an essential human endeavor, one that deserves to be represented as fully in education as every other way humans have devised to make their lives meaningful.

Can't we get along quite well without a description? Music, after all, as all the other arts, goes its merry way whether or not someone fashions a stipulative concept of it. Composing, performing, improvising, listening, and so forth, are not dependent on having worked out, or adopted, a verbal description, and few who do all those musical things are likely to have spent much time worrying about how to describe (or define) it. So why bother, especially in that the task is so difficult and precarious?

We need to do so because music educators are expected to be of some help to those they are introducing to the study of music, who, in becoming more thoughtful about it as well as skilled in it, often raise the question of its definition—or *should*. After all, it is just as human to be curious about the character, or nature, of the things we treasure in our lives as it is to just go about treasuring them. Education has an obligation to clarify the character or nature of the subjects it includes. A succinct description of science, or mathematics, or language, or geography, and so forth, can be enormously useful (however fallible) in the study of these subjects and anything else we deem worthy of learning. And if—or, better, "when"—a student asks the definition or description question about music, we should be able, as professionals, to offer some useful guidance as to how such a question might be answered intelligently.

---

[19]Morris Weitz, "The Role of Theory in Aesthetics," *The Journal of Aesthetics and Art Criticism,* 15, no. 1 (1956), 35.

"OK, Ms. Jackson," says Nick, in a middle-school general music class that has been exploring recent computer-based compositions, listening to a variety of them, composing examples of them in the computer lab, discussing their character-istics and challenges, hearing a presentation of such music by a composer from a nearby college. "You say this music is a lot like the other kinds of music we've stud-ied—jazz, rock, classical, folk, music from India. But it sure doesn't sound like all that other music. So why do you call it music? Is anything music? I mean, what makes stuff music?"

"Whoops," Jackson thinks. "Looks like the "d" word has come up. I've been waiting for it—knew it had to happen. Great. I'm ready." "Nick," she says, "you've raised a tough question: how do we define music, or describe it in a way that tells us what it is, what it does? I think I can answer the question, but let's try, as a class, to come up with an answer together. I'll help by asking a few questions to get you going.

"So, first of all, what's the one thing music depends on that makes it some-thing we're likely to recognize as this special thing music is? Something that's needed if you're going to call this stuff 'music'?"

"People," a student responds.

"Well, OK, you need people, but people do a lot of things that aren't music. We're people, but right now no music is going on. We're talking about music, but we're not making music or listening to it or anything. What would we need if music is going to happen?"

"Someone would have to sing, or you'd put on a CD, or we'd play stuff on instruments, or maybe the computer," another student volunteers.

"Does that make sense to you?" Jackson asks the class. They nod. Seems to be reasonable.

"OK. So what's going on when we sing music or listen to music or compose music or play music? What is the one thing all of that depends on?"

"Well, you've got to have something you hear."

"And what do we call stuff we can hear?"

"Well, sounds, I guess, or noises, stuff like that."

"Good. We're getting somewhere. If you're going to have music, you're going to have to have sounds going on, or noises if you want to call it that. Have all the different musics we've been studying used sounds? Can you think of any music that doesn't use sounds?"

Discussion among the students. They agree—music must have sounds. Jack-son smiles when she thinks of how she's going to hit them, later in the year, with her performance (as dramatic as she can make it) of John Cage's 4'33". They're going to love that! But the issues that piece raises can't make sense unless and until it builds on the accepted idea that music uses sounds. Cage attempted to raise issues of What sounds? Whose sounds? Any sounds at all? Happening in any way at all? That leads her to raise the next question with her class.

"OK, you've agreed, and I agree with you, that music depends on sounds. But any sounds? We're making sounds now, by talking, but are the sounds we're making music?" The class agrees that they're not. *"So what's got to happen to sounds for them to become music?"*

I won't continue the imagined scenario format, to save space and time. It gives a sense of how a teacher might explore the definition/description issue in a more active way than simply reciting his own solution. (Many other ways of doing so will be imagined by creative teachers.) I will continue now to add a few more conditions, in addition to sounds, that I think are necessary in order to usefully describe "music."

Given that sounds are music's basic—necessary—material, another distinction is needed, because, clearly, not all sounds in our world are considered to be, in and of themselves, "music" (although any sound at all can be *used* musically). Someone—some person—has to *do something* to sounds in a way she or her culture regards as qualified to be regarded as musical. (Or, as Cage did, to question a cultural assumption by transgressing it, a doing inevitably based on an existent cultural understanding.) Sounds, in all cultures, are put together, or given structure, or fashioned, in ways each culture has imagined as appropriate for music. So now we have two conditions reasonably related to what might be regarded as music: sounds, organized in some eligible way, or, sometimes, in a countereligible way or an eligibility-challenging way.

Is there any characteristic of that eligibility common to all the diverse musics around the world and throughout history? Perhaps we should stop while we're ahead, rather than raise another whole set of complex issues as to what *all* music attempts to accomplish by imagining ways to organize sounds construed to be music. But having gone this far, I am willing to take the precarious step toward a universal description, recognizing that doing so does indeed open the matter to a great many complexities. That, I believe, is a good thing (well, for philosophically minded music educators, at any rate).

So, based on the previous material in this chapter, I will propose that sounds organized in various culturally devised ways are universally intended to be meaningful in ways only organized sounds can be when they become "music." That is, musical meanings, despite being able to incorporate all sorts of additional meanings, achieve, universally, a level and kind of meaning beyond those available from conceptual reasoning, communication, conventional symbols, designations, "knowing about," and so forth, as I have tried to explain in the previous sections. Sounds, organized in culturally influenced ways, are "music" when they bring meanings into existence that are available in no other way.

Parallel to my explanation (in Chapter 4) of "when" creativity exists, it is useful to think of the question "When" is music? When do conditions exist that would cause the result to be described as music? A reasonable answer is that when sounds have been organized in some situated context to create meanings inhering within them (and including other meanings in many instances), those sounds are usually regarded to be music.[20]

To summarize: *Music can be described as sounds organized to create meanings inherent within the ways and means the sounds are organized, including all manner of additional meanings as they influence and are encompassed within that inherence.* To simplify even further: *Music can be described as sounds organized to be inherently meaningful.*

Extrapolating from that description, from the particular to the general: *The arts can be described as all the ways and means people have contrived to organize materials to produce meanings inherent within the materials and their organization.*

The visual arts use materials visually amenable to such organizations. Painting, drawing, ceramics, photography, sculpture, architecture, jewelry, and on and on with all the various ways visual arts are created, each uses characteristic materials, and organizes them in endless ways, capturing, in those organizations and their material, meanings available only in those ways. All the other arts—dance, theater, literature and poetry, various combinations and emerging technology-enabled forms—do the same with their own characteristic materials, ways to organize them, ways to include a great variety of human issues and concerns within them (perhaps *all* human issues and concerns), to add their particular meanings as those particular materials and organizations are characteristically able to do. Each art, and each specific instance of each art, is its own window onto potential meanings. That is why we have so many different arts and endless potentials of instances within (and across) them. The capacity for artistic/aesthetic meaning-making is inexhaustible, both in the human need for it and in the humanly invented ways and means to fulfill that need.

Notice that in this description of music, and of art, nothing has been said about how good the process or product must be to qualify as being music, or art. The work (noun and verb) can be good, bad, or mediocre—it is still music, or art. Music is a kind of thing, just as, say, food is a kind of thing. Food can be good, bad, or mediocre according to the criteria being applied to it. The same is true of music, and of art. Applying relevant criteria in making judgments of the quality of music making, and of the music being made, is an essential obligation of music educators, and it is also essential that their students, at every age, be clear as to why and how such judgments are being made. (I will expand on this point in my discussion of Content Standard Seven in chapters 8 and 9.)

The critical point to be made here is that when young people are engaged in organizing sounds in meaningful ways, whether by composing, performing, improvising, arranging, or whatever, they are *being musicians* and *creating music.* And when they are responding as listeners, they are *being musical* and *experiencing musically.* They may be doing these things poorly or brilliantly (taken as a whole, we can count on them falling on a normal curve). But wherever they are on that curve they are, to

---

[20]For an influential discussion of the "when" idea, see "When Is Art?" in Nelson Goodman, *Ways of Worldmaking* (Indianapolis: Hackett, 1978), and the commentary by Jean-Pierre Cometti, "Activating Art," *The Journal of Aesthetics and Art Criticism,* 58, no. 3 (Summer 2000), 237–43.

some degree, engaged with sounds organized meaningfully—with music in a genuine, authentic sense. Music, like creativity, can be and should be regarded with a small m rather than a large M, allowing it to be understood as genuinely music even when the youngest children are making or taking it. (Of course, this applies as well to all the arts.) The description of music I offer suggests that when music educators are helping their students, at any age, to pursue its characteristics, in any way, with any music, in all its settings and uses, they are dealing authentically with music and musical experiencing and therefore with musical meaning.

Using the Description to Help Explain Alternative Views

Now we have, as a tool to think with (rather than an edict to be deferred to), a three-part description of music and the arts: (1) sounds (materials), (2) organized in some invented fashion, (3) to create meanings immanent within the organization of the sounds (materials) while also assimilating any and all other meanings. We can apply the description not only to the conventionally recognized arts familiar in our own and other cultures that exemplify quite clearly how the description applies, but also to a variety of alternative views of music or art that either extend the boundaries of one or more of its three parts or attempt to do away with one or more altogether. To do this thoroughly and inclusively would require another book or several, however, so my discussion here will be only illustrative of some of these views. (In the next chapter the description is applied in a discussion of world musics in general and several tribal musics in particular.)

I mentioned John Cage as one person who attempted to open up, or to suggest the possible abandonment of, the widely accepted concept of music my description articulates. There is an important literature on Cage, too extensive to be dealt with here in any way appropriate to its seriousness and complexity.[21] But a few salient points can be made, to clarify how my description helps us think about deviations from standard expectations of what music (art) is and how it works.

Of the three components of my description of music, Cage retained, I believe, the first and the third. He continued to use sounds as his materials, although he employed, as his composing career developed, a great many far beyond those traditionally produced by the voice and conventional musical instruments, using radios, electronic and acoustic sound makers of great variety and imagination, traditional instruments altered to produce sounds never before envisioned for them (prepared piano and so forth), recorded sounds from the natural and manufactured environment, and on and on. In doing this Cage dramatically extended our notion of what

---

[21]See, for example, Marjorie Perloff and Charles Junkerman, eds., *John Cage: Composed in America* (Chicago: University of Chicago Press, 1996); Joan Retallack and John Cage, *Musicage: John Cage Muses on Words, Art, Music* (Hanover, NH: Wesleyan University Press, 1996); David Revill, *The Roaring Silence: John Cage: A Life* (New York: Arcade Publishers, 1992); Christopher Shultis, *Silencing the Sounded Self: John Cage and the American Experimental Tradition* (Boston: Northeastern University Press, 1998); Richard Kostelanetz, ed., *Writings About John Cage* (Ann Arbor: University of Michigan Press, 1993); and James Pritchett, *The Music of John Cage* (Cambridge and New York: Cambridge University Press, 1998).

"proper" sounds of music could be, now further extended by all the possibilities of computerized sound making. His contribution here was not to abandon sounds but to enlarge our conception of the sounds that can be properly employed to create musical meanings.

He did intend, I believe, for the sounds he arranged for us to hear to be meaningful—to engross us, to challenge us, to take us in directions of significant undergoings the sounds made available (the third aspect.) He wanted very much for respondents to be more participatory in the making of their own meaning from sounds than he believed traditional music allowed them to be: he wanted listeners to more "do" than "be done to," to be more a creator of the experience than a recipient. In this he also extended an existing and accepted concept of musical experience rather than abandoning it.

The second aspect of my description is the one Cage most fully challenged, at least during the times he concentrated on issues relating to the composer's role (or non-role.) He tried, in perhaps as many imaginative ways as any individual in history, to question or alter the notion that the musician (composer, performer, or improviser) was responsible for making all the substantive decisions about how to organize sounds, a responsibility we have long assumed musicians are properly supposed to fulfill.

How could he decrease or even relinquish the musician's prerogative of organizing sounds to be meaningful, as my second condition stipulates? Cage struggled mightily with this conundrum. His piece *4'33"*, with which teacher Jackson eagerly awaited shocking her students, was one such attempt. If he could arrange for an audience to expect to hear meaningful sounds organized by a composer and a performer, as would be assumed to occur when a musician sits down at a piano, but then confound that expectation by the performer's filling the stipulated time without ever playing on the keyboard, the audience, primed to listen, would hear instead all the sounds naturally occurring in a recital hall—coughing, rustlings, furnace or air conditioner humming, sounds from outside, creaking of floor boards, *whatever*. The composer and the performer would be *removed* from the three-part equation, giving ownership of meaningful, organized sound not to musicians but to the unplanned, random, indeterminate sound-world we naturally inhabit. Music can consist of any sounds, organized randomly as well as purposefully, Cage surmised as one important aspect of his creative thinking, so why not let random sounds be included as musical meaning? He experimented for many years with ways to arrange for randomization to determine the organization of sounds, using chance methods of a variety of sorts to influence the way the sounds would occur, confronting listeners with "music" in which the composer is at least to some degree bypassed, where sounds happen in ways reflecting the indeterminacy of our existence, a condition he believed is as meaningful, and as "creative," as determinacy.

Notice the oxymoron in Cage's quest. Can there be organized randomness? Cage had to work very hard to get randomization to occur, using as many clever devices as he could dream up or borrow, such as the *I Ching*, or *Book of Changes*, an ancient Chinese book in which various messages could be called up by random casting of sticks (traditionally yarrow stalks) or coins. Yes, much of our world seems random (although "chaos theory" is studying the structure, or dynamics, of seemingly chaotic systems).[22] But to "harness" randomness by making an event out of it, an event using sounds (often along with a variety of visuals) intended to be experienced as meaningful, requires all sorts of decisions to be made about how to organize to do so. Cage made such decisions—many of them—for each event: how many performers, what they would do to achieve randomness, whether to use traditional instruments or appropriated sound/noise makers, what these were to be, how many radios to record and then how to mix the sounds together and for how long, in the attempt to arrange an event that would not seem arranged—randomness.

Are the products of Cage's attempts, the sound-events he arranged and for which he set up the parameters, to be construed as "music"? In one sense it would be easy to say yes, if we are willing to include as "organization" the attempt to organize, or arrange for, randomness. Many composers in recent times, in fact, have incorporated random (or indeterminate) events as one aspect of their compositions, stipulating when and how they should occur. Randomization, or indeterminacy, in the sense Cage meant it, has become another expressive, meaningful device in the repertoire of musical meaning-making mechanisms. Perhaps, then, instead of violating aspect two of my three-part description, Cage has, as with aspects one and three, extended it in what has turned out to be a fruitful direction now employed as another expressive opportunity in creating music. Perhaps Cage's revolutionist program has defeated itself, having become assimilated as one more way to make meaning in the now expanded, culturally condoned inventory of musical gestures.

But if one chooses to apply the second condition—organization—in a more traditional way, one might decide that what Cage devised is not music, because the very concept of music requires particular, sanctioned ways to organize its sounds, and any other ways, such as randomization, are simply not to be accepted. Or, more generally, one might argue that a deviation from any of the three aspects of the description that was so divergent that it did not, or could not, become assimilated (as perhaps Cage's did become) would then disqualify that divergence from being regarded as music.

Another development in art that dissents from or radically expands upon the commonly accepted description is "conceptual art" (also sometimes called "idea art," or "information art"), a movement stemming from Surreal and Dada artists (such as Salvador Dali and Marcel Duchamp) in the first half of the twentieth century, who questioned existing beliefs about craft, beauty, inherence, and so on, as being defining or at least important qualities of art. Conceptual art, identified as such since the mid-1960s, has been most widely practiced in the visual arts although it has been influential in all the others.[23] (Cage's music, at least in some periods of his work, can be regarded as an instance of conceptual music, being based on an idea—that

---

[22]For an influential explanation, see James Gleick, *Chaos Theory: Making a New Science* (New York: Viking, 1987).

[23]For background on this movement, see Roberta Smith, "Conceptual Art," in *Concepts of Modern Art: From Fauvism to Postmodernism,* ed. Nikos Stangos (New York: Thomas and Hudson, 1994), 256–70, and Tony Godfrey, *Conceptual Art* (London: Phaidon, 1998).

everyday sounds and events, in their randomness, are inherently meaningful and qualified to be regarded as "musical"). In conceptual art the first aspect of my description—the use of material—is either abandoned (in at least some instances) in favor of a verbally articulated and communicated idea or even an idea only in the mind of an "artist," or, if not abandoned, at least considered insignificant as compared with the concept (or idea, or information) being expressed, the concept being paramount. Indeed, an attempt to overthrow the historical dependence of art on its materials, liberating art to present messages directly, was an important factor in the development of this movement.

The second aspect, organizing materials in some personally imagined way, is, curiously, still operative in conceptual art, because the idea to be articulated, even if entirely a verbal language concept, requires some formulation to exist at all. In fact, many formulations by conceptual artists use materials of a variety of sorts, including traditional ones, as the medium through which their idea is presented.

The third component, the use of the materials to create meanings inherent within the materials and their organization, is (seemingly) relinquished in favor of an idea or a concept or a message *referred to,* or *communicated* (as language does). The *inherence* is no longer the point—the *referent* is. The long-accepted practice in the arts of using references of all sorts, but taking them in directions only organized materials can do, was turned on its head, art becoming direct, communicated commentary, even philosophy, and artists becoming indistinguishable from political/social/philosophical/critical commentators.

Some conceptual artists wanted to remove any remnant of inherent meaning from their work. For example, a piece by Erika Rothenberg, in Chicago's Museum of Contemporary Art, looks exactly like a notice case, made of an aluminum frame with black felt inside and a Plexiglas cover, such as one sees in churches, announcing with white plastic letters attached to the felt, various events, or the hymns to be sung for that service, and so forth. In fact, she may very well have purchased the case from the manufacturer. The "artist" presents the following notice:

EVENINGS AT 7 IN THE PARISH HALL	
MONDAY	ALCOHOLICS ANONYMOUS
TUESDAY	ABUSED SPOUSES
WEDNESDAY	EATING DISORDERS
THURSDAY	SAY NO TO DRUGS
FRIDAY	TEEN SUICIDE WATCH
SATURDAY	SOUP KITCHEN
SUNDAY SERMON 9 AM "AMERICA'S JOYOUS FUTURE"	

This is a clever joke, calling forth a chuckle in appreciation of its ironic social commentary. It surely raises questions as to whether the decisions Rothenberg made were in any way what has been expected from visual artists, who have for many centuries taken a commentary such as this and made something visually compelling, engaging, and meaningful of it as visual artistry has been assumed to exist to do. In fact, she could easily have ordered her "work" ready-made, the letters already attached, from the manufacturer, her "idea" being her only contribution. Does this make her an "artist," and the notice board a "work of art"? Clearly the Museum of Contemporary Art thought it does, and was willing to purchase and display it as such.

Other conceptual works need not be displayed in museums. For example, Michael Mandiberg put all his possessions on sale on his Website, including updates to reflect new items he bought. The concept is that at some point when everything is sold, the "artist" will have sold his identity and can start another one from scratch. In another instance, Daniel Spoerri had dinner parties, left the table as it was when his guests left, glued and varnished everything on it (food included), and offered the results for sale as paintings.

Robert Barry's *Telepathic Piece* consisted entirely of his statement that "during the exhibition I will try to communicate telepathically a work of art, the nature of which is a series of thoughts that are not applicable to language or image." Walter de Maria's piece *Vertical Earth Kilometer* consisted of a one-kilometer brass rod, sunk into the ground (in Kassel, Germany) so that only its end, a 2-inch disk, is visible. On and on go the examples, probably many thousands having been "created" since the movement began. In each example we are faced with conundrums about what, if anything, constitutes "material," what constitutes "organization," and for what purpose any of it is being done.

Is any or all of this "art"? Perhaps, as artist Donald Judd remarked, "If someone says it's art, it's art."[24] As with the John Cage example, I have no interest in stipulating the "correct" answer to the question of whether conceptual art should be called "art." I am indeed very much interested in thinking about the question, and the difficult, puzzling, fascinating issues it raises, as are many other people involved in the arts. For example, in a program I attended on "Then and Now: Contemporary Conceptual Art," October 7, 2000, at the Chicago Museum of Contemporary Art, the panel (Byron Kim, artist, Andrea Miller-Keller, Curator of Contemporary Art at the Wadsworth Atheneum, and John Weber, Curator of Education and Public Programs at the San Francisco Museum of Modern Art) agreed that this direction in art is no longer in the vanguard, having become, because of its tendency to be academic, arid, even bankrupt, one more tool in the arsenal that artists can employ rather than an end in and of itself, as some artists, especially early in the movement, attempted to make it. Without the engagement of the artist, they agreed (meaning the attempt to make meaning through organizing materials in ways artistic decisions uniquely do), art becomes "flat," artists as strictly social commentators leaving them no function or

---

[24]This quotation, and the two previous examples, are from Smith, "Conceptual Art," note 23.

contribution better made by nonartist experts on social-political issues. "Conceptual art backed itself into a corner," said one panelist, "and could not find a way out of it." The furthest reaches of that corner had been articulated by artist Lawrence Weiner, who is said to have remarked that "a work need not be built," meaning that the idea an artist has in his head is sufficient to make it a "work of art."[25]

All panelists emphasized that the expanded potentials of using societal issues in art, as conceptual art contributed, actually enriched possibilities for art to be more inherently meaningful by opening up new aspects of human interest for artists to explore, search within, and incorporate in their works. I was struck with how much this paralleled the attempts by Cage to expand the second aspect of my description (organization), this time in regard to the first and third aspects (materials and inherent meanings), and how interests of conceptual art had become fruitfully assimilated within an expanded understanding of what music, or visual art, could be. This accommodation of meaningful form with explicit concept was clearly expressed in an interview with conceptual artist Matthew Ritchie, in which he said, "The challenge is finding the right balance between form and content. I'm trying to say you can have both, you can have something that's both beautiful and [conceptually] meaningful—and that the meaning enhances the beauty and the beauty enhances the meaning."[26]

I am not presuming that this accommodation—this consensus that the three aspects of art I propose can be expanded to encompass even radical alterations—is inevitable with all description-altering possibilities. That would be unrealistic. But I nevertheless retain an orientation to and a reliance on these three dimensions of music and the arts as a useful mechanism for sorting out issues we are presented with by important developments and deviations in the arts. I strongly recommend that, at appropriate times in music education (and education in any of the arts), this description, or others that thoughtful people might devise, be brought to the attention of students as they struggle, as we professionals do, with the very difficult but endlessly stimulating dilemmas raised by the arts. Music educators willing to tackle (and enjoy) the puzzles music and the arts continually present to our understanding, and to engage their students in doing so, are openers of doors to deeper insights into the nature of music and the arts and therefore to deeper meanings—and pleasures—they afford. My description, and alternatives others devise, can be useful instruments to aid in that adventure.

---

[25]This idea received extensive treatment in the writings of aesthetician Benedetto Croce (1866–1952). See, for an overview, Beardsley, *Aesthetics,* note 5, 318–24.

[26]Jeffrey Kastner, "An Adventurer's Map to a World of Information," *New York Times,* October 15, 2000, Art/Architecture, p. 37. An explanation of conceptual art as being present within previous approaches to art, and as now an additional dimension of art rather than a challenge to or a replacement of traditional art, is given by Roger Seamon, "The Conceptual Dimension in Art," *The Journal of Aesthetics and Art Criticism,* 59, no. 2 (Spring 2001), 138–51. For an extended, deeply thoughtful analysis of the relation of musical meaning to content, or reference, see Lydia Goehr, "Political Music and the Politics of Music," *The Journal of Aesthetics and Art Criticism,* 52, no.1 (Winter 1994), 99–112.

TEACHING FOR MUSICAL MEANING

> The query that prompted [this book's] reflections concerned the specialness of musical artworks, in particular our attention to the "feeling" ineffability in our knowledge of them. My suggestion was that music's grammatical structure creates the expectation of a semantics—something effable. What we get instead are the ineffable musical feelings of tonicity, beat strength, tension, resolution, stability, and so forth, the experience of which constitutes our conscious knowledge or understanding of the music. On the picture I am tendering, then, the yield of grammatical processing in language and music alike is *knowledge* or *understanding*—a.k.a. the grasp of *meaning;* it's just that in the musical case the knowledge is ineffable: it is sensory-perceptual or felt in nature and hence not communicable by language *ab initio* [from the beginning.][27] (Emphases in original)

Philosopher of mind Diana Raffman, in this passage from her "Language, Music, and Mind," takes us back to square one in this chapter's exploration of what and how music "means." Music "offers an alternative reality and an alternative way of being," Sparshott claimed—and all of us who have lived a life with music know exactly what he has in mind: that there is a "specialness" about music, as Raffman (and Dissanayake) note, that this specialness is related to the feelings we have of it, and we can't say, except in the crude language of emotion-category words, what the feelings are and what they mean to us. "Anything we may say of [music] in another language is pitifully inadequate to express what music expresses," Dufrenne asserted, "but this ineffable meaning . . . is what the musical object says." And we also know just what he means; that, as Raffman puts it, we hear and feel the musical gestures, we are conscious of them, we "know" and "understand" them, we "grasp their meaning," but we can't say what that meaning is because it is "sensory-perceptual or felt in nature and hence not communicable by language." Using my description, the sounds of music, organized to be meaningful, are indeed meaningful to people in all cultures, but meaningful in a way language is inadequate to express. We seem to have gotten closer to the brink of the mystery we are faced with, and to understand more clearly why it is a mystery. But, of course, that does not get us over the brink to its heart: only music itself can do that.

Music educators, in the "music" aspect of that term, help their students experience the meaning of music by immersing them directly and personally in its meanings—the felt sounds they are helped to experience. The music they make and respond to yields its mysteries—its immediately experienced ways to know—in the only ways that can happen: by direct musical experience within and how. So by taking our students into musical sounds, in all the ways our culture provides for, we allow music to speak its mystery.

---

[27]Diana Raffman, *Language, Music, and Mind* (Cambridge, MA: Bradford, 1993), 60–61. An excellent discussion of language-think and its role in knowing, including knowing in the realm of the arts, is Shari Tishman and David Perkins, "The Language of Thinking," *Phi Delta Kappan,* January 1997, 368–74.

The "education" part of our title is what raises the tough issues. People immerse themselves in the meanings of music constantly, entirely aside from our interventions, and our culture provides them with ample—we might say magnificent—opportunities to do so. We make the argument that schools should *also* do so. (I use the word "schools" here to refer to all the institutions devoted to education as their chief reason for existence, including community centers, private studios, and so forth.) But surely that implies that music education, in the professionally organized ways that schools are responsible for providing it, needs to do something in addition to what individuals and their culture are provided with outside formal education settings. If all music education did was to provide the same experiences so readily available and so widely taken advantage of outside the schools, there would be little reason for us to exist as a subject in the schools. To educate in the sense represented by schooling is to structure the enterprise—to organize it, systematize it, sequence it, assess it, research it, prepare professionally for it, do all the things required for professionalizing the act of educating.

All those doings surround and influence musical experience. They do not constitute musical experience. All those doings require language-think in addition to sound-think. Little if anything we do in teaching for musical meaning can be free of the need for what language—only language—can do. We are caught, as educators, in the paradox of language-think as necessary for more effective music-think. We can, and should, of course, use as many intramusical ways as we can to demonstrate, model, illustrate, and so forth. But sooner or later (mostly sooner) language will be needed as an essential tool. There is no escape from it.

Music in educational settings, therefore, is obligated, with the help of language, to do things with and about music beyond what individuals can do on their own in their culture outside such settings. In the context of the subject of this chapter—musical meaning and its cultivation—three obligations summarize our mission.

1. Music education should offer artistic creating opportunities *including but going beyond* those readily available in the culture. Each such opportunity provides its particular way to bring musical meaning into existence. Improvement in creating—in musicianship—is a basic goal of music education.
2. Music education should offer responding opportunities *including but going beyond* what the culture typically provides. In as many ways as can be devised, refinement in ability to gain musical meanings as responding particularly provides them is a primary aim of music education.
3. The music experienced in both musicianship and listenership opportunities should *include but go beyond* the generally available musics students are involved with in their culture(s). Each particular music provides its characteristic musical meanings. Expansion of students' repertoire of musical meanings is a foundational obligation of music education.

The Necessity of Knowing About and Knowing Why

Improving, refining, and expanding the musical meanings available to students through responding to and creating a wider variety of musics than are likely to be experienced without us, requires language to be used as a means to the enhancement of the quality of musical experience itself. The paradox that language needs to be used as a way to gain what is not available from language leads us to clarify why and how this is so. Several key ideas can help us accomplish this sufficiently for more effective music teaching.

Since the time of the ancient Greek philosophers, two dimensions of knowledge have been recognized to exist. One, identified by Plato as "episteme," focuses on knowledge as being capable of expression by propositions such as verbal languages (and numbers) present. This kind of knowledge, as I have explained, is always general. It applies to broad ranges of phenomena, and the power of such knowledge is its wide applicability as in theories and principles.

Another kind of knowledge focuses on the particular rather than the general. Aristotle included as knowledge the dimension of "practical wisdom," or "phronesis," grounded in an understanding of specific, concrete human experiences in all their complexity, ambiguity, and uncertainty. This kind of knowledge-as-wisdom is not dominantly abstract, theoretical, and general, but must be flexible, subtle, and adaptable, directed to fine details and extremely sensitive to the slightest gradations of similarities and differences in experience. This kind of knowledge is essentially *perceptual* instead of *conceptual*. Such perceptual knowledge, including sensation and feeling, Aristotle called "aesthesis," as related to the word "aesthetic."[28]

Teaching music immerses students in the realm of perceptual/sensory/affective knowing—aesthesis, or, in our case, musical artistic/aesthetic experiencing. Knowing this way is knowing music by perceiving and discriminating its *relevant details* above and beyond any generality. This kind of knowing, of *teaching*, aims toward the fullest possible development of an individual's capacity to experience the meaningful sounds of music with discrimination, sensuosity, and affective engagement. Effective music teaching brings students and sounds together in a mind-body-feeling communion with musical meaning.

What is the role of language in accomplishing this? First, musical meaning is always historically and contextually grounded. Every instance of music exists situationally and reflects its setting in its meanings. Second, every instance of music has within it a great number of possible interrelations among its sounds, as determined by history, culture, the individual(s) involved in its creation, associated ideas, references, and so forth. Musical meaning is always complex. Third, music's history, cultural setting, structure and organization of sounds, and incorporated material,

---

[28]For a more extended treatment of this material, see my "Episteme, Phronesis, and the Role of Verbal Language in 'Knowing Within' Music," *Philosophy of Music Education Review*, 5, no. 2 (Fall 1997), 101–7.

is capable of being delineated by language. The language we use to teach music is partly technical (chord, interval, major, minor, chromatic, adagio, sonata, raga, gagaku). It is also partly vernacular (introduction, pause, fast, slow, upward, downward, loud, soft, ending, repeat). It is, in addition, descriptive and informative in a great variety of ways—popular songs in Western culture often are structured in *aaba* form; the claves establish the rhythmic impulse in much Latin music; clarinets come in a variety of sizes; dance often accompanies music in African cultures; waltzes are in triple meter.

For the contexts of music, the structure of music, information about music, language is an indispensable tool. Its primary function in all such matters is to *disclose,* "to cause to appear; allow to be seen; lay open to view." Much of what we do when we teach music is to disclose by causing it to be clearer, allowing it to be more accurately created and heard, laying it open to the mind and the ear and the feelings. Doing so, as appropriate for each particular student, at the particular stage of her development, in the particular musical activity being pursued, for particular objectives in mind, constitutes a major portion of what music educators do and how we use language.

All such use of language (knowing about) can be academic when unconnected to musical meaning—the immediacy of knowing within and how. When it supports, clarifies, reveals, informs the experience of the musical sounds—when it discloses their richness of potential meanings—it is a necessary component of effective music education.

But what about the role of language in matters not specifically related to music being composed, performed, improvised, listened to? In knowing about, language clarifies (discloses) sounds in ways that affect the way they are created and heard. Can language be useful in music education even if it does not specifically relate to particular instances of music with which students are engaged?

Many knowings related to music, though not specific to disclosure about pieces and their contexts, about performing, about composing, and so on, nevertheless influence the musical experience students have when they encounter music and therefore the meanings they gain from such encounters. For example, knowing that the meanings one has in musical experience cannot be expressed adequately with words can powerfully influence how one approaches and what one seeks from any musical involvement. Many people naturally assume that some sort of "message," some meaning able to be expressed accurately by words, lurks within every piece of music (and every painting, every poem, every sculpture, every drama). If they can't figure out what that message might be, they figure they just don't "get it." Probably *other* people "get it," but they don't, and it would be too embarrassing to say anything to betray that they don't.

This misunderstanding may be more prevalent in regard to, say, painting and poetry than to music, because paintings and poems seem much more "message" prone than music. I have often heard people ask "What does this painting *mean*?"

and "What is this poet trying to *say*?" indicating that they are not able to locate an explicit, communicable idea. I have not as often heard the same sort of question directed to music (although I certainly have), perhaps because music is more easily accepted to just "be what it is." The point of encountering art, I am arguing, is not to produce a verbal message (or "interpretation"). If there does seem to be a message of that sort, it acts as an invitation to look or read or hear further until the message is "made art out of" and therefore something no longer able to be expressed by language.

That understanding can be a great relief for people. It relieves them of wondering if they are able to "get it," as if "it" were an idea, or an emotion, or information of some sort that could then be communicated by words to someone else. "What Robert Frost is *saying* in 'Stopping by Woods on a Snowy Evening' is that life . . . (whatever)." "Ah, now I get it. Thank you." What has been "gotten" is not the ineffable meanings poetry creates out of ideas, descriptions, comments, and so forth. Poets always incorporate such material as one element in meanings no longer able to be "said." Poetry uses propositions ("Whose woods these are I think I know") but is itself "superpropositional"—above and beyond propositions.

Music is, clearly, superpropositional, even when, as in vocal music, propositions are incorporated. Or a visual image ("Daybreak Express"). Or an emotion ("Valse Triste"). Or a story (*Til Eulenspiegel's Merry Pranks*). Or a gender attitude, or a political stance, or an affirmation that "We shall overcome." All these materials influence the experience, coloring and shaping it in important ways. Music can certainly enhance a message, intensify it, enrich it. But it also always adds something *beyond* it, something music is needed to do because nothing else can do it. That "something" is ineffable.

Matters such as this, consisting of language expressions about the nature of music, its values, its cultural roles, its relation, by similarity and difference, to other aspects of life, have powerful effects on how people understand and therefore experience music. The function of language in this dimension is to *explain*. This is the function of language I have called knowing why. Although knowing why is not itself perception-focused in the strict sense, it nevertheless differentiates what is perceived and how perception occurs. That is, *nonperceptual explanations have direct effects on perceptual structuring—on musical experiencing.*

Knowing why is probably the most neglected aspect of music education, both in preparing teachers to teach for it and, as a result, in the actual teaching of music in educational settings. Its inclusion in the National Content Standards—in items (7) evaluating music, (8) understanding relationships between music, the other arts, and other disciplines, and (9) understanding music in relation to history and culture—represents a major step forward in American music education history. It remains to be seen whether the profession will be able to take that step effectively.

RIFF 8: Layers of Meaning in a Life of Music

My life of music began at age twelve, when I started clarinet lessons. A new world opened to me, a world both physical (fingers, breath, tongue, lips, reeds, pads, cork grease, wood and metal, the comfortable weight of the clarinet in its case) and mental (notes, rhythms, intonation, tone, sharps and flats, etudes, etudes, etudes). Music meant clarinet. My heroes were clarinetists. I ate, breathed, slept clarinet. I loved music. That is, playing the clarinet.

Then the tenor saxophone. Sensual. Wild. A link to a whole new way to think and feel musically. Playing Stan Kenton charts, a five-piece sax section swinging in exquisitely calibrated nuance, music becoming something notes on paper couldn't encompass, a musical unity with others overwhelming in power. I didn't know music could mean this directly, beyond the politeness of my clarinet experience.

Now the oboe. Obsession with details of body and mind. Reed making: a world of skilled precision. Breath support, throat, pitch, subtlety of expressive shading pushing me to the edge of my capacity. "What do you play? The oboe? Oh, my." A very special musician. In demand. Paid. I've "arrived" as a professional, and music takes on a whole new way to mean. I supply music. I'm paid to do so. I had better produce.

I sit in the pit of the musical *Pajama Game,* hired, along with several others, to augment the travelling orchestra for a ten-day run in Richmond, Virginia. Arrayed around me are my tenor sax, alto sax, clarinet, oboe, and English horn. I start out on tenor, have two measures to switch to oboe. I barely make it. When I start playing I'm about a third flat—still set for tenor. Omigod. I learn fast. I set my mind for the next instrument during the few seconds of the next switch. That's better. That works. After the gig I write an article for *The Instrumentalist Magazine,* "Doubling on Woodwinds: Mind Over Matter." They publish it and pay me $50. I can't decide which tickles me more—being paid to play or to write. Both allow me to share what music means to me.

Teaching. Middle-school kids in a lab school. College students as woodwind instructor, band director, conducting, instrumental methods, student teaching supervision, sight singing and dictation, woodwind chamber literature, percussion class, music appreciation. Tell me what to teach: I'll teach it. I experience music as I always intended, as someone who is a teacher. Everything I know about music, everything I learn about music, everything I experience of music, is colored by my self-identification: this is what I *teach.* Music means the way teaching it means. I'm where I'm supposed to be.

I'm introduced to philosophy. Thinking *about* music and music education. A new way for music to have meaning. I'm enthralled. It hits me where I live, shifting my musical experience into another gear. Teaching philosophy is exhilarating, writing about it equally so. Now, when I experience music as a performer, teacher, conductor, I am also a thinker. What does it all mean? Why do we care? Why do we insist it be an integral part of education? "Musical meaning" takes on new meaning.

The first rehearsal of the newly formed Faculty Symphony Orchestra at the University of Illinois. I have just joined the faculty, to teach music education, and am invited to play second oboe to the oboe teacher. As we rehearse I feel a sharp pain in my left chest. It gets progressively worse. I'm short of breath, the pain travelling down my arm, up my neck. When I get home I call the hospital and describe my symptoms. "Get here now," they say.

No, it's not the suspected heart attack. My lung has collapsed. They treat it and get it back to normal but tell me not to play, at least for a while. A couple of months later, while eating lunch, it collapses again. Treatment restores it a second time. But now I'm told that playing will be very hazardous. "Do you *have* to play?" the surgeon asks? I consult with six more chest specialists in Chicago. Same story. "Well, you can play, I guess, but if I were you. . . ."

My instruments are put away, later sold. I read about "phantom limb syndrome," in which people who have lost an arm or a leg continue to feel that it's there; it's felt, it's just not able to be seen. For the rest of my life I am to suffer from "phantom performer syndrome." I still experience music, at one important level, as a performer, in all the ways performers are influenced to experience music. In a way, I'm still a performer. It's there, it's felt, it's just not able to be heard.

Sometimes, just sometimes, I am able to break through all the many ways my life in music has influenced what it means to me, and make contact with it underneath my special involvements, directly, pristinely, chastely. At such times I feel cleansed by music, washed to simplicity by its complex satisfactions. Then music speaks directly to my soul, to the me beyond my musical life. Those, too, are precious meanings. Perhaps the most precious of all.

FINALLY, WHAT MUSIC MEANS

All the theorizing in the world cannot, by itself, yield musical meaning. Such meaning occurs within each individual who experiences music, of any sort, encountered in any way. Both the music and the person engaged with it contribute to the meaning. *What music means, then, is everything a person experiences when involved with it.*[29]

Music education exists to nurture people's potential to gain deeper, broader, more significant meanings from musical involvements, by helping them know within and how, assisted by knowing about and why. Sounds simple. Few undertakings in education are as complex.

---

[29]Compare Thomas Clifton's comment "Music is what I am when I experience it." *Music As Heard* (New Haven: Yale University Press, 1983), 297.

ETUDES

1. Have you had the experience of wondering whether you were getting the "correct meaning" in a piece of music, a painting, a poem, a movie? What did you do to reach a resolution? Did you ever reach a point where you were convinced you "got it" correctly? What did you do (or what would you do) if someone else got a different "meaning"?

2. Suppose a piece of music you are teaching (whether in a performance setting, a general music setting, a private lesson, a composition lab, or any other context you choose) has in it an important message, or referent—a statement about injustice, or prejudice, or love, or whatever. Would you want to include that message as part of what you taught? All of what you taught? Would you prefer to ignore it? Do you feel, because of your background and education to be a music teacher that you are deeply qualified to discuss and teach about messages of that sort? What *do* you feel most professionally qualified to teach about music? Are you satisfied with the breadth of your qualifications?

3. If you are comfortable with the idea that music adds its special meaning to experience as only music can do, would you also argue that musical experience can contribute to meaningful experiences in other subjects, each of which has its own way to "know"? If yes, try to explain exactly how musical meaning, including its inherent and delineated dimensions, can influence learnings in, say, science, or government, or history, or a foreign language. What are the difficulties in attempting to do this with music? Any benefits?

4. Try giving your own description, or definition, of music, or the arts, incorporating the features you think are most important. Compare your description with others'. Which seems to best capture, elegantly yet powerfully, the characteristics that make music (or art) the unique phenomenon it is? (If it is better than mine, please send it to me right away!)

   Try asking a variety of people, of different ages, to define (or describe) music or art. Compare the solutions you gather with those others have gathered. What do these definitions reveal about how different people understand music (or art)?

5. Think of examples of music or art that you have found puzzling—that make you wonder whether they actually are music or art. Try applying my three-part description, locating in which aspect, or aspects, the works seem to deviate from what one might expect. There is no need to reach a definitive conclusion about the works in question. But perhaps what makes them puzzling will have been clarified.

   If you have devised your own description (etude 4) do the same using it as your guide toward clarity. Does it help make sense of how and why the puzzling works challenge expectations? If it does prove useful in that way, it may be an effective description.

   Can you envision doing this exercise with students in schools, at different grade levels? Do you think it would be an effective way to help them understand music (art) more intelligently? Do you think many students, or at least some, would find it a stimulating learning experience?

6. Try telling the story of the layers or kinds of musical meaning your own life history has brought to you, as I did in Riff 8. Share your story with others. This can be done as well with students in schools (and others). Getting to know such stories is a powerful way to confront all the many ways music "means" to people. And to teach people about musical meaning. What do you think are the earliest ages at which students might be able to do this storytelling about what music means to them? If you can, try asking students at younger and younger ages to do this. You are likely to find their stories fascinating and revealing as to how music has affected their lives.

7. Imagine a scenario in which you are teaching a music class or group. First, teach in a way that *severely overemphasizes* your use of language to disclose and explain. What effects are likely to occur on your students' learning experience?

Then teach the same scenario in a way that *severely underemphasizes* your use of language to disclose and explain. What might this cause? Now, try to get it right!

6

The Contextual Dimension
of Musical Experience

MAIN THEMES

- The cultural/historical contexts of music are a necessary but not sufficient dimension of its nature.

- Human experience includes universal, contextual, and individual levels. Musical experience does as well. All three levels need to be kept in balance, both in life and in music.

- Cultural context is a significant factor in forming human consciousness. Music, and the arts, as cultural constructions, contribute significantly to this process.

- Robert Plant Armstrong's theory raises a fundamental question: Is it possible to understand music of a culture different from one's own? The contextualist and universalist positions (the "no" and "yes" answers) are presented in debate format, and a synergistic resolution is recommended.

- In applications to teaching, a music largely "foreign" to American music education—popular music—is claimed to be a literature our profession needs to take seriously if the importance of this music in our culture is to be represented fairly.

CONTEXT IN LARGER CONTEXT

Today, in many areas of thought, not only philosophy, we are impressed by the extreme degree that most of what we encounter is culturally charged and, in that sense, meaningful. In the fifties and early sixties, attentiveness to the cultural and historical envelopment of virtually every aspect of human activity was not in the forefront of our thinking in the same way. . . . We now find it difficult to conceive of culture, history, and cultural meaning as not having bearing on almost everything we produce.[1]

---

[1]Noël Carroll, "Cage and Philosophy," *The Journal of Aesthetics and Art Criticism*, 52, no. 1 (Winter 1994), 96.

[N]*o* aspect of music is capable of being understood independently of the wider gamut of social and cultural processes . . . yet, *because* of this, it is possible that there are *aspects* of social and cultural processes which are revealed *uniquely* through their musical articulation. The *necessity* of referring to the wider gamut of social and cultural processes in order to explain "the musical" does not in other words amount to a *sufficiency*. There are aspects of affect and meaning *in culture* that can only be accessed through an understanding of the specific qualities of the signifying practices of music as a cultural form: that is, its sounds. . . . A viable understanding of culture requires an understanding of its articulation through music just as much as a viable understanding of music requires an understanding of its place in culture.[2] (Emphases in original)

When serious philosophy of music education (in the contemporary sense) got going back in the late 1950s and early 1960s, some (but not much) attention was paid to matters of music's cultural contexts (including those contexts at various times in history). As philosopher Noël Carroll points out in the first quotation, scholarship in those days did not emphasize contextual matters, having its plate full of other issues it was addressing. Music education philosophy, reflecting that stance, was caught up in attempts to explain how and why music contributes its particular meanings, how it can be and needs to be justified on that basis, how music is related to feeling in ways more sophisticated than had previously been understood, and so on. That music is necessarily enveloped in culture was not in dispute. In fact, that seemed so obvious as to be taken for granted. What has changed since then is not the belief that music, as practically everything else in human life, is grounded culturally, but that its cultural roots have bearing more widespread and more pervasive than had been explored.

Nevertheless, as music sociologist John Shepherd and theorist and popular music scholar Peter Wicke point out in the second quotation, cultural groundings, though necessary in explaining music, are not entirely sufficient. Music, in its uniqueness, contributes its own affects and meanings through its specific qualities—its meaningfully organized sounds. Music does this in all cultures, thereby contributing to making each culture what it is, just as each culture contributes to the shaping of what its music turns out to be. Neglecting the role of culture skews our full understanding of music. Neglecting the role of music in culture also throws our understanding out of balance, both about culture and about music. We achieve a more synergistic understanding when we take into account both the unique qualities of music as music, which characterize it transculturally, and the situated aspects of music, which characterize it as a culturally grounded construction. The universal and the contextual are equally implicated in a balanced view of music, and therefore both must be represented in a balanced approach to music education.

Earlier philosophical thinking in music education tended to emphasize the universal, as mentioned previously. It would be a mistake to abandon the continuing

---

[2]John Shepherd and Peter Wicke, *Music and Cultural Theory* (Maldan, MA: Blackwell, 1997), 33–34.

attempt to understand music at that level. What is needed is not a swing of the pendulum to a similarly unbalanced position emphasizing the cultural, but a recognition that the two are not in opposition, that both are necessary dimensions of the nature of music and of its significance in human experience. For humans, also, have both universal and cultural dimensions, as well as a third dimension that also needs to be acknowledged—the individuality of each human being.

In this chapter I will focus on the cultural-contextual aspect of musical experience, but within the broader purview of its relation to the universal and to the individual. There is little question that the growing attention to the cultural nature of music, with all the complex issues relating to that nature, has been a major advance toward a more complete, more persuasive explanation of how music works and why it is valuable for people. So, whereas in the previous edition of this book I included a discussion of cultural context in a section on "The Relevance of Music of Various Cultures," I now believe the contextual dimension of music and music education requires as much consideration as the dimensions treated in the previous three chapters, bringing a philosophy of music education into line with contemporary interests in the issue of how and why context is a significant factor in people's thinkings and doings.[3] But first, a few comments are needed as to why music educators are strengthened in their work and their contribution by an account that includes all three dimensions of human reality—the universal, the contextual, and the individual.

UNIVERSAL, CONTEXTUAL, AND INDIVIDUAL DIMENSIONS OF EXPERIENCE

At the universal level, the level transcending cultural differences and focusing on characteristics of music and of people held in common across the world and through history, we are reminded that music is generic to homo sapiens, as is music education. Both are panhuman constants. (I will discuss this in more detail as the chapter proceeds.) We need to be mindful of that aspect of our human condition—our deep, close kinship with all humans—if we are to achieve a world where our common humanity, recognized and cherished, allows us to share worldwide positive values, values of peace, mutual respect, mutual sympathy, openness of intercommunication, and all the other values that enhance our membership in the larger world community in which each of us must live. This is especially the case when that worldwide community has become as interlinked and interdependent as it now is. In the global culture now existing and sure to develop further in the future, the recognition that all people's needs for meaning, for significance, for sharing of experiences of feeling, are

---

[3]For an excellent account of how cultural context plays a foundational role in human cognition, and how a process of cumulative cultural evolution allowed the rapid rise of the complex cognitive capacities humans have now attained, see Michael Tomasello, *The Cultural Origins of Human Cognition* (Cambridge: Harvard University Press, 1999).

met universally through music, and are enhanced by instruction in music, adds a dimension of universality to music education that can only strengthen it politically, psychologically, and ethically. Knowing that what we do in our lives as music educators is connected to an enterprise stretching back to prehistory and extending to all corners of the earth ennobles our work, giving it a transcendent nature we should acknowledge and celebrate.

But if we overemphasize that level of our personal/professional experience, we will miss the equally powerful realization that much of the meaning of our lives, including musical meaning, stems from the particularities of our social condition—the ways we are, beyond the universal, also situated in time, in place, in an inhabited social space pervading every aspect of our lives. As precious as our membership in the universal community is the specificity of the community in which we happen to (or choose to) be a member—the distinctive, culturally defined playing out in our lives of the universal need for shared beliefs, ways to behave, ways to express ourselves, ways to organize our lives to give them order and purpose. Our culture gives us "a life"—a set of possible ways to live, to flourish, to achieve our potentials, to create meaning. Culture—the sum total of a community's ways of thinking and living—is not an option for humans. We can certainly choose the culture we prefer (within limits): we cannot choose to have no culture. That is why humans, from the inception of the species, have always had some culture or other, the expressions of it being largely a function of imagination coupled with constraining/enabling environmental conditions.

Cultures give specificity to the universal human capacity for music, and to the universal requirement for that capacity to be nurtured both for present and for succeeding generations—the universal need for music education. As varied as music can be and has been, music education has been equally varied, while at the same time all music and music education has shared universal traits. The two levels, each as valid as the other, must and do coexist.

At bottom, however, our experience must take place within our own skin, our individuality of doing and undergoing constituting our self-identity. That dimension of musical experience—what we each make it to be—must be acknowledged to be equally influential as the other two levels. Universals and contexts are, in a certain sense, constructions, or abstractions. What is "real" is the specificity of experience each of us undergoes. We recognize that others, in our particular culture and across cultures, share much of what we experience, a recognition allowing the precious gift of community. But we also recognize that our individual identity, an amalgam of biology with experience, is to some degree unique to each of us, an equally precious gift of selfhood. Different cultures emphasize or de-emphasize this dimension differently, but it is always a significant factor in musical experience and in music education. Honoring it, cultivating it, cherishing it, is the basis for a mutually respectful attitude toward all humans and toward the differences among cultures' musics and ways to educate musically.

But just as there are dangers in overemphasizing the universal, or the contextual, the individual dimension can also be too dominant. Neglecting the culture of which we are a part, and the larger world community in which our culture resides, can lead to a self-centeredness and a selfishness unhealthy both for individuals and for their culture. Enlightened self-interest is one thing, leading individuals to satisfy their own needs through fruitful contributions to and interactions with those of others. Narrow self-interest feeds on itself and diminishes the needs of others. Selfhood is precious, and in need of protection from over-encroachment from others. But we can savor our selfhood fully when we recognize that each other individual, both within our own circle of acquaintance and outside it, is also a genuine self requiring the same respect we want and need for ourselves. As with the universal and contextual dimensions of our reality, a healthy balance must be struck between individuals and the larger worlds within which they exist.

The three dimensions of human reality are, paradoxically, distinct yet compound. At one and the same time, every human being, in important respects, is like all other human beings, like some other human beings, and like no other human beings. Applying those dimensions to music, we might say that every instance of music is like all other music, like some other music, and like no other music. And for music education the paradox is the same: in certain respects all music education is like all other music education in its transcultural role of propagating music and musical experience, like some other music education in its cultural particularities as to how that role is carried out, and like no other music education in the individuality of how each human partakes of and internalizes what is being learned. In this, we as individuals, as musicians, and as music educators share fully in the common, tripartite human reality while adding our distinctive contribution to fulfilling each of its three aspects.

What are the issues particularly relating to the second dimension, the aspect of cultural context? We need to look more closely at its workings. Following that, we can return to music education and its responsibility to represent all three dimensions of music in synergistic balance, as relevant to the multimusical cultures in which most people in the world dwell.

First, a summary of what has been proposed in this book about music and its context.

MUSIC IN CONTEXT: A REVIEW

Scattered throughout the previous chapters, and here pulled together and organized, are the positions argued so far.

1. What counts as musical sounds, and as acceptable ways to compose them, perform them, improvise them, and understand and value them, are culturally based constructions rooted in the history, traditions, beliefs, self-identity, and practices of each culture.
2. Each culture defines the various musical roles expected to be played within it. In a real sense, a culture's musical life consists of the sum total of the musical roles it recognizes and provides for.

3. The choices that musicians make when creating, and that responders engage with as they internalize them, reflect the cultural influences they share, but add to and transform those influences into sounds with inherently musical meanings. Musical (inherent) meanings and culturally supplied (delineated) meanings intermingle in countless ways.

4. There is no strict line separating inherent and delineated musical experiencing but, rather, a large space allowing for a great variety of emphases on one or the other or both inseparably, depending on the people involved, the societal function of the music, the expectations particular subcultures bring to the music, and so forth. At one extreme, inherence (or "form") is supreme; at the other, delineated messages dominate. Mixtures of the two in musical experiencing range across a long continuum between the extremes, as different cultures and different individuals determine their importance.

5. In practically all cultural settings music is believed to be closely tied to the emotional dimension of experience, this being considered its characteristic sphere of influence. The success of music in capturing and displaying the depth, subtlety, and variety of feelings is widely taken to establish its valued contribution to its culture.

6. Music can reinforce cultural values and understandings but can also bring them into question and even oppose them, serving as an instrumentality for cultural self-examination and transformation. Music, therefore, contributes in important ways to both cultural stability and cultural change.

7. Every culture's music, including every subculture music within it, achieves musical meaning in its own, particular way. Each such culturally grounded meaning achievement is precious. It is unacceptable to regard any one particular music as the only "genuine" or "proper" or "important" way for music to be. Every different music shapes individual and communal experience into unique meanings it then makes available for sharing.

8. Music education exists to make experiences of musical meaning, as various cultures create them, more deeply and widely accessible, thereby contributing an essential value to each culture's and to each individual's identity and viability.

With those positions as background, we can look more deeply into how cultures affect what music can be, and how music affects what cultures can be, deeply enough to understand that interaction as affecting human consciousness.

MUSIC, CULTURE, CONSCIOUSNESS

The human genome specifies the construction of our bodies in great detail, and that includes the overall design of the brain. But not all of the circuits actively develop and work as set by genes. Much of each brain's circuitry, at any given moment of adult life, is individual and unique, truly reflective of that particular organism's history and circumstances. Naturally, that does not make the unraveling of neural mysteries any easier. Second, each human organism operates in collectives of like beings; the mind and the behavior of individuals belonging to such collectives and operating in specific cultural and physical environments are not shaped merely by the activity-driven circuitries mentioned above, and even less are they shaped by genes alone. To understand in a satisfactory manner the brain that fabricates human mind and human behavior, it is necessary to take into account its social and cultural context. And that makes the endeavor truly daunting.[4]

In this passage from *Descartes' Error,* Antonio Damasio pinpoints the relation of biology and experience, or of nature and nurture. We are determined at one level by our genes, but at another by our individual history, making each of us unique. But our history is in turn necessarily a history of our individuality in interaction with our community. To understand how our brain constructs a "mind," and behaves accordingly, requires an understanding of the influences on it of its cultural context. That is, indeed, a daunting endeavor. What can be reasonably hoped for in the context of this discussion is some clarification of how culture and music interact to make each of them what it is.

That interaction, to capture the depth and power of its influences on our achieved humanity, must be understood to operate at a level below the commonplace—at a level affecting our consciousness, our foundational awareness of ourselves as beings in a world we undergo. Music and the arts function at that depth level, where the "real" of our experience is constructed. As the cultural anthropologist Clifford Geertz puts it, the commonality of the arts

> lies in the fact that certain activities everywhere seem specifically designed to demonstrate that ideas are visible, audible—and one needs to make a word up here—tactible, that they can be cast in forms where the sense, and through the senses the emotions, can reflectively address them. The variety of artistic expression stems from the variety of conceptions men have about *the way things are,* and is indeed the same variety.[5] (Emphasis added)

Different musics, Geertz is suggesting, reflect different conceptions, culturally constructed, of "the way things are." All music, however, casts ideas into audible form, so they can be addressed reflectively through the sense of hearing and its attendant feeling. The "ideas" music deals with reach to the way things are felt—that is, directly experienced as sensible. That is the level Damasio defined as consciousness (Chapter 3). When John Blacking says "the chief function of music in society and culture is to promote soundly organized humanity by enhancing human consciousness,"[6] he is referring to how music forms experience to be affectively sensible. But in

---

[4]Antonio Damasio, *Descartes' Error: Emotion, Reason, and the Human Brain* (New York: Putnam's, 1994), 260. For another interesting treatment of the role of culture in shaping the human mind, see Leslie Brothers, *Friday's Footprint* (New York: Oxford University Press, 1997).

[5]Clifford Geertz, "Art as a Cultural System," *Modern Language Notes,* 91 (1974), quoted in *Aesthetics,* ed. Susan Feagin and Patrick Maynard (New York: Oxford University Press, 1997), 118.

[6]John Blacking, *How Musical Is Man?* (Seattle: University of Washington Press, 1973), 101.

turn, of course, each culture influences people's imagination of the forms and functions such sense can take. How does this interaction of culture, individuality, music, and consciousness take place?

So daunting is that question, as Damasio recognizes, that few people have attempted an answer and nobody has completely succeeded in formulating one. I suggest that a particular investigation of the culture/art/consciousness interface, by Robert Plant Armstrong (briefly mentioned and quoted in Chapter 2 and somewhat more extensively in Chapter 3) perhaps comes as close to an explanation, or at least to fruitful leads into ongoing investigations, as any now available. An overview of his thinking will help clarify how and why art (and music as an important component) affects human consciousness at the level of culturally grounded affective meaning—the level of psychic identity that cultures largely exist to provide.

In his book *Wellspring: On the Myth and Source of Culture,* Armstrong attempts to glimpse the deepest significance of culture's role.[7] Where in a culture can one find the strongest, most direct indications of how individuals and their contexts together forge human identity at its deepest level? This question led him to his lifelong work—the study of the arts as cultures express them. "The importance of this to the study of man is this: if one studies art one studies the externalization of man's interiority—an actuality of human experience. This one cannot do by any other means. Art is *man living.*" "Humanistic anthropology" goes beyond descriptions of activities and institutions, searching for the nature and value of human experience, toward "illuminating the lived process of being human . . . the conditions and experience of being a human being."[8]

That condition and experience is largely obscure, nonverbal, and aconceptual, Armstrong explains, but nevertheless is at the core of how cultural patterns of thinking and doing coalesce into the particular characteristics identifying each culture and each individual member of it. The underlying *quality* of situation, belief, and experience created by human contexts is what needs to be grasped if one is to grasp the "real" of a culture. That "real" is inner rather than outer. This leads to a paradox, "for in fact all that can be known of the inner is what is outer." Where can the inner be most directly encountered in outward expression? In art, conceived as "affecting presence."

And so the humanistic anthropologist makes his beginning where culture is presented to him, persuaded both that culture is experience and that it reveals itself in its own terms. Thus the humanistic anthropologist turns his attention to sculptures themselves, to music as music, to rite as enactment, to culture itself as a presentation of its own imperatives which, rather as chromosomes inform every body cell, instill each conceivable cultural action with the preconditions of its own possibility.[9]

---

[7]Robert Plant Armstrong, *Wellspring: On the Myth and Source of Culture* (Berkeley and Los Angeles: University of California Press, 1975), xi.

[8]Ibid., xii, 2.

[9]Ibid., 6–7.

Cultural imperatives, or grounding beliefs and values, are internalized not as "concepts about" (although they may be verbally articulated) but as "experiences within"—as ways to feel. No wonder Armstrong turns to the arts as the most fruitful sources of insight into "how reality feels" in a culture. But he worries that the word "feel" might be too restrictive, taken as a conceptual sign or symbol rather than as going beyond that designative function to indicate the embodiment of expressive meanings beyond verbal information. (Please review the discussion of the limitations of language in regard to artistic/aesthetic meanings in chapters 3 and 5.) In Chapter 2 I mentioned his definition of aesthetics as being "the theory or study of form incarnating feeling." He continues:

> Perhaps we ought to say "incarnating affect" since *feeling* might be construed in too restricted a sense, notably in the romantic sense of a specific emotion—of joy, sadness, or some such—about a specific situation or thing. Indeed a work may be created not to incarnate a feeling [in the sense of "an emotion"] at all, but rather an unaccountable and basic fact of one's awareness, about which one feels significantly. Thus, as we shall see, it is possible to incarnate in the affecting presence not only "beauty," which we may presume to be the result of a special relationship between the sensuous and the conceptual features of a work, a particular individualistic emotion, but also any of the infinite points on a spectrum of other realities, even including the very primal stuff of the universe as it is presumed by a particular people to be.[10] (Emphasis in original)

Here Armstrong is making the same point Damasio made and I extended (in Chapter 3): that feeling goes beyond emotion, to the level where "experienced, undergone being" is achieved, the level, we may assume, of consciousness itself. In studying the arts—the affective presences—of a culture, Armstrong provides a deep level of understanding of a culture's ineffable way to be, a way influencing and coloring the inner lives of all who are formed by that culture.

What philosophy learns from work such as Armstrong's is that the cultural basis for music is far more profound than matters of stylistic idiosyncrasies. We must understand that when a culture is effective it stamps its members so deeply in their psychic being as to form their "primal stuff"—their foundational sense of reality and selfhood. The music of a culture expresses, or captures, or formulates, or gives voice to this reality as only sounds organized to be meaningful can do (and as each other art does in its own particular way). And each instance of music contributes, in its way, to the sum total of the culture's psychic identity, because each individual's expression of artistic/aesthetic meaning affects that individual's inner world as related to his or her culture's world, whether as a mirror of it or as an alteration, an extension, or a denunciation. Music and culture exist in symbiosis, each dependent on, receiving reinforcement from, influencing change within, the other. Far below

---

[10]Ibid., 11. Armstrong is critical of Susanne Langer's position that art is "symbolic of human feeling," because of its connotation that art is "about" feeling rather than an immediate presentation of feeling. Scholars of Langer's work are likely to find his critique either mistaken or exaggerated, despite her ambiguity as to the specifics of the relation of art to affect.

the surface of different musics being, simply, alternative ways to organize sounds is the realization that these alternative ways of *musical* being are grounded in alternative ways of *human* being.

That grounding is universally shared in every culture, for in every culture the affecting presence, the work of art (please remember that "work" is both process and product), directly embodies affect (what I am calling feeling).

> It is only in this sense, namely that form does incarnate affect, that it may be said that there is a universal aesthetic. Over and above this universal fact are to be found those variations which ultimately proliferate into a particular system of aesthetics. . . . An adequate anthropological study of aesthetics, then . . . must illuminate specific aesthetic systems, and in so doing must show in detail how the cultural individuality of affecting works, in all forms, is accounted for.[11]

Armstrong's position here has direct implications for music education, in that (to paraphrase) "an adequate study of music, then, must illuminate how music operates in specific musical systems, and in so doing must show in detail how the cultural individuality of music is accounted for." What must we do to study and understand each music in its cultural individuality?

First, Armstrong insists, we must put aside any notion that what our own culture regards as "beauty" is also regarded as such in other cultures. Further, we must recognize that the power of the affecting presence is not to be found primarily or entirely in its *social* functions—its relation to the welfare and social interactions of people in a community—but that it goes *beyond* that level, to the level that "*presents those profound conditions which make social existence possible*" (emphasis his). That is, "The model of man as social animal must yield before the model of man as rich, subtle, spiritual, rational—whole, conscious, and experiencing."[12] Music, in this view, cannot be most deeply understood at the social significance level, appropriate as it is to do so as one of its important dimensions. Beyond that dimension is music's ability to formulate the experienced reality that is the *grounding of* its social utility. Armstrong pushes our conception of music down to its deepest roots, its being implicated in forming our primal consciousness, as Damasio also does.

Where in music does one find the qualities that form human consciousness?

> The chief contribution of the humanist to the study of anthropology is that he can direct attention to human phenomena in terms of their experientiality. Such a student strives to apprehend phenomena in terms of their intrinsic, unique, constitutive qualities instead of in terms of such extrinsic and alien considerations as their quantities and functions.[13]

---

[11]Ibid., 13. For an extended discussion of cultures in which art is conceived as having primarily powers of invocation, and cultures such as in the West, where powers of virtuosity are emphasized, see Armstrong's *The Powers of Presence: Consciousness, Myth, and Affecting Presence* (Philadelphia: University of Pennsylvania Press, 1981).

[12]Armstrong, *Wellspring*, note 7, 15–16.

[13]Ibid., 41.

These words should sound familiar by now, having appeared so often in various guises in previous chapters, in my attempt to articulate, often through the ideas of others (Dissanayake, Green, Dufrenne, Sontag, Miles, Dewey, Sloboda, Sparshott, Meyer, Bernstein, Wolterstorff, Phenix, Raffman, and many additional citations), that the structured sounds of music, both in and of themselves and in their capacity to include all manner of social/political/ideational matters, capture for experiencing the meanings, culturally grounded at the deepest level, that only music can make available. "The real medium of the affecting presence therefore," says Armstrong, "is consciousness itself freighted into color, tone, volume, surface, movement, word, and situation." In the expressive materials of the arts, the "immedia" directly available to experience, are found the "electricity of living consciousness."[14]

For Armstrong, the characteristic consciousness of a culture, incarnated in its arts, can be understood as the culture's "myth"; its way of encountering and understanding reality, a kind of "code of awareness." The myth, or "mythoform," is without specific content but has "a particularity of form and process." We learn our culture's myth "with awesome aptitude and hungry avidity in our earliest life, and it patterns all subsequent encounters into *experience*. . . . It exists as a deep reality which, of itself, lies forever hidden, and its sole 'language' is the totality of our existence"[15] (emphasis in original). Affecting presences—what we call "works of art"— not only incarnate their culture's myth but also celebrate it, giving each instance of art a special vitality, a special status as precious, as meaningful in a profound way. "The affecting presence is a presence and is affecting *both*, owing to the fact that it incarnates that myth which, most profoundly, we are. It shares with us the most basic principle of our humanity"[16] (emphasis in original).

THE DILEMMA OF MULTICULTURAL MUSIC EDUCATION

To the degree Armstrong (and Damasio) are correct in their argument that each culture, and its music, shapes and forms its members' particular psychic reality, we are presented with a difficult predicament. Each of us has been deeply formed by our culture, so deeply that at that level we are largely unaware of how and why we think, feel, and act as we do. If that is the case (and I believe that it is to a significant degree), how can we expect to be able to create, respond to, or understand the music of a culture not our own? If our own culture has done what it is supposed to do, does it, therefore, prevent us from being able to think, feel, "be," as a different culture does? Can we change our stripes from our own culture's to another's at will?

At the core of the idea of multicultural music education is the belief that it makes sense to do it; to include musics of a wide variety, each representing a distinct culture or subculture, so that students can share the many ways music exists as culturally deter-

---

[14]Ibid., 49–50.
[15]Ibid., 94–95.
[16]Ibid., 141.

mined. There are a great many other issues related to our professional adoption, at least since the Tanglewood Symposium in 1967, of the conviction that many cultural musics should be included in every aspect of the music program. Issues of authenticity, teaching in culturally grounded ways, availability of materials, teacher education, use of community resources, defining often ambiguous terms, bi- and multimusicality, curricular goals and objectives, providing appropriate environments, proper and improper repertoire, all have arisen and have been either well, moderately well, or poorly addressed. This is not the place for such issues to be taken up: for a comprehensive treatment of them, and others, by some of the most important leaders in the multicultural music education movement, the book *World Musics and Music Education: Facing the Issues* should be consulted[17] (among many other helpful references cited within that book). What can be and needs to be discussed in a book devoted to philosophy is the assumption underlying all these issues, the assumption that it all is valid in the first place. Are we being not only hopelessly idealistic to think we can be "multicultural" at will but also disrespectful to each culture's music outside our own, treating it as so much "material" to be homogenized, or cloned, into a resemblance of familiarity so we can treat it as a tamed, comfortable variation of what we already know?

To address this issue, I will present both sides of it—the "contextualist" and the "universalist" views—in a way that allows each to be as rigorously and forcefully argued as it deserves to be. Imagine a debate, in which two teams of multicultural music education scholars have been assigned the following propositions. Position A: Resolved, that the music of each culture is particular and unique to that culture, and therefore cannot be experienced genuinely except by people who are members of that culture. Position B: Resolved, that music is universal and transcultural, so that the music of all cultures can be experienced genuinely by all.[18]

Imagine, further, that the two teams have been given the same recording of music, from Papua New Guinea, on which to base their argument. This recording (*Voices of the Rainforest*)[19] was made by Steven Feld on the Great Papuan Plateau, just north of Mt. Bosavi, an extinct volcano towering 8,000 feet above the floor of the plateau. Some twelve hundred people live in that area of the rainforest, divided into four subcommunities, each with its own language and distinctive geography. One of these communities is called Kaluli; this recording is of their music. The teams are to listen to two examples: a song sung by its composer, a woman named Ulali, and an improvisation performed on a bamboo jaw's harp by the musician Gaima. Their arguments are to be based on these two pieces.

Here are my imagined responses by the two teams, presented as fairly and forcefully as I am able.

---

[17]*World Musics and Music Education: Facing the Issues*, ed. Bennett Reimer (Reston, VA: Music Educators National Conference, 2002).

[18]The imaginary debate is a revised version of my "Can We Understand Music of Foreign Cultures?" in *Musical Connections: Tradition and Change*, ed. Heath Lees (International Society for Music Education, 1994), 227–45.

[19]*Voices of the Rainforest*, Rykodisc RCD10173.

POSITION A: *Contextualism*

The music on which our argument is based is the cultural possession of the Kaluli. It reflects and embodies their experience of the world as presented to them by the particularities of their environment, the particularities of their history, the particularities of their social organization, customs, beliefs, ways of working, playing, birthing, marrying, living and dying, all intimately connected to the larger ecology of the rainforest they are dependent on for physical sustenance and cultural identity.

Can we, who are not Kaluli, who know little if anything about their surroundings, their history, their mental, physical, psychological, emotional, social identities, who have not *lived the lives* of the Kaluli, be expected to understand their music, which, perhaps more intimately than anything else, manifests their inner beings?

Today, in the politically correct atmosphere of the United States, in most countries of the Western hemisphere, and in many countries all over the world, music educators are expected to provide multicultural music education to all their students, under a variety of rationales and for a variety of purposes. Underlying all the pressures to be multicultural in the teaching and learning of music is the assumption that it is possible to be so, and, in fact, that it is quite easy to be so. All music educators need to do is have an open attitude to musics of cultures other than that of the cultural majority in their country, present that music to their students with a positive spirit of appreciation and respect, tell them something about the culture from which it comes, have them try composing, improvising, singing, and playing some of it as best they can and as best the teacher knows how to help them, perhaps do a report on the music, even, if possible, enlist a genuine specimen of the culture in question to come in to display her musical expertise.

From all this activity a great many good things will flow. Students will become astute appreciators of a great variety of musics, their musical tastes and preferences will be greatly expanded, they will become "world travelers" in music, sophisticated about many more kinds of music than that of their own culture, and they will also develop an attitude of respect and admiration and open acceptance of people from a diversity of cultures—an attitude of "cultural democracy," if you will, so sorely needed in the modern, multicultural world in which we now live.

All this, however, dissolves under the cold light of careful analysis. At the core of the difficulty with this politically correct view is the assumption that music can be understood and experienced authentically outside its context; outside, that is, the very thing that makes each music what it is—its cultural grounding. In fact, however, a musical culture "is a cognitive entity, defining what it is that people in a particular culture must know if they are to understand, perform, create music in a way that is 'proper' for that culture."[20] To think people can genuinely understand

---

[20]Nicholas Cook, *Music, Imagination, and Culture* (Oxford: Clarendon Press, 1990), 222–23.

the music of a foreign culture is to deal with that music with ultimate disrespect, ignoring or denying what is essential about it—its own cultural integrity, embodying a world view very different from that of cultures foreign to it.

The Kaluli live their lives against the constant backdrop of rainforest sounds—birds and insects of countless varieties, frogs, rain, creeks, and streams. To this dense and never-ending soundscape the Kaluli add their own sounds as they go about their daily activities—pounding, cutting, breaking, grinding, scraping, as they clear land, gather wood, harvest bamboo. The natural landscape of sound surrounding them becomes part of the musical consciousness of these people: they think of themselves as being, in the words of the notes to the recording, "voices in the forest." Musical sounds and natural sounds cannot be separated in Kaluli music and Kaluli experiences of music.[21]

Western concepts of music could not be more incommensurable. Western music is composed by individuals whose main purpose is to express inner, personal experience as embodied in musical works. These works, separate from and having little to do with the natural world, form a world of their own—a world of music intended for nothing except contemplation; with no functional role connecting it to the daily lives of those composing it, performing it, or listening to it. The music of the Kaluli arises naturally and spontaneously from their functions of everyday life.

Western music represents a "low context culture"—a culture in which particular contexts of particular pieces are far less important than the qualities of the pieces themselves.[22] People in a low context culture can easily understand and enjoy musical objects from different historical periods and in a variety of styles, that is, out of their contexts, so long as the pieces follow the conventions to which they have become accustomed. The music of the Kaluli represents an extremely "high context culture," closely tied to the particularities of place and time. People cannot simply pull a lever and switch into a different cultural context, high to low or low to high, no matter how eager and idealistic they are in their hopes to be able to do so.

Confronted with music of a different culture, such as music of the Kaluli, Westerners, in their attempts to understand it and teach it, will necessarily treat it as they do their own music, because that is what they know to *be* music. They will analyze it, for example, because that is what one must do to go deeper into Western music to plumb the depths of its complexities. They will find that musical complexities of the sort that Westerners value are likely to be absent or minimal in high context musics, and they are therefore likely to regard such music—Kaluli music, for example—as simple, or unsophisticated, or "primitive," and therefore inferior (although it would be hopelessly politically incorrect to express that thought).

---

[21]Steven Feld, *Sound and Sentiment: Birds, Weeping, Poetics, and Song in Kaluli Expression* (Philadelphia: University of Pennsylvania Press, 1982).

[22]Edward T. Hall, *Beyond Culture* (Garden City, NY: Anchor Press, 1976).

But, as we all know, music can arise not only from a highly rationalized sys-tem requiring elaborate notational recordkeeping, and rewarding individualistic and complex thought processes, as in the West, but also from natural responses to nature's sounds, as by the Kaluli, or from supernatural revelation as in Native American Blackfoot music, where complexity in the Western sense is not the point but the spiritual sense of humanness and "Blackfoot-ness" definitely is,[23] or from the reflection in Persian music based on the *radif* of the hierarchical interrelations of Persian social structure, and on and on with examples of musical thinking and musical practice based on principles far different from those that Westerners assume constitute what music is "really like."

To compose music as Westerners do, and think that all people compose that way, is, however unconsciously, an act of cultural colonialism. To sing and play "properly" as Westerners have learned how to do is not only to distort other ways of conceiving vocal and instrumental production but also to completely miss the point of those other ways—that the body produces musical sounds not according to some Platonic ideal but as the immediate expression of cultural beliefs reaching to the roots of how different people differently conceive what it is like to be musical and to produce "proper" musical sounds.

Different cultures, after all, are not simply variants of a common culture: they are distinct reflections of different ways to conceive human reality. A culture's music depends on and translates into sounds its ways of conceiving the world at large.[24] Because "the worlds in which different societies live are distinct worlds, not merely the same world with different labels attached,"[25] each cultural world has its decisive influence on the cognitive functioning of those who live in it. The differ-ences in brain processing cannot be attributed to physiology, because people brought up in a culture different from their own will process information as natives of that culture do. The differences stem from culture, each culture "determining how and why these uses of different parts of the brain, or 'intelligences' . . . develop."[26] To put the matter as clearly as it requires:

> It is not possible to isolate something called music from something else called culture. Musical knowledge is cultural knowledge . . . the way in which a person knows music is not different from the way he knows in general . . .

[23]Bruno Nettl, "Musical Thinking and Thinking About Music in Ethnomusicology," *The Journal of Aesthetics and Art Criticism,* 52, no. 1 (1994), 141.

[24]Ibid.

[25]Edward Sapir, "The Status of Linguistics as a Science," *Language,* 5 (1929), 207–14, quoted in R. A. Schweder, *Thinking Through Cultures* (Cambridge: Harvard University Press, 1991), 155.

[26]Robert Walker, "Music and Multiculturalism," *International Journal of Music Education,* 8, no. 2 (1986), 43.

musical knowledge is based upon the same epistemology which underlies and pervades the entire culture.[27]

Because music is so intimately bound to culture, it is facile and sentimental to believe that instructing students about musics of cultures different from their own will cause them to achieve a greater respect for and acceptance of people from those other cultures, as is so often claimed.[28] The fact is that every culture, and every subculture in polycultural societies, is constituted of insiders privy to that culture's identity and responsible for protecting that identity from erosion by the influence of outsiders. Such outside influence can be hostile and predatory, as in colonialism in its various forms—political, religious, commercial, and so on—or it can be benign, as in attempts to study a culture for ethnomusicological or educational reasons. Both influences can dilute and dissipate the integrity of a culture, the former (colonization) by intention, the latter (ethnomusicology or multicultural music education) by appropriation and distortion (in some ways, more insidious than open colonization). Whatever the form of cultural intrusion, those intruded upon are not always grateful for it, and those perpetrating the intrusion are driven by their own agenda. Resentments, misunderstandings, and stereotypes, rather than being allayed by such interactions, are often heightened by them.

There is no convincing evidence that people's resentments of, misunderstandings about, or stereotypical images of, cultural groups other than their own are changed at all by attempts to introduce them to the music or other cultural manifestations of foreign or different groups. Would that it were so easy to heal the deep, abiding divisions among peoples, so ancient in human history and so current in contemporary life, in which hatreds between differing religions, races, ethnicities, and nationalities are fairly well tearing our world apart. Let us not be so presumptuous, so inflated, as to claim that music education holds the solution to the world's problems of separatism, which have existed throughout human history and continue virulently today. We especially do not deserve to be any more than humble about this issue given the inherent unlikelihood or impossibility that we can understand music other than our own with anything approaching authenticity.

Where does all this leave us in regard to multicultural music education? What can we expect to accomplish with instruction about foreign musics, given the enormous differences that exist among different cultures' musics, reflecting the essential differences that exist among cultures themselves and the ways each culture causes its members to understand the world and to process information about the world?

---

[27]S. B. Hoffman, "Epistemology and Music: A Javanese Example," *Ethnomusicology,* 22 (1978), 69.
[28]See, for example, David J. Elliott, "Music as Culture: Toward a Multicultural Concept of Arts Education," *The Journal of Aesthetic Education,* 24, no. 1 (1990), 147-66.

We in the West cannot continue our imposition of Western thought processes on world musics, and ways to teach world musics, if we are to treat those musics, and ways to teach them, with anything resembling respect. There is no simple, singular, all-purpose solution to the reality confronting us—that foreign musics are, in essence, foreign. What we can do is honor and cherish the existence of the foreign. We can encourage diversity in music to exist as we encourage the diversity of species in the natural world to exist, by preserving and protecting each diverse manifestation of culture and of nature. We need not assume that we must person-ally benefit from the existence of foreign musics in the sense that we can own them or even borrow them for our personal aggrandizement. A world of diversity is sim-ply a more interesting world. We can be satisfied to know our part of the world, to appreciate it for what it is, and also to understand what it is *not*—a standard appli-cable to other parts of the world. The people of a particular culture must learn the fundamental lesson that their culture does not and cannot determine the rest of the world. And they cannot force the rest of the world to conform to *their* beliefs, *their* needs, and *their* practices.

We can assist in this process of reality-building by making clear to our stu-dents that each musical manifestation of each culture is the property of that cul-ture, constituting that culture's expression of its inner nature. We can know our own music, and know that others have their music. We can be exposed to those other musics, not in the vain hope that we can understand them and still less in the self-serving assumption that we can assimilate them within our own belief system, but as object lessons that we do not own the world. This relativizes our sense of ourselves. We are better able to understand what is truly the case—that our own reality is only relatively real. This is a lesson every human being needs to learn in order to grow up healthily—to lose the narcissism of youth, the idea that the world revolves around them. To understand that foreign musics are essentially foreign is to have learned a fundamental lesson about the nature of the human condition.

POSITION B: *Universalism*

This music, of the Kaluli people of Papua New Guinea, is one of a great diversity of manifestations of a universal phenomenon we call music. As such, it is universally accessible to all who care to share it. When we hear these two pieces of music—these episodes of music demarcated from other episodes of music—we know, immediately, instinctively, and with certainty, that what we are hearing is music. We may know little if anything about the details of the lives of the Kaluli. But upon hearing their music we automatically know several essential things about them.

We know that they are human beings. Music is a primal way for human beings to behave in the world, and the Kaluli share with all other human beings the capacity for and need to create music as an essential component of their lives, as these pieces immediately inform us.

We know that they are social beings. Music for the Kaluli, as we know by all our experience with music at all times and in all places, is a shared experience, in which individuals, by themselves as in these two pieces or along with others as when several people make music together, use music as a way to give form to inner experience, to represent that inner experience to themselves and others, and to build a community of shared inner experience for which music is the tangible representation.

We know without knowing anything else about the Kaluli that in addition to sharing the universal human capacity and need for music, and in addition to their creation of a body of music shared by members of their culture, each Kaluli person is also an individual, just as are all other human beings, who, while being members of the human race, and being members of some cultural group, are also individuals. We can assume confidently that the individuals making these pieces of music—these recognizable events of music—are performers in every sense of the word as it applies to all musical performers no matter where in the world or when in history. That is, they have certain skills necessary to perform, they know the tradition they must perform within, they are sensitive to the musical qualities their music employs, and they add something of their own selfness—their musical imagination—to the sounds they are forming in musical ways.

We may also assume with confidence that these performers may also be composers, either in the sense of making creative musical decisions as they are performing, in which case they are improvisers, or in the sense that they work out most or all of the decisions about a piece of music beforehand and then follow those decisions in a piece they perform, or they have their compositional decisions performed by someone else.

In the case of the Kaluli, both men and women compose songs and are well known for the songs they have composed. Ulali is a particularly well known composer in her culture: it was her song, sung by her, that we heard. The Kaluli respect particularly good composers, and sing their songs long after the composers have died. They have well-known criteria for goodness in their music, and various styles of music, and particular forms within which their music is composed and improvised.

The point is that Westerners often assume, self-importantly and incorrectly, that they are capable of composing, but that people of simpler, tribal societies just somehow "have" music—that music just "grows" in such societies. But the work of many scholars demonstrates

> that artists in traditional societies often break away from [their] traditions, that such innovations are often praised by the indigenous people, who more-over rank the art works according to aesthetic criteria; that the artists are not anonymous, except to outsiders who haven't bothered to learn their names, but exhibit distinctive styles which are readily identified both by insiders and outside observers, and that [so-called] primitive artists, like their European counterparts, often evolve, over a life-time of work, several distinct styles.[29]

It is Westerners' ignorance of other cultures that also allows them to project inaccuracies such as that foreign music is, for example, "functional" but theirs is "musical," or "aesthetic." These are completely false distinctions, in assuming, first of all, that there actually exists a "them" and "us" when it comes to fundamental matters, and also in assuming that music is not just as functional in the West as it is everywhere else. Music always serves human needs, in a variety of ways shared by all cultures. It does not require a concert hall, a stage, and quietly sitting people to experience music aesthetically, that is, as human experience given meaning by sounds organized to do so. All peoples, no matter the setting and no matter the surrounding activity, respond to, find meaning in, cherish music for its inherent power to enrich and deepen their felt experience. Westerners misrepresent and demean the music of foreign cultures, and of their own culture, when they set up false dichotomies between the functional and the aesthetic. A Brahms symphony has a function—to be listened to for the musical experience it gives. Ulali's song and Gaima's improvisation share that function: those pieces are cherished because they do precisely what the Brahms symphony does—vivify and give significance to peoples' experience of themselves as conscious, feeling creatures. All music, in all cultures, in all periods of history, serves the same underlying function—to be experienced as arranged, meaningful sound, which heightens and gives spiritual meaning to human experience, whatever other use it may happen to fulfill. At root, "music transforms experience. Music is always out of the ordinary and by its presence

---

[29]H. Gene Blocker, *The Aesthetics of Primitive Art* (Lanham, MD: University of America, 1994), 155.

creates the atmosphere of the special. Experience is transformed from the humdrum, the everyday, into something else. . . . You might even say it is an actualization of the mystical experience for everybody."[30] For the Kaluli, as for all other human beings, music embodies and communicates the most deeply felt sentiments in Kaluli social life.[31]

Every culture also differentiates among the levels of musicality of its members; every culture has some kind of hierarchy in its musical system to differentiate among styles; every culture has tradition-carrying networks; practically all cultures have some sense of the music specialist and rank such specialists according to some system; and, most telling, there are restrictions, in every culture, on how sounds can properly be used to make music. "Despite the enormous variety of musics, the ways in which people everywhere have chosen to make music are more restricted than the boundaries of the imaginable."[32] That is because all cultures have standards of goodness for their music and for their art. To think that only Westerners have well-developed aesthetic criteria is to deny the reality that all cultures have such criteria: no music exists unattached to the expectation system of its cultural setting.

How much must a person who is not a member of a particular culture know about its music to be able to share it, whether by listening to it with understanding, composing it with understanding, or performing it with understanding? It is a myth to think that music is so closely bound to a particular culture that no one outside that culture can penetrate it. A culture does, of course, give a particular character to its music, but music always transcends the limitations of that character because it also shares universal, musically determined properties, independent of this or that musical culture. To put it most strongly, all musics "are examples of basic human cognitive and social processes at work in construing and adapting to the real world."[33]

Music, then, is, to a large degree, independent from its social context. It has a life of its own. Music, therefore, becomes universally shareable when regarded as music. Musicians

> must reach beyond the conventions of their particular society to the universal mental processes of the species; and the person who is able to do this is one whose individual self-development has passed beyond the stage of lip-service

---

[30]David P. McAllester, "Some Thoughts on 'Universals' in World Music," *Ethnomusicology,* xv, no. 3 (1971), 380.

[31]Steven Feld, *Voices of the Rainforest,* album notes, note 19.

[32]Nettl, *The Study of Ethnomusicology* (Urbana: University of Illinois Press, 1983), 39.

[33]Dane L. Harwood, "Universals in Music: A Perspective from Cognitive Psychology," *Ethnomusicology,* 20 (1976), 531.

to conventional definitions of self (in terms of social status) and other (in terms of ethnic and other groupings), to an understanding of his common humanity and the reasons for variations in behavior. This is how the most individual composer can have the most universal appeal: he communicates to others at the level of the innate; he begins with cultural conventions, but transcends them by reorganizing his sound structures in a personal, but basically universal, way, rather than slavishly following culturally given rules.[34]

Another major issue must be raised in regard to the universality of musical experience. The assumption is often made that seemingly different musics are the processes and products of seemingly different cultures. That assumption also must be examined, for, like the assumption that people can understand only the music of their own culture, to assume that there are, in fact, essentially different cultures in the world is itself questionable. This world we now live in is, thoroughly and pervasively, a global culture rather than a scattering of isolated cultures. "Perhaps the most remarkable fact of the modern world is that now for the first time all the member cultures of the human race know of each other, and have, more or less, met. There really is no human Other now. . . . When we abandon the distinctions between ourselves and the Other, we will find that interaction [among cultures] comes easily and swiftly."[35] The reality in the world now is not that we must struggle to learn about foreign cultures and their exotic musics, but that there *are no* foreign cultures and exotic musics.

The process of cultural interpenetration is going on at a furious pace all over the globe. All over the world, music is becoming more homogenized, more interchangeable, more easily and casually accepted no matter its cultural origins, and an international standard of musicality is replacing local standards. Whatever may have been, at one time, a world of diverse cultures is surely no longer such a world. But of course intercultural influences have always existed: there are few if any "pure" musics in history because people have always borrowed from and been changed by other cultures with which they have come into contact. We overstate the case, and romanticize reality, when we think that indigenous musics are pristine. Music has always flowed freely across cultural boundaries. Now few such boundaries can even be identified, so accessible has the whole musical world—including the musical world of the past—become to practically everybody in it.

---

[34]John Blacking, "Can Musical Universals Be Heard?" *The World of Music,* xix, nos. 1/2 (1977), 19. For an excellent biography of Blacking, pointing out his devotion to the idea that musical meaning transcends cultural contexts, see Patricia Shehan Campbell, "How Musical We Are: John Blacking on Music, Education, and Cultural Understanding," *Journal of Research in Music Education,* 48, no. 4 (Winter 2000), 336–57.

[35]Jody Diamond, "There Is No THEY There," *Musicworks,* no. 47 (1990), 12.

Where does all this leave us in regard to multicultural music education? It leaves us with the reality that all students in schools are capable of sharing all the many musics of the world. We only need make accessible to them what they have not yet encountered in the multicultural, multimusical world in which they already live. We can help them get from all music more of what it has to give—the universally shareable experience of musical meaning. We can openly and freely encourage each student's musical experiences to be as diverse as the many musics in the world, because all those musics are the common property and heritage of all people. We can make clear to our students that they need not be limited to the familiar, because what is less familiar can become more familiar, and therefore assimilable into their experience. In a real sense, every human being can own the entire world of music. When we develop in that direction we are better able to understand what is truly the case—that our own reality is shared by all human beings. This is a lesson every human being needs to learn in order to grow up healthily—to lose the restricted view of youth that they are alone in the world. To understand that foreign musics are not in any essential way foreign is to have learned a fundamental lesson about the nature of the human condition.

A SYNERGISTIC RESOLUTION

The preceding debate between the contextualist and universalist positions raises a fundamental issue about the human condition, relating to selfness and otherness. Where does our reality reside—in our differences or our commonalities? This issue is not specific to music and not specific to education: it pervades all of our lives from birth to death, all of our relationships with others, our entire sense of our selves as individuals living among other individuals who are in some senses like us and in some senses different from us.

Music, in its closeness to the heart of what human beings are like, must, and does, manifest this paradox in a particularly powerful way. Because we are educators, everything we do being inherently and necessarily based on our values and our beliefs, we face, with particular force, the moral requirement that our values and beliefs be as fully examined as possible, and as fully resolved as possible, in light of our obligation to enhance the lives of those whose education is our responsibility.

Unfortunately, no simple, unidimensional resolution of the paradox seems to be possible in regard to music and to music education, just as it does not seem possible to fully resolve the paradox in human life as a whole. I hope readers find my presentations of both sides of the issue to be in some ways equally persuasive, as I do. I hope, also, that readers are disturbed—even distressed—by some of the positions each side takes, as I am. But although each side can become extremist in losing sight of the reality of the other, we must, finally, I believe, recognize that both, despite being contradictory, represent a piece of the truth. What we can do, therefore, is not deny the validity of either position, but avoid the extremes to which each can take us if the other position is denied.

It goes too far to an extreme, I believe, to argue that each different culture is so different that no entry into its cultural realities is possible by anyone not a full-fledged member of it. But it also goes too far to an extreme, I suggest, to argue the reverse—that every culture, no matter how different, is accessible easily if not fully to anyone desiring to enter it. I do not see the paradox as being harmful, or something to be overcome if we only tried hard enough. I believe the paradox is real and meaningful—even precious in the gift it offers humans of the possibility to become more fully self-actualized. How does that occur?

On the one hand, being a member of a culture is a prerequisite for achieving one's individual and social potentials. Whatever potentials one is born with, the culture into which one is born will be the crucial factor in allowing those potentials to be realized, and in giving them the particular character that will mark each member of the culture as a person. Personhood cannot exist in a cultural vacuum. As Elliott Eisner has often said, a culture is a place for growing things, and human cultures are places for growing human minds. A human mind, growing healthily within its culture, achieves selfhood—a personality, an identity, a place in the world where one is at home in the world.

A word often used as a synonym for the deepest essence of one's selfness is "soul." One's self-identity with various aspects of one's culture that resonate at the depths of one's being are the experienced manifestations of soul. Soul food, for example, is food pervaded with meaning—with a sense that "this is who I am." Soul music is such music—music reaching to the core of one's selfness, to one's soul. I believe it is essential for each individual to achieve a soulful identification with one or several kinds of music provided by her or his culture, at the level of feeling that this music "is who I am." Music, I suggest, exists, first and foremost, to serve our soul. Though our identities in a complex world are no longer likely to be static and singular, we nevertheless must have in our lives some self-identifications if we are to achieve a sense of soul. Music can provide an important dimension of a soulful life.

But what of the opposite aspect of the paradox—our need and capacity to encounter the other who is not just a slightly altered version of our self but a genuine other? Unless we do so we can become so insulated within our culture as to become ethnocentric or even separatist, as if what provides us with soulfulness is the only way it can be provided, and as if we were incapable of sharing anything of what others experience as soulful. In our attempts to help students identify with and "be at home" with the musics of their particular heritage we can overlook the complementary need to expand one's self by being confronted with other ways of being.

To what extent can people genuinely experience a different way of musical being—a different way that soul is achieved? I believe the answer is obvious—to *some* extent. Not to a full extent, except in rare instances, and not to *no* extent—again, except in rare instances. It is that *some* toward which our efforts at "multimusicalism" should be directed. Every addition to that "some" expands the self. In the spirit of adding to the self rather than substituting other selves for one's self, the study of the music of foreign cultures enriches the souls of all who are engaged in it. This position is argued cogently by H. Gene Blocker, whose studies of the arts in preindustrial tribal societies are among the most penetrating available. He says,

> My proposal is to face squarely the challenges of any cross-cultural study, admitting the unavoidable comparative nature of any cross-cultural study, with its inevitable and ever-present risk of ethnocentric bias, and finally to embrace what hermeneutics explains as the mutual give and take in any cross-cultural studies, whereby we open ourselves as far as possible to an alien culture which we nonetheless realize, despite our best intentions and efforts to the contrary, we are inevitably interpreting according to our own cultural bias. It is not, after all, unlike getting to know another person—we try to understand the other person from his or her unique standpoint though we know we can do this only by understanding the other person in terms of our own experience. Do we ever really know another person? Perhaps not, at least not completely; but would we want to give up the effort? In the end, what, really, is the alternative?[36]

When the song of Ulali and the improvisation of Gaima enter our experience as their way of achieving soul, touching us musically because of our better acquaintance with their music and the conditions of their lives from which it springs, our experience of soul is deepened, and commingles with theirs to some meaningful extent. We do not become Kaluli because of that, nor should we want to. We should be who we are, as the Kaluli should be who they are. But we can also be expanded in who we are by the degree we are able to share something of what the Kaluli are, as they can be expanded when sharing something of what we are.

We should continue our efforts to study musics of foreign cultures, along with our efforts to study the musics indigenous to our own cultures, because of our obligation to each of the three dimensions of the human paradox. To help our students understand that the creation of musical meaning is a universal need of human beings; that such meaning is created within the culture from which it arises; and that each individual can both find soul in the music of his or her culture and share soul to some extent with those of other cultures, is to have helped them experience musically the paradoxical—and fundamental—nature of the human condition.

---

[36]H. Gene Blocker, "Is Primitive Art Art?" *The Journal of Aesthetic Education,* 25, no 4 (Winter 1991), 97. This author's book *The Aesthetics of Primitive Art* (note 29) provides excellent insights into the artistic/aesthetic achievements of tribal societies. For another cogent discussion of the self/other issue, see Alan Simpson, "The Uses of Cultural Literacy: A British View," in *The Journal of Aesthetic Education,* 25, no. 4 (Winter 1991), 65–74.

RIFF 9

I sit in the large gymnasium of the Provincial Opera School on the outskirts of Shenyang, a large city north of Beijing in the area of China traditionally called Manchuria. I am nearing the end of my three-month research project to study the music education system of China from preschool through conservatory, sponsored by the Chinese Government, the U.S.-China Arts Exchange, and Harvard Project Zero. Along with Lyle Davidson, of the New England Conservatory, I have been in Beijing, Xian, and Chengdu, each of those places having an important conservatory, school music programs of some distinction, and the usual complement of government-run opera schools, song and dance schools, and community arts schools. The sounds of music, Chinese style, a rich mixture of types ranging from ancient indigenous musics, to children's songs both local and international, to contemporary Chinese compositions for the Western orchestra, to opera in a variety of traditional local styles, to rock and jazz, Beethoven and Vivaldi, traditional Chinese instruments and piano and guitar, ensembles of every imaginable sort both Chinese and Western—all fill my ears with their fascinating diversity and vitality. From nursery school kids singing their songs to professionals at world-class levels of attainment, the many musics of China have become, in this short but very intensive experience, part of my psyche.

Now, in this gym, the students at this long-established opera school, ranging in age from late teens through early adulthood, are demonstrating various aspects of Chinese opera for their "distinguished guests." As I have come to expect, the typical opera orchestra, some dozen players of winds, strings, and (often excruciatingly loud) percussion, are off to the side, playing their accompaniments, entirely by ear and with no conductor, as usual. The students and some faculty, singly or in small groups, perform excerpts from various operas, always including the highly stylized acting of the various roles being portrayed and sometimes the astonishing acrobatics that are part of the show.

I enjoy the presentations, the high level of achievement they represent, and my growing ability to actually make sense—musically and dramatically—of what had at first been a totally bewildering and, I admit, not entirely attractive genre. The Chinese singing voice, in its traditional guise, is more piercing ("piquant" is probably a better characterization) than the bel canto style of Western singing in which I am steeped; the acting is, for Western expectations, overly melodramatic; and the crashing, insistent orchestra is off-putting in its obtrusiveness. At first I groaned to think I would be taken to opera performances frequently, and tried to dream up ways to respond graciously to my hosts, hiding my consternation. As time went by my initial resistance softened, and I found myself not only understanding some of the intricacies and nuances but also looking forward to both opera school and professional opera house productions. I was, slowly, becoming infatuated.

As I reflected about my changing attitude, a young woman, in her early twenties, walked to the center of the gym to perform. She was dressed in Western sweats and sneakers, indistinguishable in appearance from the many Chinese and Chinese American students populating most campuses in the United States. The orchestra started up and I idly awaited her act to begin. Within a few seconds after she began I started to pay attention. A few moments more and I sat up straight. Then my eyes widened, my jaw fell, and I began to get chills up my spine. "What *is* this?" I found myself wondering. "This is like nothing I've ever heard. It's the same Chinese opera I'm getting used to, but light-years away from everything I've come to expect." I sat, transfixed emotionally, until she finished, bowed in my direction, and nonchalantly walked out.

After a moment to get myself back together I turned to the director of the school sitting next to me, an old man who, I had been told, was in his day a famous performer. "Tell me about that young woman," I said. He looked at me and smiled. "Ah," he replied. "A young person like that comes along maybe once in a century. She will become a historical figure in Chinese opera history. Maybe the best in that history."

I exulted. "Got it!" I thought. Despite my limited experience with this, to me, exotic musical genre and performance tradition, I was able to recognize, with my ear and mind and body, that something extraordinary was going on. This was a moment worth the arduous three months in China, a rare privilege I was lucky enough to have been granted that afternoon. But my exultation was tempered by the realization that this young virtuoso may have come along a bit too late. Traditional Chinese opera is dwindling in interest for younger people in that country, who are now enjoying the more up-to-date pleasures of Western musics and their Chinese adaptations. Several of the string instruments in the orchestra had been wired to amplifiers, and when I had asked about that it was explained that maybe amplifying them would make them seem more modern to young people, enticing them to attend opera performances more than they chose to do.

I was saddened that this ancient cultural practice was perhaps nearing the end of its history, ironically when one of its potentially greatest practitioners was just beginning her career. Her creativity, an amalgam of her precocious yet already musically mature craft, sensitivity, imagination, and genuineness of understanding of her culture's achievement in this particular genre, was a beacon of possibility, a testament to what humans are capable of accomplishing. But it required, as all creativity does, a fertile cultural context for it to be recognized, nurtured, and appreciated, a context now so eroded as perhaps not to be able to sustain her potential contribution. I had been remarkably fortunate to witness performance creativity at its peak, not, as so often before in my life, in the culture of which I am a member, but in a foreign land, in a foreign music, a music threatened with possible extinction. And even if it survives, as I fervently hope it will, how many people outside of

China, and the diminishing number of supporters there, will ever be exposed to this young woman's achievement, or be able, as I was luckily ready to do, to appreciate it? Since that afternoon in Shenyang the many implications of that experience, complex, puzzling, heartening yet disturbing, have continued to haunt me, with no resolution in sight.

TEACHING MUSIC IN ITS CONTEXT

As mentioned previously, many issues exist relating to effective teaching of a variety of cultural musics. Most are outside the scope of philosophy and are dealt with appropriately in books such as *World Musics and Music Education,* mentioned earlier (note 17). In the chapters on implementation of this philosophy I will return to matters of context as related to the content areas of the National Standards. Here, only three issues will be addressed. The first has to do with a music of our own culture that, despite its overwhelming prominence, is largely "foreign" to music education. The second has to do with teaching music in ways that are genuine to how it is taught within its own culture. The third raises, once again, the ever-present issue of the relation of language learnings to musical experience.

Foreign music need not be as exotic to Westerners as the music of the Kaluli. In the multimusical cultures of many or most Western nations (and others around the world) the variety of musics, each based in a particular subculture, can be so great as to make it unrealistic for people to be equally at home in all of them. So we should not assume that learning cultural background material is necessary only for musics of cultures far from our own geographically. In our own cultural home live many musics of more and less familiarity to us, and each can be better understood and appreciated when we gain more awareness of its sociocultural situatedness. I mean for this claim to apply as well to even that music, or those musics, we know best, music(s) in which we have been steeped all our lives. Even such music takes on additional breadth and depth of meaning the more we understand its complex social-cultural basis. We will never learn as much as there is to know about how our "own" music, let alone others', reflects and interrelates with its culture: all additional understandings clarify and enlighten.

In American culture one particular musical sphere has been largely, almost completely, absent from music education in any serious, deliberate way. I am referring to the musics of popular culture, those musics most, rather than least, chosen to be engaged with by the vast majority of America's populace. The musics most represented in American music education—Western classical music (including the literature of bands), songs from various folk traditions, material related to approaches such as Orff and Kodály, and, fairly recently, jazz—are all distinctly minority musics, preferred by tiny percentages of people in this culture.[37] A useful way to illustrate

---

[37]See "Table 1. Changes in American Music Preferences, 1987–1996," as reported by the Recording Industry Association of America in its *Recording Industry Releases 1996 Consumer Profile,* in Dona L. Buel

what "popular music" consists of is to peruse the list of the "Songs of the Century," the "top 365 songs of the twentieth century," compiled by the National Endowment for the Arts and the Recording Industry Association of America.[38] Although the list is criticized by some as being a "mainstream" collection (genres such as electronic dance music, punk rock, and rap seem to be underrepresented), it nevertheless is profoundly interesting for (1) what it says about the music that has most influenced the musical experiences of the majority of people in America over the course of a century, and (2) how disconnected school music has been from it. One does find on the list a few chestnuts from the classical and "light classical" canon—"Vesti la Giubba" sung by Enrico Caruso, Sousa's "Stars and Stripes Forever," *Oklahoma, Porgy and Bess, The Sound of Music*—but most are pieces/performances (the two are often inseparable in the literature of popular music) likely to seldom if ever darken the door of a music classroom or rehearsal room in the United States.

I must confess here, so that my recommendation can be viewed in the context of my personal bias, that reading this list made my heart jump with joy. Here is music of great diversity, of delightful good humor, of pathos, of sassy attitude, of endless imagination, and, most important to me, of profoundly satisfying musical value. Sentimental, exuberant, honest, outrageous, joyous, gutsy, energetic, yearning, low-down, tender, the American psyche and experience are in this body of work exemplified, warts and all, in musical expression. What a refreshing, exhilarating dose of musical reality, as compared with so much that is polite, complacent, and safe in the literature of school music. Of course much of that conventional literature is valuable, some of it supremely so. But much of the music most beloved by the majority of people in our culture is equally so. It is time—no, beyond the time—for us to embrace the foreign (to us) music of popular culture as worthy of our best efforts as educators, efforts to enhance its pleasures, broaden its understanding and appreciation, and contribute meaningfully to its ongoing vitality.

Doing so will force us to face many vexing questions of the relation of music to social issues, to morality in the commonplace sense, to politics, decorum, and on and on with the interface of music and life so explicitly present in this literature.[39] We will also have to confront the issue of what our culture regards as appropriate in schooling.

---

and Samuel C. Welch, "Improving Music Appreciation Class Using Cohort Analysis," *General Music Today,* 13, no. 3 (Spring 2000), 14. Preference/purchase of Rock and Roll, Country, Urban Contemporary (R&B), Pop, Rap, and Gospel add up to 81.9% in 1996. For Classical music it is 3.4%, and for Jazz 3.3%. (The remainder is scattered among Oldies, Soundtracks, New Age, Children's, Ethnic, Standards, Big Band, Swing, Spanish, Electronic, Instrumental, Folk, and Holiday music.) In the 2000 *Consumer Profile,* Jazz had slipped to 2.9% and Classical to 2.7%.

[38]The list of songs is available on the Recording Industry Association of America Website, riaa.com.

[39]An indispensable source of insight into the complexities of popular musics and of their cultural roles is Simon Frith, *Performing Rites: On the Value of Popular Music* (Cambridge: Harvard University Press, 1996). This book should be studied by all music educators concerned with issues of popular culture as related to music and music education. Other worthy books on this topic include Peter G. Christenson and Donald F. Roberts, *It's Not Only Rock & Roll: Popular Music in the Lives of Adolescents* (Cresskill, NJ: Hampton Press, 1998); *Sound Identities: Popular Music and the Cultural Politics of Education,* ed. Cameron McCarthy, Glenn Hudak, Shawn Miklaucic, and Paula Saukko (New York: Peter Lang, 1999); and *Adolescents and Their Music,* ed. Jonathan S. Epstein (New York: Garland, 1994). Each of these books cites many others of value.

We will have to add to our expertise in both creating and responding to music the authenticity of how this particular music is created and shared, just as we must with every other music in which the practices of making and taking are not based on the Western classical model. The closer we get to the ways of creating, responding, and teaching/learning in each particular musical practice the closer we get to the genuineness and singularity of musical experience it offers. We cannot, to be specific, teach popular music (creating it, responding to it, understanding it, critiquing it) as if it were classical music, just as is the case with jazz (a lesson we are well along in learning) and with every other music not of the Western classical tradition. And, with popular music, as much as with all others including classical, understandings of its cultural situatedness will add dimensionality to the meanings to be gained from it.

How can we do all this effectively? The four ways of knowing music discussed in previous chapters can help answer this question. Knowing within a particular music requires some measure of internalizing, in one's mind, body, and feelings, the particular "flavor"—the characteristic musical qualities—of that music. For popular music our students are already deeply immersed in at least some styles and types, far more, of course, than we teachers are likely to be. But many other popular music styles are likely to be relatively unfamiliar, as is the case with music of other cultures. To internalize any unfamiliar music it is necessary to get that music "in one's ears"— to immerse oneself in what it sounds like. That is the precondition for all understanding: without it any understanding can only be empty. Clearly, listening, listening, listening, is the direct route to knowing within any music. But now we must include in listening, in addition to increasing perceptual awareness of what those sounds are doing and how they are doing it *in the ways each music defines its own expectations*, a sense of the cultural/social environment within which music lives. Knowing about and knowing why—about the conditions of life, belief, behavior, and values of its culture, and why the conditions add up to a particular "way to be" in the world and in music—become powerful components of understanding, of gaining musical meaning as fully as that music makes it available.

Knowing how to create an unfamiliar music internalizes it in a very powerful way. But notice: knowing how, without deep immersion in knowing within, where saturated listening provides the essential basis for creating, can only be empty, trivial, and disrespectful. Creating a music one has not been immersed in through sufficient taking within of its musical ways to be can only yield superficial results. This is not to say that one cannot try to create a music one is getting to know until some magic moment when one has internalized its soundscape to "x" level. It's an acknowledgment that knowing within must be a constant accompaniment to, and springboard for, the knowing of creating if the attempt to create is to be honest.

All these balances among the four ways to know music—like juggling four balls at the same time—take considerable musical/pedagogical skill and insight if learning is to be optimal. How nice it would be if there were a neat formula we could follow—such and such degree of this, such and such degree of that—to achieve a guaranteed result. But of course if that were the case our work would be easy, and therefore unlike the teaching of every subject, each requiring, in its way, the same exquisitely sensitive juggling of its component aspects. For us in music education the worst errors tend to occur, I suggest, when balances become extreme; when one or another focus of learning so dominates that the others are unattended to, rendering them powerless to add their necessary dimensions.

In the matter of social/cultural contexts, the risks are heightened because of the need to use language to do what it uniquely does—to disclose and explain. Language-knowing is so dominant in education, so highly respected and supported, that we can be seduced into relying on it too much, overbalancing the experiential foundation our subject requires. So we need to be careful here, using disclosure and explanation sufficiently for them to enrich, but sparingly enough that they do not interfere with what matters most in music—the experience of its meaningfully organized sounds in their embodiment of the culture from which they spring.

ETUDES

1. Armstrong argues that the arts of a culture embody the deepest characteristics of human feeling, or affect, in that culture. Do you think a culture's feeling potentials can be gained completely by experiencing just one of its arts, such as music? Or would a more complete sharing of potentials be gained by involvement with more than one art, or all? How does your answer play out in its implications for education? What would be an ideal education that made artistic/aesthetic meanings most fully available to all culture members?

2. Where do you stand in the Contextualist-Universalist debate? Does one position seem more attractive to you than the other? Why?

   Try taking one side and debating the issue with someone who takes the other, building on and extending the arguments I offered. Instead of using the musical examples I chose, try using a couple of examples of popular music—say, contemporary rock, or reggae. How does this music exemplify all music, in the sense of its universal musical characteristics? How does it exemplify a particular cultural playing out of the larger sphere of music? And how do the pieces you chose exist as incomparable? Does seeing the pieces in all three dimensions increase your understanding and respect for them?

3. Imagine, or if you can, try out a debate similar to the one above with students of your choice, and with musical examples appropriate for those students. How would you prepare your students for their debate? What instructions would you give each team to help them get ready and to present a strong case? What discussion might take place after their presentations? Would you support one or the other position if the students asked your opinion? Are you comfortable with recommending to both that they consider a synergistic resolution?

4. Do you feel "at home" with more than one kind of music? How did your identification with the music most familiar to you come about? Did any music that was once quite foreign to you ever become very familiar, sufficiently that it feels like it is now "yours"? Was that a difficult process?

In teaching music, requiring that we expand opportunities for musical experience and enjoyment, how can we smooth the way for our students to open themselves to, and incorporate more of, musics different from those with which they are already comfortable? Can we do this *without trying to diminish their enjoyment of and respect for the music(s) they presently regard as "theirs," in fact heightening that respect and enjoyment?*

5. How do you relate to the position I've argued that popular musics have been largely and unfortunately neglected—even spurned—in American music education and in many other places around the globe? To what extent do you feel we need to rectify this situation? If we do attempt to include this literature as a basic part of school music education, what issues will we have to face that its exclusion has allowed us to ignore? How would teacher education programs have to change to best prepare knowledgeable and effective teachers of these musics? What research would help us? What resistances from our communities might we expect, and what might we do about them? What would the impact be on students at different school levels and from different cultural/ethnic/racial backgrounds? What resistances from the music education profession itself might occur?

All these questions raised by including popular music as relevant for music education suggest important, even fundamental changes in traditions of music education in many cultures. Do you think such changes need to be made, despite their problematic nature?

7

From Theory to Practice:
Musical Roles as Intelligences

MAIN THEMES

- There is not a single "musical intelligence," as Howard Gardner has proposed. Music offers a wide range of ways to be intelligent.
- Similarly, each domain (subject) taught in schools contains a variety of ways to exercise intelligence. And human endeavors outside those taught in schools also are ways to be intelligent.
- Intelligence includes both a general factor, applicable to all intelligences, and a contextual factor, recognizing the multiplicity of distinctive ways that the general factor can be applied in the many roles humans play.
- Intelligence embraces imagination, culture, individuality, opportunity, the body, the feelings, and several other factors. All are implicated in and determinants of the ways individuals are able to be intelligent and the varied degrees of their intelligences.
- Composing, performing, improvising, listening, music theory, musicology, and music teaching each call on a particular yet related way to demonstrate intelligence.
- The theory applies to several perennial issues in music education: teaching for parts and wholes, assessment and testing, transfer, "integration."
- Music education should help individuals achieve whatever potentials they have to be musically intelligent—able to more fully experience musical satisfactions—in whatever ways they choose. Achieving such a vision will require serious reexamination of present music education beliefs and practices.

BEYOND THE THEORY OF MULTIPLE INTELLIGENCES

> Precisely because [music] is not used for explicit communication, or for other evident survival purposes, its continuing centrality in human experience constitutes a challenging puzzle. The anthropologist Lévi-Strauss is scarcely alone among scientists in claiming that if we can explain music, we may find the key for all of human thought or in implying that failure to take music seriously weakens any account of the human condition.[1]

In this statement from his influential book *Frames of Mind: The Theory of Multiple Intelligences,* Howard Gardner suggests that an understanding of music may be the key for understanding all human thinking, and that to understand the human condition we must take music seriously into account. Few of us in music education would not feel ennobled by his bold—even breathtaking—claim, valuing music as we do. But few of us, or of the many thinkers about music throughout history, have been quite so ambitious about music's nature and value. We have intuited that music is more central to humankind than is generally thought, and we have struggled to explain why, but we have generally stopped short of identifying music as the one sure clue to unraveling the mysteries of the human mind, intriguing (and self-justifying) as that may be.

I do not intend to pursue Gardner's perhaps grandiose claim (although I would certainly not dispute it). I hope this book, to this point, has clarified and strengthened our understandings of why musical experience is central to the condition of being human, allowing us to know ourselves in the world as nothing else can. I do intend, in this chapter, to offer an explanation of how diverse musical involvements are demonstrations of diverse intelligences, and how such an explanation applies to all human involvements. That is, I will use music as the basis for explaining and exemplifying what intelligence consists of and how it permeates all that humans do. So although I will not claim that music is "the key for all of human thought," I will indeed claim, and demonstrate, that musical involvements are clear and illustrative instances of how humans are intelligent. I will clarify how musical experiences represent, as much as anything else humans can do, the essential characteristic—intelligence—that marks us as *Homo sapiens*—that is, creatures capable of wisdom and judgment.

This explanation will serve as a pivot point between philosophy and educational practice, leading directly to issues of curriculum, teaching, and learning in the following chapters. As will become clear, my theory of intelligence, as particularly manifested in the ways music is encountered, is not by any means a strictly theoretical construct. It is, instead, a way to understand how we act effectively—with wisdom and judgment—in the real worlds human cultures provide us. The discussions of teaching music in the previous chapters, focusing on issues relating to each chapter's topic, will here be pulled together into the larger construct of musical intelligences. That construct will serve, in the following chapters, to illuminate the nature of the challenges facing us if we are to take the national content standards for music education as seriously as I believe they deserve and need to be taken.

---

[1]Howard Gardner, *Frames of Mind: The Theory of Multiple Intelligences* (New York: Basic Books, 1999), 123.

My starting point for the theory of intelligence I will offer will be the one Gardner has proposed in the book previously quoted (and in subsequent books and other writings). I will expand on and add precision to the concept of intelligence he has formulated, developing the proposition that musical intelligence, and by extension, human intelligence in general, is better understood as constituted not of "frames" conceived as stable mental structures but of "roles," conceived, according to the dictionary, as "proper or customary functions." I will argue that Gardner's notion of musical intelligence, helpful as it has been in certain respects, is not sufficiently descriptive of the diverse ways intelligence is manifested in the domain of music, and, by extension, how intelligences are manifested in other domains and outside what are typically conceived as domains in the academic community. The limitations of Gardner's conception, I will suggest, stem from a concept of intelligence so general as to not define precisely what constitutes it, leaving its application uncertain and confusing. This leads him to a description of "musical intelligence" that cannot be sustained. I will offer an alternative definition of intelligence (and, by extension, of musical intelligence) that provides sufficient specificity to allow a much needed refinement in our understandings of the diversity of musical intelligences, and, extrapolating from that, of the diversity of human intelligences as they operate in all aspects of human life. My definition, and the theory it undergirds, will provide a manageable set of constructs for understanding both the specificities of what intelligence is and how education can enhance the scope and quality of each of the many ways intelligence can be manifested.

THE MANY CONCEPTS OF INTELLIGENCE

Given the innumerable definitions of intelligence proposed over the centuries, one may well ask why still another is needed. After all, a great many major thinkers have turned their attention to the issue of human intellectual capacities and the essential characteristics that seem to underlie them. Gardner's chapter on "Intelligence: Earlier Views," in his *Frames of Mind,* mentions more than thirty important views of intelligence over the centuries, and more than forty characteristics that have been attached to it. His chapter is only the tip of an iceberg. The appendix of John B. Carroll's monumental *Human Cognitive Abilities: A Survey of Factor-Analytical Studies*[2] lists 205 factor classifications explored in the research on cognitive abilities, many of them containing several subfactors. In the book *What Is Intelligence? Contemporary Viewpoints on Its Nature and Definition,*[3] editor Robert Sternberg provides a framework for the two dozen definitions the book's authors propose, identifying three sources of intelligence—within the individual, within the environment, and within the interaction between the individual and the environment—each of which contains a number

---

[2]John B. Carroll, *Human Cognitive Abilities: A Survey of Factor-Analytical Studies* (Cambridge and New York: Cambridge University Press, 1993), 791–95.
[3]Robert J. Sternberg and D. K. Detterman, eds., *What Is Intelligence* (Norwood, NJ: Ablex Publishing Corporation, 1986).

of more specific sources. His 56-item framework is extremely useful as a way to conceptualize the larger field: it also gives a sense of the daunting complexity of that field. A perusal of the two-volume, 1,235-page *Encyclopedia of Human Intelligence,*[4] and of the bibliographies following each entry, gives still more evidence of the enormity of the effort made by so many scholars over so many centuries to attempt to delineate the workings of the human intellect. Few issues, it would seem, have engaged the efforts of so many thinkers, over so long a time, with so many questions still unanswered, as that of the nature of human intelligence.

Musical Intelligence

In the field of music the use of the word "intelligence" as the key concept for understanding the musical mind and its workings has been only sporadic.[5] Certainly Gardner's 1983 book, with its chapter on musical intelligence, has brought more widespread attention to this concept than any other single event. But a diverse set of terms relevant to musical capacity has existed for a very long time. Gardner's chapter on musical intelligence uses, as synonyms for or designations of musical intelligence, talent, gift, prodigy, precocity, competence, accomplishment, ability, skills, achievement, musical imagination, core abilities, auditory sense, feeling, sensitivity, apprehension, promise, proficiency, musical thinking, appreciation, intuition, fluency, perception, capacity, aptitude, and memory. Gardner's particular contribution is his argument that all such common terms for musical ability can be understood as descriptors for what in other fields of mindful ability, most notably the linguistic and the logical-mathematical, is regularly called intelligence. In his inclusion of music among the basic ways humans can be intelligent he has dramatically altered the perception of many people both inside and outside the academic world as to how music can be regarded and valued.

Why should the word intelligence be applied to music? Why not continue to rely on the terms historically applied to competency in this field—ability, talent, musicality, sensitivity, aptitude, and capacity being among the most common?[6] After all,

---

[4]Robert J. Sternberg, ed., *Encyclopedia of Human Intelligence* (New York: Macmillan, 1994).

[5]The term "musical intelligence" can be found in Carl E. Seashore, *Psychology of Music* (New York: McGraw-Hill, 1938); in H. D. Wing, *Standardized Tests of Musical Intelligence* (The Mere, England: National Foundation for Educational Research, 1939, 1961); in Jack Heller and Warren Campbell, "Models of Language and Intellect in Music Research," in *Music Education for Tomorrow's Society,* ed. A. Motycka (Jamestown, RI: GAMT Music Press, 1976); in W. Ann Stokes, "Intelligence and Feeling" (Doctoral diss., Northwestern University, 1990); and in several other sources. The term "musical intelligence" is not, however, a common one in the scholarly literature on music and music education, nor has it achieved a commonly understood meaning. I am not aware of any previous treatment of musical intelligences as I am suggesting they should be construed.

[6]An excellent discussion of the meanings of and controversies surrounding such terms is given in J. David Boyle, "Evaluation of Music Ability," in *Handbook of Research on Music Teaching and Learning,* ed. R. Colwell (New York: Schirmer Books, 1992), 247–52. It may very well be that each such term has particular shadings of meaning worthy of retaining. For example, "aptitude" usually refers to musical potential, and "musicality" suggests a sensitivity to expressive nuances. My purpose in this paper is to develop a concept of musical intelligences that, as will be explained, subsumes all these other descriptors.

"What's in a name? That which we call a rose / By any other name would smell as sweet."[7] Well, in the field of education, some names emphatically smell sweeter than others. Music, I believe, along with the other arts, has been ghettoized in education to a large degree because it has been considered to be different from—usually radically different from—those subjects that require intelligence. As I have mentioned previously in other contexts, education has labored for centuries under limited notions of how intelligence is manifested, resulting in effective division of the school curriculum into the basics—the subjects for which intelligence is the key factor—and the specials—all those subjects not requiring intelligence but instead depending on the existence in some children of ability, talent, aptitude, and so forth. The Bloom *Taxonomy of Educational Objectives*,[8] so influential for so many years until recently, added credibility to that bifurcation of subjects, conceptualizing the human mind as comprising the cognitive domain, consisting of progressively more complex verbal/conceptual constructs and therefore synonymous with intelligence, and the affective and psychomotor domains (in which the arts primarily dwell), *ipso facto,* not cognitive and therefore not to be conceived as requiring intelligence.

In recent years our understandings of the diverse ways the human mind is cognitive—that is, capable of knowing, perceiving, reasoning, and constructing meaning—have opened up, largely as a result of work in the cognitive sciences, finally leveling the playing field for music and the arts, allowing us not only to make the case for the arts in entirely new ways but also to reconceive our own understandings of the musical mind and how it might be cultivated. Chapter 5 laid the groundwork for how we can now regard musical thinking, knowing, and doing as acts of cognition in which intelligence is manifested. We are ready to shift the previous boundaries of our beliefs, and open up new territories in which we can begin to explore a host of heretofore unnoticed issues as to the variety of ways musical intelligences can be and need to be developed and, as a direct consequence, how the human mind in all its manifestations can be and needs to be developed. All who are interested in the workings of the human mind should welcome the opportunities, challenges, and far-reaching implications of redefining musical engagements as requiring the operation of intelligence.

A DEFINITION OF INTELLIGENCE

In chapters 1 and 5 I discussed the hazards of definitions—their tendency to delimit ongoing understandings and therefore growth and change. In my attempt to distinguish the salient characteristics of aesthetic education, music, and art, I suggested

---

[7]William Shakespeare, *Romeo and Juliet,* act 2, scene 1.

[8]Benjamin S. Bloom et al., eds., *Taxonomy of Educational Objectives, Handbook I: Cognitive Domain* (New York: David McKay, 1956); David R. Krathwohl et al., eds., *Taxonomy of Educational Objectives, Handbook II: Affective Domain* (New York: David McKay, 1964); Anita J. Harrow, *A Taxonomy of the Psychomotor Domain* (New York: David McKay, 1972).

that conceiving a definition as, modestly, a description, softens its often rigid demeanor. I referred to my delineations of aesthetic education, music, and art as descriptions, to avoid a feared rigidity and to emphasize their use as tools for thought rather than as prescriptions to be followed slavishly.

That position applies as well to my definition of intelligence. But here I am more willing to go out on a limb and call my proffered description a definition, largely because so many others have done so in a free marketplace of theorizing. There seems to be less concern in intelligence scholarship (or perhaps less modesty) with diverse definitions presented as such. So, in that spirit, I will use the term definition here and willingly accept its risks.

First, however, some qualifications. Various definitions of intelligence are not necessarily, and in fact not usually, competitive. With all highly complex concepts, such as education, democracy, truth, and value, differing definitions may be understood as complementary attempts to illuminate the multifaceted nature of each of them. So definitions of intelligence have historically ranged from very broad to very specific, and have pinpointed a great variety of mental functions as being the salient ones.

At what point on the continuum of very general to very specific definitions has one gained optimal utility? Probably no single correct answer exists to this question. Different points on that continuum are usefully generative of different levels of insight and application. (I will return to this issue shortly.) At what point in history will we know, with finality, exactly how the mind functions so that we can stipulate exactly which factors are most implicated in intelligence? I suggest we should not hold our breaths. We can only try to take best advantage of what is credible during the time we happen to address the issue, recognizing that credible knowledge is always in process of becoming.

With these caveats in mind a proposed definition of intelligence can be understood modestly rather than grandiosely, as complementary rather than as exclusionary, as derived rather than unprecedented, and as an attempt to make a pragmatic rather than an absolute truth-claim. In that spirit I proffer the following definition:

> *Intelligence consists of the ability to make increasingly acute discriminations, as related to increasingly wide connections, in contexts provided by culturally devised role expectations.*

EXPLANATION OF THE DEFINITION

My definition of intelligence has two aspects, the first dealing with discriminations and connections, the second with the contexts in which they are made. I will discuss each aspect in turn.

By the term "discriminations" I mean primarily differentiations. A major, necessary component of intelligence, I suggest, is the ability to perceive differentia—

"The character or basic factor by which one entity is distinguished from another."[9] Mindful functioning requires distinctions to be made, differences to be noted, particularities to be registered, whether consciously or tacitly. This process of noting distinctions—making discriminations—ranges across a wide continuum from the very obvious to the very subtle. A person's capacity to discriminate differentia at increasingly acute levels of precision, nuance, refinement, particularity, and meticulousness is one essential dimension of the level of that person's intelligence.

By the term "connections" I mean primarily interrelations. The second necessary component of intelligence is the ability to perceive how and to what degree entities are interrelated with each other by identity, similarity, affinity, association, proximity, relevance, pertinence, difference, contrast, dissimilarity, incommensurability, polarity, and so forth. Mindful functioning requires, as much as the making of discriminations among particularities, the making of connections among particularities. The process of making connections ranges as broadly as does the process of differentiation, from noting obvious identicalities, to understanding complex, tenuous correspondences and implications, to recognizing differences, incompatibilities, oppositions, and divergences of the most subtle and complex sort. A person's ability to apprehend connections at increasingly comprehensive levels of interrelatedness is a second essential dimension of that person's intelligence.

The term "as related to" joins discriminations of differentia with recognitions of connections. Human intelligence is characterized by the remarkable—even astounding—capacity not only to differentiate acutely but also to recognize how that which is differentiated is connected with other differentia. That capacity to perceive more precisely while at the very same time comprehending more inclusively may well be the defining quality of human intelligence. Discrimination brings to consciousness the details of the world and of the self within it, without which our minds would be empty of content. Interrelation brings to consciousness the patterns in the world and of ourselves as part of it, without which our minds would be devoid of coherence, understanding, meaning, and wisdom.

The key factor in the making of connections among discriminations is imagination. By this word I mean far more than the commonplace use of it to denote fanciful or creative thinking. I mean imagination to be understood as the foundational operation of the human mind in its function of making meaning, making sense—the fundamental requirement for sapience. Unlike animals or machines (computers, for instance), humans can add determinants made from choice to the hard-wired determinants of connection-making (such as instinct, involuntary responses, and chaining). The choices are supplied largely by cultures and by individual interactions with them. So while imagination in the "creative" sense is one dimension of its functioning, as explained in Chapter 4, I mean it in this context as the basis and possibility for all meanings of which humans are capable. This is what Mark Johnson so clearly explains as the deepest meaning of imagination, not just as "artistic creativity, fantasy,

---

[9]*Random House Dictionary,* 2nd ed., s.v. "differentia."

scientific discovery, invention, and novelty," but also as "our capacity to organize mental representations (especially percepts, images, and image schemata) into meaningful, coherent unities."[10]

> We are thus brought to a momentous conclusion about the importance of human imagination, namely, *there can be no meaningful experience without imagination,* either in its productive or reproductive functions. As productive, imagination gives us the very structure of objectivity. As reproductive, it supplies all the connections by means of which we achieve coherent, unified, and meaningful experience and understanding. We are talking here about operations of the imagination so pervasive, automatic, and indispensable that we are ordinarily not aware of them. Nevertheless, our ordered world, and the possibility of understanding any part of it, depends on the existence of this synthesizing activity.[11] (Emphasis in original)

The capacity to discriminate connectedly or to interconnect discriminatingly is the basis for all so-called higher-order cognitive functions. Cause and effect, categorization, metaphor, problem solving, problem finding, synthesizing, judging, interpreting, theorizing, model-building, critical thinking, creating—all these and many other complex cognitive operations are built on a foundation of fine discriminations connected in a variety of generative ways for particular purposes. Therefore, I intend the first aspect of my definition to be understood as identifying the general factor underlying all intelligent functioning.

The second aspect of my definition calls attention to the necessity that the general factor—discriminations and their connections—be actuated in particular contexts. The general process of discriminative connectedness, underlying all intelligent functioning, is differentiated by and particular to the role a person is playing—that is, the setting, task, and purpose of the engagement being pursued. There can be no discriminations made without a particular content of and context for them: one cannot simply "discriminate." There can be no making of connections except when particular discriminations are connected in a particular way and for a particular purpose: one cannot simply "make connections." Therefore, the general factor of intelligence exists as the substratum within, and attains reality and functionality within, domain-specific, task-specific, role-specific cognitive operations. In my theory there is no separation at the functional level of the general, foundational factor of intelligence from its special, diversely characteristic applications. Human intelligence, I suggest, is manifested in a great variety of ways, each being an instance of the complex, multifaceted nature of human cognitive potentialities. Each potential of the mind—each way to manifest intelligence—depends, at bottom, on the general capacity to discriminate and interrelate as pertinent to that potential. This general factor

---

[10]Mark Johnson, *The Body in the Mind: The Bodily Basis of Meaning, Imagination, and Reason* (Chicago: University of Chicago Press, 1987), xv.

[11]Ibid., 149–51. This material is from Marian Dura, "The Kinesthetic Dimension of the Music Listening Experience" (Doctoral diss., Northwestern University, 1998), 181.

can be separated from its functional reality-base theoretically, as I am attempting to do to explain my view of the nature of intelligence. In the actual manifestation of intelligence there can be no separation of the general factor from its particular, specific applications in the roles that cultures provide people to play.

Further, and crucially, intelligence as I conceive it always exists *to some degree*. It is not something that comes into being only when some specified level of it has been attained, such that those who have demonstrated *x* amount of ability to discriminate and interconnect in some particular field of endeavor (role) are regarded as "being intelligent" in the endeavor (role), while those falling below that level are "not intelligent." Whatever level one has achieved (I will discuss both innate and environmental contributions to achievement further on), at whatever age one happens to be, is the level of one's intelligence in that role context at that point in time. Intelligence exists on a continuum from very low to very high in all the many roles in which it can be manifested, and is in a continual state of development. The major point here is that the stereotypical view that intelligence is a unitary constant—something a person has or does not have (or is or is not), to a stipulated, permanent degree—is unacceptable in my theory.

Although the general factor of discriminative connectedness is, by definition, universally applicable to the functioning of all human minds (or else it would not be a general factor), it is always embedded in influences that shape human minds, such as culture and individuality.

The Influence of Culture

Culture provides perspective. At the physiological level of sensory discrimination or sensory perception, there may indeed be a stratum common among all humans across cultures. Physiology, of course, influences the discriminations potentially capable of being made: a person with a fully functioning, completely healthy system in any particular sensory modality will be capable of making more acute perceptions than someone who is impaired in that modality. But the physiological level of sensory perception is not yet at the level at which I conceive human intelligence to operate. After all, many living creatures possess perceptual acuities beyond those of humans. These, by themselves, do not fulfill my definition of intelligence. Physiology is one enabling factor of intelligence and therefore impinges transculturally on intelligence. (I will discuss other enabling factors further on.) But something has to happen to physiology in order for human intelligence to come into being. Culture enters the scene.

As explained in Chapter 6, human cultures are aggregates of shared human beliefs, behaviors, values, and ways of living. Although human physiological characteristics are pan-cultural, the uses to which they are put are always embedded in particular cultures. In the context of this chapter a culture can be conceived as a setting in which human intelligences can be developed. In specific terms, cultures are a major determinant of what discriminations get made and the manner in which they are made, and of what connections among them get made and the directions in which those connections are expanded. That is, culture largely determines how the general factor of intelligence plays out functionally.

In broader terms, cultures give people the possibility of achieving a coherent selfhood. Human experience, I suggest, is unique because of its capacity for the kind of intelligence of which humans are capable—an intelligence in which meanings arise out of connected discriminations. Without a culture to provide guidelines within which order may occur out of an infinite number of possible discriminations and connections, thinking and doing could only be chaotic. For humans, culture is not optional. A humanly meaningful life is one in which intelligence is given opportunity to develop as connected with culturally grounded arrangements of meaning potentials.

Such arrangements of ways to achieve meaning—of ways to develop the coherent discrimination/connection matrices constituting intelligence—are the roles humans play as actors within their culture. Each cultural role—each of the many components of a life experienced as meaningful—is the basis for the kinds of discriminatory connections required to be made and to be developed in order to fulfill that role with intelligence. The degree to which a person is able to fulfill a particular role with discriminative acuity coupled with relational expansiveness (including, in some cases, adding new dimensions to or significantly altering the role in question) is the degree of that person's intelligence in the role being played.

The general factor of intelligence, I am proposing, resides within and is activated by the various roles a culture affords its members. (Of course, new roles and various new combinations of roles continually appear in viable cultures.) Given that each person must play a variety of roles to be a functional member of her culture, each person is likely to demonstrate a variety of levels of intelligence. Like Gardner, I suspect that each person's "intelligence profile" is particular to that person. Unlike Gardner, however, I connect ways to be intelligent to roles people play rather than to frameworks of mind. Gardner implies something like role-based intelligence in claiming that within a particular frame of mind, the linguistic, for example, a person's intelligence can be manifested in a variety of ways, such as by being a poet, or a philosopher, or a journalist. So the notion of intelligence as being role-based is, at least to some degree, commensurate with Gardner's thinking. But he also claims that there are specific criteria (or "signs") to be met for a frame of mind to qualify as an intelligence.[12] He also admits that "the selection (or rejection) of a candidate intelligence is reminiscent more of an artistic judgment than of a scientific assessment."[13] This cautions us to be at least somewhat skeptical about the criteria he proposes. I am suggesting an alternative construct for what an intelligence is and how intelligences

---

[12]Gardner, *Frames of Mind*, note 1, 62–67. His criteria, or signs, by which an intelligence is designated as such, are (1) a faculty that can be spared or destroyed by brain damage, (2) a faculty existing in idiots savants, prodigies, and other exceptionalities, (3) a core operation or set of operations for the faculty, (4) a developmental progression in fulfilling the faculty, (5) a prehuman evolutionary history of the faculty, (6) support from experimental psychology, (7) support from intelligence testing, and (8) capacity of the faculty to be encoded in a symbol system.

[13]Ibid., 63.

function: that there is a core set of operations underlying all intelligences and that all intelligences are functionally role-based. Gardner's and my conceptions should not be understood as incompatible; they are different perspectives on this complex phenomenon. As I will attempt to explain, the concept of role-based intelligences as manifestations of a general factor of intelligence adds a powerful dimension to both our understanding of the human mind and our effectiveness in attempting to educate the human mind.

The Influence of Individuality

In addition to the cultural dimension, the dimension of the individual shapes human minds in their manifestations of intelligence. More than any other species on earth, individual humans are different from one another. Though cultures provide coherence through the particular roles that must be played for the culture to be viable, the people playing those roles display a high degree of variability as to how those roles get played out. As pointed out in Chapter 6, some cultures place a high value on individuality, although there are always limits as to how much divergence from role expectations will be tolerated. Other cultures, more tradition-oriented, accept less variability in role fulfillment, rewarding conformity more than divergence. Whatever the cultural expectations, however, the complexity of the human organism, especially the complexity of the human mind, fairly well ensures a high level of diversity between people and therefore a high level of diversity in the levels at which people can display intelligence in whatever roles they play.

This diversity stems from a host of factors, important among them that of genetics—the innate capacities with which a person is born. Clearly "nature" is influential in determining the level of intelligence a person is likely to achieve in any particular role context. In music, the terms "aptitude," "talent," and "capacity" are commonly used to designate this innate dimension of ability.[14] A good deal of interest in this dimension exists both among professionals in music and among the general public, reflecting long-held beliefs that success in this field is to some significant degree determined by natural endowment. My theory of intelligence includes the factor of innateness as one determinant of the degree to which individuals will be able to discriminate finely and interrelate widely: advances in scholarship in this area advance our understandings and ability to take best account of the nature factor in intelligence.

In addition to nature, building onto it through lived experience, are all the "nurture" factors also crucial in determining the extent to which individuals are able to function at higher levels of intelligence, and also accounting for the wide diversity that exists in people's intelligences. Factors such as motivation, preference, attitude, interest, ambition, learning style, and a host of additional psychological/emotional elements, implicated in myriad combinations and permutations in each individual's personality, inevitably influence the levels of intelligence people attain in the various roles they play.

---

[14]See Boyle, "Evaluation of Music Ability," note 6, for a succinct review of research on this topic.

The Influence of Opportunity

For those of us in education, an essential factor relating to the variability of intelligence is opportunity. At the macrocultural level the diversity of roles available to be played in a particular culture determines the ways intelligences can be manifested. Compare life in a poverty-stricken village in an isolated country with life in a major world capital city. Both settings require intelligence of their inhabitants and there are likely to be the same potential degrees of intelligence in both locations; it is in diversity of opportunities for intelligences to be fulfilled that they differ.

At the microcultural level opportunity has to do with access to whatever degree of diversity a culture provides. The simpler the culture, by which I mean the lesser variety of roles available to play, the more likely all inhabitants will be expected to participate in many or most roles. As cultures become more complex, specialization increases: some roles continue to have to be played by most or all members (son or daughter, friend, nurturer, provider, and so forth), but more and more societal roles become the province of only those who devote particular efforts to cultivating one or another of them. Society becomes increasingly dependent on specialization as the major way its needs are met, rather than on equal sharing of many or most functions. Opportunity increasingly becomes a pressing issue. Are some roles reserved for some people but not others? On what basis? Accident of birth into a particular socioeconomic class? Accident of birth in a particular location? Race? Sex? Religion? The ambitions and values of one's parents?

I am stressing here that the development of intelligences entails far more than the genetic endowments with which a person happens to be born and the personality each individual develops through his or her life experiences. I am suggesting that all aspects of culture, including governmental systems, belief-systems, moral and ethical systems, value systems, economic systems, educational systems—all major societal mechanisms—can be conceived as determinants of and monitoring instrumentalities for the apportionment of opportunities for intelligences to be developed. Given all these forces at work in who gets to do what—who gets the opportunity to develop whatever innate and accrued potentials they have—it is no mystery that high levels of diversity, approaching chaos, exist in complex cultures in this regard.

How can some semblance of order be constructed out of all these infinite possible permutations of individual potentials as influenced by the vagaries of how each potential of each individual might be even noticed, let alone given full nourishment? One major answer to this question has emerged over the past century or so in some societies. To ensure the greatest possibility that each individual's intelligence potentialities might be fulfilled, a society must provide universal education equally available to all citizens to as high a level as the society can afford; a general education component required of all students, to provide basic acquaintance with and basic development of intelligence in those roles most valued in that society; and a specialized, elective component in which preferred or particularly high intelligence potentials can be fulfilled optimally. The attainment of that ideal vision is, perhaps, the major challenge of any society in which full achievement of human potential is a grounding value.

Several additional explanations of my definition of intelligence will be given before I turn my attention to the specifics of musical intelligences.

The Body in Intelligence

The first explanation is that my proposal to regard intelligence as consisting of the ability to discriminate finely, and to interrelate those discriminations widely, applies equally to physical and mental operations. Of course, in a profound sense there can be no actual separation of the physical and the mental—of the mind and the body— physiologically or psychologically or philosophically, as I have explained in several contexts previously. That is not the issue I am dealing with here. My point here is a limited one, essential as it is: manifestations of intelligence frequently entail particular bodily actions. That is, fine discriminations embedded in wide connections must often be made in the body's operations in the particular ways called for by the intelligence in question. The high level of intelligence of a world-class athlete, for example, depends on, is manifested in, and in fact is defined by the exquisitely fine discriminations being made by the body within the particular context of the connections called for by a particular sport. Opportunities to manifest intelligence as expressed in bodily actions exist in a great variety of ways, most notably, perhaps, in athletics, the manual/mechanical trades, certain roles in medicine such as surgery, and the performing and visual arts (including crafts). It is important to understand that my conceptualization of intelligence most emphatically includes the operations of the body (as in performing music) as being, often, the essential grounding within which discriminations and connections are made. Intelligence, in my theory, is not, as so often assumed, located "from the ears up," as strictly a function of an isolated brain exercising its rational logic. Intelligence, instead, involves all that makes us human—our minds, bodies and, as I will discuss next, our feelings—in the fullness of meanings that saturate our lived experience.

Feelings and Other "Enablers" in Intelligence

In addition to intelligence including the body's actions, feeling is deeply implicated in my concept of intelligence. In Chapter 3 I made a distinction between emotion and feeling, based largely on the work of Antonio Damasio, whose research on brain function as it relates to consciousness has clarified emotion as the substratum from which feeling arises. Feeling carries the generality of an emotional state to the level at which particulars are noticed, processed in awareness, and therefore made conscious. Feeling, then, can be understood as the central, essential portal to conscious awareness, and therefore the basis for the noticings on which discriminations and their connections depend.

Such noticings need not be accompanied by conceptual identifications, instead being "noticing without naming," as I attempted to explain in Chapter 5. Much of what we notice, as in music, remains tacit but "still" meaningful, as Dufrenne argued in his phenomenological explanation of aesthetic meaning. Discriminations and their meaningful interconnections are felt and perceptually structured in much of our experience, including our experiences of music. As I labored to explain in my discussion of musical meaning, such structuring pervades our lived experience: we know much of ourselves and our world through immediate apprehensions, comprising discriminations we tacitly make and the interconnected structures of meaning they form. In all our conscious experience, not just in music and the arts, distinctions and their interrelations, experienced in an amalgamation of mind, body, and feeling, are the foundation for what we know and process as meaningful.

I am not persuaded, therefore, that "emotion" is fruitfully regarded to be a separate intelligence, as Daniel Goleman has suggested in his book *Emotional Intelligence*.[15] (What is dealt with in that book is, essentially, emotion rather than feeling. Music and the arts are not mentioned.) Instead, I prefer to conceive feeling as an underlying enabler of or precondition for the discriminations and connections on which intelligence is based. Intelligence depends on a variety of enablers—conditions related to the ability to make discriminations and configure them meaningfully. For example, one important enabler of intelligence is memory. By itself memory is not an intelligence but an essential tool, or mechanism, allowing discriminations and their meanings to be held in mind, recalled, and made use of in particular ways (that is, in particular roles). Sensation—hearing, for example—is another enabler of intelligence (especially in music but in much else we experience). If we are unable to hear particular sounds because of a faulty sensory apparatus, we will be unable to make the aural discriminations and their interconnections on which intelligence depends in the particular role calling for them to be made, just as if we are not able to remember a discriminated set of sounds we will not be able to make something of them in their interconnections as called for in a particular role.

Still another enabler of intelligence is knowledge—the mental material one has available to draw on to make connections. By itself, knowledge is inert and piecemeal, as in quiz show experts who have an impressive assortment of facts, or information, on tap. When knowledge is connected in meaningful configurations it becomes an essential component of intelligence, so long as "knowledge" is conceived to include the body's operations and the role of feeling in awareness and perceptual structuring, and is inclusive of all the many ways—roles—in which humans act meaningfully, including but going beyond those academic domains usually associated with the term "knowledge."

"Understanding" is another way to identify the configuring of connections to create meaning. Understanding can be conceived as the ability to make relevant, genuine connections among discriminations. The amount of understanding one has about something is the level one has achieved of pertinent, authentic interconnections of the salient characteristics of that something, both in and of itself and as

---

[15]Daniel Goleman, *Emotional Intelligence* (New York: Bantam, 1995).

related to other things. Understanding, therefore, like intelligence, which subsumes and depends on it, is best conceived not as a fixed entity but as a process in ongoing development. When has one reached the end of possibility to "understand"—to grasp meaningful connections about, say, the teaching of music? Or about tonality? Or about any of the content standards for music education? Or (to be less parochial) having a successful relationship with one's parents?

Conceiving knowledge, understanding, feeling, memory, sensory processing, attention, energy, interest, intuition, and so on, as *implicated* in intelligence, as *enablers* of intelligence, permitting it to be manifested in ways called on by particular roles, allows each enabler to contribute an essential dimension to the inclusiveness of human intelligence. Which brings me back to feeling as an essential enabler of intelligence. In all we do in our lives, our feelings operate as a basis for the meanings we experience. In music and the arts feelings play two additional, distinctive functions. The discriminations and connections we make in all musical experiences depend on feeling as a primal mechanism determining what and how we perceive and what and how we "make something of" what we perceive, something we call "musical."

Further, feelings are the primary *content* of what we experience musically, that is, the "musicalization" of sounds (and incorporated materials including ideas, emotions, and so forth) into the felt meanings music exists to provide. (Please review Chapter 3 as to what I mean by that assertion.) This dual function of feeling in the aesthetic domain, as both means and end, in which feeling (conceived as a union of mind with body) is the sine qua non of that domain, constitutes the "specialness" the arts add to our meaningful experience, as the previous chapters, each with its own focus, have attempted to explain. In music, the general factor of intelligence, the ability to make meaning by acute differentiations and increasingly inclusive interconnections among sounds, founded on feeling-awareness, is situated within each musical role a culture provides, each role requiring its own playing out, in its own particular way, of the general factor. (I will be more specific about this shortly.)

Intelligence in music, then, is the ability to experience music as fully "within" and "how," with unified engagement of mind, body, and feeling, as potentially possible in every musical role a person plays. That potential is unlikely to be entirely fulfilled by any person in any particular musical role, so rich with possibilities are various musical involvements, provided by various musical roles. The degree of one's discriminative meanings/understandings in a particular musical involvement is the degree of one's intelligence at that time and in that case. This is a very different concept from the one that considers musical intelligence to be one's fixed capacity as measured by a set of tasks. Musical intelligence as I conceive it is the level of one's ability to experience music as meaningful, informed by sensitive discernments and broad understandings, in each particular musical role engagement in which one becomes involved. The flexibility, breadth, inclusiveness, and role specificity of this concept allows musical intelligence to be regarded as being based on the reality of how people actually experience music as a meaningful cultural artifact, capable of being assessed in ways authentic to its complex nature, related to different musical roles one can play, and amenable to improvement through systematic, experience-focused education.

Intelligence as Communal

In addition to the body as implicated in intelligence, and feeling and other enablers as also contributory to it, my theory of intelligence recognizes its essentially communal nature. Some manifestations of intelligence, such as that of the theoretical scientist, or creative artist, or visionary philosopher, are often conceived as occurring in splendid isolation, the person in question drawing from his or her unique brain a new discovery or insight arising as if out of nowhere. We might think of instances of this as being the staggering depth, breadth, and imaginativeness of Einstein's mathematical discriminations and connections leading to his theory of relativity, or of Michelangelo's equally staggering manifestation of artistically interrelated perceptions in the ceiling of the Sistine Chapel, or of the moral-ethical-societal connections to proper human behavior articulated by Martin Luther King, Jr., or of Emily Dickinson's astonishing sensitivity to the differentia and connections among human relationships and feelings as transformed into poetic utterance.

However, these geniuses (persons of extraordinarily high capacity to discriminate and interrelate in a particular endeavor) were steeped in, influenced by, and nurtured by the cultures in which they worked, which provided the basis for the discriminations they were led to make and the relations among them they were able to conceive. Their achievements, and all others of similar nature, however individual they may seem, were and could only be the products of what communities of human beings engender.

Many manifestations of intelligence, unlike the preceding, implicitly communal, instances, are explicitly so, depending not only on a social background from which they arise but also on cooperative interactions for intelligence to become operative. Clear examples are team sports, musical ensembles, and theater and dance productions. In such instances an individual's discriminations depend on and are intimately tied to those being made along with the other individuals simultaneously engaged in the event, and their interconnections are also being made both individually and communally. What is generally called "distributed cognition" in the cognitive psychology literature is comfortably assimilable to my notion of intelligence as essentially communal, my definition adding specificity to the operations underlying the intelligent functioning being displayed.

The solitary thinker and the jazz ensemble represent ends of a continuum, connected in that both depend ultimately on human communality for the intelligence they call for to become functional. In between are most human roles, neither as strikingly solitary nor as interactive as these, yet always playing out against a background of shared discriminations and connections. My theory of intelligence, then, acknowledges the aspect of individuality but also recognizes the ultimate dependency of individuals on others in many ways and at many levels.

Intelligence and Creativity

The next explanation of my theory to be given here has to do with the relation of intelligence to creativity. This is a venerable topic, of course, on which a great many scholars and researchers have energized. A few salient points will help clarify my thesis.

As pointed out in Chapter 4, conceptions of what constitutes creativity vary across cultures. The Western view is captured accurately by the *Random House Dictionary,* which, being a dictionary of the English language, embodying Western perspectives, defines creativity as "the ability to transcend traditional ideas, rules, patterns, relationships, or the like, to create meaningful new ideas, forms, methods, interpretations, etc.; originality, progressiveness, imagination." Practically all scholarly work on creativity in the West is based on this general conception of its nature.

The relation of this conception to my definition of intelligence is quite clear. As I mentioned previously, all so-called higher-order cognitive functions, including creativity, are built on the foundation of the mind's capacity to discriminate connectedly, or to interconnect discriminatingly. What differentiates various cognitive functions such as problem solving, hypothesizing, theorizing, and creating are the directions, purposes, and motivations of each, depending on the role being fulfilled. Creativity can then be defined, using the Western construct as a basis, as the making of discriminations and connections that "transcend those traditionally made in regard to ideas, rules, patterns, relationships, or the like," and in which those discriminations and connections bring "meaningful new ideas, forms, methods, interpretations, etc." into being, the discriminatory connections having been made with "originality, progressiveness, and imagination."

Creativity, then, is a particular kind, or manner, or style of intelligent functioning, with (culturally) characteristic, identifiable attributes. Therefore, a person may be recognized to be, say, a highly intelligent biologist but not a particularly creative one, or a very intelligent cook but not a very creative one, or an extremely intelligent teacher but not a notably creative one. This applies even in domains in which all or most roles are considered to require creativity, such as in the arts. It is perfectly reasonable to judge that such and such a person is an intelligent painter (or dancer, poet, pianist, composer, conductor, and so forth) but not very creative. We would find such a comment meaningful. (In the arts, because creativity as conceived of in the West, embracing originality, divergence, and so forth, is an important virtue, such a judgment would not be considered entirely positive.)

Similarly, we could judge a person engaged in a particular role to be quite creative at it but not very intelligent about it. In this case, the creativity, though imaginative, divergent, novel, and so forth, would not be judged to be sufficiently based on the fine perceptions and their credible interconnections that would make that person's work convincing and well grounded. The person's creativity, lacking in supportive intelligence, would seem superficial, or unaware, or, perhaps, "off the wall." The creativity would be "out of sync" with the intelligence needed to undergird it. An excellent example of this is given by Gail Zweigenthal, editor-in-chief (at that time) of *Gourmet Magazine,* who, in discussing a particular dessert of a famous New York chef, says,

> It's exactly the sort of culinary creativity we wanted to include in this issue celebrating the restaurant. We looked for chefs who can dazzle, but whose flair is grounded in solid technique, a keen sense of flavor, and respect for tradition. Otherwise, as we realized when collecting and testing these recipes, the food can be shallow; what should be great entertainment is merely slapstick.[16]

Just as manifestations of intelligence are specific to particular roles, creativity is also role specific. As Gardner says, "A single variety of creativity is a myth."[17] Although he identifies domains or disciplines as providing the boundaries within which intelligences and creativities reside, my thesis suggests that his analysis is not sufficiently fine-grained, about either intelligence or creativity, to best illuminate the diversities of each as they exist both within domains or disciplines and outside the domains or disciplines commonly recognized in the academic literature. Getting to the specifics of the many, diverse roles humans play, and recognizing each as a particular opportunity for intelligence and creativity to be demonstrated and developed, gives, I would argue, a far more accurate, more useful, more educationally suggestive, and, not least, more appreciative picture of human capabilities than the more limited view of domain specificity.

The important educational implication of the argument that intelligence and creativity are not identical is that each role that education attempts to cultivate—such as, in music education, the role of the composer, the performer, the improviser, and the listener—requires attention to both intelligence in that role and creativity in it. Developing one does not automatically develop the other. But deficiency in either seriously impedes artistic/aesthetic accomplishment. Clarity about developing the creative aspect of musical role expectations, as Chapter 4 attempted to provide, will not by itself satisfy the need for clarity about developing the intelligence aspect of each role. The latter is what this chapter addresses.

Specificity/Generality

The level of specificity of a definition is a key factor in its utility, very general definitions being useful for certain purposes, very detailed definitions being useful in other ways. My definition is not as detailed as some others, aimed at specifying the individual component operations underlying our ability to discriminate and to interrelate. For example, according to John B. Carroll, there are ten types of cognitive components by which we process information: monitor, attention, apprehension,

---

[16]Gail Zweigenthal, *Gourmet Magazine,* October 1997, 34. Copyright © 1997 Condé Nast Publications. All rights reserved. Reprinted with permission of *Gourmet.*

[17]Howard Gardner, *Creating Minds: An Anatomy of Creativity Seen Through the Lives of Freud, Einstein, Picasso, Stravinsky, Eliot, Graham, and Gandhi* (New York: Basic Books, 1993), 7.

perceptual integration, encoding, comparison, co-representation formation, co-representation retrieval, transformation, and response execution.[18] These may very well be the underlying elements that allow for discriminations and connections to take place, or perhaps other analyses are more apt. I take no position about how best to identify the elemental, operational details underlying my definition. I am aiming for a level of generality I believe more useful for understanding the overall nature of intelligence, recognizing its many functional manifestations, and planning ways to cultivate it through particular educational interventions, than more detailed analyses are likely to be, necessary as these are for different purposes.

At the other end of the spectrum are definitions more general than mine. Howard Gardner's is a good example. In his discussion of prerequisites of an intelligence, in *Frames of Mind,* he suggests that

> a human intellectual competence must entail a set of skills of problem solving—enabling the individual *to resolve genuine problems or difficulties* that he or she encounters and, when appropriate, to create an effective product—and must also entail the potential for *finding or creating problems*—thereby laying the groundwork for the acquisition of new knowledge.[19] (Emphases in original)

This is an explanation of *how intelligence is applied.* I find it rich with implications for educational practice, in its emphasis on the resolution of genuine difficulties with which students must grapple, in its recognition that making things can be construed as acts of intellectual competence (I am thinking of the making of music, of course), and in the implication that students must be actively engaged in working out solutions to problems they present to themselves as they seek new insights. All these are articles of faith for those of us, such as Gardner and me, steeped in and devoted to Deweyan progressive education principles.

Unfortunately, this application does not constitute a definition. Nowhere does Gardner provide one (as he does not anywhere for creativity). To suggest that "a human intellectual competence" (is this a synonym for "intelligence"?) entails a set of "skills of problem solving" is no doubt true, but it does not tell us what intelligence consists of that allows us to exercise those skills effectively. After all, given a problem to solve, a person can go about doing so very intelligently, moderately intelligently, or minimally intelligently. What, exactly, is that thing called intelligence that

---

[18]Listed and explained in Robert J. Sternberg, "Cognitive Approaches to Intelligence," in *Handbook of Intelligence,* ed. Benjamin B. Wolman (New York: John Wiley, 1985), 60, 61. For a different exploration of information-processing components (among many others) see Robert J. Sternberg, *Metaphors of Mind: Conceptions of the Nature of Intelligence* (New York: Cambridge University Press, 1990), 121–22. For a thorough, penetrating analysis of research on the operations underlying musical pattern recognition, pattern comparison, and decision-making mechanisms, including an explanation of his own carefully researched theory that explains the underlying factors in musical processing of tonal-rhythmic material, see Harold Fiske, "Structure of Cognition and Music Decision-Making," in *Handbook of Research,* note 6, 360–76.

[19]Gardner, *Frames of Mind,* note 1, 60, 61.

enables the problem to be solved effectively and aptly rather than clumsily and ineptly?

The same applies to "creating an effective product," and "finding or creating problems." All these are ways to *use* intelligence, to *bring intelligence to bear*. Gardner's "definition" does not tell us what it is we are using, or bringing to bear, on doing these things that would identify our doings as being, to some degree, intelligent. We desperately need, in Gardner's work, a clear definition of intelligence itself—not just how it gets used. We do not receive it.

Therefore, there is an empty place at the core—a hole needing to be filled if Gardner's (admirable) agenda is to be achieved. His application, absent a clear description of *what* gets applied, leaves us without guidance for either grasping what intelligence consists of or nurturing it effectively. I believe this to be the case as well with other positive suggestions Gardner has made for education, including his insistence that understanding is a key component in effective education (most notably in his book *The Unschooled Mind*), but with no clear definition given of what understanding consists of so that we can use it to aim for and achieve effective education.[20] What is needed for "intelligence," "creativity," and "understanding" are clear-cut definitions providing explicit guidance toward educational interventions that can help learners exercise higher degrees of each as they apply them to their studies and lives.

In regard to intelligence, I believe my definition is useful for doing this. In transcending the elemental details of cognitive operations, it attains a holistic level immediately related to how we actually go about "being intelligent" in the lives we live. But in identifying the particular, foundational functions on which all intelligent activity depends, it makes tangible both the conditions of intelligence and the cultivation required if it is to be developed. That is, to solve problems, of any sort and at any level, one must discriminate the factors, issues, or phenomena needing to be identified as being problematical. Without such selective discrimination—an essential requisite for intelligence—no problem can be solved, brought to an acceptable resolution. But in addition to making the appropriate discriminations, problem solving requires that those discriminations be interrelated in ways particular to and pertinent for the solution being sought. The second requisite for intelligence, being able to make meaningful and relevant connections among discriminations (understanding), leads these discriminations in the generative directions necessary for problem resolutions.

This applies equally and precisely to "creating an effective product" and to "finding or creating problems," both of which require that appropriately fine distinctions as related to pertinent connections among them be made—that is, that intelligence be activated through the core operations on which effective thinking and acting depend in all the roles one plays in life. To help students solve problems, find problems, create products, achieve understanding, as Gardner correctly insists education must do if it is to be meaningful, educational encounters must be so arranged that each student is led to and provided with the particular experiences that will

---

[20]Howard Gardner, *The Unschooled Mind* (New York: Basic Books, 1991).

enable discriminations and connections to be made as relevant to whatever is being learned, to whatever is being encountered, to whatever challenges are being set, to whatever problems are being addressed. My definition, I believe, provides a foundational structure and an operative mechanism for both unifying smaller details of cognitive functioning and operationally specifying how to fulfill larger goals of effective learning. Among the many extant definitions of intelligence, each helping to clarify its complex nature, the one I propose seems to me both optimally specific and optimally general, to provide useful guidance both theoretically and practically.

MUSICAL INTELLIGENCES

The level of specificity of one's definition of intelligence will inevitably influence one's conception of musical intelligence. Gardner's (overly) broad definition (if definition at all) led him to the recognition that music is, indeed, a way to manifest intelligence. That, I believe, has been his major contribution, along with his recognition that there are other ways to be intelligent beyond those measured by IQ tests and other traditional intelligence identifiers. However, the generality and imprecision of his concept of intelligence allowed him to be satisfied with a singular intelligence covering all who are engaged with music. This is a counterpart in music to the IQ concept in intelligence theory—an oversimplification so severe as to seriously misrepresent what intelligence is and how it manifests itself in human endeavors. Gardner does mention, in passing, that "there are several roles that musically inclined individuals can assume," these being, in hierarchical order, composing, performing, and listening.[21] But his analysis provides few distinctions as to the different ways intelligence is exhibited in these different musical roles, and how each requires particular applications of the cognitive operations entailed in intelligence.

It is precisely in these differences among musical thinkings and doings—differences among musical minds—that the multiple realities of musical knowing and experiencing come to light. To think that those engaged in each of the many different musical roles our culture makes available are all intelligent in precisely the same way is to seriously misconstrue what each of those roles particularly calls on if it is to be played intelligently. If there were a singular musical intelligence that each role manifests identically, a person who was highly intelligent as, say, a composer, would therefore be equally intelligent, or potentially equally intelligent, in every other musical role.

All our experience tells us that this is not the case; that, in fact, it is highly unusual for a person to be equally competent, or intelligent, in more than one musical role. When that happens, as, say, with Leonard Bernstein, highly intelligent as a composer, conductor, performer, teacher, writer, we are likely to shake our heads in wonderment—the exception proving the rule. For another example, one thinks of

---

[21]Gardner, *Frames of Mind,* note 1, 104. The notion of a "hierarchy" of musical roles seems to me both artificial and unhelpful.

Michael Jordan, incomparably intelligent in basketball (yes, I am describing his achievement as intelligence) but, despite his fondest wishes and extraordinary efforts, unable to achieve professional levels in baseball or golf. Of course, given his magnificent athleticism he was able to go further with these other sports than most ordinary people (that is, normally intelligent in them) are likely to do. Of course, a musician such as Bernstein is more likely to excel in several musical roles than someone not particularly intelligent in any such role. And, naturally, the education of a person pursuing, say, musical performance, will include far more opportunity to develop intelligences in related roles such as conducting, musicology, and music theory than will an education not pursuing a music specialization.

The point is not that people are necessarily limited to only one way of achieving high intelligence but that each role requires its own way to apply and develop its characteristic intelligence. Most important, *each role requires its own way to educate for the development of the intelligence upon which it calls.*

Gardner, in his discussion of musical intelligence (in *Frames of Mind*), claims that there is a set of "core abilities that underlie musical competence," these being pitch, rhythm, and timbre.[22] However, pitch, rhythm, and timbre (along with other musical elements) are not abilities. They are aspects of music *upon which people can exercise their abilities.* It is precisely what such "exercise of ability" consists of that a theory of intelligence is supposed to stipulate: that exercise, after all, is the exercise of intelligence. Gardner, unfortunately, in not addressing the fundamental issue of what intelligence is, leaves us with more confusion than clarity, especially in how we should educate to develop musical intelligence in regard to pitch, rhythm, and so forth, and, in addition, in regard to all the many other aspects of music implicated in musical knowing. Each way to be musically intelligent—each way to play a musical role with discriminative understanding—requires, for its fullest possible (or feasible) development, an education focusing on the particular differentiations and interconnections characterizing that role.

Because we music educators, along with Gardner, have not made sufficiently critical distinctions among the various musical intelligences our culture both provides for and requires to be fulfilled, our practices as educators have been too limited, too narrowly conceived, to serve the differing needs of our students in the multiplicity of ways our culture provides for them to engage themselves intelligently with music. We have so emphasized the role of the performer as, mistakenly, the sole way to experience music genuinely, or, equally mistakenly, as the core way on which all other musical involvements depend, as to have seriously depleted the opportunities for musical intelligences to be developed in the variety of other ways our culture affords. Our "one size fits all" level of understanding and acting has inevitably fit some of our students quite well, others moderately well, and many more quite poorly. It is time now, with our growing awareness of the multidimensional nature of musical cognition, to become more aware—more intelligent, if you will—of how we can serve the varying musical capacities and interests of our students more effectively.

MUSICAL ROLES AS INTELLIGENCES

In all cultures diverse roles exist within the general domain of music, each requiring distinctive discriminations and connections to be made as pertinent to that role's differentiated involvement with expressive sounds. Each role embodies an elaborate system of beliefs and practices, including how initiates can be educated to become competent in that particular role. I will explain how seven selected musical roles require intelligence, so as to give a broad sense of how my definition plays out in the multiplicity of ways discriminations and interrelations can be achieved in this domain. I will start with the four roles most immediately connected to the making and receiving of expressive sounds in Western cultures, and therefore most commonly conceived to require musical intelligence. These are composing, performing, improvising, and listening. Having discussed (in Chapter 4) the particular creativities called on by each, my treatment of them here will be brief, sufficing only to call attention to the particularities of discriminations and connections necessary to each role.

I will then turn to comments about three other roles within music also connected to the defining characteristic of the domain, in less obvious ways than the previous four but nevertheless serving important musical functions in what our culture has defined as the domain of music. Two of them, music theory and musicology, raise important issues about transfer among intelligences and about general education and specialized education. The intelligence required to be a music teacher particularly calls for explanation, to clarify how that role requires a variety of intelligences in addition to specifically musical intelligences.

1. Composing

All people dwell within a world of musical sounds provided by the culture or cultures impinging on their lives. Composing requires a particular approach to such sounds—an attempt to formulate combinations of them potentially meaningful to the composer and others. Anyone attempting to do this—to construct some sequence of intrinsically meaningful sounds, and to preserve them in some way, as in memory, in a notation to be performed, or in a recording made from electronically generated sounds, so they subsequently may be shared with listeners—is, when engaged in the act of so doing, "being a composer." To do this, at any level of competence from the most rudimentary to the most masterful, and at any level of ambition from the simplest to the most lofty, requires a particular combination of musical discriminations and interrelations, in which each particular sound chosen, with its pitch, duration, timbre, volume, articulation, and expressive effect, is chosen also as linked with every other particular sound in the event being formed.

The linking of sounds into meaningful configurations through a process of decision making, reflections about previously made decisions, and altering and adding to and deleting sounds previously decided on as new implications and possibilities arise requires both memory for what has transpired and imagination for what might transpire next. As mentioned previously, these two mental operations—memory and imagination—are enabling conditions for all manifestations of intelligence because no successive acts with meaning could take place without a memory of what one has already thought or done and a projection to what might then be thought or done as a consequence. The particular discriminations on which one is focusing, and the connections being made among them, are what determine the particular intelligence being manifested. The particular role a composer plays is to exercise the intelligence necessary to bring meaningful and completed sound structures into being as events subsequently to be shared with others. Doing so successfully requires making the exquisitely subtle and sensitive discriminations among sounds that music depends on for its existence, and connecting them in ways that both embody and expand personal/cultural meanings as only music can do. This exercise of intelligence, along with other musical roles/intelligences, is as distinctive a capacity of being human as can be imagined, and as impressive. Music-think becomes specific here, as composer-think. And, as all human thinking, composer-think engages the mind, feelings, and body in the making of meaning.

It is important to understand that every person's capacity to be musically intelligent in this way, whatever that capacity might happen to be, is amenable to fulfillment through education. Education for composing has not been provided, except sporadically and perfunctorily, in American music education. The attempt to rectify this shortcoming needs to be, I suggest, a major characteristic of music education in the United States in the foreseeable future.

2. Performing

Performing music, construed here as the practice in Western and many other cultures of bringing previously composed and variously notated musical events to completion in actual sounds, involves two dimensions of musical intelligence.

The first has to do with discriminating the particularities of each sound to be made and how each needs to be connected to all others in the musical event being performed. Guiding the many decisions required in this dimension of performance intelligence are both the notations/instructions the composer has supplied and the experience and insight the performer has amassed about the appropriate ways to construe them; that is, relevant performance practice for the particular music in question. But additional to the performer's ability to make the "proper" sounds as indicated by the instructions a composer has provided and the accrued set of musical expectations surrounding those instructions and how they are to be carried out appropriately, is the expectation that the performer will add something original, or personal, or distinctive to the composer's thoughts—that the performer will "interpret" the music (as discussed in the context of musical creating in Chapter 4). So the first dimension of a performer's intelligence is the ability to discriminate and interconnect the sounds a composer has indicated in ways appropriate to the accrued expectations surrounding a particular composition, but also with a personal flair that throws the performer's individual illumination on the composer's thoughts.

The second dimension of performance intelligence is connected with the physicality by which sounds must necessarily be produced. Sound does not occur without vibrations being set in motion. Performance requires the conscious and controlled setting in motion of the physical energies required to produce desired sounds and to shape those sounds artistically—imaginatively, sensitively, and skillfully. The involvement of the intelligent body—the body as the medium in which discriminations and connections are actualized—is requisite for all musical performance. This requirement shapes the life of all who perform, who must, by the very nature of the intelligence required to do so, achieve such a unification of body and mind that, in the act of producing sounds artistically, the two are indistinguishable.

The mind/body integration of thinking and doing required for performance is a fundamental aspect of the intelligence on which this musical role depends. Within the thinking, feeling body, performers bring exacting, exquisitely controlled, discriminative qualities of sounds into being, and connect them into meaningful personal/cultural events. Music-think as a generality becomes, specifically, performer-think, a way to be and do particular to this musical role, this musical intelligence.

Whatever a person's capacity to be intelligent as a performer, that capacity can be led toward fulfillment through education. American music education has achieved great success in making performance opportunities available to all who choose to pursue them; music educators all over the world, in a variety of ways, have made performance accessible to those who choose to be involved in this way. However, recognizing performance to be a mode of intelligence, and as being defined by the characteristics I have briefly enumerated here, would enable us as professionals to better cultivate the artistry performance requires beyond proficient sound-making, to include the integration of mind and body in acts of bringing personal musical meanings into being. That, in turn, would help elevate performance in education from the "activity" it is often considered to be to its rightful place as a powerful and unique way for humans to be intelligent.

3. Improvising

Improvising, of course, is performing, and therefore shares the characteristic bodily intelligence of performing. However, as discussed in Chapter 4, whereas performers of composed music must "interpret" the music, performers as improvisers must supply the consequential musical ideas themselves. Further, those ideas must be generated *during the act of performing*. The "as one plays or sings" requirement of improvisation separates it, as I explained in Chapter 4, from the performance of composed music, because the making of discriminations among sounds, and connecting them into meaningful events, must occur instantaneously. It is this astonishing capacity to think-in-the-moment, in all the discriminatory, interconnected ways music requires, and to produce the thinkings bodily *as they are being thought,* that accounts for the unique excitement—the risks at the edges of human capacity—that improvisers engender. Few human roles provide this risk/satisfaction opportunity as richly as musical improvisation. Improvisation-think, with its challenge of instantaneous mind/body/feeling acts of intelligence, presents endless opportunities for musical exploration and excitement.

The musical mind of the improviser, then, combines, in an authentic way, the intelligence of musical decision making with the intelligence of the body as executive ("executive" meant here as both noun and verb). The capacity to be intelligent in this musically challenging role has been largely limited, in American and other Western cultures, to the relatively few students who get involved with jazz improvisation. Expanding opportunities to develop improvisatory intelligence remains an important goal for the profession.

4. Listening

For music to exist, sounds must be heard, either in imagination or in actuality. Composers, while composing, hear—listen to—the sounds they are discriminating and connecting, inwardly perhaps (as Beethoven had to do when he became deaf) or actually, as, for example, when using a keyboard while composing. Listening is an essential component of the compositional act, providing the sonic material itself to the mind working with that material in the unique way composers work with sounds.

When composers listen to music composed by others, as they must continually do to absorb within themselves what is possible for them to utilize in their own musical thinking, they are likely, by virtue of their particular perspective on music, to "listen as composers." That is, the experience of music they receive as listeners is likely to be shaped by the particular musical perceptions and connections to which composers must attend because of the particular musical role they play.

Precisely the same circumstances apply to performers and improvisers. They listen to the sounds they are making as they are making them, those sounds providing the essential feedback as to what they are doing and must therefore do next. And when performers and improvisers listen to music performed or improvised by others, as they also must do continually to remain viable in their roles, they are likely to listen as performers or improvisers listen—that is, by exercising the particular intelligence each brings to music because of the particular musical role each plays.

Listening to music, however, does not require that one be a composer, a performer, or an improviser. This should certainly go without saying, given that all people, or practically all people in Western cultures and most others around the world, listen to music, often regularly and devotedly. But only a very small percentage of listeners are in any substantive way composers, performers, or improvisers, and, therefore, only a very small percentage of listeners listen to music from the perspectives of the composer, performer, or improviser.

Listeners who do not bring any of those perspectives to the listening act (including, of course, composers, performers, and improvisers when they do not happen to listen through their particular role-perspective) listen as listeners. That musical role, the most widespread of all, is, as much as any other, the manifestation of a genuine way to be musically intelligent—a way in which musical discriminations and interconnections are the basis for the experience gained.

When listening to the performance of a composed piece, or to an improvisation, the listener is presented with sounds assumed by those making them to be potentially meaningful to others; after all, that potential for musical meaning to be gained by listeners is the point of making them available to be heard. But the sounds being made are, as sounds, only *potentially* meaningful for those who listen. If the listener has previously absorbed sound-gestures construed to be meaningful by his culture, discriminates the sounds being heard as instances of such sound-gestures, is able to make the relevant interconnections among those gestures as his culture sanctions and as the particular sounds heard are able to be interrelated meaningfully by this particular listener, the listener in question then shares, to some degree, the musical significance of the sounds being presented.

Listening, then, is an act of co-construction of musical meaning. Every act of listening requires the operation of musical intelligence—the discrimination and interrelation of sounds imaginatively, sensitively, and skillfully, paralleling (but not duplicating), in the act of receiving, the acts of generating accomplished by composers, performers, and improvisers. Given the high levels of intelligence achieved by many composers, performers, and improvisers—that is, the complexities, depths, breadths, and subtleties of the musical differentiations and interassociations they have brought into being—the challenge to the listener's musical intelligence to rise to those achievements is daunting, and, perhaps, seldom entirely fulfilled. After all, practically everyone in today's world has easy access to a broad range of the world's music, including the most profoundly intelligent instances of it.

Clearly there is a great deal of room for the improvement of the distinctive intelligence the role of the listener entails. A major obligation of the music education profession, I would insist, is to foster that improvement for all students, and to do so largely in the most efficient possible way, which is, for listening as for all other learnings, *directly.* Incorporating performing, composing, and improvising within listening instruction is essential to clarify and experience how those roles require special listening perspectives and to point up particular qualities of music being explored. But listening instruction must always exceed in breadth, complexity, and divergence that which students are capable of performing, improvising, or composing themselves. The entire body of music, historically and culturally, can be directly experienced and more fully shared by even young children through listening. Very little of that music will ever be encountered by most people in any other way. The development of every student's listening intelligence, therefore, is a crucial obligation of music education. Listening-think, as much as any other way to think musically, deserves the fullness of respect and cultivation that all musical intelligences require.

5. Music Theory

As with all musical roles—all ways to be mindful within the realm of music—that of the music theorist has its particular set of characteristic preoccupations. Music theory, to be explicit, is not simply a subsidiary aspect of other musical roles, existing only as contributory but ancillary to them. The authentic intelligence of the music theorist focuses on the interplay between the processes by which musical sounds achieve meaning, and the products that embody those meanings. Recognizing the necessary interdependence of process and product, theorists explore, articulate, and to the extent it is possible and useful to do so, hypothesize processual/structural principles for, the operations by which sound-gestures and their organizations (both as compositions and improvisations) produce their expressive effects.

There are a great many ways to pursue such interests, of course, accounting for the wide diversity of approaches and involvements among theorists (just as similar diversities exist among composers, performers, improvisers, and listeners). The community of theorists, as for each of the other roles, is a community (or "field") because it shares a characteristic concentration of discriminations and interconnections within the larger domain of music. The important point in regard to the conception of intelligence I am proposing is that the role of the music theorist is identifiable and distinctive, and therefore requires cultivation according to its particular way of manifesting musical intelligence.

Others in music—composers, performers, improvisers, listeners, and so forth—may certainly benefit from enhancing their own capacities to be intelligent as theorists are intelligent, and from making connections from theory to their own field of expertise. After all, the making of interconnections among the various musical roles is part and parcel of the process of developing broad musical understandings beyond the particularities of those within each role. But to think as theorists think is to be intelligent in a way that is authentic to theory. Transfer of such thinking to other musical roles requires that the particular kinds of perceptions and connections theorists make also be made by those intending to use theory as an aid to other involvements. Further, the transfer from "theory-think" to, say, "performance-think" must be built carefully from a foundation of accurate discriminations of the links between the two, and thoughtful identification of the connections between the two. That is, links between theory and (in this case) performance can be unintelligent or intelligent. There is no guarantee that simply studying theory will then magically assist people in whatever other roles they are pursuing. (I am assuming here, perhaps wildly optimistically, that such study will be authentic to the intelligence that theory requires rather than, as so often happens in the name of theory, an accumulation of so-called music fundamentals separated from the particular roles within which they achieve meaning.)

Transfer from one role of intelligence to another, even within a particular domain such as music let alone across domains, requires its own exercise of intelligence—its own making of fine differentiations and carefully built interconnections among the roles in question. The difficulty of doing so, the care, meticulousness, and insight needed to do so, account, perhaps, for the superficiality of so many off-handed attempts to "integrate" learnings. The case of music theory in the domain of music, so often considered only a handmaiden to other musical roles, raises clearly and succinctly the issue of transfer, central to but often ignored within proposals for "integrating the curriculum." I will return to this matter of integration in the next discussion and further on.

6. Musicology

Definitions of musicology are often very broad, encompassing any and all scholarly study of music in any and all of its many dimensions. My focus here is on musicology as an authentic mode of exercising musical intelligence through its focus on the contexts of music, historically, culturally, and individually. Musicologists typically study influences—the forces that cause or help determine why and how music became what it was, or becomes what it is, at various times, in various places, and among particular people. As has been pointed out often in this book, music, like all other human endeavors, exists in particular environments impinging on what it can be and what it can become. Attending to those environments, or contexts, or settings, with all their historical, cultural, psychological, political, aesthetic aspects, is an important defining characteristic of musicological activity, the basis for the particular discriminations and connections upon which this role focuses.

As with music theory, musicology, especially in its historical dimension, is often conceived to be foundational for any and all specialized study of music. After all, a basis in theory and history would seem to be necessary for whatever musical role one is to play. I do not intend to dispute that widely held assumption, but I do want to reiterate in regard to musicology (or music history in particular) what I argued in the case of music theory—that "thinking musicologically" is a genuine way to be musically mindful, requiring its own mode of discriminating and interconnecting. Transfer from this particular mode of musical intelligence to others is certainly possible and desirable but, unfortunately, not likely to occur automatically.

Typical courses of study for music majors in colleges and universities require both theory and history for all specializations, under the assumption that their efficacy for each of the other specializations will be manifested in some mysterious but inevitable way. But, as we know from a good deal of experience, only occasionally do students experience a revelatory connection from theory or history to each other or to a particular specialization. We should not be surprised by the disconnected nature of music curricula and the musical learnings they produce. Connections must be *achieved*—they are acts of intelligence requiring careful, conscious cultivation. Comprehensive musicianship, defined as broad-based musical intelligence in which a variety of modes (roles) of musical thinking/doing are mindfully subsumed within one's own specialization, remains an ideal seldom reached, except in rare instances of individuals who somehow seem to have "gotten it together."

Getting it together—connecting a variety of relevant intelligences—requires nurturance specifically provided for that purpose. Until we pay serious attention to what that nurturance consists of, and how best to provide it in education, we are likely to have to settle for random moments of illumination when genuine connections somehow appear. That we did not provide such nurturance in the attempts to achieve "comprehensive musicianship" in the 1950s and 1960s,[23] and do not do so

---

[23]See the discussions of this important initiative in music education in Michael L. Mark, *Contemporary Music Education*, 3rd ed. (New York: Schirmer, 1996), 28–34, 162–66.

now, accounts for the disjointedness of so much musical learning among both professionals and students in schools. If we are ever to take seriously the coordination (a term I greatly prefer over "integration") of musical learnings on which broad musical intelligence depends (the making of meaningful interconnections among various musical roles), we must seriously address how such coordination can be achieved. It does not, except haphazardly, "just happen."

7. Music Teaching

The role of the teacher is ubiquitous in all human societies, for a culture cannot survive if it is not transmitted to future generations. In an informal sense all humans, at least on attaining adulthood, play the role of teacher in some manner and under some circumstances. But as with many if not most other societal roles in cultures of some complexity, specialization of the teaching role occurs, formalizing it, institutionalizing it, and differentiating it into a great variety of subspecialties.

Common to all teaching is the core requirement that decisions be made as to how to effectively influence students to acquire desired learnings. Three factors are involved in such decisions—a grasp of what is entailed in that which is to be learned, sensitivity to what is occurring to and within the person(s) being taught, and awareness of the larger context in which the teaching–learning process is being undertaken. From these three factors springs the infinitely complex domain of education with all its elaborate systems, beliefs, traditions, and structures. Control over these factors constitutes the particular intelligence entailed in being an effective teacher.

As with all intelligences, the intelligence of teaching exists in degree. A highly intelligent teacher is one who discriminates very fine and subtle details within both the material being taught and the responses of the learners, along with broad and complex connections of a great variety of sorts having to do with the nature of the learners in question, where they are in their development of these particular learnings, what their background has been in the material being learned, how this learning fits into others in which they are involved, what beliefs and values exist in the learning community and the larger community about such learnings, what issues and problems exist in the material being learned, how such material interconnects with similar and different material to which it is related. A teacher of low intelligence, in contrast, is able to make few discriminations beyond the obvious, either about the material, about the learners, or about the context, and only limited connections in regard to the interactions among them.

Music education is that field devoted to the systematic, intentional development of intelligences in the domain of music, each of which entails its pertinent manifestation of creativity. I use the plural, of course—intelligences—because of the multiplicity of ways one can be intelligent in this domain, including, as one essential way, being a music educator, a person who helps learners develop one or several musical intelligences.

This all-too-brief overview of seven selected intelligences in the domain of music gives, I hope, a sense of how my definition of intelligence helps us identify and understand the many role-based intelligences existing in this particular domain, and the authenticity—the unique characteristics—of each, related within the domain of music by their shared foundation in involvement with expressive sounds. I hope that this explanation of multiple intelligences within music will also suggest parallel multiplicities in every domain of human knowing and doing. Among the most powerful implications of my theory (and, for me, among the most attractive) is its capacity to bring to awareness the intelligence-saturated nature of human life, in which much of our existence can be played out in the context of the uniquely human meanings our capacity to be intelligent affords us. Most or all of what we do in our lives can be done more intelligently; intelligence as I conceive it is not limited to the traditional academic disciplines, nor is it manifested only in the traditional behaviors associated with them. My theory, I believe, democratizes the concept of intelligence.

TEACHING FOR MUSICAL INTELLIGENCES

To thoroughly apply my theory of role-based intelligences, and of musical intelligences in particular, would, of course, require a major effort, one I hope the profession of music education and education as a whole will take on over the years as the theory develops and its applications become apparent. At this point, a few illustrative implications will be offered to demonstrate the theory's efficacy.

Parts and Wholes

A long-standing dichotomy has existed in music education between focusing on the particular (or parts) and focusing on the general (or wholes). To what degree do parts (skills, facts, information, details) have to be firmly in place if wholes, made of aggregates of those parts, are to be firmly grasped?

Recognizing from a great deal of accrued experience that all direct musical engagements require highly focused and concentrated attention to be paid to all the complex, subtle, interactive dimensions of the musical sounds being dealt with, music educators and others interested in the details of musical interactions, such as music psychologists, music evaluation specialists, and music researchers of various methodological persuasions, have tended to expend major efforts exploring and defining the detailed specifics of musical discrimination processes.

Given the persuasiveness of the evidence that acute discriminations among sounds are indeed essential for intelligent musical experience (as stipulated in my definition of intelligence as it applies to music), it would seem logical on the surface to assume that a prerequisite for any intelligent musical engagement would be that a high degree of differentiation among musical sounds must occur, and the more specific the differentiations the better for musical experience. So if we can discover more and more about the specifics of musical perceptual processes through research, and devise tests that measure with accuracy the levels of perceptual acuity individuals can demonstrate in as many as possible of their responses to a variety of musical dimensions (such as pitch, time, volume, and timbre), we can then reap the rewards of those labors by devising teaching and measuring methodologies that systematically, sequentially, and painstakingly build up the specifically identified and taught perceptual skills of students, whose musical capacity will then improve accordingly.

In fact, this line of reasoning has been extremely influential in music education in Western and other cultures, most recently with the advent of narrowly scientific approaches to the study of human functioning and of education. The height (or depth, if you prefer) of mechanistic science applied to education occurred during the middle of the twentieth century with the rise (and then fall) of methodologies based on behavioral psychology.[24] Music education has regularly included a great deal of attention to the very small details on the discrimination side of the discrimination–connection relation. A focus on parts, often to the neglect or even exclusion of wholes (that is, the structures of meaning arising from the ways parts are interrelated in a variety of culturally determined role configurations) has characterized a great deal of music teaching, to the point where the term "training" often seems more apt than "education" to describe the endeavor.

I will discuss further on some of the problems caused in present-day music education by an overemphasis on parts and a neglect of wholes in music assessments and music teaching, and the deleterious effects of ignoring the differences among the ways people can be musically intelligent. Here I want to point out that views emphasizing the "training" aspects of education as being either sufficient or at least foundational for learning have largely been replaced by more unitary, cognitivist beliefs about effective education, as exemplified by Howard Gardner's work, by the national standards for each of the subject matter fields in education, and by the general attempt throughout education to confront and influence the human mind at its most comprehensive levels of functioning rather than dominantly at the level of particles.

The key, in this matter of focus on parts or on wholes, is to recognize and honor their interrelation, while also recognizing that the nurturing of intelligence requires that parts be made whole by infusing them with the meanings found in connections. Learning, from the start and in all instances, aims toward meaning; in our case, musical meaning, the making of which, and the sharing of which, in all the roles in which that occurs, are demonstrations of musical intelligences. When teaching situates details within meaningful contexts—real music being dealt with in ways that enliven our experiences of it—and when that experience is enriched by the many discriminations it requires, musical intelligence is being well served and well cultivated. A blueprint for doing this both deeply and broadly is provided, I will argue, by the musical content areas enumerated in the national standards.

---

[24]For a discussion of the background of this movement, its applications to music education, and the dangers it raised, see my "Aesthetic Behaviors in Music," in *Toward an Aesthetic Education,* Bennett Reimer, Organizing Chairman (MENC, 1971), 65–87.

Assessing Musical Intelligences

The old, positivist idea that anything that exists must exist in some degree and therefore be capable of being measured has exerted strong influences in the field of intelligence theory, resulting in a long history of tests and measurements developed not only for practical purposes but also as ways to help define and operationalize just what makes up intelligence. Hence the tendency in that field to equate intelligence with scores on intelligence tests. My intent here is not to propose guidelines for testing musical intelligences as I define them: I would hope that those in music education who are experts in such matters might accomplish that task. A few ideas related to that challenge will be offered.

In a recent discussion about applications and misapplications of his theory of multiple intelligences, Howard Gardner emphasizes the specificity of intelligence.

> It makes little sense to think of intelligences in the abstract. Intelligences only come into being because the world in which we live features various contents—among them, the sounds and syntax of language, the sounds and rhythms of music, the species of nature, the other persons in our environment, and so on.
>
> These facts lead to the most challenging implication of MI [Multiple Intelligences] theory. If our minds respond to the actual varied contents of the world, then it does not make sense to posit the existence of "all-purpose" faculties. There is, in the last analysis, no generalized memory: there is memory for language, memory for music, memory for spatial environments, and so on. Nor, despite current buzzwords, can we speak about critical or creative thinking in an unmodified way. Rather, there is critical thinking using one or more intelligences, and there is creativity in one, or in more than one, domain.
>
> Powerful educational implications lurk here. We must be leery about claiming to enhance general abilities like thinking or problem solving or memory; it is important to examine *which* problem is being solved, *which* kind of information is being memorized. Even more important, the teacher must be wary of claims about transfer. Though transfer of skill is a proper goal for any educator, such transfer cannot be taken for granted— and especially when such transfer is alleged to occur across intelligences. The cautious educator assumes that particular intelligences can be enhanced, but remains skeptical of the notion that use of one set of intellectual skills will necessarily enhance others.[25] (Emphases in original)

As I have explained, I believe Gardner is entirely correct in this position, but I argue that he does not go far enough. It is not sufficient to posit a generalized musical intelligence, as Gardner does, different from others equally general. We must probe beneath the surface to the reality that different musical roles, and equally distinctive roles in all other domains and role contexts, call for particular ways to be intelligent,

---

[25]Howard Gardner, "Probing More Deeply into the Theory of Multiple Intelligences," *National Association of Secondary School Principals Bulletin,* 80, no. 583 (November 1996).

requiring diverse ways to think, to solve problems, to employ memory, to implicate bodily actions, to engage feelings, to make decisions. We should be as wary about claims of transfer between roles as Gardner appropriately is at the more general level of transfer between domains. The implications for assessment are clear.

Past and present attempts to test for musical ability, aptitude, talent, musicality, and so forth, have suffered, I believe, from two crucial weaknesses. First, they are, with few exceptions, not role-based, assuming (incorrectly, I would claim) that whatever they test for is applicable across the board to any and all musical involvements, as Gardner seems to imply. I want to emphasize the point that although all musical intelligences—all the many ways to be competent in the many roles music affords—center on interactions with expressive, meaningful sounds as cultures define what these are, each interaction, or role context, determines how and to what purpose that interaction takes place.

Assessment of musical intelligence, then, needs to be role-specific. The task for the evaluation community (those whose intelligence centers on issues of evaluation) is to develop methodologies and mechanisms for identifying and assessing the particular discriminations and connections required for each of the musical roles their culture deems important. As evaluation turns from the general to the specific, as I believe it urgently needs to do, we are likely to both significantly increase our understandings about the diversities of musical intelligences and dramatically improve our contribution to helping individuals identify and develop areas of more and less musical capacity.

The second weakness from which music testing, evaluation, assessment, and so forth, has suffered, in addition to its neglect of role specificity, has been its concentration almost exclusively on the discrimination aspect of intelligence, leaving the necessary dimension of the connections among discriminations largely unexamined. By definition (the definition I am proposing) it is insufficient—even misleading—to assess just one aspect of the differentiation/interconnection complex of which intelligence consists and then assume one has assessed all that matters. The one-sided nature of practically all our music assessments or evaluations, focusing on the particles and ignoring the ways they are connected to make meanings, severely misrepresents the phenomena they purport to examine, whether musical aptitude, talent, capacity, ability, or achievement. It also severely undermines the validity of our evaluation instruments.

The task for the evaluation community, then (in addition to developing instruments and procedures related to particular musical roles), is to include as an essential dimension of assessment the processes used and levels attained in the connections forged—the organization and structure developed—among that which is being perceived, along with, and as an integral component of, the depth and subtlety of those perceptions. This is indeed a challenging agenda, but until it is tackled successfully we will achieve neither the veracity our assessments require nor the utility they can provide. Our task is to better identify and clarify just what these interrelating processes are, how they function, how they can be cultivated, and how they can be assessed in ways authentic to their particular musical contexts.

We do not start from scratch in this matter. We know a great deal about functions of the mind and the making of meaning, especially as cognitive science has developed in recent years. The application of such knowledge, and the extension of it into musical evaluations of a variety of sorts, is likely to significantly improve not only professional evaluation capacities and contributions within the field of music education, but also professional understandings in the larger sphere of human mental functioning, given the centrality of musical intelligence in human culture and history.

The So-Called Integrated Curriculum

My theory of intelligence suggests that a music program must have, as its primary mission, the cultivation of musical intelligences, along with the creativities associated with them. The primary mission of every other domain and role a culture chooses to include in education is the same—to develop the particular kinds of intelligences each domain and role encompasses. As pointed out earlier, there is no "general domain" or "general role" in which some sort of "general intelligence" can be developed, because there are no "general discriminations" to be "generally interconnected." Discriminations are always tied to specific ways of thinking and doing as called for by particular roles being played in pursuit of particular ends. The interconnections among roles may branch out in countless closely related or distantly related directions, but those interconnections are empty, or academic, or ungrounded, if not firmly rooted in the particular differentia on which each set of interconnections is based. That is, whereas focusing on discrete discriminations devoid of their interconnections produces people trained but uneducated (unintelligent), focusing on connections devoid of the discriminations out of which they arise produces people with a shell of what might seem to be education but is empty of the substance on which genuine education depends. Such people have also and equally been left uneducated, or unintelligent.

If one desired to build a curriculum (a program of studies) more comprehensive than for one single domain—say, the single domain of music with its characteristic roles—one is likely to include in that curriculum at least the domains (and their roles) most closely related to the one in question. In the case of music the domains sharing more of its characteristic ways to be intelligent than any others are the other arts. The kinds of discriminations—not the particular discriminations but the sort of discriminations focusing on expressive, meaningful gestures culturally supplied—made in the arts are comparable among them: that is what makes the arts a natural family. A comprehensive arts curriculum would be one in which all (or at least more than one) of the arts are included for study; in which the particular roles each calls on are systematically encountered; and in which connections are made, *both by similarities and by differences,* among each of the arts and roles included. Such a curriculum, it could be fairly argued, would, if effectively carried out, positively influence the intelligence of its participants within, how, about, and why for each of the arts included and for the arts as a domain.[26]

---

[26]For my articulation of such a curriculum, see my "A Comprehensive Arts Curriculum Model," *Design for Arts in Education*, 90, no. 6 (July/August 1989), 2–17, and Janet R. Barrett, Claire W. McCoy, and Kari W. Veblen, *Sound Ways of Knowing* (New York: Schirmer Books, 1997).

Education can include a diversity of domains and their roles in a comprehensive, interrelated format if it chooses to do so, but it can do so effectively only if it carefully retains and depends on the specificities of functioning of each manifestation of intelligence included, and just as carefully cultivates interconnections (understandings) of both the similarities and the differences among them. Such a vision, or general conception, for inclusive learning is radically different from the scheme most commonly implemented in current educational practice, in which some overarching theme or idea provides a mechanism for so-called integration, but in which the various subjects focusing on the theme or idea are not developed both in their veracity as ways to be intelligent and as related by the similarities and differences in which they treat or become involved with the theme or idea. Comprehensive understanding—broadly based and firmly grounded intelligence—does not arise from the pursuit of generalities to which undeveloped particular intelligences are assumed to contribute.

To achieve intelligence wider than that encompassed in any particular domain and its roles requires cultivation of intelligence in roles specific to a domain and those in related domains. A person of broad intelligence is a person of relatively high intelligence within one role or several in a domain, who understands the linkages to various roles in other domains, and is cognizant of the existence of many more intelligences, and interconnections among them, than one can possibly encompass oneself. To foster such far-ranging intelligence is a noble ideal. We must recognize, however, that whereas in simpler times and in simpler societies (times and societies in which roles were more delimited) it may have been possible to approximate omniscience, as in the legendary "Renaissance man" (now to be corrected to "Renaissance person"), that kind of all-encompassing intelligence is no longer likely, at least in complex societies. However, grounded connections among a variety of roles in addition to the one in which a person specializes remains a viable and important aspiration for education, both to minimize the limitations of narrow, provincial, and short-sighted specialization, and to encourage fruitful cooperation and coordination of efforts and understandings in endeavors more inclusive than a single role or domain can encompass.

Learnings across domains/roles, I suggest, are most fruitfully and validly understood as a means to accomplish the aspirations identified in the previous sentence. Although specialization is a necessity for the viability of the complex cultures now existing all over the world, there is a substantive difference between a narrow-minded and a broad-minded specialist. The former is limited to a single intelligence (that is likely to be itself limited). The latter is able to connect a specialized intelligence to the broader vision of others with which it interrelates, thereby enriching both the experience of that specialist and her ability to cooperate meaningfully with others when that is desirable. The point and purpose of interrelations among roles, and of an education that nurtures them, is precisely to enrich the personal experience of those able to make the discriminative connections such interactions call for, and to enable coordinative endeavors among specialists as so many complex tasks and institutions require in the world in which we live.

Notice that I have not used the term "integration" to describe broadly based intelligence and its uses. Integration is often taken to mean the unification of different subjects or roles such that the identity of the subjects and roles is lost in the creation of the new one that replaces them. I find that (common) notion of integration both unrealistic and potentially harmful. In many cases of human doings, the roles we play and the venture we pursue call on a variety of discriminations from which meanings must be made, each set of distinctions/connections contributing to the totality of that role or venture. The specialized role of "teacher," for example, calls on subject matter expertise, psychological sensitivity, pedagogical understanding, social finesse, assessment skills, curriculum comprehension, and so forth, each identifiable and learnable, and each contributing its dimension to the totality of a teacher's effectiveness. We can tell when one of them is impeding that effectiveness because of deficient grasp or use, and intervene to strengthen it so it can contribute more fruitfully to the whole, a whole that, when functioning optimally, coordinates them—brings each to bear as needed. When a venture, such as starting a community-based arts program for special needs children, calls for a variety of people intelligent in various particular roles—fundraising, politics, real estate, budgeting, special education, special education in each art, publicity, facility management, and so on—each must coordinate his or her contribution with the others, working cooperatively to achieve a goal dependent on many intelligent inputs. Even the project coordinator exercises a particular intelligence defined by her role. Success occurs through fruitful, supportive collaboration among diverse roles/intelligences.

Successful functioning in a complex role, and in complex endeavors organizing a variety of intelligences as each contributes its particular aspect, seldom if ever reduces each aspect to, or causes it to disappear within, others that unitize, or "integrate," it out of existence. Perhaps the most penetrating discussion of this matter is offered by Edward O. Wilson in his book *Consilience: The Unity of Knowledge*.[27] In his deeply intelligent treatment (remarkably acute discriminative observations and broad-ranging interconnections), Wilson attempts to counteract the fragmentation caused by narrow specialization, by demonstrating how linkages can be and need to be made among the sciences and the humanities (particularly the creative arts). The term "consilience" was first used by William Whewell in 1840, who said, "The Consilience of Inductions takes place when an Induction, obtained from one class of facts, coincides with an Induction obtained from another different class. This Consilience is a test of the truth of the Theory in which it occurs."[28] In that spirit of "coinciding" (rather than integrating into a different unity), Wilson traces the history of the disciplines of Western thought, seeking the underlying "co-incidences" that demonstrate their affinities, all of them being grounded in human biology. The point of consilience as being coordination, or alliance, is made by Wilson explicitly in the case of science and the arts. Understanding of the arts, he suggests, relies on scholarly analysis and criticism—what he calls "interpretation." Such interpretation

---

[27]Edward O. Wilson, *Consilience: The Unity of Knowledge* (New York: Knopf, 1998).
[28]Ibid., 8.

"will be the more powerful when braided together from history, biography, personal confession—and science,"[29] making allies of the arts and sciences rather than competitors. But alliance, in which insights from one illuminate the nature of the other, does not reduce one to the other or both to some form of hybrid.

> The key to the exchange between them is not hybridization, not some unpleasantly self-conscious form of scientific art or artistic science, but reinvigoration of interpretation with the knowledge of science and its proprietary sense of the future. Interpretation is the logical channel of coherent explanation between science and the arts.[30]

Wilson argues that we can better understand the arts when the insights of biology and other sciences are brought to bear to demonstrate that art, as everything else human, dwells in a coevolution of genes and culture. But that does not reduce—integrate—art to science or science to art.

> While biology has an important part to play in scholarly interpretation, the creative arts themselves can never be locked in by this or any other discipline of science. The reason is that the exclusive role of the arts is the transmission of the intricate details of human experience by artifice to intensify aesthetic and emotional response. Works of art communicate feeling directly [nonconceptually, unmediated by language] from mind to mind, with no attempt to explain why the impact occurs. In this defining quality, the arts are the antithesis of science.[31]

Wilson's treatment of what he calls "the unity of knowledge" is in no way a call for "integration" as commonly understood. It is, instead, a plea to view human life, including the distinctive and "special" experiences and roles provided by the arts (he quotes Dissanayake's "art makes special" idea), through the illuminating lens of scientific insights about the nature of being human. For me this is "coordination" at its best and most far-reaching, in which the distinctiveness of different intelligences is recognized and treasured, and the connections among them (by similarity and even antithesis) are deeply grasped. Preserving this foundational position, in all the many ways intelligences within music, between music and other arts, and between the arts and disciplines outside the arts, can be broadened and deepened by more wide-ranging interconnections (as content standard 8 calls for), allows music (and the arts) to be understood as part of the larger human endeavor but also as a distinctive contribution to that endeavor. All learnings, in any program attempting to place music in larger context, will be authentic and humane, and will have musical veracity, when founded on a coordinative, cooperative, interrelated stance, enhancing musical intelligence by demonstrating its broad connections to others but without subsuming or "integrating" its unique ways to be intelligent. (Of course, if the term "integration" is used to mean what I am calling coordination, no conflict exists. The

---

[29]Ibid., 211.
[30]Ibid.
[31]Ibid., 218.

more useful term, I suggest, is whichever one clearly captures the distinction I am proposing needs to be made. Experience leads me to prefer coordination, but particular circumstances may favor integration. The term, of course, is only a tool. The principle is what needs to guide our actions.)

Our contribution as music educators is specific to the intelligences with which we deal. It is also connected to the contribution of all who educate, all whose mission is to assist in the development of the multitudinous intelligences of which humans are capable. The concept of intelligence I offer here receives tangible embodiment when applied to a domain such as music, illuminating how this particular domain embraces multiple roles our musical culture has sanctioned, each representing a distinctive way intelligence can be demonstrated. The parallels in all other domains our culture deems worthy of inclusion in its schools are clear. Each domain encompasses a diversity of roles/intelligences: each can be and deserves to be cultivated by attending to its distinctive ways of manifesting intelligence.

In addition, my theory calls attention to the operation of intelligence in all aspects of our lives, reaching far beyond the academic disciplines or domains we choose to include as part of formal education. Just as a culture is enhanced as a humane environment by the success of its formal education endeavors, it also benefits from the achievement of higher levels of intelligence in all the pervasive nonformal or nonacademic roles on which it equally depends for both its survival and its quality. All members of a culture benefit from, and have an obligation to support, all possible societal mechanisms devoted to the enhancement of human intelligence in its myriad manifestations.

However, intelligence is not the only human capacity worthy of cultivation. Being loving, generous, trustworthy, nurturing, kind, and so forth, are, no doubt, at least equally desirable human traits. And there is no necessary correlation between being highly intelligent in a particular role and being a humane person. A brilliant physicist or painter or politician or plumber or plasterer or performer may also, alas, be a despicable individual. Conversely, an admirable human being may also be markedly less intelligent than most in several or many important endeavors. Intelligence is not the only characteristic of value in human life. It lies, however, at the core of the human condition, and the quality of both our individual and our communal lives depends in large part on its optimal development. The theory of intelligence offered here provides, I believe, a powerful, useful, and attractive basis for advancing theoretical understandings about intelligence and practical efforts to cultivate it in all possible ways, both inside and outside formal education structures.

My theory of multiple musical intelligences invites the music education profession to reexamine a great many of its assumptions and practices, to determine which would benefit, both theoretically and practically, from being understood in connection to this theory. Such a reexamination would, I suggest, transform our field in many positive ways, immeasurably enhancing its contribution to the quality of people's lives and thereby immeasurably enhancing its status in the larger domain of education. The foundational premise underlying my theory is that the role we play as music educators is to help others achieve their various potentials to be musically intelligent, along with being musically creative. This can best be accomplished through a general education in music for all students and through specialized education in music for as many as possible. The following chapters address those topics.

ETUDES

1. Have you believed, or have you encountered people who believe, that being involved with music (or the arts) does not depend on intelligence but on "talent," or a "gift" or an "endowment"? Why do you think some (many) people seem to make that distinction? What effect has this had on the ways music is treated as a subject worthy of inclusion in the schools?

2. Is there a risk that conceiving musical roles as intelligences will cause people to think that music will then become "academic," or "intellectual," ignoring or short-changing its affective, creative, humanizing dimensions, making it just another theoretical subject at which students have to grind away? How can we make clear that intelligence does not exist just "from the ears up," but entails our body, mind, and feelings working together to create meanings, and that music is a prime example of this? How must one teach music to exemplify this?

3. Do you feel that your experience as a student, in the schools and beyond, gave you rich opportunities to discover and cultivate the musical role/intelligence for which you might have been best suited? What would have needed to happen, for you and others, to provide such opportunities? If they had been provided in effective ways, do you think many more students would have chosen to involve themselves in some musical role?

4. Apply question 3 to the larger context of all the arts. What might have happened if, for you and all others, opportunities to explore a great variety of possible role involvements in the arts had been available, so that each student had the best possible chance to discover a particular role in the arts in which interest and intelligence merged? Does that vision of comprehensive arts opportunities in music education excite you? Do you think it can ever be attained?

5. In the roles providing immediate involvement with musical sounds (composing, performing, improvising, listening, conducting, arranging, and so forth), intelligence and creativity must support each other. Do you feel your education in music provided optimal development of their interdependence? Imagine a scenario in which you are teaching (level, setting, lesson of your choice), and in which you (1) overemphasize discrimination/connection aspects to the exclusion of creativity, (2) overemphasize creative aspects to the exclusion of intelligence, (3) achieve a fruitful balance between the two. Compare your solution with others', to expand your repertoire of effective practices.

6. Have you had experience with an "integrated" curriculum of any sort? How did it (they) compare with my explanation of the need for role expertise, coordination of roles, and focus on explorations of similarities and differences among the

roles included? What are some dangers of "integrated arts" approaches, given my position? What are some advantages? Ditto for music (or the arts) integrated with other subjects. Can we cooperate in a variety of ways with other domains and their roles while also not endangering the veracity of the particular intelligences on which each role calls? Try making a list of (1) what to emphasize in an effective coordinated curriculum or unit, and (2) what to avoid in it. Again, compare your lists with others'.

Advancing the Vision:
Toward a Comprehensive
General Music Program

MAIN THEMES

- A seven-phase model of the total school curriculum, applicable to the music curriculum as well, provides a basis for understanding strengths and weaknesses in our present offerings and for constructing a comprehensive music program.

- The traditional goal of music education, to foster active musical involvements, has been based on a narrow view of what "active" means, leading to equally narrow opportunities for musical learning and to a remarkably disunified general music program that is largely unconnected to the musical culture in which it exists.

- The U.S. National Content Standards for Music Education can serve as a useful conceptualization of what a comprehensive general music education should include, representing the major musical roles in many cultures around the world.

- Rebalancing present general music programs to represent each content area equitably constitutes a radical departure from tradition.

- Musically active involvement exists at three levels—aficionado, amateur, and professional—all sharing several attributes of focused engagement. The general music program must balance attention to the three levels appropriately.

- Each of the musical roles identified by the content standards plays its important and characteristic part in a comprehensive general education in music.

- The vision of general music proposed here presents significant, far-reaching challenges to the music education profession, particularly in how we conceive teacher education, research, and the operational program in the schools. To the extent we meet the challenges we will strengthen our position as a basic school subject.

Chapters 1 through 6 of this book offered a philosophical basis for music education, and answers to questions of why people value music, why musical education enhances the value of music to people, and why all people, especially young people in schools, deserve to study music in ways that will nurture their abilities to gain the special satisfactions it offers.

Chapter 7 explained what an effective music education attempts to accomplish at the broadest, most inclusive level—the nurturing of each individual's capacities to be musically intelligent (and musically creative) in the variety of roles that can be played in music as each culture makes them available.

Now it is time to be more specific about how the philosophy offered here, and the theory of intelligence providing a basis for cultivating the many ways music can be experienced thoroughly and meaningfully, can be activated. What we need is a music curriculum sufficiently comprehensive to encompass the diverse opportunities music offers people to share its special satisfactions. Nothing less than inclusiveness, in both our concept of what an effective curriculum is and how our programs can best carry it out, will be sufficient for accomplishing what people learning music deserve—the broadest possible opportunities to discover and fulfill their potentials to incorporate fulfilling musical experiences in their lives. That our curriculum concept, and the programs we have devised to carry it out, have not been appropriately comprehensive accounts in large measure for the less than optimal effects we have had on the musical well-being of our students. Historically, our goal has been to enhance the musical knowings and doings—the musical pleasures—of all students in schools. Few would argue that we have achieved this goal as fully as we are capable of doing. This chapter, and the one following, are intended to give an overview of how we might make significant progress toward achievement of the noble goal of nurturing all students' ability to share music as fully as they might wish.

A MODEL OF THE TOTAL CURRICULUM

Four sets of questions, dealing with why, what, when, and how, provide a basis for identifying seven phases of a comprehensive curriculum. This seven-phase model will be useful for conceptualizing the major aspects of the total educational enterprise and understanding its complex workings. The model applies not only to education as a whole but also to every subject included in education, such as music. A summary diagram appears on page 242.

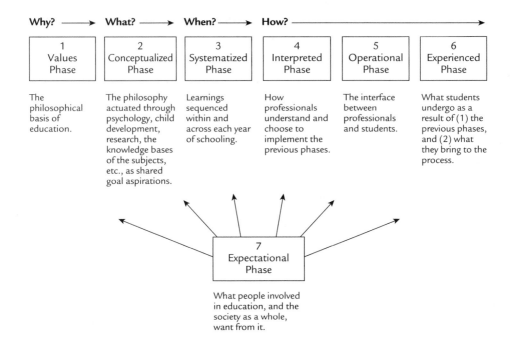

Why? ———▶   What? ———▶   When? ———▶   How? ————————————————————▶

1 Values Phase	2 Conceptualized Phase	3 Systematized Phase	4 Interpreted Phase	5 Operational Phase	6 Experienced Phase
The philosophical basis of education.	The philosophy actuated through psychology, child development, research, the knowledge bases of the subjects, etc., as shared goal aspirations.	Learnings sequenced within and across each year of schooling.	How professionals understand and choose to implement the previous phases.	The interface between professionals and students.	What students undergo as a result of (1) the previous phases, and (2) what they bring to the process.

7
Expectational
Phase

What people involved in education, and the society as a whole, want from it.

1. The "Why" questions—the questions addressed by philosophy—are the starting point for all conceptualizations of education, whether in music, other subjects, or education as a whole. Answers to these questions—questions of value—provide the purposes of education, purposes dependent on what people in a culture regard to be so important that education must focus on them. Without a unified vision of what is valuable, education can only be haphazard. With a strong, grounded set of beliefs as a guide for action, education as a whole and in its significant parts, such as in music, can proceed in coherent directions toward achieving its aspirations.

2. The "What" questions—questions of what education must do to fulfill its purposes—provide broad guidelines (as conceptualized goals education should attempt to achieve) from which actions can proceed effectively. A theory of intelligence provides a solid underlying basis for such goals. On that basis each subject included in education can conceptualize its knowledge base, its functional ways of knowing and doing that characterize its nature and that provide the guideposts for what needs to be taught and learned in operational programs, taking into account factors such as child development, educational psychology, research, assessment, and so on. In recent years each subject in schooling has made an extraordinary effort to clarify its knowledge base—its "standards"—conceived as the basic contents of what students need to know and be able to do if they are to grasp the nature of the subject in question.

3. Given a philosophy—a set of values directing the educational endeavor—and given a conceptualization of what needs to be achieved, the learnings to be pursued need to be arranged in some order, some rationalized plan over time, allowing and promoting the ongoing accumulation of competencies. The systematized phase of the curriculum, addressed to the question of "When?", is now called for, in which a map of sequential learning is provided, yielding directionality to teaching and learning over the span of the school years.

4. With the "Why," the "What," and the "When" in place, issues of "How" can be addressed coherently and effectively. The first aspect of the How phase of the curriculum is how the professionals responsible for providing schooling interpret the previous phases. If teachers, administrators, and supporting personnel are all deeply intelligent about the values that education is pursuing (as a whole and in each subject), about the goals through which those values can be achieved, and about the accumulative nature of learning generally and in each domain, they are likely to be able to work in effective and mutually supportive ways toward providing students with important, functional, effectual educative experiences in the real world of schooling. That is, teaching and learning are likely to be as successful as they can be.

If, however, the interpretations about why, what, and when by those who deliver education through their immediate interactions with students are poorly grounded, confused, or thoughtless, their efforts are likely to be ineffectual. Their effects on their students cannot help but reflect their faulty grasp of what constitutes an effective curriculum. The best possible curriculum conceptualization, in philosophy, in goals, in sequences, will fall dead in the hands of such teachers and others whose responsibility is to bring it to life in the learning experiences of their students. Good teaching, supported by good school leaders, remains a key factor—no doubt *the* key factor—in successful education. Of course, all phases of the total curriculum must be in excellent order if the endeavor is to be excellent. But teachers hold the fate of any curriculum in their powerful hands. As is fitting.

5. Finally we arrive at the operational phase of teaching and learning—the interface of professionals and students. This is the phase of the curriculum most obvious to those who look at education from the outside. What are teachers doing? How are students responding? Is everything going well? In this phase "the rubber hits the road" in real-time doings and undergoings in school settings.

What is not seen by many observers of schools in operation are the previous phases and their powerful influences on what teachers do, how well they are enabled to do what they do, and the level of effectiveness they are able to achieve. Those previous phases of why, what, and when, including the interpreted aspect of how, are hidden from view, despite their crucial function in determining the operations of teaching. This leads to the misperception that the work and competence of teachers is limited to the operational phase, that schooling is simply a matter of teachers teaching and students learning, blind to the complex but unseen initial phases that determine the schooling operations so readily visible to the unthoughtful eye. It is easy, then, to regard teachers as technicians and teaching as largely the transmission of measurable learnings for which teachers should be held accountable.

In actuality, teachers in genuine educational settings are the bearers of their culture's deepest values as captured in an educational philosophy; are guided by a conceptualization of education formulated into guidelines for cultivating the foundational knowings and doings of each subject included in education; are striving to nurture students' intelligences in as many dimensions as possible, those intelligences involving the students' fullest humanity rather than only their rational intellect; and are keenly aware of the developmental reality of every student as an individual in each of the diverse challenges with which each student is being presented. Such teachers, in such educational circumstances, represent the highest cultural achievements humans can attain. And they deserve all the respect such attainment represents. The goal of all education, and of each of its particular aspects (such as music education), is to attain that genuineness of aspiration and achievement. Doing so depends on excellent operations of teaching but also has deep roots and reliance for validity in the just-discussed dimensions of the curriculum.

6. Even if every phase of the curriculum to this point is as excellent as humanly possible, with a strong guiding philosophy, a solid conceptualization of goals, a psychologically astute developmental plan, and deeply understanding teachers and school leaders who are also excellent in all the operational tasks of teaching and supporting teaching, there is no guarantee that all students will learn optimally. At the experienced phase of the curriculum—what students take from and make of their education—how well learning will take place and what will be learned depend on all that makes each individual student what she is. Here we are presented with one of life's many ironies, that the best-laid plan (in this case, curriculum) can become a shambles when put into operation for reasons having little to do with its inherent quality. Or, on the other hand, it can succeed beyond its own quality if and when conditions for it happen to be optimal with particular individuals. The point is, much in life is beyond our control, in education no less than in everything else. We are obligated as professionals to do everything we can to achieve excellence in what we undertake, but must recognize with humility that complete success is unlikely no matter how hard we try, given that students, as individuals, will ultimately determine the outcomes of our efforts.

7. Finally, underlying all these phases of the total curriculum is another dimension that has significant determining influences on each of them—the expectations people have of education. The culture as a whole, special interest groups within it, parents, students, education professionals, all bring to the enterprise their beliefs and values and needs from it. Education in every culture exists not in a vacuum but in a ferment of influences affecting what it can be and do. At both the theoretical and the practical levels, education reflects the expectations of all who have a stake in it. In this sense education, inevitably and no doubt appropriately, is a political phenomenon.

THE GENERAL MUSIC PROGRAM AS VIEWED
THROUGH THE CURRICULUM MODEL

The model just articulated can provide us with a clear, penetrating view of the state of music as part of general education for most of the twentieth century and up to the present, allowing us to clarify both its strengths and its weaknesses.

1. Values Phase

In pre-twentieth-century America (and all over the world) the music that the vast majority of people were able to have in their lives was the music they made for themselves. Learning music, whether informally or in school settings, quite naturally had to focus on the ways music could come into existence, most readily through singing. Singing schools in the American colonies, and, eventually, music programs in the schools, consisted essentially of "vocal music," a term still heard to this day. Learning to sing, with all the attendant knowings that requires (the so-called fundamentals, especially how to read music), were quite logically and practically the major interests pursued by music educators. Philosophical thinking largely consisted of explaining why those interests were valuable and worthy of being cultivated in education.

With the advent of the twentieth century and of recorded music, the school music program expanded to include listening and also other ways to perform, such as on classroom and accessible instruments (Autoharp, recorder, piano, guitar, and so forth). Making music—performing—remained the primary involvement, along with related learnings supportive of it, supplemented by listening, movement, and "creative activities" of a variety of sorts. The opportunity to elect to learn to play orchestral and band instruments, and to play in those ensembles, emerged over time.

In classrooms (general music), the singing-playing-moving involvements, supplemented by listening, remained dominant, and became codified and contextualized into two highly influential and individualistic approaches to them associated with two European musicians/educators—Carl Orff and Zoltán Kodály. Each of these pursued the long-standing value of making music—performing—as the basis of what music education should consist of, and each added a variety of related involvements to implement and supplement that value.

Another important influence on what general music became was the variety of music textbook series published over the years, which began as primarily song collections and continue as such to the present, but with the gradual inclusion of other involvements reflecting advancing recording technologies, interests in diverse cultural musics, and a wider variety of creative activities. Whatever the approach taken, the major underlying philosophical value for the enterprise was to cultivate active musicianship, construed primarily as the ability to perform.

2. Conceptualized Phase

The goal of general music, then, came to be conceptualized as promoting and enabling active musical involvement. A good general music program was one that did so, in any way that teachers could envision, so long as "active" was the key. But little philosophical attention was paid to the notion of musical action and what it might consist of beyond the "hands on" level so clearly demonstrated by performing. As a result, any and all ways of hands-on involvement were taken to be qualified as valid—as promoting musicianship and therefore what is most to be valued.

Given this interpretation of "active," listening to music, not requiring the "hands" (body) to make sounds, was regarded by many to be passive and by some to be even antimusical, fit only for those who occupied the lowest possible rung of the musical ladder—consumers, or, synonymously, musical couch potatoes. Also to be regarded with suspicion if not contempt were attempts to include reflection—careful, probing thinking about and why—as an essential ingredient of musical learning. "Students don't want to think about or talk about music," it was often said. "They want to *do* it."

The doings in general music evolved into a great diversity of approaches, each claiming to do what a good music education should do and each logically convincing because each could demonstrate that it required musical action. Whether focused on and organized around hand bells, guitar, dulcimer, singing, or Orff or Kodály configurations of such activities and others particular to each approach, general music became remarkably disunified, based as it was on a conceptualized goal too limited to provide coherence beyond the unexamined dictum of being "musically active." The concept of the knowledge base of music was restricted to one of its aspects, an aspect that, though essential, is insufficient to provide an education reflecting the ways music actually is pursued in the larger culture in which the schools exist.

3. Systematized Phase

With being musically active as the general goal, the most widespread basis for sequential learning was the development of the skills of performance, including associated notation skills, terminology, and theory concepts. In this the music education profession succeeded in achieving high levels of expertise in teaching for and assessing sequential progress. But general music usually ends during the middle school years. Performance specialization opportunities in the upper elementary grades siphon off students interested in pursuing them. General music in and after those grades often found itself rudderless, no longer responsible for "serious" musicianship teaching but with few alternatives to provide relevance and excitement beyond a continuation of earlier grade activities that were increasingly ineffectual for the maturing students and their maturing musical interests. The dominant goal of performance instruction and related matters was too limited to sustain a viable general music program into the middle school/junior high school, accounting for the ongoing and deep uncertainty of what the program should consist of at that level.

It also led to the virtual absence of music learning opportunities other than in performance at the high school level, where the culmination of musical learning and involvement became performance ensembles, the possibility of other offerings being simply unperceived. If students were not, by then, performers, what else could they possibly need to learn? Theory perhaps, but that was mostly for those performers gravitating toward being college music majors and needing preparation for the rigors of the content of typical college theory courses (also for guitar players and whoever else wanted and needed better harmony understandings and skills). "Music appreciation" perhaps, under a variety of guises but with little solid grounding as to what it needed to be beyond either an extension of earlier general music or an adaptation of college history or literature courses. A smattering of other courses could be found here and there, but total enrollments in all of them approached indiscernibility. In short, a sequence of learnings for general education in music encompassing grades K–12 has never been envisioned securely, let alone actualized.

4. Interpreted Phase

Inevitably, with the prevailing disunity of approaches to general music, interpretations by teachers of what it should contain were hit or miss, dependent in good measure on the approach in the college methods courses they happen to have taken or by the proclivities of the school(s) in which they happen to have worked. Of course, diversity may be conceived to be a virtue, and certainly a uniform, undeviating interpretation of what constitutes a valid curriculum would stifle individuality. What the profession has lacked, I suggest, is sufficient depth of reflection about the aims of general music to have achieved a foundational conceptualization providing consistency, in which that consistency promotes wide leeway for individual teachers' adaptations. Until such unity with diversity has been attained, I would argue, general music, the only aspect of the curriculum in which music is taught to 100 percent of students, will never be regarded—and should not be regarded—as worthy of core subject status. That it has not been regarded as such should not be surprising given the lack of a solid, comprehensive basis for program development and the extreme variability, approaching disarray, to which that led.

5. Operational Phase

At the level of classroom operations I believe a remarkably high percentage of general music teachers have been extremely good at doing what they have chosen to do, certainly at least as good as teachers of other subjects, if not considerably better. Of course, a normal curve of teaching effectiveness is always likely to exist, but in the case of general music I feel it has been skewed toward the high end. The problem, unfortunately, is deeper than occasional incompetent or marginal teaching, problematic as that always is. The ineffectuality of general music, I would argue, is rooted in our historical weaknesses in all the previous phases, not in ineffectual teaching skills. The lesson here is that without a solid foundation for the operational phase, teaching expertise in itself is likely to accomplish less than it deserves to accomplish.

6. Experienced Phase

What students experience from general music has been, predictably, as varied as the programs they have undergone. Certainly in every program, no matter how idiosyncratic, many useful, musically important, stimulating learnings are likely to have occurred. But just as certainly there has been a high degree of waste, and of efforts expended to teach and learn materials, skills, and understandings having little to do with the knowings and doings students would find influential for a lifetime of musical enjoyments. Identifying those materials, skills, and understandings is, precisely, what we have historically been unable to do.

7. Expectational Phase

What have people other than music educators wanted from or expected from general music? One answer to this question, often given by music educators, is, Who cares? After all, we are the experts, the people endowed by talent and training to provide what we, in our wisdom, conceive to be what they need. So we are the ones to be entrusted with the substantive decisions as to what a good general education in music should comprise. Never mind that our decisions have ranged all over the map of possibilities and we have been unable to articulate a persuasive argument as to why this should be so, despite that, in all the basic subjects, a high degree of common expectations by both professionals and laypeople has existed. The will of the people—of students, parents, community members, as evidenced by the musical lives they have chosen to live—need not be consulted let alone followed in matters musical. In fact, we have often deprecated their choices, attempting to elevate their musical lives by substituting our own choices, reflecting our superior tastes and enthusiasms. In the old music education motto "Music for every child and every child for music," there has been some unnoticed small print: "But on *our* terms, with *our* preferred music, and with *our* preferred way to be involved with music."

I have stated this situation starkly to dramatize the point that in the inevitable and healthy interface between what communities desire from education and professionals' aspirations for it, there will always be some level of tension, but for education to be effective both perspectives must be considered in a synergistic spirit. If the expectations of the lay community so dominate that the expertise and devotion of professionals have little or no influence, education is likely to stagnate and vacillate, unable to muster the guiding energies to move in fruitful directions guided by the wisdom of specialists. But when community values are ignored or denigrated, as has happened to uncomfortable levels in music education, especially in regard to general music where students cannot vote with their feet by not electing it, the gap between what teachers consider musically valuable and what students/communities regard as such has tended to be intolerably wide.

I believe this has occurred too often in regard to general music largely as a result of two realities. First, as explained previously, the profession has not succeeded in fashioning a general music program both sensitive to and supportive of community musical life and representative of a comprehensive perspective of musical knowings and doings. This two-pronged consideration is needed to expand community values and musical experiences in productive directions.

Second, those who teach music in schools tend to be people who poorly represent the musical realities of the communities they serve. Most were, as students, the most successful in elective performance involvements, and their success in pursuing those involvements determined and intensified their musical interests, tastes, and values. For the majority of music educators, what they themselves needed to know and be able to do, primarily focusing on becoming good performers both individually and in ensembles, tended to become, quite naturally, their vision of what is "fundamental" for all people to know and do. So performance-centered learnings, with all their needs for technical expertise with notation, craft, music theory knowledge, and acquaintance with the musical literature of the Western classical tradition and how it works, dominated the content of general music. This was exacerbated, of course, by the pressures exerted by some secondary school ensemble directors who regarded the general music program as a feeder mechanism for supplying and preparing their players and singers.

The upshot of all this has been, historically, a strong tendency to conceive general music in elementary and middle schools as needing to be performance oriented in a variety of ways, despite that most students do not choose to become involved with music as performers, especially in the ways bands, orchestras, and choruses deal with music and with the particular musics they perform. A healthy percentage of students do elect school performance offerings (estimates range from 9 to 15 percent overall who become involved with ensemble programs), but the great majority who do not opt to be performers are often left with introductory learnings leading in directions irrelevant to what they want and expect music to be in their lives.

Some better accommodation is needed between the actuality of our culture's musical existence and the interests of general music educators. We cannot go on ignoring the reality so obvious to the objective observer—that general music as conceived and delivered by professionals has often been unacceptably discordant with the ways music exists outside schools, ways we cannot dismiss on the basis that our interests are the only valid ones. In the elective music program a different situation exists, a situation I will address in the following chapter. In general music the reality gap causing many programs to be painfully out of touch with student desires and enthusiasms remains a major issue the profession needs to address directly and substantively. Fortunately, we now have the means and the basis for doing so.

ACHIEVING COMPREHENSIVENESS

As explained in Chapter 1 and here, the standards movement in education caused each school subject to examine its knowledge base—its foundational knowings and doings—and to provide guidelines for how teaching and learning could give all students a comprehensive education focused on what matters most in each domain. The document doing this in music (also in dance, theater, and visual arts) delineates nine dimensions that cover the major ways people in our culture engage themselves with music.[1] Here is a listing of the nine as they were originally conceived.

U.S. NATIONAL CONTENT STANDARDS FOR MUSIC EDUCATION (ORIGINAL)

1. Singing, alone and with others, a varied repertoire of music.
2. Performing on instruments, alone and with others, a varied repertoire of music.
3. Improvising melodies, variations, and accompaniments.
4. Composing and arranging music within specified guidelines.
5. Reading and notating music.
6. Listening to, analyzing, and describing music.
7. Evaluating music and music performance.
8. Understanding relationships between music, the other arts, and disciplines outside the arts.
9. Understanding music in relation to history and culture.

In music the content standards generated a large number of auxiliary documents covering a great many details of teaching, assessing, securing optimal opportunities to learn, and so forth.[2] This response is quite typical of the desire of music educators for a high level of specificity in regard to program implementation. Interestingly, controversies over the standards movement as a whole, including the arts, have arisen not so much in regard to the contents proposed for each subject as about matters of standardization, testing and accountability, equal opportunity, teacher education, and on and on with many issues at the implementation level. Unfortunately the word "standards" has caused a great deal of confusion, because it is generally understood to mean stipulated levels of expected achievement. To reach a standard is to achieve a specified, consensually determined degree of competence. So the initial use of the term as referring to content soon shifted, no doubt inevitably, to matters having to do with degrees of expected learning, with all the convoluted, politically charged, psychologically and emotionally volatile issues always surrounding attempts to set achievement expectations and to measure (test) how well they are being reached.

I hope I will be excused for not wading into those waters here, because doing so would take me into complex discussions not central to my focus, which is on how comprehensiveness of content needs to occur if a general education in music is to be valid and useful. I urge music educators concerned with the many political issues surrounding the implementation of the standards (in education as a whole and particularly in music) to express themselves in our journals and forums, and I will gladly

---

[1]*National Standards for Arts Education: What Every Young American Should Know and Be Able to Do in the Arts* (Reston, VA: Music Educators National Conference, 1994).
[2]For complete listings, see the MENC *Professional Resources Guide,* published yearly.

do so as well.[3] Here I will return to the initial intent of the standards movement to provide descriptions of the knowledge bases of the school subjects and to the initiative to do so in music as well.

Critiques of the nine music content areas identified in the U.S. standards as to their validity and suitability for music education curricula have been remarkably absent. Indeed, I have had the opportunity to discuss and explain the U.S. content standards in many places around the world, and always ask the same two questions of the music educators involved: (1) Are any of these nine content areas irrelevant or inappropriate for music education in your culture? (2) Should anything else be added to the nine to fully represent musical learnings important in your culture? In all cases the answers to both, after thoughtful reflection, have been no. I do not presume that my experience is definitive, of course, but I also do not presume that the contents in the U.S. standards are in any substantive way idiosyncratic or partial or insignificant. No doubt time and experience will cause us to add to them or alter them in ways reflecting changing musical possibilities. At the moment they seem useful, defensible, and very widely acceptable to professionals in divergent societal situations over the globe as providing a model for comprehensivity in musical learnings.

Further, I believe that, worldwide, the goal of comprehensiveness, rather than restrictiveness, is being recognized as the appropriate basis for meeting the widely varied musical needs of individuals and for nourishing the healthy state of multimusicality as it exists in most cultures in today's world. In practically every culture there are diverse ways to be involved with music—diverse musical roles people can play—and diverse musics in which these roles are actuated. If music education is to honestly represent the musical realities of the culture it exists to serve, rather than to reflect the interests of those who choose to be music educators as a way to serve their own personal musical interests, it will have to provide, in the general education aspect of the program, a far more inclusive curriculum than it has offered in the past. A new vision of general music is now called for, one aimed toward enabling all students to (1) gain a grounded understanding, through direct experiences of knowing within and knowing how, supplemented by knowing about and knowing why, of the fullness and diversity of musical satisfactions their culture makes available, and (2) discover if any particular music and role is so personally compelling and fulfilling as to warrant elective study building on and taking further their individual interests and proclivities.

---

[3]For discussions of the politics of standards in music education, see Catherine M. Schmidt, "Who Benefits? Music Education and the National Standards," *Philosophy of Music Education Review,* 4, no. 2 (Fall 1996), 71–82, and the rejoinder by Paul Lehman, *Philosophy of Music Education Review,* 5, no. 1 (Spring 1997), 55–57. Also see Richard Colwell, "The Meaning of the National Standards: Are We Ready for the Consequences?" *Maryland Music Educator* (January/February 2000), 32–35. A biting indictment of the politics of assessment and the reductionism of achievement standard-setting is given by Anthony J. Palmer, "Consciousness Studies and a Philosophy of Music Education," *Philosophy of Music Education Review,* 8, no. 2 (Fall 2000), 105–6. A rebuttal, pointing out the benefits of assessing by standards, is offered by Christine Brown, "A Response to Anthony J. Palmer," *Philosophy of Music Education Review,* 8, no. 2 (Fall 2000), 118–19.

REDEFINING AND REBALANCING GENERAL MUSIC:
A RADICAL PROSPECT

The vision just articulated challenges the traditional performance-dominated general music practices in the United States and in many other cultures around the world, not by eliminating performance as one essential way to be engaged with music (as the content standards certainly recognize it to be), but by shifting the focus to a more equitable balance among the content areas. Rather than the program's being conceived as devoted primarily to performance, with all the others seen as, simply, supplementary to it, each content area should be regarded to be authentic, all the others serving it as enrichment.

That vision, particularly in the United States given its historical performance-focused conceptualization of music education, is nothing short of revolutionary. Surely, the ingrained tradition assumed, the point and purpose of all music education, general or elective, is to make each person into a musician. Being a musician means being a performer. So the general music program existed to introduce students to the "fundamentals of music"; to provide experiences of singing and playing and teaching the basis of doing those things well; to listen to and learn about the kinds of music represented by the preferences of music educators and pursued in secondary school music offerings; and to demonstrate through performances at a variety of school functions that the children were learning what most matters—to be able to sing and play with some acceptable level of competence.

It will be difficult, I recognize, to rebalance this long-held view by placing it in a larger perspective, and anyone attempting to do so is at risk of being regarded as subversive. But the advent of the content standards, and their overwhelming acceptance by music educators in America and around the world as being a valid delineation of the important ways music can be experienced, calls all of us to at least begin to reconsider our traditional stance and its unfortunate limitations. We need to embrace all the important musical roles in our culture as genuine and valuable ways for people to be actively engaged with music, each in its own way and each with its own characteristics.

The goal of general music, in this conception, is to enable all students to develop their awareness of the roles that music encompasses in their culture, so that those roles can be appreciated, understood, and seen as the repertoire of musical possibilities open to all. In addition, they will be introduced to how and why music specialists in each role do what they do. Such an education provides access to and the ability to take full advantage of all the important ways their culture provides for making and sharing musical meanings by the ways the culture operationalizes its musical values.

To capture this conceptualization graphically, I propose a restructured format for the standards, retaining the basic contents but emphasizing that each represents a role in which a particular musical intelligence and creativity is manifested.

U.S. NATIONAL CONTENT STANDARDS FOR MUSIC EDUCATION (RESTRUCTURED)

A. Musicianship Roles (Intelligences)

1. Singing, Playing   (Performer)
2. Improvising   (Improviser)
3. Composing   (Composer)
4. Arranging   (Arranger)

↑

(Reading and notating music)

↓

B. Listenership Roles (Intelligences)

5. Listening   (Listener)
6. Analyzing, Describing   (Theorist)
7. Evaluating   (Critic)
8. Understanding relationships between music, the other arts, and disciplines outside the arts   (Psychologist, Philosopher, Neuroscientist, Educational Theorist, etc.)
9. Understanding music in relation to history and culture   (Historian, Ethnomusicologist, Anthropologist, Sociologist, etc.)

I suggest that this restructuring of the standards gets us closer to what general music needs to accomplish if it is to realistically serve the musical needs of all students. As will be explained in the following chapter, it also delineates what a comprehensive program of musical electives will make available to all students. Before discussing each of the musical roles as part of a general education in music, however, we need to clarify the issue of active engagement with music, not only as it exists beyond the musicianship roles, but also as it exists at different levels of musical involvement.

Developing musical intelligences in the general music aspect of the program does indeed require that students be actively engaged with music in all the important ways music can be encountered, understood, and enjoyed. Such engagements, though not aimed toward producing professionals, nevertheless include, as one aspect, gaining a sense of what professionals do and how they do it in each culturally important role. But the professional's perspective—how professionals must be active—is not the primary one taken. Two other levels need to be influential.

The first is that of the amateur, the person who engages in a musical role for the sheer delight and satisfaction it affords rather than as a professional career. Of course, professionals can and do delight in their role and gain much satisfaction from it. But being a professional requires attainment and maintenance of a level of competency, and the fulfillment of a great many obligations when payment is a basic component, that separate the two roles in a fundamental way. What is at stake is simply different in the amateur and professional levels of musical involvement, related as they are. Understanding what the difference is, and how amateurs in various musical roles are actively engaged with music—the amateur's perspective—is an important component of general music.

Despite the hopes of many music educators that all students will choose to be at least amateurs in some musical role, devoting significant time and effort to it in their lives because of the musical (and associated social, psychological, etc.) rewards it brings, most students will choose a different level of musical involvement from that of either the amateur or the professional. They will be quite content with the role of partaker of the musical pleasures offered by amateurs and professionals. I suggest that we call such people "aficionados"—that is, enthusiasts who eagerly, delightedly, and *intelligently* seek musical experiences in their lives in one or several or many of the ways their culture makes them available other than by being amateurs or professionals. Cultivating the active responses to music required if aficionados are to be intelligent as well as committed partakers of the efforts of amateurs and professionals is a foundational goal of a general education in music. Foundational because that involvement is, in fact, the central one in Western cultures and in many if not most others in the world in which we live. It is central in being the most widely and actively pursued and on which the others depend for their existence.

The activeness of the aficionado—of all who willingly and heartily enjoy partaking of music but not as amateurs or professionals—has identifiable characteristics, equally shared by amateurs and professionals but not by doing what they do. All who are active in their musical engagements, at whichever of the three levels previously discussed, and at whatever age, demonstrate high levels of the following attributes:

1. They attend to music with mental, emotional, and physical energy. Their engagement with music, at whatever level, is marked by absorption, by giving themselves fully to the experience, immersing themselves wholeheartedly and "wholemindedly" in whatever musical event is occurring and whatever engagement they are having with it.

2. They are discerning about what is occurring, both in the music and in all the ways the music entails and embodies its cultural surrounding. They notice with discriminative awareness, absorbed in the many significant components that, together, constitute the identity of the musical event.

3. They are imaginative with what is being discerned, connecting parts into meaningful wholes, experiencing the music in light of its scope as a singular occurrence and how that occurrence relates to others both alike and different.

4. They are engaged with feeling, necessarily therefore with their body, experiencing musical events as suffused with affective undergoing they welcome and are willing to have taken in whatever directions the music leads them.
5. They are musically courageous and curious, seeking not only comfort and the pleasures of the familiar but also expansions of what they already are capable of experiencing musically. They are open to new musical challenges and are knowledgeable about where and how to discover them.
6. They seek and incorporate diverse musical satisfactions as an ongoing facet of their lives, valuing musical experiences as a source of pleasure, personal growth, community with others, and spiritually fulfilling meaning. They are aware that attaining the many satisfactions music offers calls on continual efforts to learn more about it in its many dimensions, and are open to becoming more educated musically as appropriate to their life circumstances and their level of musical obligations.

A valid general education in music aims to enhance every person's abilities and natural propensities to be actively engaged with music in the ways described (and others), recognizing that most will be involved as aficionados, some as amateurs, and a (very) few as professionals.An education in consonance with that aim will also enable the attainment of amateur and professional levels of involvement when coupled with the offerings in the elective aspect of the music program, as will be explained in the following chapter. General education, in any subject, cannot be sufficient by itself to prepare students for all three levels: that is why specialization is a necessary dimension of education. The mistake we have made in general music, often made in other subjects as well, is to have so overemphasized the professional/amateur aspects of education (that is, the specialized knowings and doings those levels demand) as to have overly neglected the base of our responsibility—the overwhelming majority of people who do not and will not aspire to those levels.

We can represent an appropriate balance of emphases in general music as follows:

This implies that, while the general music program attends to the cultivation of active engagement with music at the core aficionado level, it also includes and enables possibilities for the other levels, both explicitly by targeted instruction about and experiences of what those levels entail, and implicitly by providing a foundation of learnings as relevant to those levels as to the central one. Everything aficionados learn about experiencing music within, how, about, and why, in its feeling dimension, its creative dimension, its meaning dimension, and its contextual dimension, is equally relevant and important for amateurs and professionals if they are to fulfill their roles intelligently. But not sufficient. That is why specialized experiences are needed, and a program devoted to supplying them.

IMPLEMENTING A COMPREHENSIVE GENERAL MUSIC PROGRAM: THE RESTRUCTURED CONTENT STANDARDS

This book, obviously, is not a general music methods text, so it will not attempt the kind of specificity such a text needs to contain. Instead, it will give an overview of how the content standards (roles) identified in the restructured format can function to provide what an effective general music program should make richly available—learnings in music that are

1. Grounded in a philosophically compelling position about the values of music
2. Focused on the most salient roles in music as they function in the culture in question
3. Based on musical experience in its inherent and delineated dimensions, in which knowing within and how are central and knowing about and why are supportive
4. Sequenced both developmentally and by the nature of each of the various roles
5. Presented in ways that engage and nurture the musical intelligences and creativities of each student as each interacts with each role
6. Balanced toward the development of musical aficionados supported by and extended to understandings of the ways amateurs and professionals function in their culture
7. Representative of the ways people in a culture actually participate in music and of the musics they choose as valuable to them
8. Enriching of the experience of those musics and ways to be engaged with them and also expansive in introducing diversities and challenges of musics and roles beyond those presently familiar

For learnings in general music to be as musically powerful as possible, each of the dimensions of musical experience identified in the standards needs to be treated as a genuine and characteristic role in which to be engaged with music, with its particular demands of intelligence and creativity, and as related to and supported by learnings in all the others. That is, a general music program of optimal educative influence will not be simply a collection of various areas of study, each treated as separate and distinct from the others, nor will it be a kind of fusion of all in which the differences among them are ignored. The key to effectiveness is to make explicit to students in appropriate ways at each grade level that each particular engagement is at one and the same time a special way to know and experience music and is also enriched in its specialness by learnings in the others.

Effective teaching, then, calls on the ability to teach each of the roles in and of itself, to bring the others into play by coordinating them with whichever is the focus, and to apportion all of them equitably so that none is overly dominant or largely ignored over the course of each grade level.

Given those guiding principles we can now examine the nine roles, or content areas (plus reading and notating), as to their function within the overall general music program. The musicianship roles, those in which music is created, are grouped as 1–4. The listenership roles, 5–9, are not focused on the creation of music but on roles in which various responses to created music are made.[4] (Please review the discussions of the creativities entailed in musicianship and listenership in Chapter 4.)

1. Singing and Playing

I will discuss these together, as appropriate for my focus on musical roles as intelligences. Taken together they constitute the basis of traditional general music programs in the United States and in much of the world, as has been pointed out. They are listed first in the original and restructured standards, not, as often assumed, because they are the most important of the nine, or the most basic or essential or necessary, but because they are the most familiar, being the most widely dominant aspects of the established program. When presenting the content standards to the profession for approval (and feedback) the task force (see Chapter 1) needed to balance a sense of security and confidence with a sense of newness and challenge: overemphasis of either would have met with strong resistance or at least consternation. Starting the list with security—"We can do this"—was important to avoid potential anxieties and negative reactions. So

---

[4]The term "listenership" is used often in David Elliott's writings, his concept of it in some ways similar to mine and in other ways quite different. As explained in Chapter 2, he usually explains it as a necessary dimension of the performer's (and sometimes other music-producing roles') know-how, as I do as well, and he continually points out that musicianship always includes listenership, a point also central to my view of what musicianship requires. But it is not always clear whether he believes that listenership can exist as a genuine way to be musical if not demonstrated within the contexts of performance/composing, and so on. For example, in his article "Modernity, Postmodernity and Music Education," *Research Studies in Music Education*, no. 17 (December 2001), 39, he insists that listening must be "grounded in active and critically reflective music making, by which I mean: performing-listening, improvising-listening, composing-listening, arranging-listening, and conducting-listening."

My own view is that, though performance (and every other standard area) is important in the education of listenership, each aspect of music adding its dimensionality to listening, those who do not play a musicianship role can in a real and full sense be intelligent and creative listeners: in fact, most people in the world actively, intelligently, and creatively engage themselves as listeners but not as performers (or composers, and so forth). Enhancing their expertise as listeners is the major task of the listenership standards (5–9 in the restructured format), supported and enriched by associated learnings in standards 1–4, just as 1–4 are supported and enhanced by 5–9.

the safe course—I believe the wise course—was to start the list with present strengths and move on to areas of lesser experience/expertise.

The risk, of course, was that this would perpetuate long-standing general music practices, singing and playing seemingly being given top billing and the other areas able to be assumed to exist as supportive of their primacy. Given most music educators' high levels of devotion to and expertise with performing, it is comforting to interpret the standards as giving permission to remain firmly in that groove and to simply add a bit more of the other seven when appropriately related to performance learnings. In and of itself that does indeed broaden and strengthen performance experiences, a result all to the good. The issue is whether it is sufficient for a genuinely comprehensive general music program.

I suggest it is not. Singing and playing will naturally be present in abundance throughout the elementary years and on into the middle school years. The other content areas need to support and enrich the performance-focused experiences as we are increasingly learning how to accomplish.[5] However, the balance between the performing standard and the others must shift significantly if the potential intelligences, creativities, and interests of all students are to be discerned and given a chance to be developed. I do not believe it is possible to stipulate an "ideal" distribution of time among the nine roles because different ones need to be stressed at different times and for various purposes, flexibility being necessary at every grade level. Nevertheless, it is the very point of the standards that greater parity among them be achieved. In regard to singing and playing, it will be important to maintain and refine the high levels of effectiveness already established; more fully coordinate the other roles to deepen and broaden performance understandings; incorporate a greater diversity of styles and types of music reflecting the realities of what the out-of-school musical culture contains; and extend the repertoires to musics less familiar, including, emphatically, performable musics of the Western classical music tradition and its contemporary manifestations. All this will ensure that performance will be as powerfully influential in the experience of all students as it deserves to be, whether their lives lead them to be aficionados of others' performances or to be amateurs or even professionals.

2. Improvising

Given its shared basis in performance, it seemed sensible to the task force that wrote the original standards to list improvisation after singing and playing. Nevertheless, the fact that it was not incorporated as just a variant of those two testifies to its singular characteristics and the need to attend to them if education for improvisation is to be effective.

In the general music program, improvisation experiences have been offered in

---

[5]Many articles have appeared in our professional journals on how to incorporate learnings from the other standard areas into the first two, and many workshops, convention sessions, and so forth, continue to be offered. For a focused treatment of issues and implementations, see *Performing with Understanding: The Challenge of the National Standards for Music Education,* ed. Bennett Reimer (Reston, VA: Music Educators National Conference, 2000), and the many MENC publications dealing with implementing the standards.

Orff contexts and to some degree in others. Given the rich intelligence and creativity characteristics of this musical role, and the exciting challenges it offers, it needs to play a far more important part than it has traditionally been given. Orff experiences provide secure introductory engagements. More extensive possibilities and pleasures are available in the Western style largely dependent on it—jazz—and in the many musics around the world that are improvisatory in essence. In this we must be careful to avoid the assumption that jazz improvisations or Orff improvisations are models for how other culturally embedded ways to improvise are to be conceived and taught. Each improvisatory repertoire around the world is likely to share some characteristics with others, but also to be indigenous, requiring acquaintance with its musical ways to think and act as particular to its setting. Standard 9, focusing on cultural understandings, comes immediately into play.

The point here is to give all students a genuine taste, both by improvising and by learning about its nature, of what this musical role is like around the world, the diverse musical pleasures it affords, and what amateur and professional attainment in it requires. That goal calls on understandings of how and why improvising is similar to but also different from singing and playing composed musics; how and why it is similar to and different from composing and arranging; how and why notation is either irrelevant or used in very special ways; how it can be examined and described; how its quality is to be judged; how and why improvisation plays important roles in other areas and in various other aspects of life; and, as previously mentioned, the historical/cultural learnings related to the many ways improvisation is manifested at different times and in different places.

I have left the relation of listening to improvising for last because of its central, essential role, no matter the age of the students or their level of musical development. As I have emphasized before (and will continue to do as appropriate) a foundation of "having the sounds in the ears" (the mind, body, and feelings) is the basis for any genuinely intelligent, creative, improvisatory experience. Listening to improvisations of all sorts and styles to get its sounds internalized is a fundamental component of learning what it is all about.

Opening up improvisation to the world's possibilities can go a long way toward revivifying the general music program. It would also identify those students, previously invisible, who might well choose to go from aficionados of improvisation to amateurs or professionals and deserve the opportunity.

3. Composing

Here, as with improvisation, an endlessly fertile domain of musical possibilities for intelligence and creativity exists, a domain severely limited in school opportunities in the past, although some countries (such as Great Britain) have gained more experience with it than others (such as the United States).[6] Now, in the age of the technological

---

[6]An excellent overview of composition as a component of British music education, and the continuing effort to achieve success at it, is the research report *Composing in the Classroom: The Creative Dream*, Anice Patterson, Author and Research Fellow, George Odam, Editor and Project Director (National Association of Music Educators, 16 Pinions Road, High Wycombe, Buckinghamshire HP13 7AT, England).

transformation of music and how it can be composed, new attention is being paid to offering school curricula focusing on this foundational musical role. All over the world music educators devoted to composing have either begun to develop or are further developing their expertise and making contributions toward establishing thoughtfully devised composition curricula at all levels of schooling. In addition, research on composing with young people has increased dramatically both in quantity and in quality.[7]

All this adds up to a level of energy, and a sense of new potential, that, along with increasing activity in improvisation, can significantly elevate general music to unprecedented levels of relevance in the musicianship aspects of learning. As composition experiences become more available, challenging, and satisfying, both through technological means and in traditional settings, this mode of primal musical intelligence and creativity can finally begin to reach all students in genuine rather than artificial ways. As a result, aficionados of a new sort can be expected to appear, with insights into musical thinking and doing that equip them to understand and enjoy music at higher levels of sophistication than had ever before been attainable. The ensuing ripple effect can lift the quality of musical experience in all its aspects, as this inherently creative way to be engaged with music (along with the creativity of improvisation) infuses more and more people with expectations that their musical experiences should satisfy their needs for creative challenges and who therefore seek such challenges from their musical culture.

Successful composition instruction in general music will incorporate each of the other standards as each relates to compositional creativity. Singing and playing experiences impinge directly on composers who create music for performance. Similarities and differences between composing, improvising, and arranging need to be understood. Notations of various sorts need to be called on as relevant to what is being composed, and skills developed accordingly. Analyzing, describing, and evaluating, as will be discussed further on, are essential components of the compositional act. Understandings about how composition is comparable (similar and different) in various ways to creation in the other arts and creativity outside the arts broadens the perspective of youngsters about what composing is and does. And viewing the role of the composer in history and in various cultures also situates learnings within a base of reality.

Listening, of course, is a primal requirement, not only within the act of creating compositions, but also as the basic source from which ideas and possibilities spring. Composing absent a broad repertoire of listening experiences is composing in a vacuum and therefore in a real sense composing in ignorance. Composition experiences need to be saturated with associated listenings.

4. Arranging

Arranging serves an important function in a variety of musical styles and is likely to intrigue students given the opportunity to experience it.[8] The creation of various

---

[7]A useful overview of composing approaches and research is Joanna Glover, *Children Composing 4–14* (London: Routledge-Farmer, 2000).

[8]For an excellent and concise discussion of arranging, see David Elliott, *Music Matters: A New Philosophy of Music Education* (New York: Oxford University Press, 1995), 170–72.

popular musics, as discussed in several places previously, involves students in a compositional/improvisatory/arranging-like/technology-enhanced mixture of creative thinkings and doings attractive to many youngsters, who pursue it avidly but usually outside the schools. Incorporating this creative opportunity in general music would not only spread its availability to all but also enhance the musical insights relevant to discerning the quality of music in these styles, as it does with such insights about musical quality in all styles about which learning has occurred. Experiencing the creation of popular musics inevitably affects the intelligence of aficionados about it, thereby influencing both their discriminations and their enjoyments. General music programs including experiences in composing/arranging popular musics are likely to be not only musically exciting for students but also educative in important ways for their musical futures. Additionally, special elective offerings are required in which enthusiasms for it can be developed beyond what general music can provide, opening still another opportunity for music education to be of service.

(Reading and Notating Music)

This standard is a special case. The issue of whether notation deserved a separate category or whether it was more sensible to include it as one of the aspects connected to singing, playing, composing, arranging, and analyzing occupied the standards task force in many discussions. Eventually the decision to list it separately was made, largely because so many music educators regard it as central to musical learning that not doing so might have caused a strong negative reaction. Notation is functional for particular purposes in particular musics. Those purposes and those musics have been so dominant in traditional music education in America and in many other countries as to have led to the notion that notation skills must logically be "fundamental" and therefore an important—even central—aspect of a general education in music.

I seriously question that assumption and the values on which it is based. The old notion that musical literacy equates with language/notation literacy seems to me fallacious. I have argued for a very long time that the narrow view of literacy, in which the term is taken to mean the ability to read and write, leads to the mistaken conclusion that musical literacy means the ability to read and write music notation. But reading and writing function in fundamentally different ways in language and in music. Language deals with conceptual material and requires a symbol system as its primary medium for containing conceptual meanings and making them available. Music does not operate conceptually, instead being based in a medium—sounds—not organized as language must be. In music, the meanings do not come from a symbol system but from directly experienced sounds. (All this is explained in some detail in Chapter 5.) Western classical musics developed in a particular way, in which the sounds composed had to be captured in a medium—written in a notation-language—that performers could "read" and transform into the sounds the composer had in mind. Notation skill is necessary for composers who "write" music (no longer necessary with technologies that capture and present composed sounds directly) and for those who must read their notations in order to make the sounds they signify.

So long as notated compositions continue to be created and performed and so long as the music that was conceived that way in the past is preserved for experiencing, some musicians will continue to need the "literacy" connected to writing and reading a notation system. But literacy in the broader sense consists of musical intelligences—the ability to discriminate sounds and make meanings out of them as various roles require. Those discriminations and meanings do not come from a system of notation but from the ways heard sounds are perceptually structured intelligently.

Reading and notating music are special skills required by people who compose and perform and arrange the kinds of music that are notated, and are useful (perhaps essential) in the pursuit of various other roles. Therefore I now believe those skills are best attained as needed for the various roles in which they function and best learned in connection with those roles rather than as a separate role in and of itself. For general music, instruction in notation should be relieved from the obligation to teach it in the ways and to the degrees amateurs and professionals dependent on notation must learn it. Instead, generally educated aficionados must learn about the roles notation plays in particular kinds of music that are conceived notationally, its nonuse in many musics, and how it functions as connected to both musicianship and listenership roles, and must develop enough skill in those contexts to appreciate and understand what amateurs and professionals are doing when writing and reading complex musics.

This reconsideration of the role of notation study in general music situates the program realistically in regard to how the vast majority of people participate in music—with notation playing no part whatsoever. It also alters our expectation of what to assess in our attempts to appraise our effectiveness as teachers and our students' success as learners. Notation skills, notoriously poorly attained by the great majority of students no matter how hard music educators have tried to cultivate them throughout our history and no matter what clever systems we have tried to employ,[9] can with good conscience be regarded as a contributory aspect of a useful general education and be evaluated in that realistic light. It is a different story for amateurs involved with notated musics, of course. But evaluations of their competence should rightfully and relevantly be undertaken within the specialized programs in which they have chosen to become involved. This shift in expectations, I believe, can go a long way toward uncluttering traditional general music programs, freeing them to deal with what is important to educated enthusiasts—the quality of their musical experiences as they overwhelmingly opt to pursue them, which is emphatically not through reading and writing music notation.

5. Listening

Listening pervades each of the standards as a foundational involvement without which none could be pursued validly. Singing, playing, improvising, composing, and

---

[9]Descriptions of various schemes in early American music education history to enable note reading by all, and various systems intending to simplify notation, can be found in Edward Bailey Birge, *History of Public School Music in the United States* (Reston, VA: Music Educators National Conference, 1939).

arranging, each requires its particular listening perspective focused on the sounds being created and whether they are being created meaningfully and effectively. Each also requires, through listening, a broad background in and continual exploration of the creations of others in each of those roles, to ground further explorations securely. The study of notation, as that occurs in musicianship contexts, needs to be immersed in listening if it is not to be entirely sterile. And to analyze and describe music, to evaluate music and performances, and to understand it in its relations to other domains, to culture, and to history, requires that experienced musical sounds be an integral component of learning.

Those sounds will sometimes be provided through students' own performing, improvising, composing, and arranging. They will always, however, go beyond self-made music to the musics existing as cultural capital on which all can draw. The musical treasures of the entire world can readily be incorporated into the experience of all students through listening. And much if not most listening will of necessity be through recordings. This source of musical experience must not be considered only a poor substitute for listening to live performances, necessary as that experience is in every person's musical life. As Theodore Gracyk powerfully explains, "It is only in the aberrant case that one experiences music in a live, group format. Recording technology is our dominant mode of musical reception."[10] Far from recordings being inferior to live performance, Gracyk argues, or, as many have claimed, that recordings have made the world aesthetically poorer, they have instead opened the entire world of music to all people instead of only to the very few who can possibly have direct access to the world's musics or even to all the musics in their own culture when that culture is as complex as many now are. Because of accessibility and convenience, recorded selections from any music literature can be brought to bear on the learnings of students at any time and in any place.

Further, a growing musical literature, especially in popular styles but in others as well such as computer-generated musics, depends on technological manipulations for its veracity. The recording in such music is the genuine instance of the music, the sound engineer being an essential contributor to the creative result. As the British composer Edward Williams puts it,

> [T]he importance of the verisimilitude of the *recorded* sound of the orchestra to the direct *acoustic* experience of it has slowly become less important, and it is often now replaced by the expressive potential of the electronic medium itself—a classic case of the transfer of the message to the new medium, with its expanded range of possibilities. Today, the recordist is often an equal, even occasionally the dominant partner, in the creative musical team, contributing an ever-growing palette of sound-processing technique to recordings of instrumental and vocal material.[11] (Emphases in original)

---

[10]Theodore Gracyk, "Listening to Music: Performances and Recordings," *The Journal of Aesthetics and Art Criticism*, 55, no. 2 (Spring 1997), 139–50. The comment "It is only . . . group format" is a quote from Kathleen Marie Higgins, *The Music of Our Lives* (Philadelphia: Temple University Press, 1991), 150.

[11]Edward Williams, "Obsolescence and Renewal (Musical Heritage, Electronic Technology, Education, and the Future)," *International Journal of Music Education*, no. 37 (2001), 21.

Denigrating recordings, as too many music educators tend to do, is elitist, illogical, backward-looking and unrealistic, and contemptuous of one of the most important culturally democratizing occurrences in recent human history. Of course, there are unique, powerful benefits from live music—obviously. Those benefits are not compromised in any way by the benefits of musical experiences unavailable live. As Gracyk concludes after a sophisticated analysis and critique of claims for the superiority of live music,

> I have not claimed that recordings are, on balance, a superior mode of access to music. But I have asked why others regard live performance as superior, and have identified some counterbalancing merits and parallel experiences furnished by technological mediation. Perhaps we are best off taking advantage of both, but it is less than clear that the proliferation of recorded music leaves the world aesthetically poorer.[12]

Throughout the curriculum, at every grade level, focused instruction in listening, supported and enriched by each other musical role as it illuminates and vivifies that instruction, will ensure that what occurs in general music will be as pertinent to the real musical lives of students as it needs to be while also adding precious dimensionality to their lives.

6. Analyzing and Describing

Analyzing and describing are important, even essential, functions in every musical role. No musicianship role can be successfully played without the careful examination and differentiation among sounds called on by each, allowing decisions about those sounds to be made creatively and discerningly. And every listenership role also depends on careful attention to musical detail as relevant to the particular music being experienced and studied.

Analysis and description should not be limited in their meaning to the particular kinds and ways of carrying them out associated with Western classical music. That is, analysis as appropriate to the characteristic complexities of that particular cultural milieu does not fully encompass its widespread use throughout world musics. In every music, attention is paid to its components by those playing both musicianship and listenership roles, that attention being determined by what the salient details happen to be in each music as its history and cultural setting have led them to be construed. Westerners do not own analysis and description, or the only proper ways to carry them out. Wherever and whenever musicians and partakers exist—that means everywhere and always—scrutiny, sometimes greatly detailed, is required, each music relying on it in its characteristic way. When teachers help students at every age and in every role pay appropriate attention to the workings of the music they are experiencing, they are using what we in the West call analysis and description to do what all music deserves to have done—to be taken seriously and

---

[12]Gracyk, "Listening to Music," note 10, 148.

with respect for what makes it tick so that its enjoyments can be more fully shared. That can be and needs to be accomplished with no imposition of any particular system of analysis on musics to which it does not appropriately apply. All musics call on attention. Helping students attend in relevant ways to a wide variety of music is a basic obligation of the general music program.

For some, analysis and description are in themselves fascinating ways to approach music, and they will desire specialized experiences in doing so. Music theory electives then enter the scene.

7. Evaluating

Performing composed music and improvising require constant evaluation, both during the act and retrospectively. Listening to what one is doing as one is doing it, and shaping the sounds according to how one judges their effectiveness (and affectiveness), is the primary doing–responding synthesis occurring within the act of creating performed sounds. And afterward, by reflecting about what was done and how it might be improved, the subsequent doing can become closer to one's deepening understandings of what is possible.

That experience, so basic to musicianship, is available genuinely in the general music setting even at the earliest ages. Performing composed music (singing songs, for example), and improvising (both by singing and by playing simple instruments) engages all who do so in the exploration/discovery process constituting creativity. That process is infused with judgment-making.

Composing and arranging also require ongoing evaluations as decisions are made about what to do next. Developing the expertise to guide such decisions sensitively in classroom settings remains a major challenge—and opportunity—for the profession.

In all these cases, that is, evaluating in standard areas 1 through 4, one's own doings call forth the evaluations needing to be made. In addition to providing that opportunity is another that standard 7 requires: the opportunity to learn how to evaluate the quality of what musicians have accomplished—their performances, improvisations, compositions, and arrangements. Although aficionados need to experience being musicians, they also need to develop their capacities to partake of the work of musicians: that, after all, is how they primarily choose to be involved with music. Intelligent and creative responses to music, both as process and as product, require judgments to be made, to guide choices as to what will provide most satisfaction and also to grow in discernment and therefore depth of enjoyment. By what criteria can those who partake of the work of musicians evaluate that work?

An important issue is raised by that question. Given that each cultural/historical music has its own way to "be" musically—its particular character as meaningful sounds—is it possible to apply criteria across different musics? Would it not be more logical to expect that each music will have devised its own, particular criteria, as idiosyncratic to that music as is the music itself? How can there be universal or at least widely applicable criteria given the great diversity in the world's musics? The issue of universal and contextual, discussed at some length in Chapter 6, reappears pointedly in the matter of evaluating music. Especially when music education attempts to be inclusive of many styles and types of music and to regard each with the respect it deserves, it seems reasonable to assume that criteria for judging quality must be distinctive to each music and therefore incomparable from one to another.

In the synergistic spirit in which the issue of universal and contextual was dealt with in Chapter 6, and as an extension of that discussion, I suggest that there are indeed universal criteria applicable to diverse musics but that these criteria must be applied distinctively in each. (This is a parallel to the theory that there is a general aspect of intelligence but that it takes its reality from each different role to which it applies.) At the universal level, the same criteria applied to their work by musicians all over the world are the criteria that can be applied to evaluating the results of their work.

1. Was there sufficient ability, in the singing, playing, improvising, composing, or arranging, to have managed the challenges the music was presenting, so that the music was not impeded or diminished by lack of the craft it required? Craft, the internalization within the body of the ways and means to make the sounds the music calls on to be made, is a foundational criterion for successful musicianship. This is the case whether the musician is a first grader "being a musician," a seasoned virtuoso, or anything in between. It is the case whatever the music, of whatever style or type, from whatever culture or time.

But crucially, what *counts* as craft is particular to the particular music being evaluated. The general criterion, then, must be applied by anyone doing so—not just musicians but all who partake of their efforts—in light of understandings of what *in this particular music* good craft is considered to be. Learning the variety of ways craft is conceived in diverse musics is a basic goal of a general education in music. It enables all, whether they are to become aficionados, amateurs, or professionals, to do something all must do if they are to be optimally intelligent in their dealings with music—that is, be able to judge the sufficiency of craft to the demands made on it.

2. Was there sufficient responsiveness to the affective potentialities in the music as to give them fullest expression, capturing and displaying with sensitivity the richness of feeling the music was capable of presenting? Sensitivity to musical feeling, the ability to shape sounds so as to embody their affective energies and make them available to those partaking of those sounds, is a second basic criterion for musicianship, again, whether of young children or professionals. And, again, what counts as sensitivity, as particular musics embody it, is a function of each particular music and must be evaluated accordingly. Learning the many ways various musics approach and actualize affect is a second foundational aim of the general music program for all students no matter their musical futures. Learning to judge the sensitivity of what musicians do is a powerful dimension in the cultivation of musical intelligences.

3. Was there sufficient imaginative exploration of the possibilities in the music to have given it the fullest realization of its potentials? Musical imagination—

projecting and realizing musical meaning as fully as the particular musical event enables—is an obligation all musicians assume, the achievement of which gives vital energy to their doings. No matter their age or experience, people making music must imagine its potential meanings and bring them to life in the sounds they create. Judging whether this was done optimally, as particular musics construe and display imagination reflecting the belief systems in which they operate, adds another key dimension to all students' developing musical intelligences. It therefore is a key aspect of what all must learn in their general music education.

4. Was there a "genuineness" displayed in this musical event—a sincere, authentic investment by those creating it to do so with all the powers they could bring to the challenge, honoring both what the music demanded of them and their own selfness as it met those demands? We know when music is being treated authentically—that is, honestly and respectfully, allowing it to be what it needs to be in the individuality of its particular setting and its way to offer its meanings. We can tell when music is dealt with disrespectfully, forcing it to be something it is not or using it to do something not germane to its nature. Developing that sense of authenticity is something all children studying music must accomplish if any level of their involvement with music is to be genuine. It is, therefore, an obligation of the general music program.

I suggest that a useful set of criteria such as the four I have explained—craft, sensitivity, imagination, and authenticity—or whatever other conceptualizations thoughtful people can devise, can add a much needed degree of specificity to the complex and confusing issue of how music is to be judged. We must help our students understand that judging music is not a matter just of deciding what one likes but also of developing criteria that are as respectful of the complexities of music as music deserves.

We must also be more helpful than to settle for the pluralist cliché that every different kind of music has its own criteria. Every different music is also music, I would argue, and therefore exists at universal, contextual, and individual levels, as explained in several places in this book, particularly in Chapter 6. Identifying some practicable dimensions at the universal level, recognizing that they are played out differently in different contexts, and that individual instances of music can be reasonably judged in light of those two dimensions, allows us to teach what is actually learnable and manageable, and as well, I suggest, philosophically defensible.

In the matter of evaluating music some students may become so interested in its challenges and pleasures as to aspire to be amateurs or professionals in doing so— that is, music critics. In the next chapter I will include a discussion of our obligation to make the cultivation of this particular musical role as available as all others.

8. Understanding Relationships between Music, the Other Arts, and Disciplines Outside the Arts

Fulfilling this standard requires thinking about the nature and values of music, the nature and values of the other arts, and the nature and values of all the other subjects. It also entails differentiating among those three sets of conceptualizations and understanding their interconnections—that is, the ways they are related by similarity and difference. We are thrown, here, into the domains of knowing about and knowing why, and into all the risks and benefits of language-think as it relates to what is central in music—sounds-think. The discussions throughout this book dealing with knowing about and why are here put to work at the level of the music program, raising again the issues of how music relates to the larger world of which it is one part.

Why do the standards recognize, as an equal with all the others, the need for understandings of this sort to be cultivated in music education? Does this not lead the music program away from musical knowing and doing toward abstract learnings that are irrelevant to musical experience? For many music educators there is a suspicion, even a fear, that giving this much attention to learnings that require thinking in language can only make the program academic in the worst sense. Associated with that suspicion or fear is that many feel inadequate to deal with the issues raised in this standard. If asked, themselves, to explain how and why music is both similar to and different from the other arts and nonarts subjects, they would likely feel quite inadequate to offer a knowledgeable, reasoned answer, and would therefore feel very insecure as to how they would help their students learn something they themselves find confusing if not daunting.

The inclusion of this standard as being a necessary component of the knowledge base of music culminates, I think, a slowly accumulating philosophical shift from what generally existed previous to the standards movement. It calls for situating music in a larger context than its traditional separatist posture had attempted to do. Recognizing intuitively (and correctly, I believe) that music is a unique way to think, act, and experience, its teaching tended to occur in isolation from its contexts among the other school subjects. This relieved music teachers from having to deal in any substantive way with those subjects except at the rather trivial level of occasional overlaps, such as when music had obvious references to or clear similarities with material in various subjects.

Now we are being challenged, not to abandon our long-held and defensible conviction that music is a genuine domain with its singular nature and values, but to recognize that understandings about music are deepened and broadened when related to other human endeavors both similar (although not identical) and different. We are being led, by this standard, not to diluting music, but to strengthening it by helping students understand it more clearly as it relates to and interacts with the other important domains in schooling and in life.

Accomplishing this in general music contexts requires teachers sophisticated about the complex issues of the ways of knowing and being—the roles to be played—that music, each of the other arts, and each of the other school subjects make available. They must also be able to translate their understandings into explanations, demonstrations, and involvements appropriate for the developmental level of whatever grade(s) they are teaching, and to do so without watering down or misrepresenting the ideas they are raising. In a very real sense the younger the student the more clearly and accurately the teacher must understand the material to be taught, so that it retains its veracity while being presented as simply as is required.

The skills and insight needed with young children to accomplish this simplification with no loss of validity is among the most challenging tasks in all of education. How are we to enable general music teachers to infuse their instruction with understandings about relationships of music to the rest of the curriculum that are both well grounded and pedagogically effective?

Well, probably with some difficulty. This challenge goes beyond training in some skill or methodology. It raises issues of generally educating music teachers about the other arts and other subjects, enabling them to grasp the intelligences and creativities necessary to each. That, in turn, entails reconceiving the typical technically oriented teacher education program in music education, broadening it not only in all the ways the previous standards call for but also outward to an encompassing vision of the larger world in which music exists. Certainly good materials, workshops, clinics, courses, and so forth can help cut down to reasonable size the magnitude of this obligation: it is important that we not abandon it in face of its many complexities. If we genuinely want to educate all students, at every grade level, to be as intelligent about music as well-grounded aficionados (and amateurs and professionals as well) must be, we must attend to the reality that musical experience, as I have attempted to explain, is both unique and situated, encompassing within it many dimensions and meanings of life and carrying them to musical conclusions. Those conclusions will be more powerful, and valid, when encompassing a broad vision of music as part of a larger world of meanings, a vision seldom as fully developed as the standards now ask us to accomplish.

For some, the studies and experiences embodied in this standard will be fascinating, with a desire for specialized instruction to pursue its values. The elective program will have to provide such opportunities.

9. Understanding Music in Relation to History and Culture

Enough has been said throughout this book about music as historically and culturally grounded to make further substantive discussion here unnecessary. The profession has well accepted the need for infusing its programs with learnings relating to contexts and is making progress toward doing it effectively, although we certainly have many challenges as yet not overcome. Effectiveness here, as in every other standard area, requires making all pertinent use of each other standard to bring learnings about history and culture vividly to life in musical experience. "Teaching history," if it becomes a verbal exercise unrelated to music being internalized by active participation (please review the previous discussion of what "active" entails), cannot further musical knowings within and how, and therefore runs the real risk of being irrelevant to musical pleasures. Ditto "teaching culture" separate from direct experiences of music.

In the general music context our continual efforts to represent music as being situated in history and culture is very likely to uncover and encourage interests in pursuing musical roles focused on these matters, in courses and experiences devoted to music in various historical settings and cultural settings. This opens a broad array of opportunities for the music education elective curriculum to serve the special needs of many students to go deeper into music and roles to which they particularly relate, building on their effective general music education.

THE CHALLENGE OF COMPREHENSIVENESS

I am well aware that the vision of general music I have presented is more ambitious and inclusive than has traditionally been articulated, taking the profession far beyond its tendency to focus on a few of the standard areas and conceive the others as simply supportive of those few. I am aware also of the scope of challenges this vision presents. It raises difficult issues having to do with (1) teacher education, (2) research, (3) time and resources for general music programs, and many others connected to these. In the context of this book only a few comments about these three can be offered.

1. In regard to the education of general music teachers it seems clear that the broad-ranging demands of the nine content areas require a broader background than typically has been provided in teacher education programs. That cannot be achieved when balances in these programs are as heavily weighted toward performance requirements as they tend to be, learnings in the other areas left with little if any time for development. Performance remains a critical aspect of general music, of course, so must receive its due. But so must all the other aspects, equally worthy of attention in preparing teachers responsible for instruction in them. We cannot simply retain the performance-dominated teacher education programs we have devised, embodying that particular orientation of what music education comprises, and add to it everything else we now recognize must be included. Something's got to give. A more equitable balance must be achieved.

That challenges our long-standing belief that every teacher, even in nonperformance settings such as general music classes (when they are not conceived as mini–performance groups, at any rate), must be, first of all, a good musician, meaning, we have narrowly assumed, a good performer. When that is accomplished, we have assumed, everything else of value will just naturally follow. Well, not so. Each of the other areas is equally demanding and equally worthy of attention if it is to be nurtured appropriately for general music teachers. We are called on, by the standards, to do for general music teacher education precisely what they require us to do for the school program—widen its scope to reflect a significant advance in our understanding of what constitutes the knowledge base of music as functionally manifested in its roles.

That is the radical aspect of the standards, not only for the general music program, but for the specialized elective program as well. We can ignore, or go into denial about, what they require of us, adapting them to our present prejudices by sweeping their demands for comprehensiveness under the rug. I believe we have done this to a large extent, quite naturally under the circumstances of our previously limited vision of what a general (and special) education in music entails and the challenge to that vision the standards represent. Advancing our vision in the direction of a general education in music that is fully representative of music in its many dimensions, and relevant to the actual musical lives of our citizenry, calls us to a thoroughgoing reconsideration of teacher education—as thoroughgoing as the standards demand.

I hope and trust that such a reconsideration and reconstitution of teacher education for general music will take place in all its complex dimensions. Reforming general music, with reconceiving teacher education as a crucial component, is an agenda central to the viability of music education in a musical world that has changed and continues to change significantly all around us but to which we have not appropriately adapted. We have begun the movement: it is time for major, consolidated new efforts.

2. To succeed in this reform we will need the help of research. But it, too, will have to reconsider its role and function. Heavily focused on performance aspects of music education, research will need to broaden its interests to all of the standard areas. Progress has been made in this direction, especially in regard to composing, as has been mentioned, and aspects of listening have also received attention. But comprehensiveness of scope has still to be achieved optimally.

Also yet to be achieved is a sufficient level of coordination, such that each topic of importance to reforming general music (and the elective program) is pursued by large numbers of interrelated studies, over time, all aiming in a consistent and accumulative direction. That is what scientific research does, accounting for its remarkable achievements. So long as we continue to produce isolated studies representing each researcher's particular interest, rather than congruent, corroborating studies representing the profession's major issues, research will remain as tangential to the larger enterprise as it has tended to be.

The musical roles identified in the standards provide a powerful unifying mechanism for research, each role calling for concerted efforts to clarify its teaching–learning mechanisms and how each contributes to the others. The music education research community, so impressive in size, in output, and in expertise, can make a significant—no, necessary—contribution to reforming music education in the direction of comprehensiveness if it takes full advantage of the content standards as focal points for coordinated efforts employing all modes of research interactively.

3. How might a "re-formed" vision of general music, operationalized by competent teachers and supported by relevant research, play out in school settings? No doubt in a great variety of ways. But all programs will give full due to all of the many roles that demonstrate and develop musical intelligence and creativity the standards identify, thereby being relevant to all students with their diverse musical potentials. The multidimensionality of musical knowing, doing, and enjoying will be demonstrated and cultivated, allowing students to discover ways to be engaged with music appropriate to their interests and capacities. What we can hope for as a result is not homogeneity in how people can participate but increased heterogeneity, in which the perspectives on music people choose to favor, the musics they select to enjoy, the

levels of involvement they elect, are as varied as music is and as people are, empowered by a comprehensive general education in music that cultivates all rather than only one or a few of its diverse pleasures.

Is this feasible given the limited time for general music in schools all over the world? First, we must address the common idea that "we don't have time to add all those other learnings to the program—we don't even have time to teach what we're already teaching." This assumes that what we do now is, somehow, sacrosanct; that we have already discovered the one inviolable truth and therefore nothing can be changed. In that case we simply must do what we do because we do it. Case closed.

The standards open the case. They demonstrate that it is no longer acceptable to assume that our present programs represent any sort of ultimate ideal. They do not. The standards call on us to reexamine our preconceptions and to be open to the need to approach the idea of general education from different premises, premises of choice, of inclusiveness, of nonuniformity of outcomes as a goal, of diversity not just as a platitude but as a fact of life. We need, in short, to better align ourselves with the realities of what music actually has become in our world and the realities of how it is actually partaken in our culture. Whatever time we do have in schools will then, at least, be time more realistically and functionally spent. Of course, we must do this by building on the foundation of those programs and practices that are already congruent with comprehensiveness. But we also need the courage to look carefully at everything we presently teach as to whether it is really indispensable and which other possible involvements from the standard areas might be included more fruitfully if time for it were made available.

As we open ourselves to the broad array of ways to know and do that are identified as foundational in the standards, and reconfigure our programs accordingly, we may find, because of our increased relevance and therefore heightened enthusiasm for our contributions, that there are greater demands for our offerings. I am suggesting that our limited time in the total curriculum may not be entirely attributable to all those insensitive people out there lacking the capacity to appreciate the gifts we have been offering. Some, at least, of our marginal status might fall on us, in having offered a limited array of gifts, many of them reflecting our own rather than the recipients' desires. Not a pleasant realization. But one that should energize us toward building general music programs so vital to our musical culture and to the many enthusiasms they cater to as to make us more central in education than we have ever succeeded in being. No one will do that for us. It is time we do it ourselves.

ETUDES

1. Think about the general music classes you took when you were a student in the schools. Do you think they were based on convincing positions on the seven phases of the curriculum? Were you helped to be aware of the positions being taken about the why, what, when, and how of your musical learnings taking place? Would you have appreciated your learnings more, or have made more

sense of them, if you had been informed about such matters? How can you help your students, even at early levels, be aware of what is behind the learnings they are undergoing?

2. Are any of the content standards unnecessary for general music programs in your opinion? Why? Would you add any to them? What? And why? Try restating them to fit your conception of what the musical roles in a general education in music should be. How would a program including all of yours be implemented? What changes from present practices, if any, would have to occur? (If you are perfectly satisfied with the original nine, you can skip this question!)

3. Are you persuaded that, as argued, a more equitable balance among the nine standards is needed for general music? If not, what balance do you envision as being desirable, and why? If you are convinced of the need for a more balanced program, what changes would be needed in present programs with which you are acquainted (or that you teach)? Do you think the present overwhelming dominance of performance and related learnings will be difficult to change? What are some gains and losses if that change occurred? Do you think the trade-offs are necessary?

4. If you are (or hope to be) a general music teacher, does the prospect of developing the musical intelligences and creativities of students who are most likely to be aficionados (and are quite happy to be that), with fewer aspiring to be amateurs and very few to be professionals, provide you with the challenges and satisfactions you seek as a music educator? In what senses can your role be conceived as foundational for achieving a healthy, thriving musical culture? How would you make a case for that if you were (or are) preparing future teachers for general music settings so that their enthusiasm for the challenge could sustain them happily in their work?

5. Reflect about your personal relation to each of the roles identified in the restructured version of the standards—how each fits you as an individual. Assume that the full complement of musicianship and listenership roles were available to you when you were a student in the schools, taught by qualified music educators. Are there any you feel you might have gravitated toward as being particularly compelling or "natural" for you other than performance, and that you then might have been delighted to become a teacher of in the schools? Can you envision a future in which that would be possible for aspiring music educators?

6. What will we need to do as a profession to move in the direction of a more comprehensive concept of general music? Do you think we are capable of accomplishing real change in doing so, and in changing our programs accordingly? Or do you think we are so comfortable with, and steeped in, our present posture of imbalance as to make significant change unlikely or impossible? What are the implications for the future of music education of the position you take about our capacity and willingness to change?

9

Advancing the Vision: Toward a Comprehensive Specialized Music Program

MAIN THEMES

- The music elective program needs to be as comprehensive as the general music program, not by balancing the content areas (roles) equitably as general music must do, but by representing the breadth of the standards in specialized study opportunities.

- The seven-phase curriculum model from Chapter 8 provides a basis for an examination of present and potentially more inclusive elective offerings.

- That examination raises the issue of, and need for, a reconceptualization of what the specialized music program in the schools should consist of, departing in significant ways from our present limited offerings. Bold plans are needed to restructure elective music programs, teacher education, research and scholarship, and organizational support.

- The need for a synergistic approach to philosophy and for a comprehensive approach to curriculum is reiterated, now able to be seen in light of the specifics delineated in this book. Pursuing this vision is the central task of music education at this stage of its history.

This chapter builds on and applies the ideas and arguments in Chapter 8. I strongly urge readers not to skip that chapter even if they are particularly interested and involved in specialized music electives. That material underlies and gives substance to the discussion here, which will make far more sense when understood in light of what was explained previously.

In Chapter 8 I argued that an effective general music program needs to be inclusive of a culture's varied musical roles so that all students can become cognizant of the many opportunities for musical satisfactions their culture affords them and can also discover whatever particular role(s) might suit their particular capacities and interests. The restructured national content standards (page 253) provide a delineation of basic musical roles needing to be included in a comprehensive general music education.

The specialized music program, meaning elective experiences beyond general music, also needs to be comprehensive but in a different sense. Here, rather than study being inclusive of all musical roles in an equitable, feasible balance, comprehensivity means including as many specialized involvements as possible as choices for focused, delimited attention. The aim here is not for learnings to be extensive and inclusive, as general education must be, but to be intensive and selective within each different role. That is why general education and specialized education are distinctive and necessary: each aims for a different result. General music emphasizes the cultivation of the most widespread involvement with music, that of the aficionado, while including amateur and professional commitments as an aspect of study and experience. The elective program rearranges that balance, emphasizing the most widespread special involvement—that of the amateur—with concomitant attention to the professional and aficionado. Those who elect a music specialization want to experience music in a concentrated way through the role in question. Some are likely to continue their involvement as amateurs long after leaving school. A few will gravitate toward being a professional in that role. Most tend not to continue their participation after graduation, becoming aficionados but often with a special relationship to the role they chose to experience more deeply. Here is a representation of the balance in emphasis the electives strive to offer, as appropriate to the realities of those who choose them:

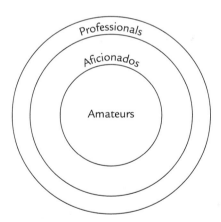

THE SPECIALIZED MUSIC PROGRAM AS VIEWED THROUGH THE CURRICULUM MODEL

With that overview of the different mission and emphasis of the elective music program from that of general music, the issue of conceiving specialized experiences as instances of curriculum, appropriately for schools, needs to be addressed. Important questions and problems will be raised by doing so. The model of the total curriculum presented in Chapter 8, with its seven phases (page 242), will be employed as the basis for this discussion.

1. Values Phase

Why is specialized music study of value for students drawn to elect it beyond the general music program? Two dimensions of value can be identified: personal and societal. On the personal side at least some students will find an aspect of music so fulfilling, or potentially fulfilling, as to seek out the challenges of pursuing it to discover whether it might play an important or even dominant role in their lives. The opportunity to do this—in every field of study education offers—allows students to become who they may potentially be, to fulfill whatever promises of intelligence, creativity, and curiosity they possess. Among the many ways to conceive what a good life consists of, surely the fulfillment of one's potentials and enthusiasms must rank high. Schooling, in a real sense, is a culture's way to provide that opportunity and resource for every person.

When that is done, the culture's values and needs are best served as well. Everything studied in its schools reflects the values and needs of the culture, the fulfillment of them being essential for the culture's viability. Successful education, in this sense, enables every person to discover a role or roles both personally satisfying and culturally important. General education provides the comprehensive foundation for that goal, in its introductory study of a broad range of roles of societal value, both to impart what those are so that the culture can be fully savored, and to allow for informed individual choices. Specialized education takes the next step, allowing particularly compelling possibilities to be experienced more fully to determine if one or another catches hold. A fully functioning education for all citizens will provide both levels of opportunity—the general and the special—in abundance.

In most cultures in the world some degree of general education in music is offered, ranging from insignificant to significant. Few offer specialized music instruction as part of the school day by teachers who are prepared specifically to offer it. That achievement has been most strikingly attained by schools in America, where one aspect—performance—has managed to become ubiquitous at upper elementary, middle and junior high school, and high school levels, taught by music educators who have majored in choral or instrumental (band or orchestra) specializations. The opportunity of having this option as part of public, tax-supported education is remarkable, given its rarity in the world. That it continues to be supported both in teacher education and in school programs on the basis that, as has been mentioned, some 9–15 percent of students elect to become involved in it is even more remarkable. Clearly the value to enough students, and to the culture that benefits from their experience, is sufficient to keep the program going. The support of performance as a recognized school elective has demonstrated, at least in a particular culture, that it is possible to hope that study of the full knowledge base of music can be provided at both the general education and the specialized education levels as integral parts of schooling. We should be emboldened by the success of performance to explore the ramifications for a more comprehensive approach to specialized music offerings. I will do so in the section starting on page 281.

2. Conceptualized Phase

The values of diverse specialized learnings in music, and the possibility that they can be made available in schooling, call for a reconceptualization of what constitutes those learnings. If the one musical role at which success has been achieved in making it widely available as an elective—that is, performance—were the only one worthy of attention, the content standards would not be what they are. The knowledge base of music would consist of performance, all other ways to know and do music simply being subsumed within it as subsidiaries. If we take the standards seriously as describing the ways music actually exists in the world, as I have suggested we must do if the realities and opportunities of music are to be acknowledged and taught, our work as exemplified by performance has only just begun. Building a general music program fully representative of our culture's musical roles is one foundational task, as discussed in Chapter 8. The other is to do the same for elective offerings. We have never fully envisioned what a program of electives would look like when conceived as broadly as the content standards delineate, and what it would do both for students and for the music education profession. Advancing the vision of comprehensiveness requires that we now do so.

3. Systematized Phase

That vision must include attention to the systematized phase of the curriculum, the organization of learnings over time. When performance is the only elective, sequential learning is driven by its special requirements. A brief look at those requirements will raise important issues related to sequential learnings in a comprehensive program of specializations.

Two demands have guided approaches to ongoing learnings in performance. The first is for skill development—the accumulation and refinement of culturally relevant techniques of singing and playing, increasing in control and finesse as students are presented with gradually increasing challenges.

The second sequential dimension of performing is the graduated difficulty of the literature chosen, expanding in both interpretive and technical challenges as craft, sensitivity, and imagination become available to meet those challenges. This, too, is a necessary aspect of performance education, accounting for a major portion of what sequence consists of in this musical involvement. Traditionally, the combination of skill acquisition matched with literature interpretation difficulty has been the foundation for developmental performance learnings.

Now, with the advent of the standards, a radically expanded conception of sequence for performance enters the scene. The demands of skill development and literature interpretation appropriate to it cannot be ignored. Yet integrated within that context must be all the other learnings the standards demand. Each of the other roles and the learnings they entail must influence performance learnings, saturating them with understandings that go far beyond the skilled, creative makings of the sounds each piece calls for while also preserving that foundation. When, and how, and in what order, and to what degrees of difficulty, and to what extent, should the knowings and doings embedded in each of the other standards be incorporated within the knowings and doings of performance itself? Remember, in the specialized performance program, unlike the general music program, performance creativity and intelligence, dependent on and grounded in the skilled doings of the body, is the point and purpose of all learnings, the others serving to deepen and broaden those learnings. The result aimed for is not a series of separately learned matters attached to performance, but an infusion of performance with learnings that transform its quality by their being absorbed within the performance act. By what sequence of learnings can this be best accomplished? Well, no doubt in a carefully planned, research-based, programmatically progressive format in which both structure and spontaneity play appropriate roles—that is, an effective curriculum.

Clearly we have our work cut out for us if we are to devise an educational program of study relevant to the fullness of knowings and doings musicianship in the performance mode entails. That work deserves our best efforts because performance deserves our best efforts: it is too important, too basic in music to be dealt with in anything less than a full-fledged curriculum devoted to cultivating its satisfactions. I believe the profession is addressing this broader conception of what performance entails by attempts to be more inclusive about it than ever before in its history. Focused research on issues of developmental acquisition of associated learnings and their influence on performance artistry would be of enormous help in this enterprise.

The very same effort is needed for each of the other musical involvements the standards identify. Each has its veracity requiring its own characteristic ways to develop competence through sequential learnings. Each requires all the others to be absorbed within it if it is to be as replete as it deserves to be. Performance, so familiar to us, provides a powerful example of how each other way to be engaged with music will call on our expertise and ingenuity to forge a developmental program of studies particular to each.

What we do in performance, however, does not simply transfer intact to the others, and vice versa. It is likely that as we gain experience in comprehensive program development some or many commonalities will be recognized. But many substantial differences among each content area and its developmental learning progressions are likely to become clear. Research can be a strong ally in helping us maximize our teaching effectiveness by clarifying effective sequences of learning for each musical role. That agenda is surely challenging, but just as surely necessary if we are to fulfill the promise of specialized studies that are as valid and effective as students who engage themselves in them deserve to be offered.

4. Interpreted Phase

The ways teachers interpret their mission, here having to do with the level of inclusiveness of the elective program, is a crucial dimension of success. Two layers of inclusiveness are at play as we move toward a comprehensive elective program. One is to recognize the possibility, and the need, for each of the roles to constitute a program of study in and of itself. The other is to incorporate the support of all the other roles in the study of each. That double obligation constitutes comprehensiveness in its full sense.

It also constitutes a major change in our interpretation of what music in the schools should be. We are so accustomed to a conception of school music as consisting of general music and performance electives as to simply not notice that it is, indeed, a conception rather than a necessity. We have become conditioned to think of the duality of classroom and rehearsal hall as constituting the universe of music study in schools. Now the standards are telling us a different story, and, as with all paradigm shifts, this one will inevitably be wrenching. If this particular phase of the total curriculum—teachers' interpretations of what music education should properly consist of—cannot adapt itself to an advancing vision of wholeness, little can be expected to happen, conceptually or practically. I will return to this crucial issue in my conclusion to this chapter, a conclusion also fitting for this book.

5. Operational Phase

At the operational level of teaching and learning a world of new challenges awaits. Our expertise in teaching performance has accumulated over a long period of time, and a great deal of talent and effort has gone into developing it. Certainly there is more to learn, but we can be deeply proud of the profession's attainments in bringing youngsters to admirable—often formidable—levels of performance know-how within the inclusiveness of the school setting. That has been, unquestionably, a major triumph of American music education and of other countries around the world, now being brought to fruition as the wide scope of learnings connected to performance is being recognized and pursued.

Can we accomplish parallel levels of success in each of the standard areas? Clearly not if we do not attempt to do so. But if we do, as I devoutly hope we will, there is no reason to doubt that our operational teaching expertise can be extended to embrace each dimension of musical knowing/doing, each musical role. No doubt it will not happen automatically or swiftly or easily—nothing this important and complex ever does. But conceived as a goal worthy of our profession's full potentials, our work toward attaining it can revivify us, opening whole new areas of growth and satisfaction for us to attain. Seen as an opportunity for us to become something we have never been, both for ourselves and for the contribution we can make, rather than as a threat to our comfortable status quo, a new perspective opens up, one of new significance personally and professionally for each of us and for all of us collectively. Becoming excellent music educators in ways we have seldom if ever conceived possible is now a real prospect. What could be more exciting?

6. Experienced Phase

To the extent we succeed, the musical experiences of our students—the opportunities we give them to learn and how we expertly help them to learn—will expand dramatically. As mentioned in several contexts previously, musical possibilities to develop potential intelligences and creativities have poorly represented all the ways our musical culture makes available. How many students over the years may have discovered ways to become musical amateurs (or professionals) other than in the single opportunity we have provided? We'll never know, of course. But it seems reasonable to assume that at least as many if not substantially more than have done so to date could have enjoyed the self-identification with a dimension of music that amateurs might seek, a dimension discovered through a wide variety of musical engagements offered as electives. When we have in the past expanded our offerings to embrace a previously unavailable opportunity, such as, notably, performance of jazz, many students have leaped to the chance and have benefited enormously by our expert instruction, a whole new school music undertaking having come into existence. This has been healthy both for all the students who would never otherwise have become involved and for our profession, which has expanded its contribution in a culturally grounded, musically important way.

The standards open up possibilities for similar new initiatives in a broad array of musical experiences to which many students are likely to gravitate. Whether as amateurs with long-term, devoted involvements, as aficionados who add depth to various areas of their musical enjoyments, or as professionals whose careers are discovered and energized by their school involvement, all would benefit from the diversity of offerings a reconceived elective program would make available.

All the previous curriculum phases aim toward this experienced phase—the payoff in student learning of everything that leads to and supports it. In the established performance electives we have had the time, the research, the teacher education, the support of communities financially and psychologically (although, of course, not to the extent we would prefer), and the professional infrastructure, to have created admirable opportunities for students to elect and learn from our programs. The last thing we need is in any way to diminish this most successful of our contributions. We do need to deepen and expand it as the standards prescribe, and we are well on our way to doing so. Adding new dimensions to our contributions and expertise should not be conceived as a threat to our present structure—it is hard to imagine that the number of students presently desiring performance electives would be negatively affected by similar opportunities being available in other musical involvements. But if some were to find more satisfaction in a different involvement we should be pleased rather than disgruntled: serving students' needs, not our own, after all, is the point of education. An elective program representing all the musical roles would surely attract far more students to music as amateurs, as curious aficionados, and as potential professionals than our single-focus offerings can ever hope to do.

7. Expectational Phase

The expectations we have of school music have been shaped by its history. The content standards represent a significant departure, calling on us to be more than we have ever been, requiring a shift toward authentic inclusiveness. Of course, that is likely to cause puzzlement, even anxiety, both within the music education profession and outside it in the larger educational and general communities. "This is new. This is uncertain. Can it be done? Should it be done? How would it be done? Should the schools support it? Who would teach it? Who would take it?" On and on with the fears of the unknown, as is inevitable with any departure from tradition. Just as inevitable will be a host of objections caused by insecurity: "Well, good idea, but, but, but, but. . . ." We can all think of endless "buts" that can protect us from change.

That's not necessarily bad: we do have to be cautious in the face of the unknown. We don't want to endanger what we have, there being some wisdom in "a bird in the hand." Of course, the opposite is just as wise: "nothing ventured." No doubt the prudent course takes account of both. We need to protect what is successful while also recognizing the need for thoughtful improvement and even innovation. Changing expectations, as an advancing vision requires us to do, is difficult and not necessarily pleasant. It is also, however, rejuvenating, allowing us to recognize in ourselves the capacity to keep growing, to make deeper and broader contributions, and thereby to strengthen ourselves as individuals and as a profession.

I do not believe we can ignore the challenges the standards present and simply rest on what we have accomplished so far. Doing so, I am afraid, will cause us to stagnate, continuing to make our admirable contribution as we now do but also becoming less and less relevant to a significantly changing musical world. We are facing a growing crisis of dispensability, as music in our culture thrives while music education faces constant uncertainty as to its value. Every change we have succeeded in making toward relevance to our culture's musics and musical practices has kept us going, has kept us viable, while also allowing us to continue to strengthen values of long-standing worth. But change has occurred faster and more diversely than we have been willing to acknowledge. We need to be more courageous in what we expect of ourselves, what we can offer including but going beyond our traditions. The standards give us a workable, musically defensible, philosophically grounded basis for significant growth, being practicably, musically, and philosophically in tune with a more inclusive, synergistic stance about what we can offer our culture through education. Changing our own expectations of what music education can be, and also the expectations of the larger community by our explanations and actions, can indeed allow us to keep faith with established values while opening ourselves and our communities to broader expectations of what we have to offer. An overview of a comprehensive specialized music program, as was proffered for a comprehensive general music program in the previous chapter, can give a sense of both the challenges—and the feasibility—of meeting those expectations.

IMPLEMENTING A COMPREHENSIVE SPECIALIZED MUSIC PROGRAM: THE RESTRUCTURED CONTENT STANDARDS

Just as this book is not a general music methods text, it is also not a text on the music electives. But enough can be said here connecting principles to implementation as to give a sense of what a comprehensive approach to a curriculum for special music offerings would consist of, an approach in which the enhancement of musical experience in all its dimensions is the point and purpose of each involvement. In short, a curriculum devoted to the development of the wide variety of musical intelligences and creativities the restructured standards identify, each directed primarily toward cultivating amateurs with concomitant benefits for aficionados and professionals.

1. Singing and Playing

The central point to be made in regard to the performance program is that it cannot and should not be made to bear the burden of primary responsibility for teaching all the standards. That is an important reason for widening the scope of musical electives. When only one specialized way to be involved with music is available, as is presently largely the case, the rest of the standards have to be crammed into performance or left unattended to. But the performance program, though enriched by learnings from the other standards, is not the general music program. It is an elective with its own integrity, its own ways to be musically creative, its own ways to act intelligently. Students electing it want and deserve to learn to be performing musicians as their primary goal, other learnings being supportive of that goal.[1] It is simply unfair (and unrealistic) to think that under our present practices performance can be expected to do justice to the breadth of learnings the standards represent.

The integrity of the performance program deserves protection in another important way. The standards stipulate that singing and playing should utilize "a varied repertoire of music." Surely musical learnings of those in choruses, bands, and orchestras will be as broad or as narrow as the selection of music they learn to perform creatively and intelligently. A repertoire focusing on the tried and true will certainly serve an important purpose in providing a needed foundation. But exploration of divergent styles and types of music is also necessary if the broad range of musical experiencing available through performance in the standard ensembles is to be enjoyed and found instructive. But that said, how far toward divergence is far enough?

I believe we must recognize about our own culture's musical identity what we recognize about the musical identity of others'—that their culture should be honored and appreciated not for trying to become what we are but for being what they are. Every music is inevitably a product of particular ways of being its cultural basis supplies, and each such way of being has produced music valuable in large part for its individuality. As argued in Chapter 6, it goes too far to assume that a culture's music is so insular as to be inaccessible to others, but it also goes too far to assume that all musics are as readily assimilable to the experience of people as the music of their own culture. In fact, if a foreign music is not genuinely "other," confronting its genuineness will not cause us to expand our sense of the multiplicity of musical

---

[1]For an extended explanation of the influence of the other roles in achieving performances infused with understanding, see my "What Is 'Performing with Understanding?'" in *Performing with Understanding: The Challenge of the National Standards in Music Education,* ed. Bennett Reimer (Reston, VA: Music Educators National Conference, 2000), 11–29, along with all the other chapters offering specifics of achieving understanding in performance.

meanings and thereby our own potentials for expansion as feeling beings. So we need other cultures' musics to be what they are, as a foil to our own and as an opportunity for musical/human growth.

We also need for our own music to be what it is. "Our own" music, in this context, is the music culturally associated with the Western repertoire of choruses, bands, and orchestras. These groups are not only "Western" but also genuine cultures in and of themselves. Each of them represents a value system, a belief system, and a community of aficionados, amateurs, and professionals bound together by shared enthusiasms and ways of acting. Choruses, bands, and orchestras in schools are cultures. There are unique characteristics surrounding our performance enterprise—its home within the school structure, the youth of the participants, the combination of educational and public presentation emphases, the psychological/emotional needs of the participants as novices who are being faced with complex challenges to their emerging self-image. All conspire to establish a special culture; a real world of meanings, aspirations, ways to behave and think, rewards and recognitions, demands and expectations, interpersonal associations, and on and on with what a culture supplies—a way to live a life.[2] Those of us who have lived the life of a school student deeply involved with a performance ensemble, and as a director of such an ensemble, know very well the precious dimensions, both musical and personal, it has added to our lives.

Central to what makes school ensembles cultures are their characteristic repertoires. I suggest that these repertoires, inclusive of the diversity each ensemble's music embraces, are the foundation for its cultural veracity. These repertoires deserve to be regarded and enjoyed as being the musics of particular cultures, as all musics are. They deserve to be cherished for the ways they add their musical dimensions to the identity of those who participate in these ensembles, as all viable cultures and subcultures do. Of course, there are opportunities for each to include exploration of relevant musics from other cultures, "relevant" meaning musics existing for these particular performance configurations when and if they exist in cultures outside the West, explorations that can be accomplished within the standard makeup of Western choruses, bands, and orchestras. Often, however, adaptations, if they are to be musically trustworthy,[3] require specially configured ensemble groupings and additions of instruments or vocal practices not indigenous to Western music. An example is the International Vocal Ensemble established by Mary Goetze at Indiana University, a group that specializes in the performance of musics from around the world.[4] That

---

[2]An excellent discussion of school ensembles as cultures is given by Steven J. Morrison, "The School Ensemble: A Culture of Our Own," *Music Educators Journal*, 88, no. 2 (September 2001), 24–28, in which he clearly explains the many ways school performance groups constitute genuine cultures, with all the musical and human benefits these cultures provide for their members.

[3]I borrow this term from Rita Klinger, "A Materials Girl in Search of the Genuine Article," in *World Musics and Music Education: Facing the Issues,* ed. Bennett Reimer (Reston, VA: Music Educators National Conference, 2002).

[4]Goetze's experience in forming and sustaining this ensemble, and of performing choral musics not conceived in Western terms, is vividly described in her "The Challenges of Performing Choral Music of the World," in *Performing with Understanding,* ed. Reimer, note 1, 155–72.

group does not substitute for the traditional Western choral experience—it adds to it, and that is much to be admired. But so is the Western chorus with its indigenous repertoire, and bands and orchestras with theirs. A "varied repertoire of music," I am suggesting, need not force our traditional ensembles to become something they are not: it encourages them to become all that they are.

In regard to performance, then, our remarkable success will be enhanced, and our attractiveness to a wider population of students increased, by (1) respecting the cultural veracity of Western ensembles and their indigenous musics; (2) representing the full diversity of those musics historically and stylistically; (3) concentrating on performance itself, including all its complex interrelations with the other standard areas (but not by attempting to duplicate what general music is responsible for); (4) balancing large ensemble configurations and literatures with those calling for a greater diversity of solo and small groupings representing both Western composed musics and composed musics of other cultures; (5) including instruments and vocal practices called on by other cultures; and (6) working closely with (or perhaps taking primary responsibility for) improvisational musics of other cultures and popular musics of our own and other cultures, requiring ways to create and perform quite different from that of the composer-conductor-performer tradition of Western groups. This set of aspirations both preserves the excellence of our traditional approaches as they fully deserve and adds important opportunities that can appeal to many students' musical creativities, intelligences, and interests beyond our traditional offerings.

Performing is likely to continue to be attractive as an elective for at least the percentage of students now opting to become involved in exploring it as amateurs (and potential professionals), and can appeal to many others with those aspirations if it adds new opportunities beyond its present configurations and literatures. Within an expanded elective program, performance will then continue to be an essential component.

2. Improvising

Electives focusing on improvising may well be offered and contained within the performance program itself, as already mentioned, if that program is expanded beyond performing composed musics. This has already occurred with the inclusion of jazz as integral to, although identifiable as a distinct offering within, existing performance programs. What structures for providing improvisatory experiences emerge as they are broadened to include traditions beyond jazz depends on factors beyond the focus of this book. I would only emphasize here what has already been pointed out previously, that the musical thinking and doing constituting intelligence and creativity particular to the role of the improviser requires instruction specific to this role.

The sequence of improvisatory learnings that best provides for optimal development especially needs to be taken into account. As we have learned from the jazz improvisation experience, the nurturing of skills, understandings, and creativity in that role requires approaches quite different in many important ways from how they are nurtured in performing notated compositions (and even different, I suggest, for performing notated jazz). Added to the complexity of appropriate sequential development is the issue of culturally embedded practices for each different improvisatory musical tradition, needing to be understood and applied as culture bearers of that tradition exemplify them. That is, transfer from jazz improvisation practices to other culturally derived improvisation practices is not likely to be absolute. Here is a fascinating issue crying out for research and scholarship of a variety of sorts, and its application in a variety of ways, if an improvisation program of substance is to be added to our elective offerings as the standards mandate and as all of us should wholeheartedly desire.

Teaching our students to create music improvisationally as it is done in various cultures around the world entails our approximating as best we can what seem to be best practices in each culture as far as we can determine what they are. We also, however, need to apply our own professional know-how in assessing whether the practices in question make best pedagogical sense, giving them all due respect but not blindly, just as people not native to the West should do when learning, say, jazz improvisation. If we taught it perfectly they could simply imitate exactly what we do. Because we don't, they have to exercise judgment, just as we also must do. With an open and respectful attitude, recognizing that natives to a culture know what we cannot equally know despite that they, like us, are not perfect, we can give ourselves up to other practices of teaching and learning without giving up our professional awareness. And we can pass on to our students the same receptive, appreciative embracing of different ways to approach learning to improvise while acknowledging that no way achieves perfection.

Expanding improvisation opportunities to better represent its many styles, including innovative manifestations beyond the traditional, will no doubt attract many students, both those involved in the established ensemble electives and others who are not. The exciting nature of improvisation—its requirement for creative immediacy—has a great deal of appeal for students, an appeal of which we have not begun to take full advantage. Taking that advantage will allow us to cultivate a new and significant population of aficionados who explore it, amateurs who develop significant expertise, and, perhaps, future professionals. It will also provide an opportunity to extend our own musical and pedagogical expertise.

3. Composing
4. Arranging

The comments in Chapter 8 about composing and arranging in the general music setting apply equally to the elective setting, except that here students demonstrating these particular interests can be given all the challenges they seek in concentrated programs specifically devoted to them. Each of these concentrations must incorporate all the standard areas as necessary supplements, of course, but nevertheless the specialized nature of each should dominate. Here I will concentrate on composing, with the understanding that my suggestions apply to arranging as well.

In composing we are faced with professional challenges and opportunities unprecedented in our history. Four are of particular interest: fostering individuality, nurturing cooperative creativity as called for in popular musics, capitalizing on technology, and supporting a potential new school music culture.

1. Teaching composing in classical and many other styles requires intense focus on individual creativity, unlike performance, where group creative musicianship has been the norm. Individual performance has of course continued to be cultivated when possible in the school setting but is far outstripped by ensemble experience. And although composing can profitably occur in groups, especially for teaching purposes, the main characteristic of this mode of musicianship is its individuality. Teaching composition is much more similar to what occurs in the art studio than to what occurs in the rehearsal room. This has profound effects on sequence, methodology, assessment, the teacher–student relationship, and every other dimension of pedagogy. The nearest approximations in music are perhaps piano instruction and guitar instruction, which, though often carried out in class settings at the level of amateur education, are often an individual endeavor.

But piano and guitar performance are still performance, whether of composed music or of improvisation. Composing, as I have argued in regard to both creativity (Chapter 4) and intelligence (Chapter 7), is a genuine and specialized role requiring development of its own ways to think and act. We have begun to develop some impressive expertise in how to teach for this special musical role, especially in classroom settings at the introductory level. Now we face the need to take that further, as we have done impressively with performance and to some degree with improvisation.

In that task we would do well to learn as much as we can from our art studio colleagues, both in how to structure the program appropriately in schools to account for the need to teach in groups while concentrating on individuals, and in how to cope with the cultivation of divergence in creativity as the primary goal rather than, as in the ensemble experience, convergence of creativity as a necessary basis. The composer, as the visual artist, pursues an individual vision, influenced and constrained by all the cultural forces at work that impinge on artistry, of course, but nevertheless incorporating the culture in ways particular to the individual's imagination, personality, beliefs, interests, and ambitions. The psychology of nurturing the individual to become what he or she artistically needs to be is significantly different from that of fostering a group endeavor that includes individuality while also depending on communality. How do we begin to acquire the pedagogical/psychological/artistic wisdom to achieve success in a musical role in which we have precious little experience ourselves, both as musicians and as teachers, especially at the amateur level of attainment that elective offerings should cultivate?

We do, of course, have composition teachers in colleges and universities we can call on for assistance, both in how to compose and in how to teach it. But few of those are acquainted with or interested in teaching youngsters in school settings. (Of course, when that expertise and interest are present in a college composition teacher we should leap at the chance to exploit it!) The issue of finding the help we need to gain our own necessary competencies is central, because composing, and teaching others to compose, is as complex and demanding as performing and teaching others to perform. Think of the elaborate system in place to meet the needs of performing and performance education in the schools. Students at around the fifth grade have the opportunity to begin specialization and to continue it through high school. The most devoted—a small percentage—major in music at the college level and study performance with teachers who are often professional performers as well as faculty members and who sometimes, as well, have school teaching experience. Some graduate to become school music educators, supported not only by all their performance experience and instruction but also by specialized methods courses and by student teaching. From elementary school through college they have accrued their expertise both as musicians and as teachers for their specialized role.

In a comparable way, future composition teachers in the schools would have taken the opportunity to begin elective study with specialists at some appropriate point (perhaps at the upper elementary level). They would have continued their study in both group and individual settings through high school, majored in music education at the college level and studied composition as their primary emphasis, taken supportive courses in the teaching of composition in the schools, done their student teaching in composition settings, and then taken jobs as composition specialists at whatever school levels best suited their temperament. That would put the teaching of composing in the schools in parity with the level of expertise presently existing in performance. If teaching composing is indeed comparable to teaching performing in its challenges, as I believe it certainly is, we should expect nothing less than comparable competence to what we have achieved in our excellent performance programs. A new vista opens up.

2. As with performing, improvising, and composing, the comments made in Chapter 8 about creating in popular styles in the general music classroom apply as well to electives, but in this setting at more intensified and advanced levels. Popular music creating can be discussed as reasonably in connection to performing and improvising as composing, of course, given the interactive nature of all these doings in bringing it into being. And although it may sometimes be included in a "Be a Composer" elective as one style explored among others, it is likely also to stand on its own as a particular elective devoted to this style, given its singular multifaceted challenges so different in many respects from traditional composing, and given its, well, popularity.

Who would be qualified to offer popular music creating courses? Perhaps some who specialize in teaching composing. But, realistically, not many of those would have the background to do so as genuinely as it deserves. The people described in the previous discussion are those focusing on composing as traditionally conceived (and, as I will explain next, as related to the tradition but expanding it in directions allowed by computer technologies). Their knowledge of, experiences in, and identification with popular musics may very well be minimal or nonexistent. (Of course, there will be some who are steeped in popular music as well.) But to do justice to the many styles of popular music and the creative traditions they represent, there is a need for people whose histories parallel those who become composing teachers as described previously. That is, they would have early on chosen to elect study in the creation of popular music, continued that study through high school, majored in music education at the college level with emphasis on popular music and its creation as taught by specialist faculty, taken a sequence of courses on teaching it in the school context including student teaching with that focus, and been hired to teach it (and, perhaps, related courses) in schools. Their specialization would be parallel in all significant ways, both in their own development to become professional music educators and in the array of course offerings they then were able to make available from (probably) middle school through high school. And some of them, as some school performance teachers, improvisation teachers, and composition teachers, are likely to want to return to universities for advanced studies in their specialty and become teacher educators themselves. The pattern we now have in place for performance, then, would apply to comparable patterns in these other specialized areas. The vision continues to expand. As does our ability to serve the many musical needs and interests actually existing in our multimusical culture.

3. Adding to the challenge of developing traditional composition and popular music programs taught by specialists is the central role likely to be played by technology in both. As discussed previously in this book, in many popular music styles, technology has become an essential ingredient in a variety of ways ranging from performance to recording. Clearly, those teaching such electives will have to be well prepared to incorporate technology in the variety of ways popular musics have come to depend on it. My comments now will focus on technology as related to composing outside the popular genres.

Although composing music for performers to sing and play is likely to continue, at least for the foreseeable future, there are fast-emerging technological opportunities for young people to compose at levels of complex musical thinking far beyond their abilities to notate that thinking or of performers to perform what has been composed. The capacity for computers to provide traditional staff or other notations for what has been composed so that performers can interpret it is growing dramatically. But when the full capacity of technology is used to create whatever the musical imagination can conceive, notated versions are likely to be extremely complex to the point of unperformability, especially by amateurs.

At any rate, freedom from the demands of notation, and from the need for the intermediary of performers if a composer's music is to be heard, affords composers an entire new world of possibility. They can now exercise the fullness of their musical imaginations and have their creations immediately available to be shared, without having to enlist competent performers, rehearse them, find a place to have the work performed, entice people to be at that place at a stipulated time and perhaps to pay for the privilege, print a program, and on and on with all the complicated necessities, both musical and practical, involved in getting their composition to be heard by listeners—

the goal of every composer. Equally complex matters (and equally daunting financial outlays) must be attended to if, instead of a public performance, a recording is to be made of the performance and then marketed. All these complications allow only a very small number of compositions to ever reach their goal of being performed and heard.

For professional composers the struggle to get performed and to get a performance recorded is a major and ongoing reality of their lives. Few ever attain the level of being heard by a widespread public. But amateurs, though they may harbor grandiose dreams, are in it not to make a living at it or with expectations for broad impact but for the deep satisfaction of creating and having some people—family, friends, acquaintances, groups of which they are members—share the products of their efforts. Some lucky (and very persistent) amateurs can manage this to some modest degree with performed music. But technology allows full exercise of compositional creativity without regard to performability (especially the need for finding very competent performers), and inexpensive and immediate recordings of their work able to be heard by people willing to listen, including other amateurs eager to hear one another's music (and, of course, everyone else whose arm can be twisted). Few experiences are as exciting and as fulfilling as creating something and having others share what one has accomplished. Children who proudly bring home their art class creations, displayed on the refrigerator by their equally proud parents, know this thrill. That ease of sharing one's creations can now be accomplished with music, with all the joy it brings.

4. As technology continues to improve to enable sophisticated composing in genuinely creative ways; as composition teachers learn how to use it effectively; as popular music creating incorporates it optimally; and as students in schools continue to take to technology as fish to water, elective offerings in composition can be expected to become more and more in demand. A new school music subculture of composing, as exists now with performing, is likely to arise, with all the activities, organizations, reward systems, industry affiliations, and so forth, now established in performance. Already in the exhibition areas at MENC conventions at state, regional, and national levels composing technologies are set up next to instrument displays, people "doodling" at both.

Whatever forms it takes, we may find ourselves with opportunities for serving musical/social/educational involvements related to composing and to improvising that are as attractive and significant as now exist with performing. And therefore needing parallel structures of teacher education, research and scholarship, graduate studies, organizational systems, and on and on with all that subcultures need for sustenance in order to thrive. An exciting challenge appears, one that can elevate the music education profession to new levels of contribution, relevance, and importance.

(Reading and Notating Music)

As discussed in Chapter 8 in connection with this standard, my position is that it should be considered an aspect of those musical involvements in which it plays a part rather than as a separate role within music. For amateur performers, composers, and arrangers, it continues to fulfill an important function, so of course must be learned, and assessed, as one component of those programs. Some musicologists and theorists have developed high levels of expertise in early notations, the history of musical notations, comparative notation systems, contemporary notations, and so forth, and if some students express an interest in such topics efforts should be made to provide them with elective study.

5. Listening

Listening, as I have discussed in a variety of contexts, is an essential ingredient of all musical learning and therefore of every standard. What is its role as a separate domain among electives?

First, no matter how much the general music program balances its attention to all the standard areas, including listening, it is unlikely to be able to satisfy all the interests of aficionados as those interests develop. Special focused listening electives of a great variety should be offered, both as standard courses often available and as special courses reflecting special curiosities. The variety is potentially as great as the variety of music itself. When aficionados become enthusiasts about a particular music or aspect of music—early jazz, folk music of a particular sort, madrigals, musical acoustics, popular music around the world, romantic opera, the history of rap, musical theater, computer music, music and race, music and gender, minimalist music, the music of ancient and contemporary Japan, and on and on indefinitely—that enthusiasm begins to qualify as amateurism. In fact, many nonmusicians—that is, nonperformers, composers, improvisers, arrangers, and the like—are expert, devoted, and sophisticated lovers of some aspect of music—often to a degree surpassing that of their teachers—that satisfies them in a variety of ways. Their needs—often hunger—for specialized music study in which listening is the central engagement (supported and enriched by all the other standards, of course) should be met by the elective program. Such offerings, when generously available, may well be the most popular of all, elected not only by aficionados but also by many involved in the musicianship programs, who are likely to be aficionados of various musics and musical topics as well.

Who would teach a broad array of such courses, offered at least at the high school level if not earlier? Under present circumstances few music educators would leap at the chance or even be interested, at least if our history is an indication. Occasionally we get energized about the need for non-performance-based courses at the secondary level and show some life about trying to develop them. But little has changed: only a tiny percentage of students in high schools have access to such courses. Performance directors, after all, have their hands more than full with their own responsibilities and few have had any training in how to teach such courses. Because they are the only music teachers in practically all high schools, the need and interests of the majority who are not enrolled in the performance program simply go unmet.

Some would argue that performance directors can learn to teach such courses and be expected to do so. But that simply imposes an additional burden on the existing program, already challenged to incorporate all the other standards. We are in the position now of an inverted pyramid, all the needs for comprehensiveness resting on the narrow base of the performance program. Performance is not able to support that weight of expectations, nor should it. Perhaps if we succeed in adding other musicianship specialists they could share in offering listening-focused courses open to all. That would certainly ease the crunch and widen the variety of course choices reflecting a more diverse music faculty.

Going further, however, opens up a whole new way to think, newer even than preparing teachers as specialists in all the musicianship roles. It suggests a specialization in the teaching of a variety of listening-oriented courses. (Remember, please, that these need to include learnings in all the other standards, including singing, playing, improvising, composing, and arranging, as relevant to the topics being explored.) Parallel to what presently occurs for future performance teachers (and, as I argue, needs to occur for future improvisation, composition, and arranging teachers), students at an appropriate grade level (probably middle or high school) who were pursuing aficionado/amateur status by taking and being enthused with a variety of music courses, would decide to become teachers of such courses. They would enroll in a music teacher certification program with a specialization in the teaching of courses for aficionados and amateurs outside those in aspects of musicianship, take a variety of such courses as their major, as well as specialized courses on how to teach them, including student teaching with that specialization, and then find employment as music course teachers in the schools. They might well enroll more students than any other music elective.

I am avoiding the term "general music" teachers for such people because general music is a foundational, inclusive course of study essential in the elementary grades, probably continuing to be relevant in the middle school/junior high school grades along with specialized musicianship and listenership electives, and one among many course offerings at the high school level for those needing and desiring continued inclusive study such as general music exists to provide.

The listening-focused courses, however, are outgrowths of and deeper probings of topics introduced in general music, as appropriate for specialized study by aficionados and amateurs at the secondary level. General music combines musicianship and listenership learnings in a balanced representation, as a general education needs to do. Listening specialization teachers are not general music teachers, just as teachers of composition and improvisation (and guitar, handbells, dulcimer, etc.) are not. Specialized listening courses (and the other listenership specializations to be discussed next) require teachers specially trained to offer them, just as general music requires its specialized expertise.

6. Analyzing and Describing

When people listen to music they generally and appropriately do not do so through analyzing and describing. They listen, just as performers perform, improvisers improvise, composers compose, and so forth. All those musical roles *benefit from* close examination and explanation of what is musically transpiring. In fact, improvement in all musical roles and with all musics depends to a significant extent on probing carefully into what is going on musically (always including the contextual/delineated dimensions of music, of course). As pointed out in Chapter 7 and elsewhere in this book, analysis and description, appropriate to the particular characteristics of each music in its particular contextual setting, are important tools for musical learning.

For some, a specialization in analyzing and describing will be compelling, offering musical/contextual challenges they find fulfilling and significant. Those who pursue this specialization play the role of the music theorist. Courses in theory for those whose interest and intelligence lead them in this direction will be an important dimension of listenership offerings, for aficionados broadening their musical acuities, amateurs developing special expertise, and potential professionals. We can expect some of these students to enroll in a teacher education program with a specialization in music theory education, leading them to be school music teachers as fully prepared to offer their particular contributions as those in all the other roles discussed so far.

7. Evaluating

In all cultures people are faced with choices in many dimensions of living, and develop an evaluation system guiding them in directions of their preferences, whether in ways to cook food, to dress, to seek amusements, to support political stances, and so on. In complex societies such as now exist all over the globe, choices in many areas of life are so numerous that expert guidance becomes a necessity if they are to be made with more than randomness. In America, for example, there are restaurant critics, movie critics, TV critics, automobile critics, book critics (reviewers), wine critics, art, dance, architecture, and theater critics, political critics (columnists, editorial writers, TV pundits), and, among many more, music critics of a variety of sorts—classical, country and western, rock, jazz, pop, and so forth. In every case the expert critic applies criteria of goodness as pertinent to the field in question and to the critic's value system, often a system shared widely among critics in a particular field. (My suggested criteria for musical judgments are offered in the previous chapter's discussion of this role.)

Music critics must be able to discuss levels of quality in music both as product and as process, and to place their judgments in broad perspectives of history, culture, aesthetic expectations and values, political-social issues, the status of those who create the music (whether novices, amateurs, or professionals), and other related matters having to be taken into account. We value their informed expertise because few of us are able to devote ourselves as fully and concentratedly to achieving such expertise as professionals do, as is the case in practically every aspect of our lives where we ourselves are not experts.

Courses in evaluating musical products and processes, both general to music criticism as a whole and particular to specific genres, can be challenging and very appealing to aficionados, to those who aspire to amateur status, and to some who might become professionals, including those who desire to become music educators devoted to this specialization and take a college certification program preparing them as fully for their professional role as those in the other roles the standards identify. Music teachers prepared by their background and training to offer courses in criticism would fulfill a much-needed function in enhancing the musical satisfactions of all who learned from them. What a shame that we in music education have seldom if ever recognized an obligation to offer this important contribution to our students' lives and to our society. A comprehensive curriculum cannot neglect the central role of the music critic in the functioning of a healthy musical culture.

8. Understanding Relationships between Music, the Other Arts, and Disciplines Outside the Arts

In Chapter 8 I pointed out the complexities of this standard, both conceptually and practically. The understandings it calls for—the ability to make relevant connections among fields that are both similar to and different from one another—are not easily gained, and teaching such matters is equally challenging. This is especially the case in a field such as music education that tends to value musicianship above all, listenership less enthusiastically, and the language understandings on which this standard depends with some suspicion. However, imparting such understandings, we have come to believe, is not just a decorative addition to musical learnings. It is an important obligation if we are to recognize music as part of a larger world of human values and therefore to understand it as precious in and of itself while also kindred to other values that are also distinctive and precious. The learnings entailed in this standard heighten the quality of both musicianship and listenership, casting them in a clear light so they can be appreciated fully for what they add to our lives.

For some this is a compelling, fascinating topic. It is approached in a variety of ways by people in a variety of disciplines—psychologists, cognitivists, philosophers, philosophers of art or aestheticians, educational theorists interested in curriculum coordination (or integration), and even neuroscientists dealing with brain function, all of whom are interested in the many ways humans create and share meanings. For some music educators the opportunity to develop particular expertise in this field will be a delight, and they will pursue study in it at the college level (if not before) and will want to offer electives, probably at the secondary level, although possibly earlier, that share their enthusiasm. We should do all we can to encourage and enable them to add this dimension of musical knowing to our repertoire of contributions to youngsters whose intelligence and creativity lead them in this direction, thereby enabling them to fulfill their capacity. And, perhaps, to become music educators able to further spread the availability of this significant mode of musical cognition, exploring how music is an essential way to know among others like and unlike it.

9. Understanding Music in Relation to History and Culture

As explained in the discussion of this standard in Chapter 8, the profession has for some time recognized, supported, and acted in a variety of ways appropriate to the importance of knowing and doing music informed by its setting in time and place. There is no need to repeat here the material from all the discussions in this book regarding music as situated, especially in Chapter 6. What needs to be emphasized is that, in addition to all the ways that history and cultural settings need to be attended to in musicianship aspects of the curriculum if singing, playing, improvising, composing, and arranging are to be accomplished genuinely, they also need to be studied in courses devoted to developing genuine listenership. This means that aficionados, many of whom pursue specialized interests leading toward amateur status and some who aspire to be professional music historians or musicologists focusing on particular cultural musics (whether of the West or elsewhere), need to have their proclivities developed in a wide variety of offerings centered in listenership. Such offerings need to serve the interests of students in local situations reflecting particular cultural identifications. But they also need to provide opportunities to explore musics less known if known at all, to widen horizons and challenge too-comfortable assumptions.

Electives in historical periods and genres and in culturally based musical beliefs and practices, along with their social-political assumptions, values, and controversies, are likely to be a core component of listenership programs, along with a variety of other topics sampling the endless array of fascinations music arouses. We have historically been unconscionably limited in our offerings for aficionados and amateurs in the ways most pursue, regard, and enjoy music, thereby ensuring limited participation. Opening our electives to the realities of diverse musical enthusiasms young people possess, and teaching them with the specialized expertise they need and deserve, would transform our curriculum, our value, and our status in education.

RECAPITULATION AND CODA: PURSUING THE VISION

In this book I have attempted to forge a philosophical foundation for the enterprise of music education as it exists and functions in the world of the early twenty-first century. I have argued that a viable philosophy of music education for these times needs to take into account several realities affecting our professional thinkings and doings. One is that general philosophies—thoughtful arguments about the nature, values, and purposes of human life—have become increasingly diverse and conflicted, calling into question a great many assumptions previously accepted as unassailable or at least persuasive. Uncertainty, ungroundedness, and disaccord permeate philosophical discourse, creating an atmosphere of ferment and therefore excitement but also of insecurity about what we can or should believe and how we should properly act.

That atmosphere inevitably seeps into the world of music education, causing similar doubts and reexaminations of long-held beliefs and practices. On the positive side, we benefit as a profession from the need to clean our house when we have allowed it to become a bit musty. We share in the excitement and challenge of new and sometimes unsettling ideas that cause us to reassess our ingrained, comfortable habits. Opening our windows to the fresh air of philosophical debate can blow away some cobwebs in our thinking and our acting, letting us see our environment more clearly so we can better decide whether we need to clear out some old furniture, add some that is new, and rearrange our rooms so they can function more effectively and satisfyingly.

On the negative side, the philosophical air blowing through the windows is sometimes acrid, stinging our eyes and therefore impeding our vision rather than clarifying it. We can act hastily, losing important values and substituting questionable ones, giving up successful practices in favor of some too shallow and narrow to sustain themselves beyond initial glitter. We can lose our balance, our focus, our sense of who we are, what we want, what our mission should be.

I have suggested that in times of uncertainty and of diverse, sometimes competing belief systems, we are well served to adopt a synergistic position, seeking below the surface level of discord to explore potentials for accordance of values beyond seeming conflicts. I believe many common beliefs and purposes pervade the positions of thoughtful music educators, despite inevitable and fruitful disagreements. Recognizing common values, tempering extreme views, seeking concurrence whenever it is positive to do so, will allow us to maintain a shared basis for our beliefs about why we exist and how we might best make our contributions.

A synergistic spirit requires, also, an openness to and a positive attitude toward diversity, in which inclusiveness, or comprehensiveness, is seen as a guide and a goal. The nature of music, in this spirit, is likely to be multifaceted, music being identifiable as a special domain while manifesting its singular nature in a great variety of ways. The values of music, likewise, depend on its specialness but also exist and are attained in multitudinous ways, shapes, and forms. Music education, then, reflecting the diversity of music, can best serve its educative function when it incorporates as many dimensions of musical value as it can, seeking extensiveness in its offerings and goals so that it can serve the widest possible spectrum of people's musical needs and interests.

Those needs and interests are served musically, in the ways music can fulfill so powerfully, when the feeling dimension of music—its capacity to explore and make available a broad range of affective experiences—is regarded as a primary contribution it makes to the quality of human life and is cultivated in all musical learnings. We serve people musically when the creative dimension of music—how musical meanings are brought into being—is available for them to experience in as many as possible of the ways musical creativity can exist and with as many as possible of the many musics that are the result of creativity. We add musical values to people's lives when we focus their learnings on musical meanings—the special ways music incorporates the world in which it exists, allowing us to know ourselves and others through mind, body, and feeling—so that the meanings in their lives are enriched by those that music particularly offers. And we make our contribution to people authentically when helping them understand musical feeling, creativity, and meaning as the processes and products of people existing in particular times and places, both contributing to and reflecting their universality as human beings, their particularity as members of a culture, and their individuality as unique persons.

The role of education in a democracy is to cultivate, with equal opportunity for all young people, their capacities to share fully in and contribute meaningfully to their culture's values, personal and social needs being fulfilled complementarily. Music education, as one important dimension of the education enterprise, needs to offer to all students the opportunity to share their culture's musical riches as fully as possible and to contribute to the viability of their musical culture as their interests and capacities allow, whether as engaged partakers (aficionados), as devoted partici-pants in musicianship and listenership activities (amateurs), or as earning their livelihood from their particular musical expertise (professionals). No matter their level of participation or their particular role, all should have received an education that cultivated their musical intelligences and creativities optimally, enabling them to fulfill their chosen role(s) effectively and with satisfaction.

A valid curriculum in music, then, needs to satisfy three long-held and often articulated conditions: it needs to be comprehensive, sequential, and balanced. It is comprehensive when it regards all substantive musical roles in a culture as worthy of cultivation, both at the general education level of inclusiveness and at the specialized education level of focused learning. It is sequential when human developmental fac-tors and the particular ways and progressions of learning in each musical role inter-act to nurture capacities and provide challenges effectively. It is balanced when all substantive musical roles are accessible to be experienced, when all culturally signif-icant musics and as many as possible of other cultures are represented fairly, treated with respect, and studied accordingly, and when each level of musical involvement—aficionado, amateur, and professional—is cultivated with the fullest devotion and expertise the music education profession can bring to bear.

The vision articulated in this book, in both its philosophical and its practical dimensions, builds on historical and successful traditions while also advancing them into largely unexplored territories. Should our profession attempt to achieve this very challenging and idealistic aspiration? Or should we settle for the successes we have already achieved, counting our present blessings rather than reaching for the moon?

In a real sense we have indeed been successful, no doubt far surpassing the wildest dreams of those who initiated the field of school music education in the United States in the first half of the nineteenth century[5] and their counterparts around the world. But we are also, I am afraid, creaking in our joints. We tend to con-tinue in well-worn paths, with "tried and true" programs and methodologies. We generally offer reactive rather than proactive rationales to both ourselves and others. We have built an admirable, impressive superstructure of professional organizations, undergraduate and graduate degree programs, research and scholarship, worldwide

---

[5]This history is well recounted in Michael L. Mark and Charles Gary, *A History of American Music Education*, 2nd ed. (Reston, VA: Music Educators National Conference, 1999).

intercommunications, a supportive and thriving music education industry, and many profession-sustaining traditions. I often marvel at the many successes music education has achieved and the stunning expertise it demonstrates in a great variety of ways both musical and educational. Yet underneath that warranted admiration is a school program of very limited scope in its lack of comprehensiveness, its narrow view of sequential learning therefore, and its striking, perhaps dismaying, imbalance. We serve very few students, with very few options, with restricted kinds of music and a limited number of ways to develop musical creativities and intelligences. Our apparent health is founded on a base too meager to sustain the growth we deserve to experience.

Yes, we are improving in comprehensivity in the face of difficult obstacles, and are therefore maintaining our viability for the present. But as our culture changes and as its musical realities change we must strengthen both by positioning ourselves at the forefront, leading those changes in thoughtful, musically expert ways that recognize both the potentials of what is emerging and the values of our traditions. We must be closer to reality—the reality of the actual musical life of our culture and how we can extend, refine, and deepen it. In light of how music exists outside schools and what it tends to be inside schools, we must acknowledge a disparity too severe to be sustained. Our culture is remarkably and vigorously musical, despite our complaints that it does not support our particular preferences to the degree we would desire, a degree perhaps unrealistic given the excellence of our culture's achievements in the realm of classical musics. We are obligated to sustain those achievements and to do the same with all the other musical practices so plentifully represented in the multimusical cultures now existing in America and around the world. Our contribution needs to be more adequate to the musical actualities in which we exist.

Are we up to that challenge? The vision of comprehensiveness I have proposed requires significant changes in how our profession thinks and acts and in how the field of education regards and supports us. I believe the latter depends on the former; that is, what we do to make ourselves more relevant to our culture's musical needs will procure concomitant support, support we long for but often on our own too self-serving terms. A more broadly based music education, philosophically, musically, and educationally, can only strengthen our often precarious position in the schools, our wider contribution warranting wider appreciation.

But comprehensiveness is not only a political tactic. It represents a vision more adequate to music and to music education than we have so far been able to imagine, a vision, like others of magnitude, perhaps not entirely achievable but certainly pursuable. Advancing the vision of a more vital music education is a cause to which we can dedicate ourselves wholeheartedly, a cause worthy of our art, of our devotion to sharing it as abundantly as possible, and of our remarkable and wide-ranging expertise. I earnestly hope that the early twenty-first century will be regarded as the time when the music education profession purposefully began to become what it fully can be.

RIFF 10

I am captive, still, to the physical effort of wringing words out through the ink marks my fingers direct as they grasp the pen. Ideas tied to body, given reality by the actions of muscles at work. Once "ex-pressed"—pressed out—they live independently, claim their selfhood, demand their progeny. The writer follows them, their servant while their master. Will the children of mind be welcomed in their world of thoughts? Be helpful in that world? If they are, an alchemy of transformation will occur, teachers turning ideas into actions, actions into musical sounds created, shared, "joyed," by more people, in more ways, with more satisfactions, than would otherwise be the case. I am proud to be among the fellowship of music educators, the professionals devoted to thought and action in pursuit of that ideal.

ETUDES

1. In which of the nine content areas do you feel you are (or will be) qualified to teach challenging, sequentially valid elective courses for students who will have had solid and comprehensive general music classes? Try to rank-order your degree of confidence in the nine. Then compare your ranking with others'. If possible, get a group ranking and compare yours with the group's. What does this say about the challenges we face if we are to achieve the vision of comprehensiveness in elective offerings?

2. Try going through each of the standards and sketching which of the others would support learnings in each. Do some standards seem to rely more on particular supporting areas than do others? That is, perhaps the balances among those supporting each might be different depending on the nature of each. But can all still play a helpful, enriching role for each?

3. Given the complexities of pursuing a comprehensive vision of elective offerings, what would you hope the music education research community might offer so as to make our efforts as valid and effective as possible? What contributions might our national, regional, and state organizations make? the international music education community? colleges and universities preparing music teachers? graduate programs preparing teachers of teachers? the music industry including publishers? Can you envision a coordinated effort to pursue this vision? How might that occur?

4. If the aspirations for music education expressed in this book appeal to you, what role might you envision playing in helping the profession pursue them? After all, pursuing them in one's own work, though an essential basis for progress, is difficult if not impossible without a supporting context in the larger profession.

What strengths and interests do you possess that could be of value to the larger community in working toward these aspirations? How might you assert your competencies in ways that would be welcomed by other professionals? And what do you hope, or expect, from present leaders in music education whose influences affect us all?

Index